Dance in the
Vampire Bund

Age of
Scarlet
Order

02

story & art by
Nozomu
Tamaki

CONTENTS

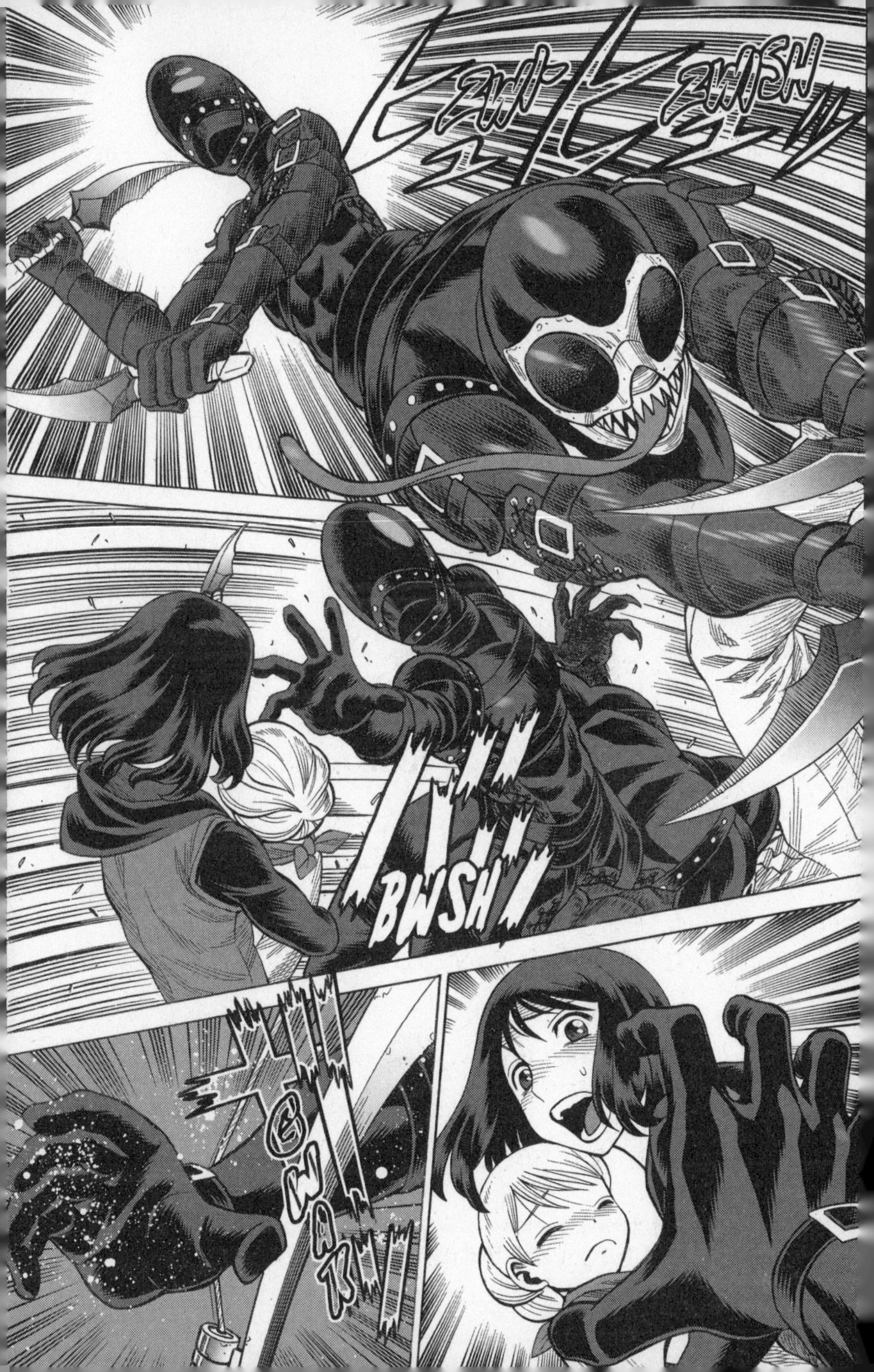
ZWISH
ZWIP
BWSH
GWAK

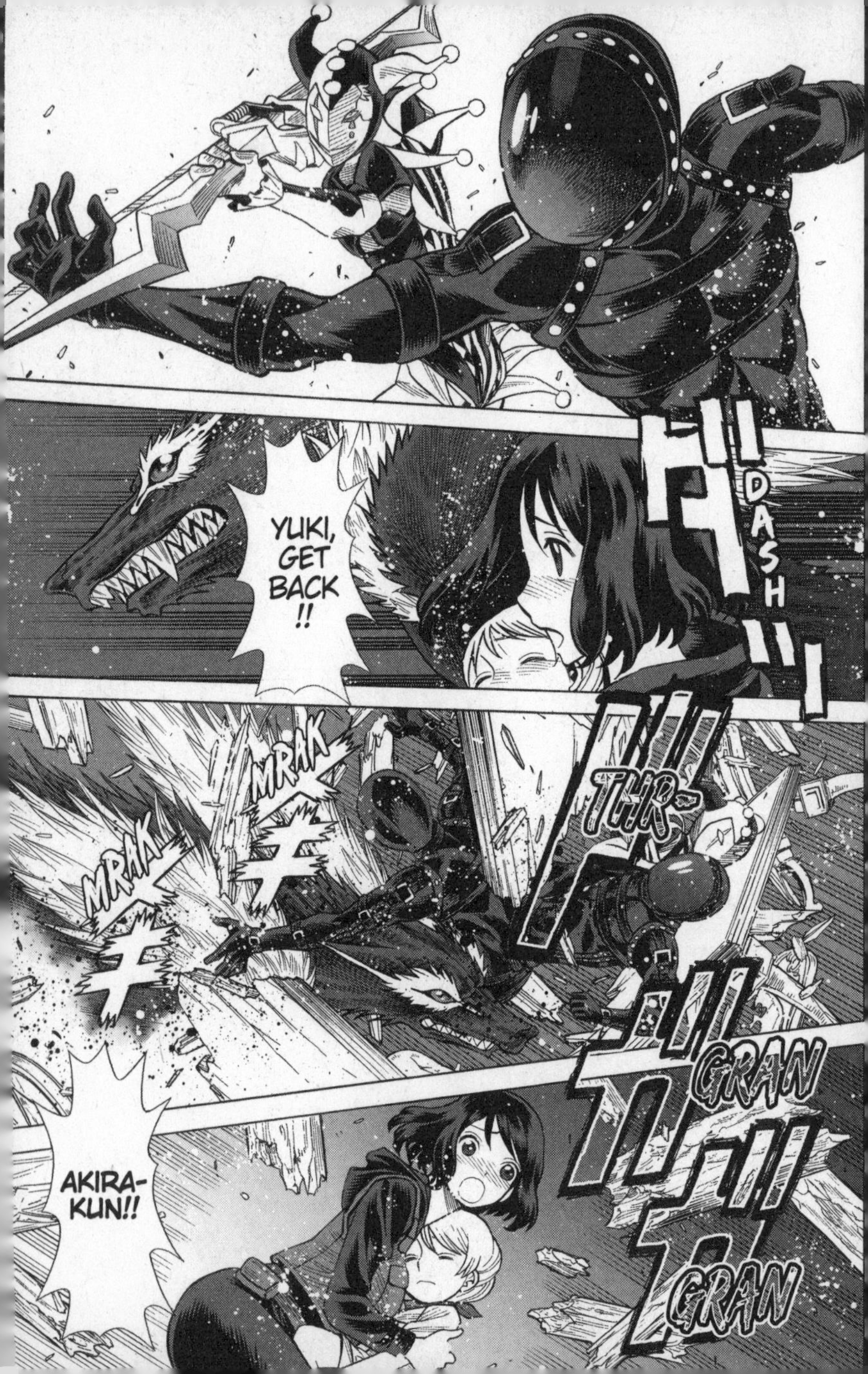
DASH
YUKI, GET BACK!!
THR-
MRAK
MRAK
GRAN
GRAN
AKIRA-KUN!!

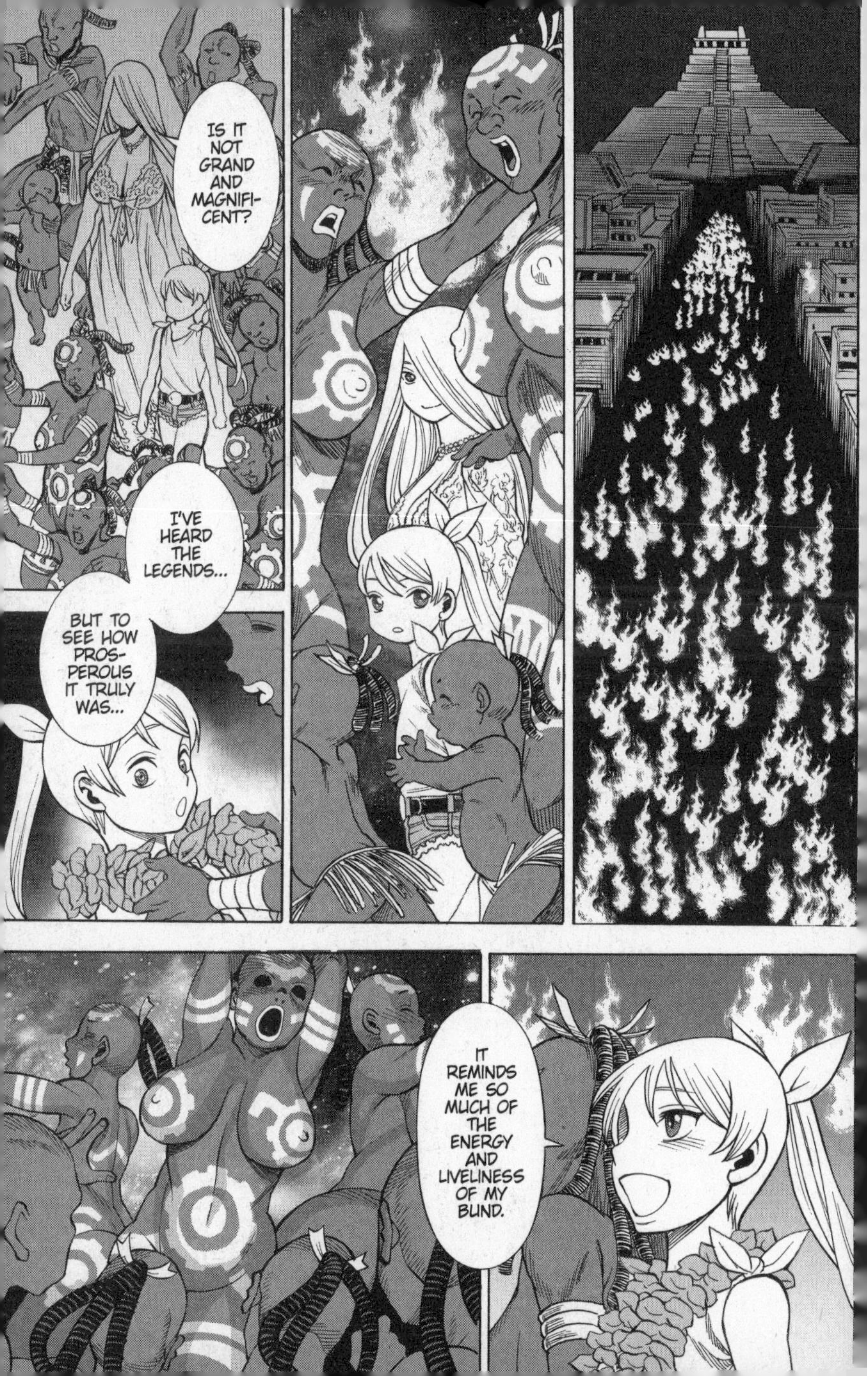
IS IT NOT GRAND AND MAGNIFI-CENT?
I'VE HEARD THE LEGENDS...
BUT TO SEE HOW PROS-PEROUS IT TRULY WAS...
IT REMINDS ME SO MUCH OF THE ENERGY AND LIVELINESS OF MY BUND.

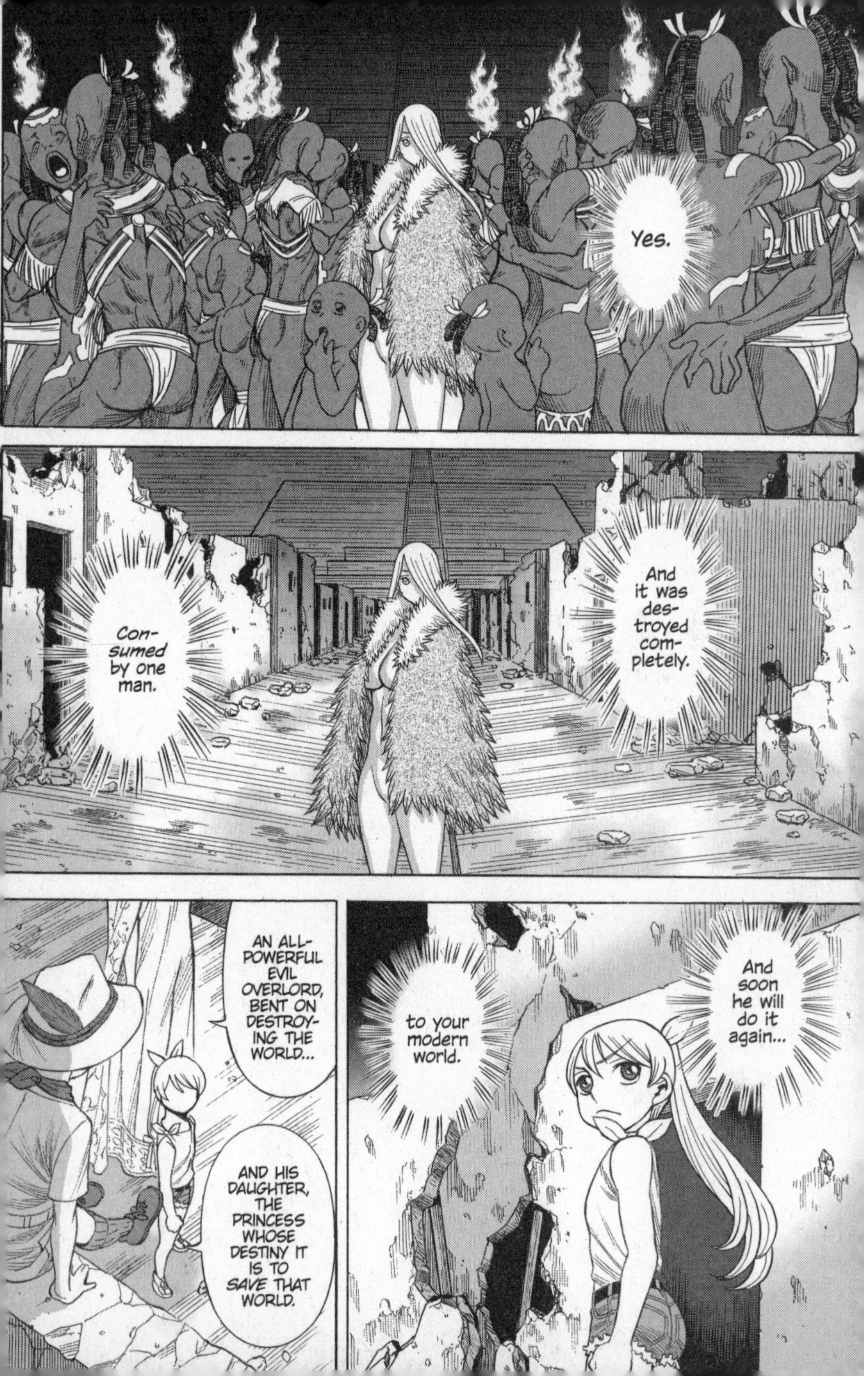
Yes.
And it was destroyed completely.
Consumed by one man.
And soon he will do it again...
to your modern world.
AN ALL-POWERFUL EVIL OVERLORD, BENT ON DESTROYING THE WORLD...
AND HIS DAUGHTER, THE PRINCESS WHOSE DESTINY IT IS TO SAVE THAT WORLD.

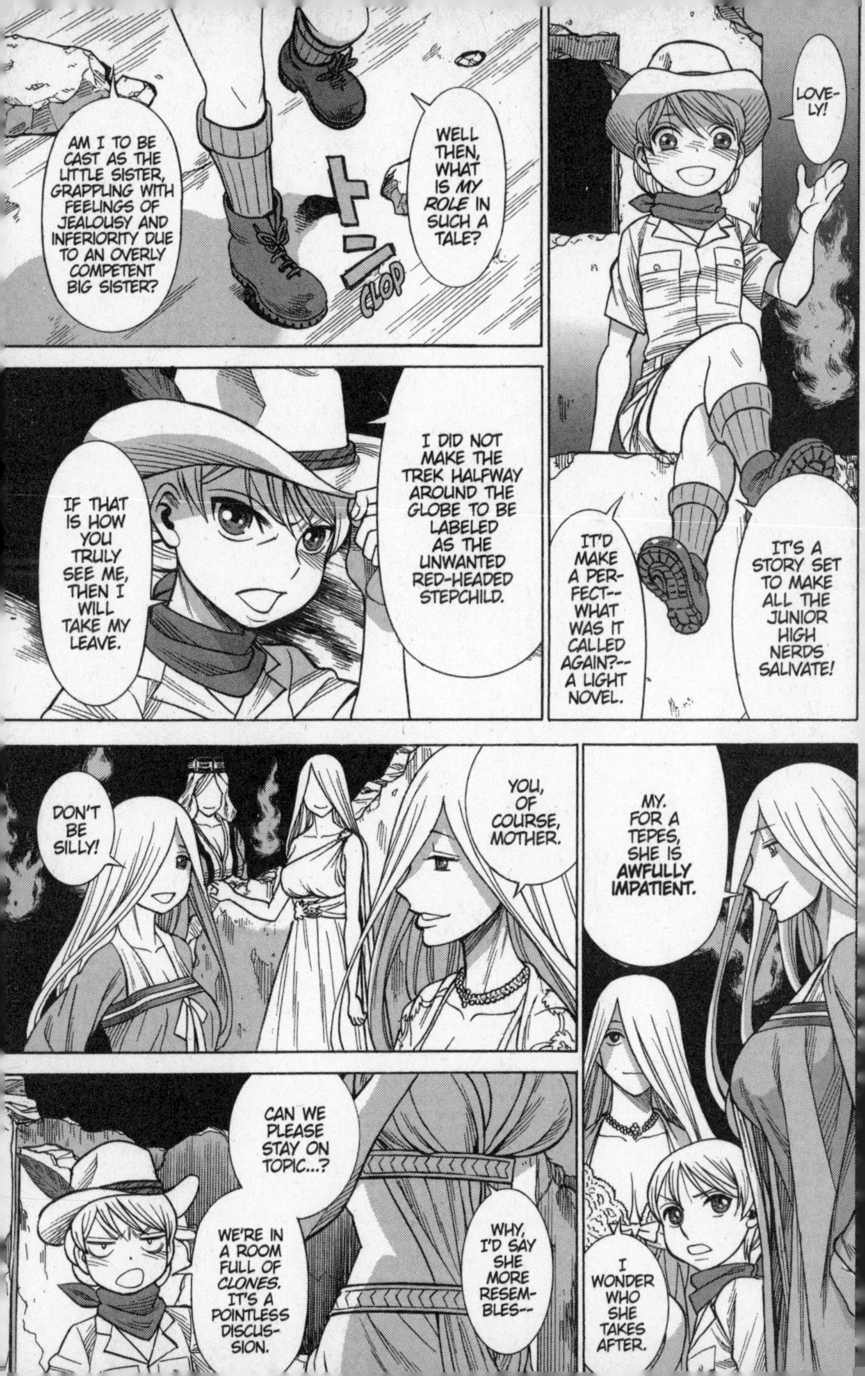
LOVE-LY!
IT'S A STORY SET TO MAKE ALL THE JUNIOR HIGH NERDS SALIVATE!
IT'D MAKE A PERFECT--WHAT WAS IT CALLED AGAIN?--A LIGHT NOVEL.
WELL THEN, WHAT IS *MY ROLE* IN SUCH A TALE?
AM I TO BE CAST AS THE LITTLE SISTER, GRAPPLING WITH FEELINGS OF JEALOUSY AND INFERIORITY DUE TO AN OVERLY COMPETENT BIG SISTER?
CLOP
I DID NOT MAKE THE TREK HALFWAY AROUND THE GLOBE TO BE LABELED AS THE UNWANTED RED-HEADED STEPCHILD.
IF THAT IS HOW YOU TRULY SEE ME, THEN I WILL TAKE MY LEAVE.
MY. FOR A TEPES, SHE IS **AWFULLY IMPATIENT.**
I WONDER WHO SHE TAKES AFTER.
YOU, OF COURSE, MOTHER.
DON'T BE SILLY!
WHY, I'D SAY SHE MORE RESEMBLES--
CAN WE PLEASE STAY ON TOPIC...?
WE'RE IN A ROOM FULL OF *CLONES.* IT'S A POINTLESS DISCUSSION.

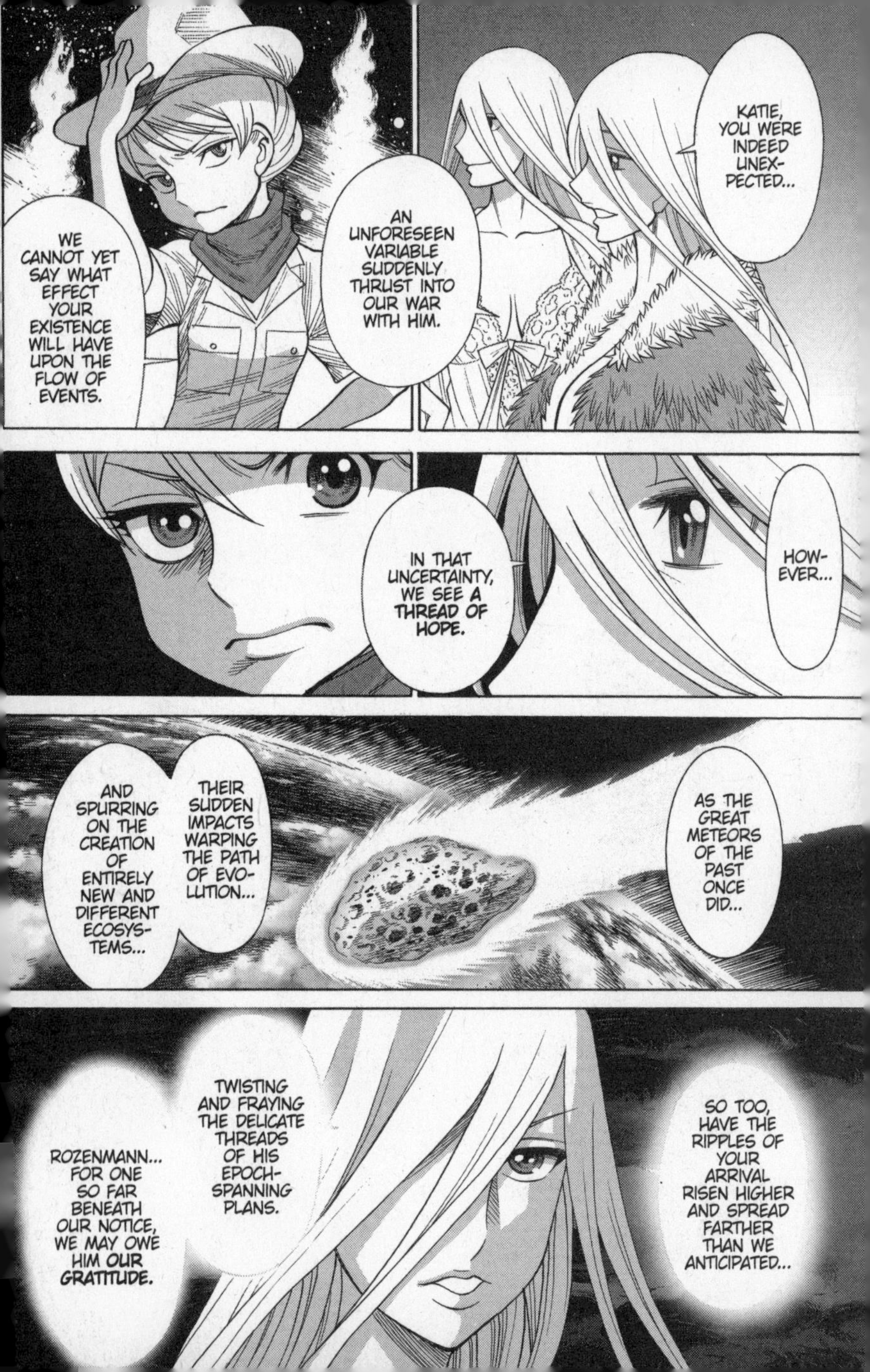
KATIE, YOU WERE INDEED UNEXPECTED...
AN UNFORESEEN VARIABLE SUDDENLY THRUST INTO OUR WAR WITH HIM.
WE CANNOT YET SAY WHAT EFFECT YOUR EXISTENCE WILL HAVE UPON THE FLOW OF EVENTS.
HOWEVER...
IN THAT UNCERTAINTY, WE SEE A THREAD OF HOPE.
AS THE GREAT METEORS OF THE PAST ONCE DID...
THEIR SUDDEN IMPACTS WARPING THE PATH OF EVOLUTION...
AND SPURRING ON THE CREATION OF ENTIRELY NEW AND DIFFERENT ECOSYSTEMS...
SO TOO, HAVE THE RIPPLES OF YOUR ARRIVAL RISEN HIGHER AND SPREAD FARTHER THAN WE ANTICIPATED...
TWISTING AND FRAYING THE DELICATE THREADS OF HIS EPOCH-SPANNING PLANS.
ROZENMANN... FOR ONE SO FAR BENEATH OUR NOTICE, WE MAY OWE HIM **OUR GRATITUDE.**

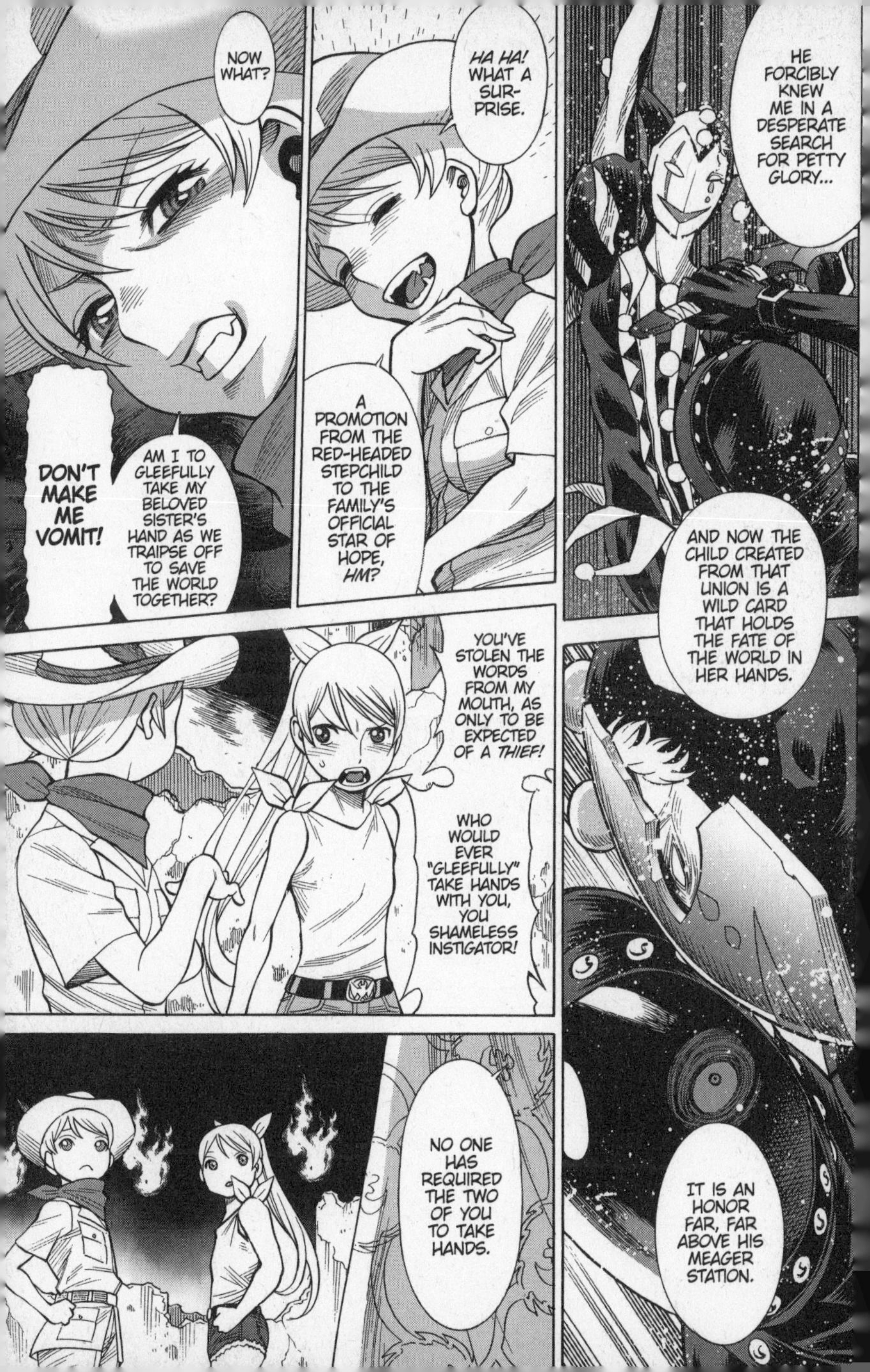
HE FORCIBLY KNEW ME IN A DESPERATE SEARCH FOR PETTY GLORY...
AND NOW THE CHILD CREATED FROM THAT UNION IS A WILD CARD THAT HOLDS THE FATE OF THE WORLD IN HER HANDS.
HA HA! WHAT A SUR-PRISE.
A PROMOTION FROM THE RED-HEADED STEPCHILD TO THE FAMILY'S OFFICIAL STAR OF HOPE, *HM?*
NOW WHAT?
AM I TO GLEEFULLY TAKE MY BELOVED SISTER'S HAND AS WE TRAIPSE OFF TO SAVE THE WORLD TOGETHER?
DON'T MAKE ME VOMIT!
IT IS AN HONOR FAR, FAR ABOVE HIS MEAGER STATION.
YOU'VE STOLEN THE WORDS FROM MY MOUTH, AS ONLY TO BE EXPECTED OF A *THIEF!*
WHO WOULD EVER "GLEEFULLY" TAKE HANDS WITH YOU, YOU SHAMELESS INSTIGATOR!
NO ONE HAS REQUIRED THE TWO OF YOU TO TAKE HANDS.

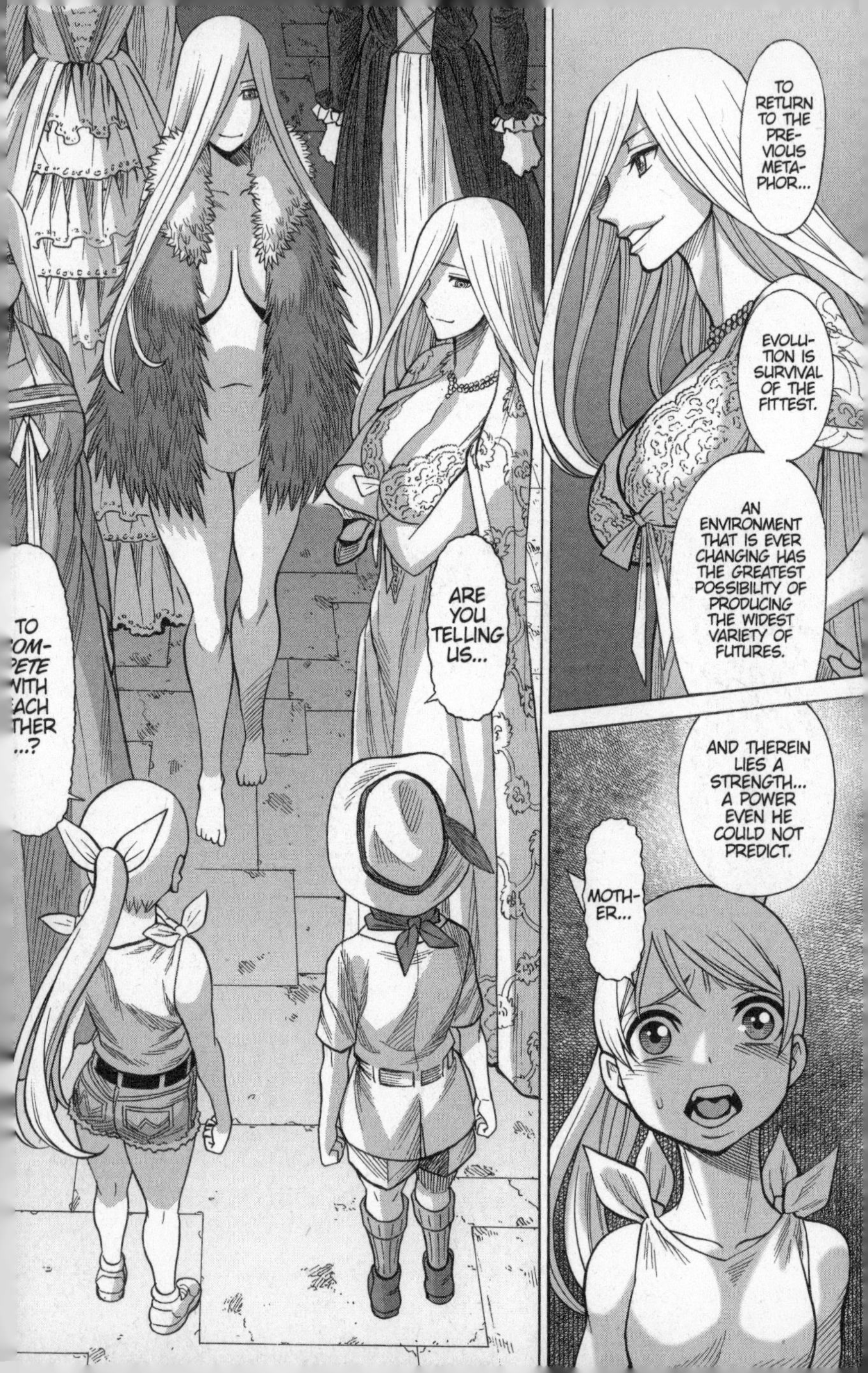
TO RETURN TO THE PRE-VIOUS METAPHOR...
EVOLUTION IS SURVIVAL OF THE FITTEST.
AN ENVIRONMENT THAT IS EVER CHANGING HAS THE GREATEST POSSIBILITY OF PRODUCING THE WIDEST VARIETY OF FUTURES.
AND THEREIN LIES A STRENGTH... A POWER EVEN HE COULD NOT PREDICT.
MOTH-ER...
ARE YOU TELLING US...
TO OM-PETE WITH EACH THER ...?

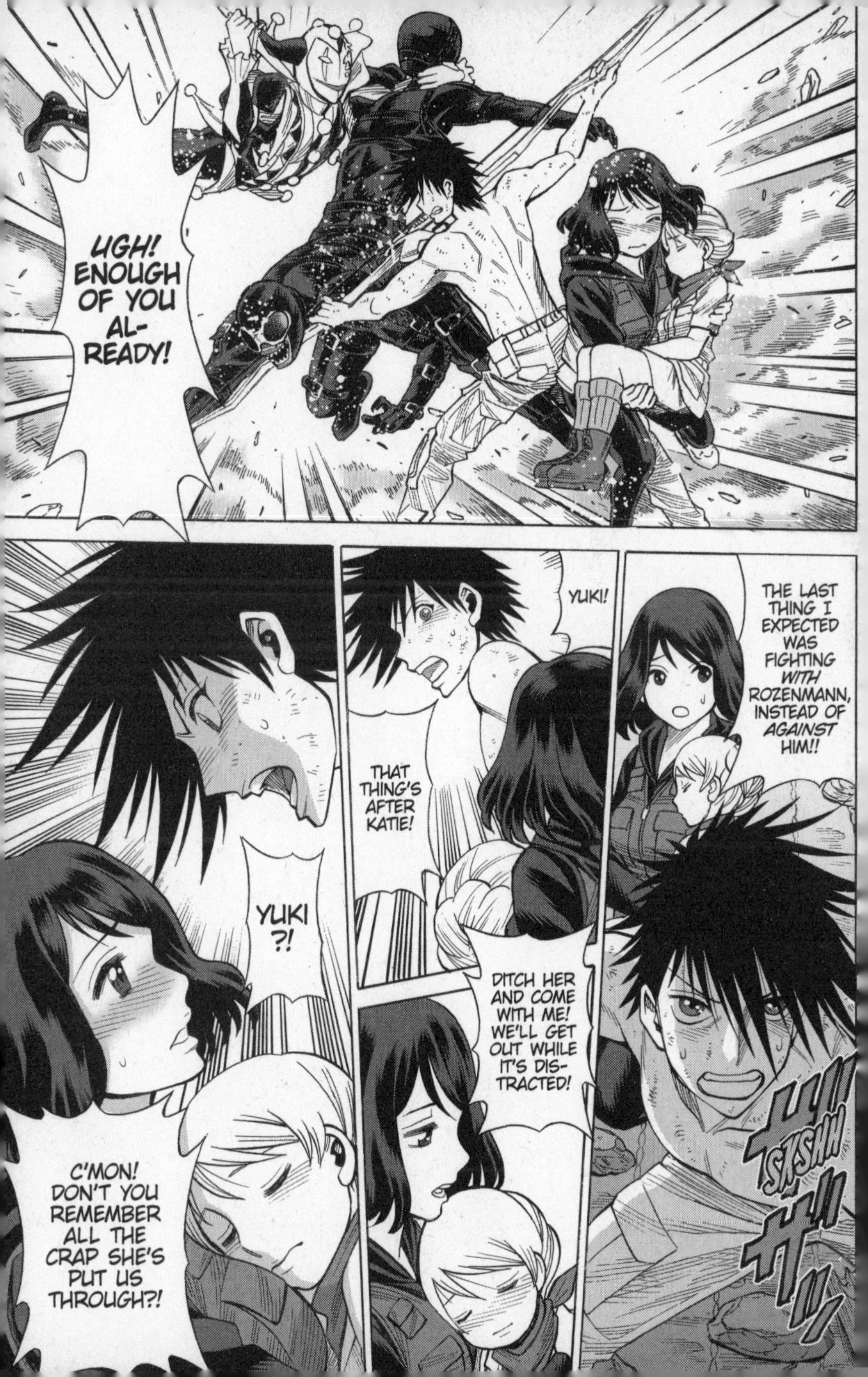
UGH! ENOUGH OF YOU AL-READY!
THE LAST THING I EXPECTED WAS FIGHTING WITH ROZENMANN, INSTEAD OF AGAINST HIM!!
YUKI!
THAT THING'S AFTER KATIE!
DITCH HER AND COME WITH ME! WE'LL GET OUT WHILE IT'S DIS-TRACTED!
SKSHH
YUKI ?!
C'MON! DON'T YOU REMEMBER ALL THE CRAP SHE'S PUT US THROUGH?!

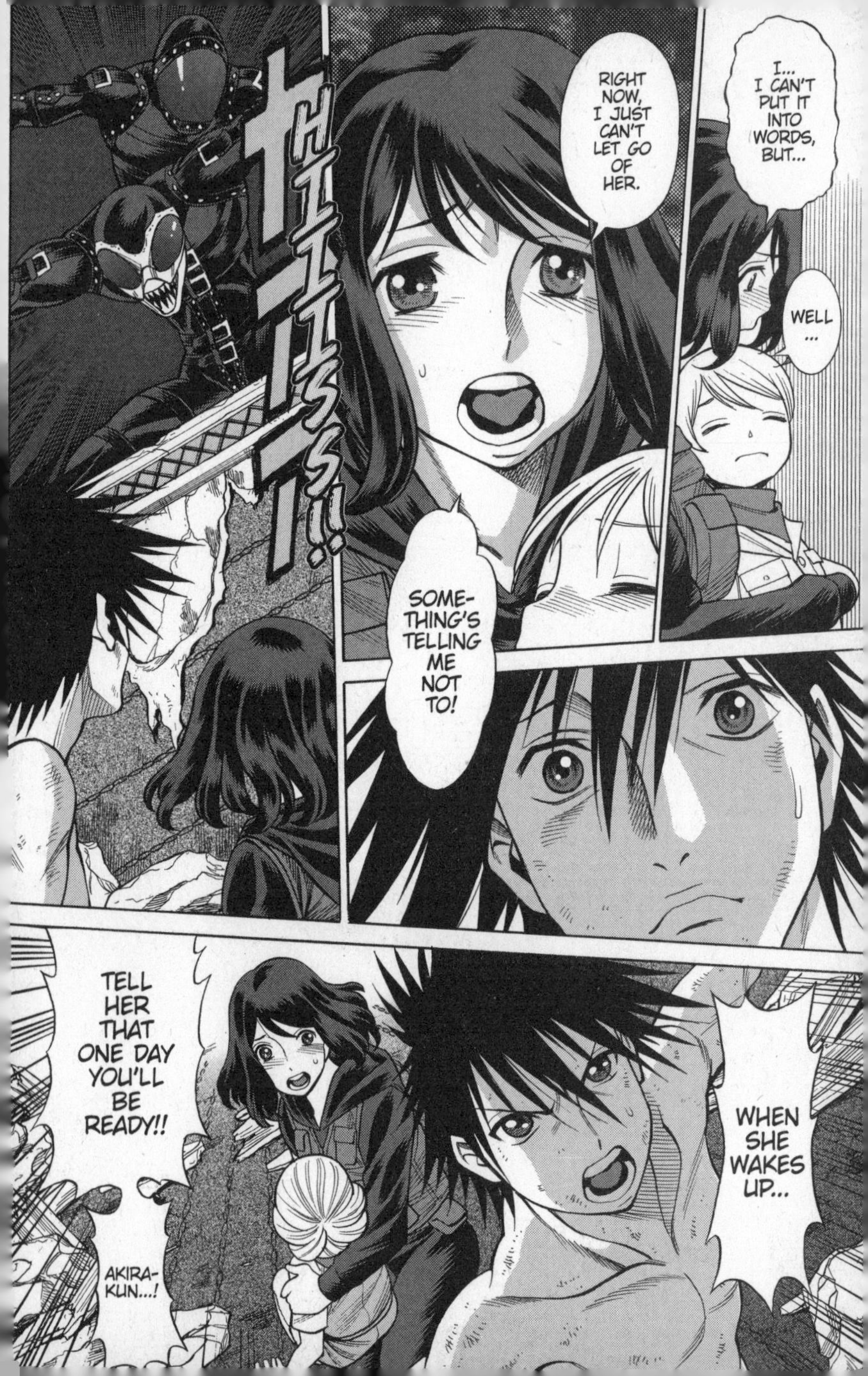
I... I CAN'T PUT IT INTO WORDS, BUT...
WELL ...
RIGHT NOW, I JUST CAN'T LET GO OF HER.
SOME-THING'S TELLING ME NOT TO!
HIISS!!
WHEN SHE WAKES UP...
TELL HER THAT ONE DAY YOU'LL BE READY!!
AKIRA-KUN...!

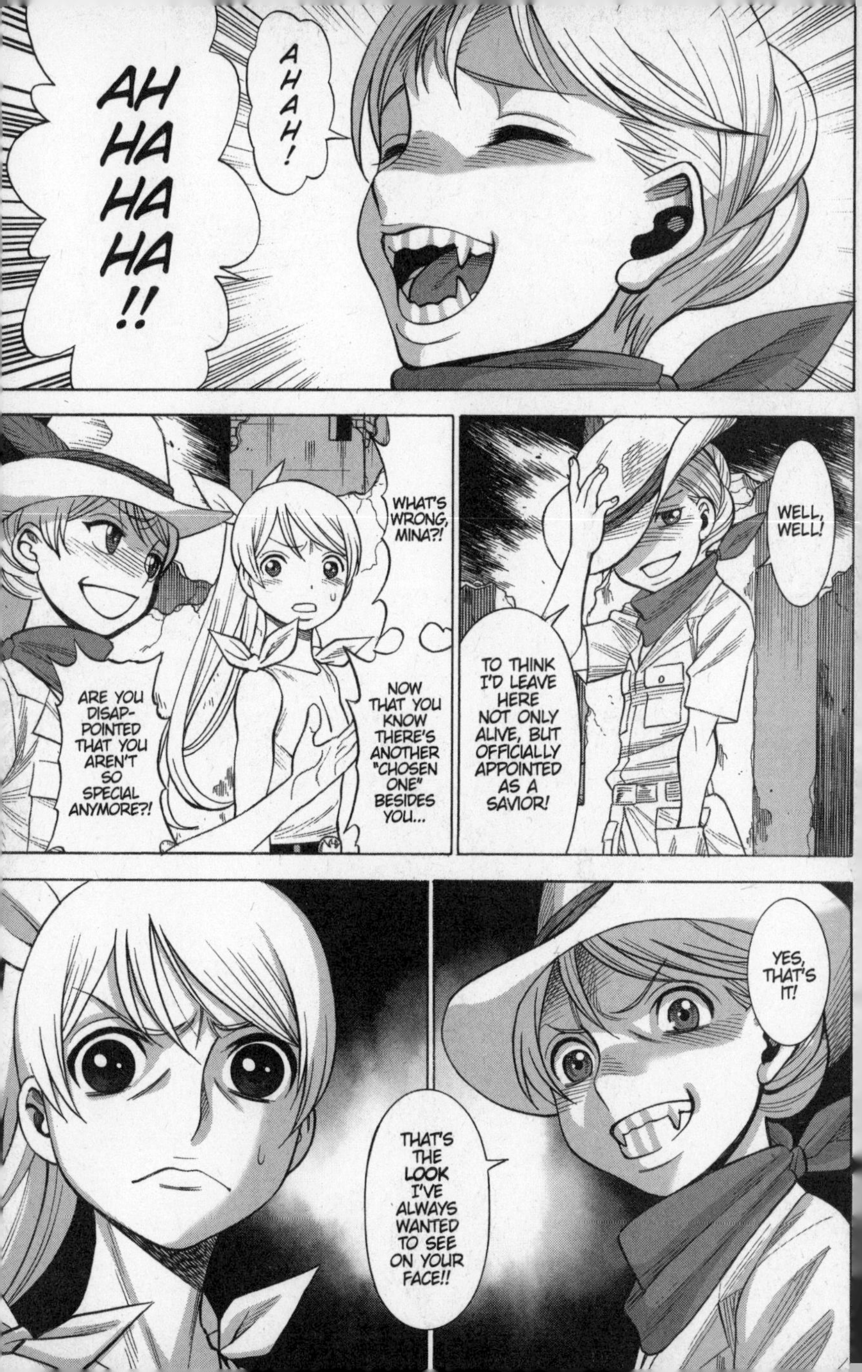
AHAH!
AH HA HA HA!!
WELL, WELL!
TO THINK I'D LEAVE HERE NOT ONLY ALIVE, BUT OFFICIALLY APPOINTED AS A SAVIOR!
WHAT'S WRONG, MINA?!
NOW THAT YOU KNOW THERE'S ANOTHER "CHOSEN ONE" BESIDES YOU...
ARE YOU DISAP-POINTED THAT YOU AREN'T SO SPECIAL ANYMORE?!
YES, THAT'S IT!
THAT'S THE LOOK I'VE ALWAYS WANTED TO SEE ON YOUR FACE!!

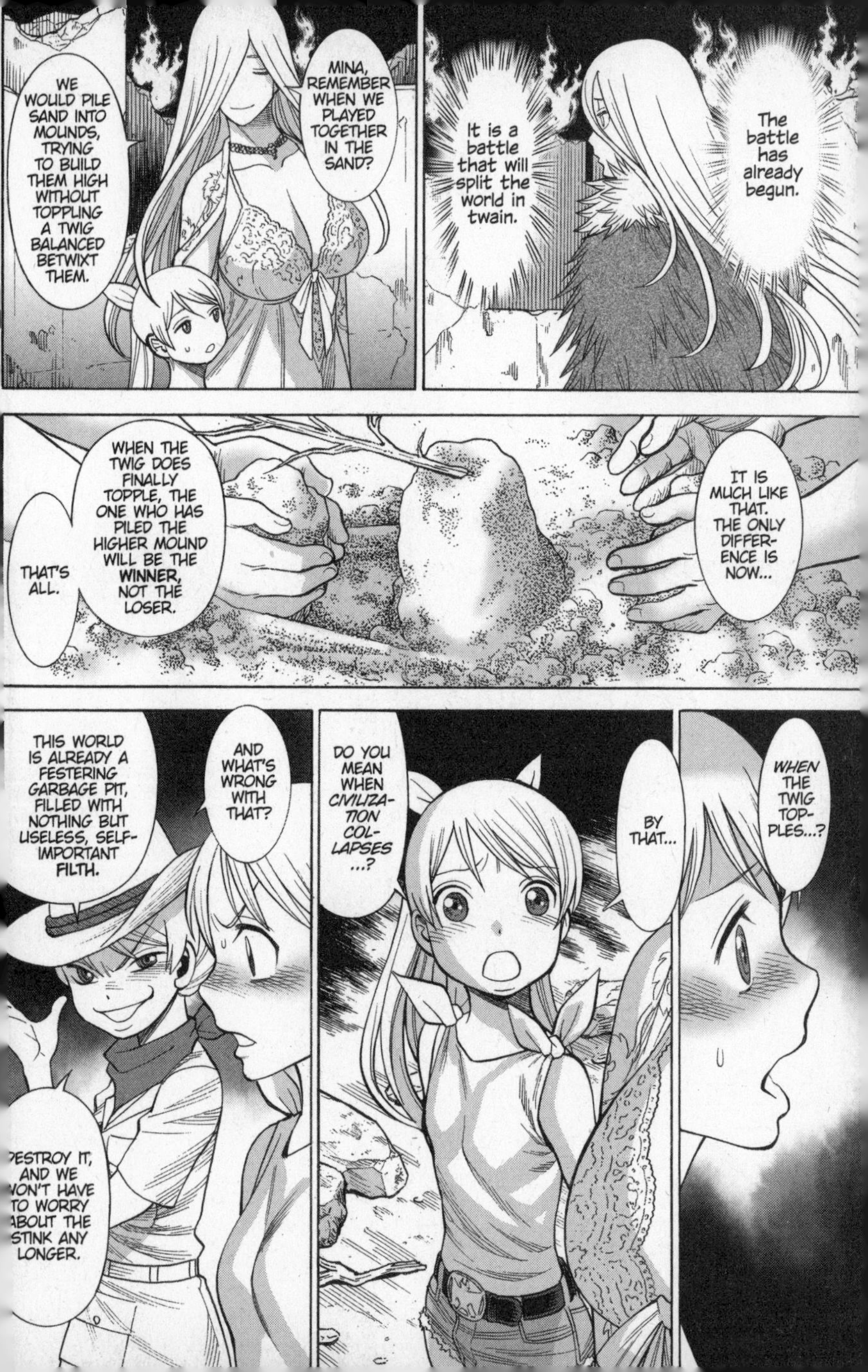
The battle has already begun.
It is a battle that will split the world in twain.
MINA, REMEMBER WHEN WE PLAYED TOGETHER IN THE SAND?
WE WOULD PILE SAND INTO MOUNDS, TRYING TO BUILD THEM HIGH WITHOUT TOPPLING A TWIG BALANCED BETWIXT THEM.
IT IS MUCH LIKE THAT. THE ONLY DIFFERENCE IS NOW...
WHEN THE TWIG DOES FINALLY TOPPLE, THE ONE WHO HAS PILED THE HIGHER MOUND WILL BE THE **WINNER**, NOT THE LOSER.
THAT'S ALL.
WHEN THE TWIG TOPPLES...?
BY THAT...
DO YOU MEAN WHEN *CIVILIZATION COLLAPSES*...?
AND WHAT'S WRONG WITH THAT?
THIS WORLD IS ALREADY A FESTERING GARBAGE PIT, FILLED WITH NOTHING BUT USELESS, SELF-IMPORTANT FILTH.
DESTROY IT, AND WE WON'T HAVE TO WORRY ABOUT THE STINK ANY LONGER.

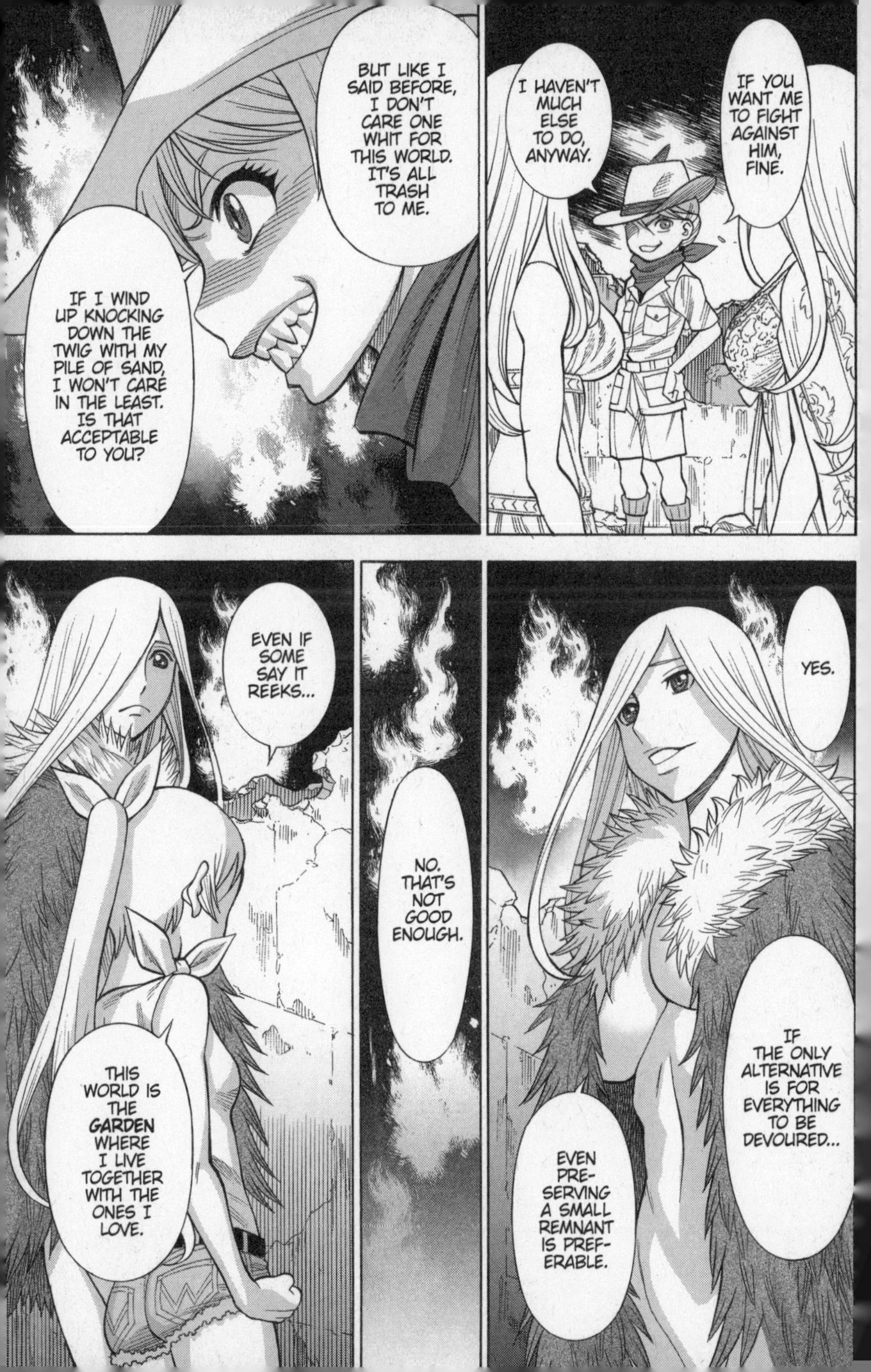
IF YOU WANT ME TO FIGHT AGAINST HIM, FINE.
I HAVEN'T MUCH ELSE TO DO, ANYWAY.
BUT LIKE I SAID BEFORE, I DON'T CARE ONE WHIT FOR THIS WORLD. IT'S ALL TRASH TO ME.
IF I WIND UP KNOCKING DOWN THE TWIG WITH MY PILE OF SAND, I WON'T CARE IN THE LEAST. IS THAT ACCEPTABLE TO YOU?
YES.
IF THE ONLY ALTERNATIVE IS FOR EVERYTHING TO BE DEVOURED...
EVEN PRE-SERVING A SMALL REMNANT IS PREF-ERABLE.
NO. THAT'S NOT GOOD ENOUGH.
EVEN IF SOME SAY IT REEKS...
THIS WORLD IS THE **GARDEN** WHERE I LIVE TOGETHER WITH THE ONES I LOVE.

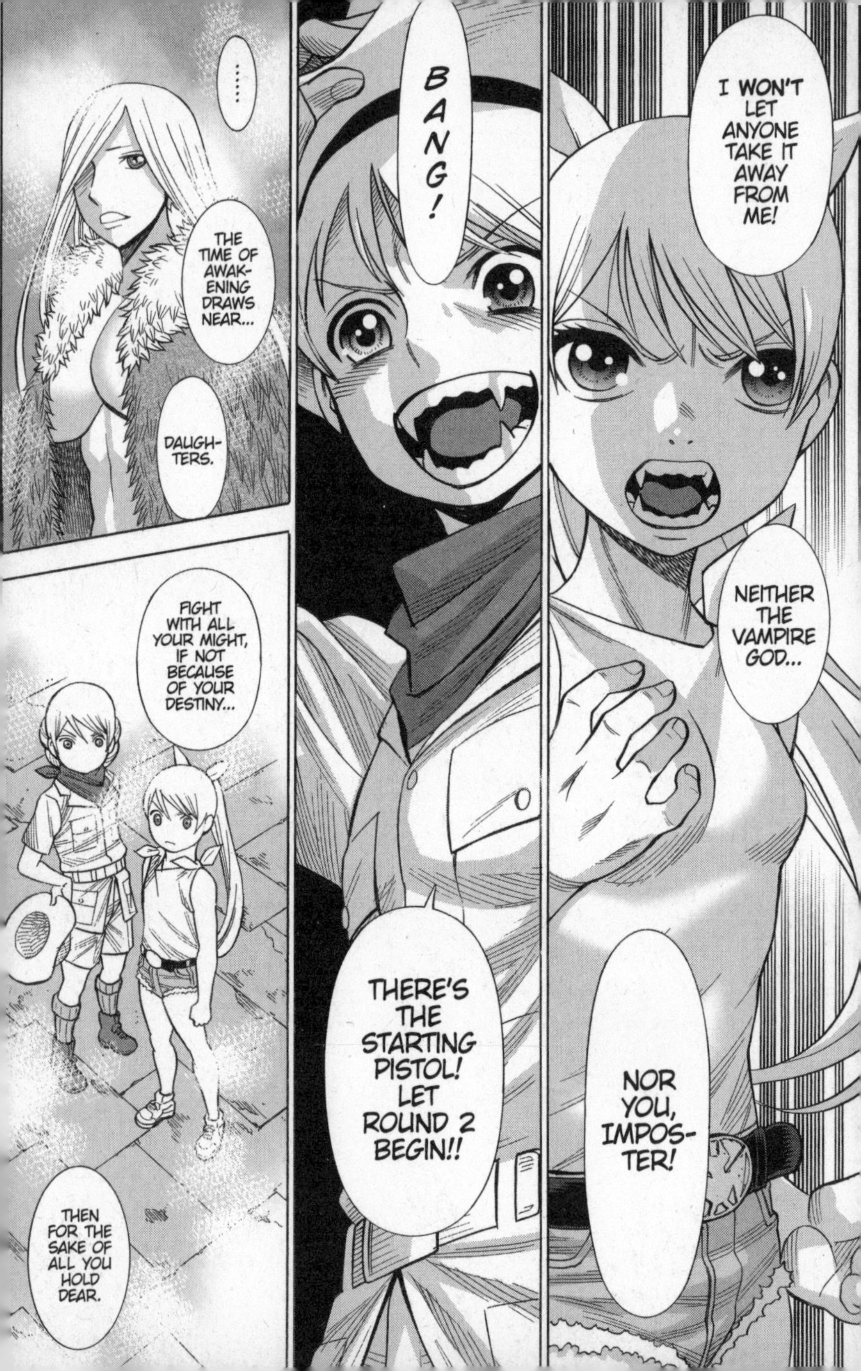
I WON'T LET ANYONE TAKE IT AWAY FROM ME!
NEITHER THE VAMPIRE GOD...
NOR YOU, IMPOS-TER!
BANG!
THERE'S THE STARTING PISTOL! LET ROUND 2 BEGIN!!
......
THE TIME OF AWAK-ENING DRAWS NEAR...
DAUGH-TERS.
FIGHT WITH ALL YOUR MIGHT, IF NOT BECAUSE OF YOUR DESTINY...
THEN FOR THE SAKE OF ALL YOU HOLD DEAR.

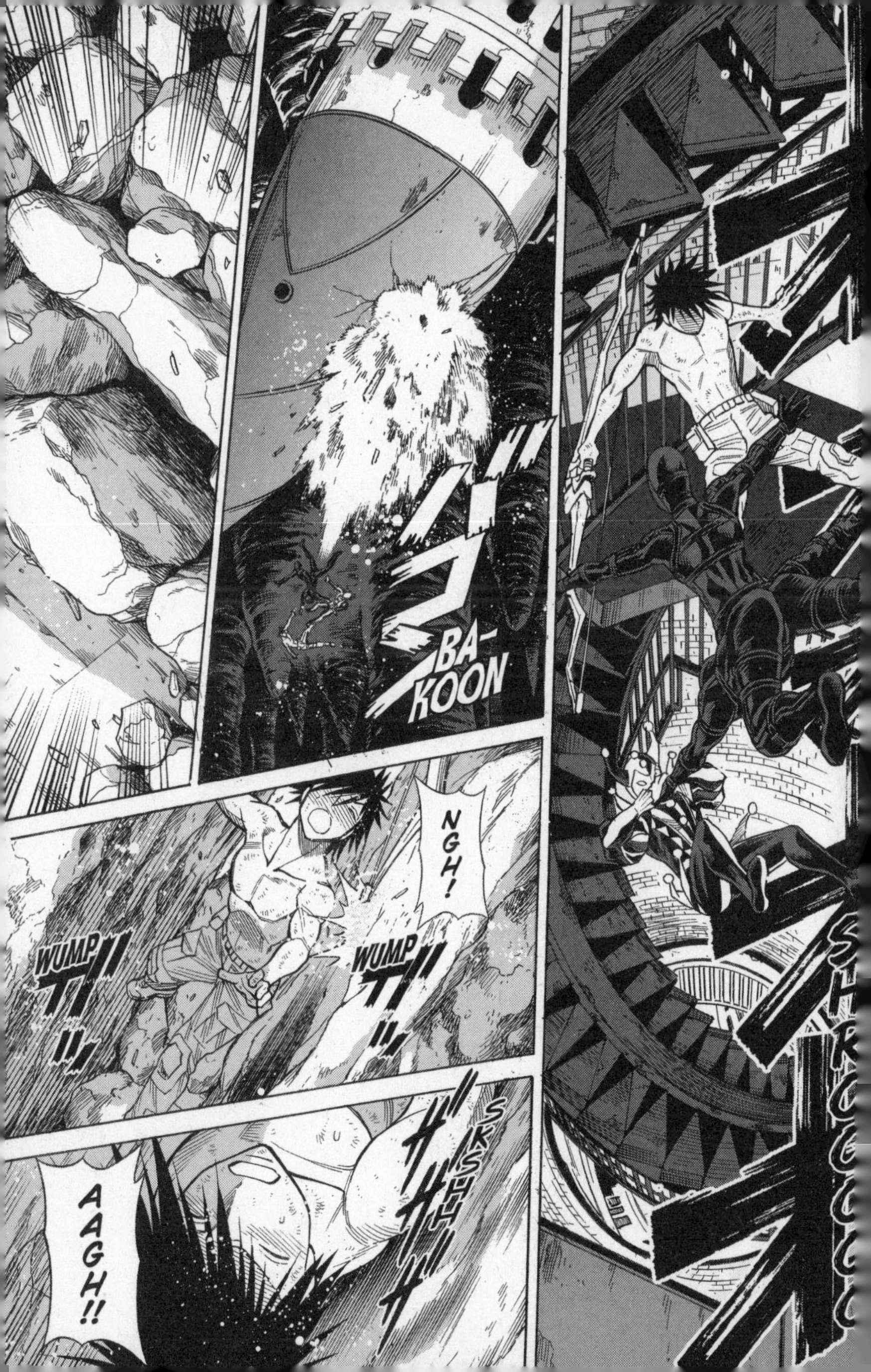
SHROOOOO
BA-KOON
NGH!
WUMP
WUMP
SKSHUH
AAGH!!

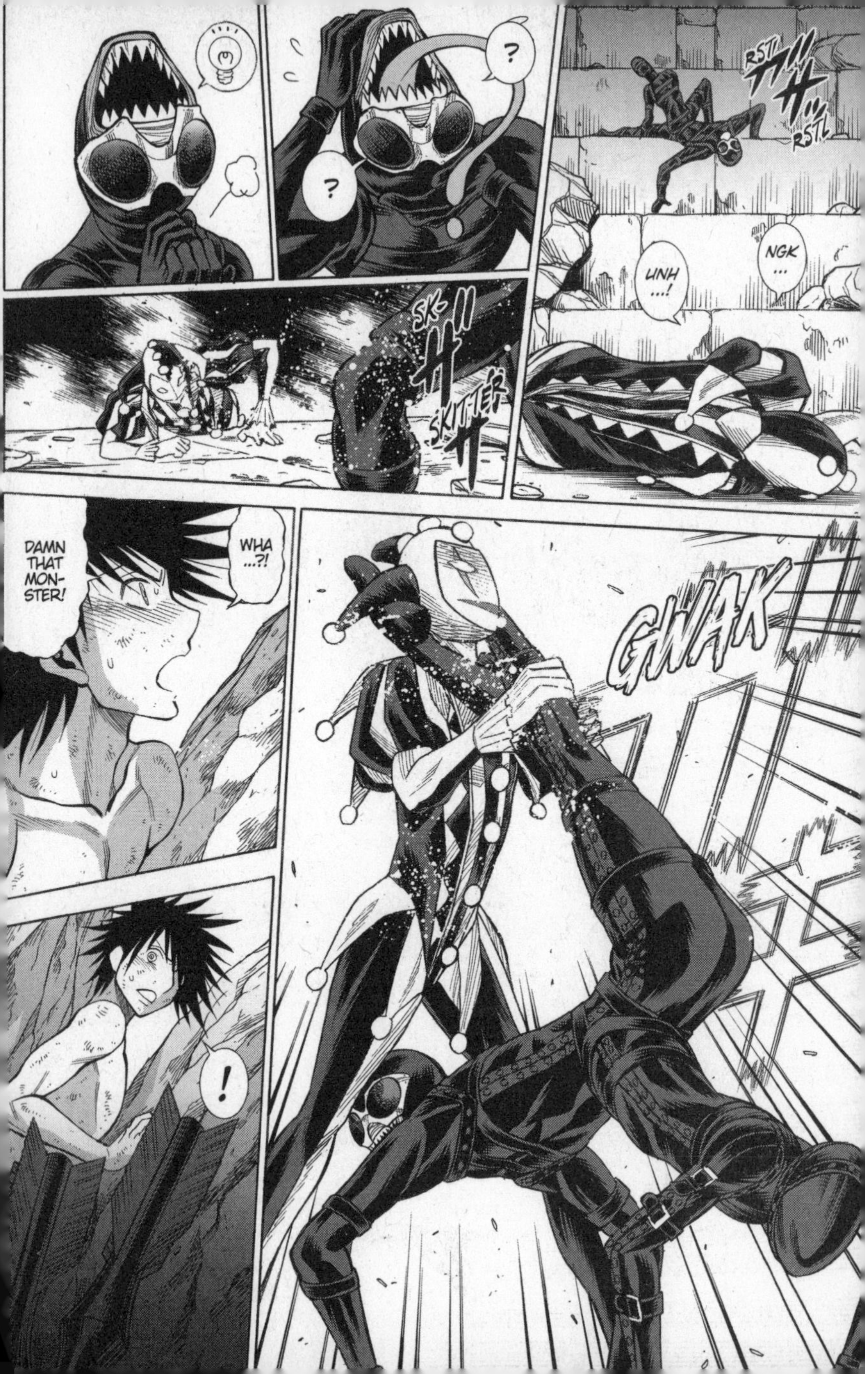
RSTL
RSTL
NGK ...
UNH ...!
?
?
SK-!!
SKITTER
GWAK
WHA ...?!
DAMN THAT MONSTER!
!

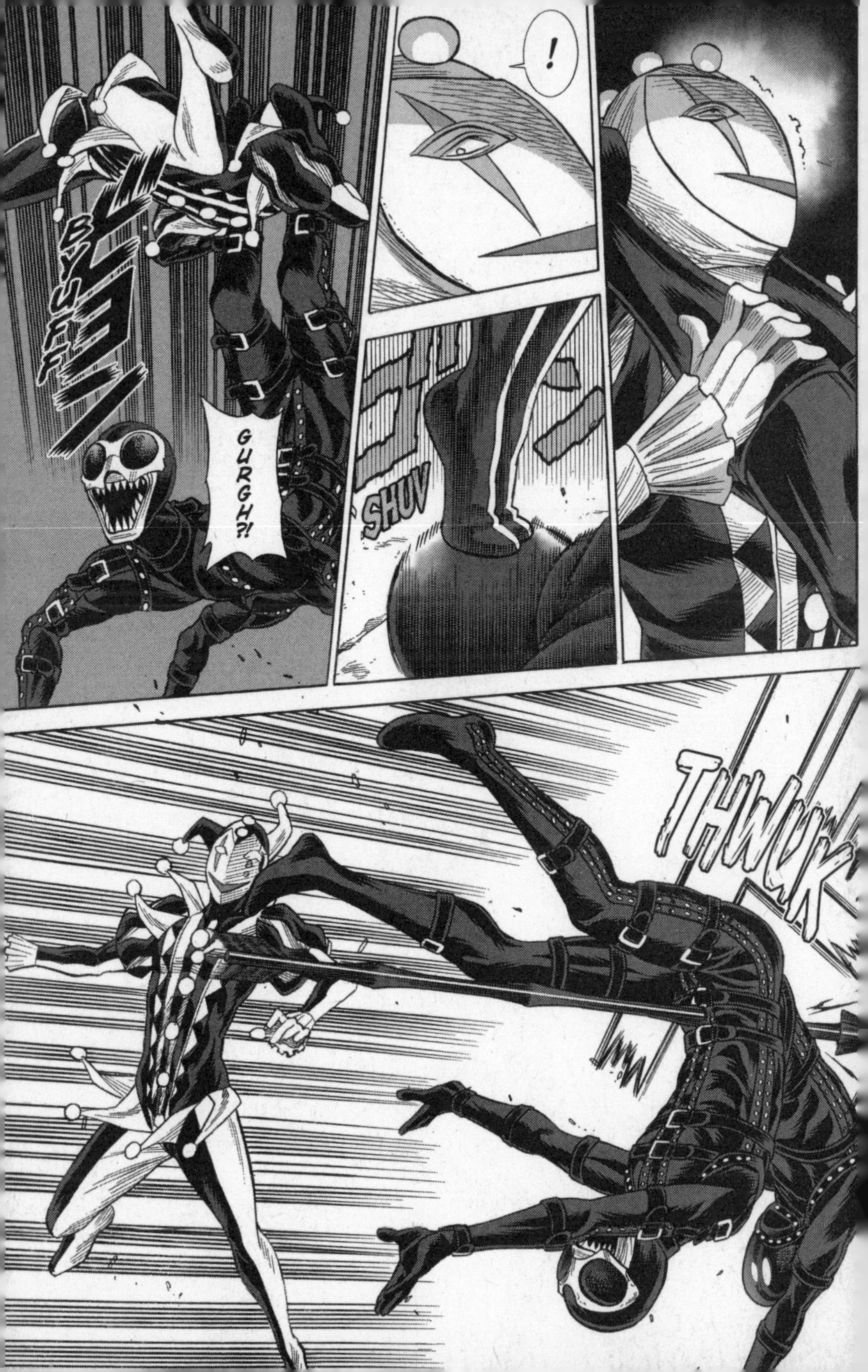
!
SHUV
BYUFF
GURGH?!
THWUK

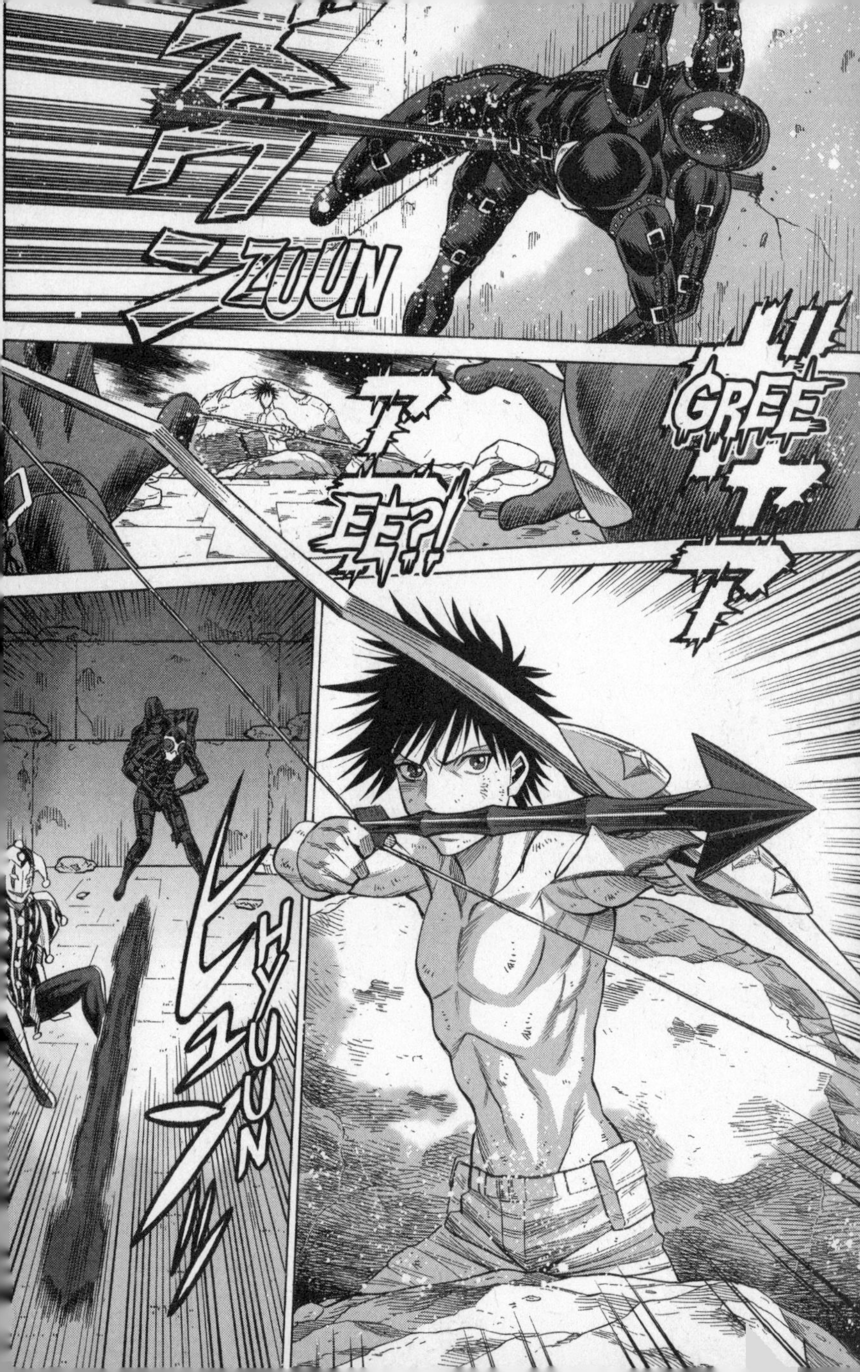
ZUUN
GREE
EE?!
HYUUN

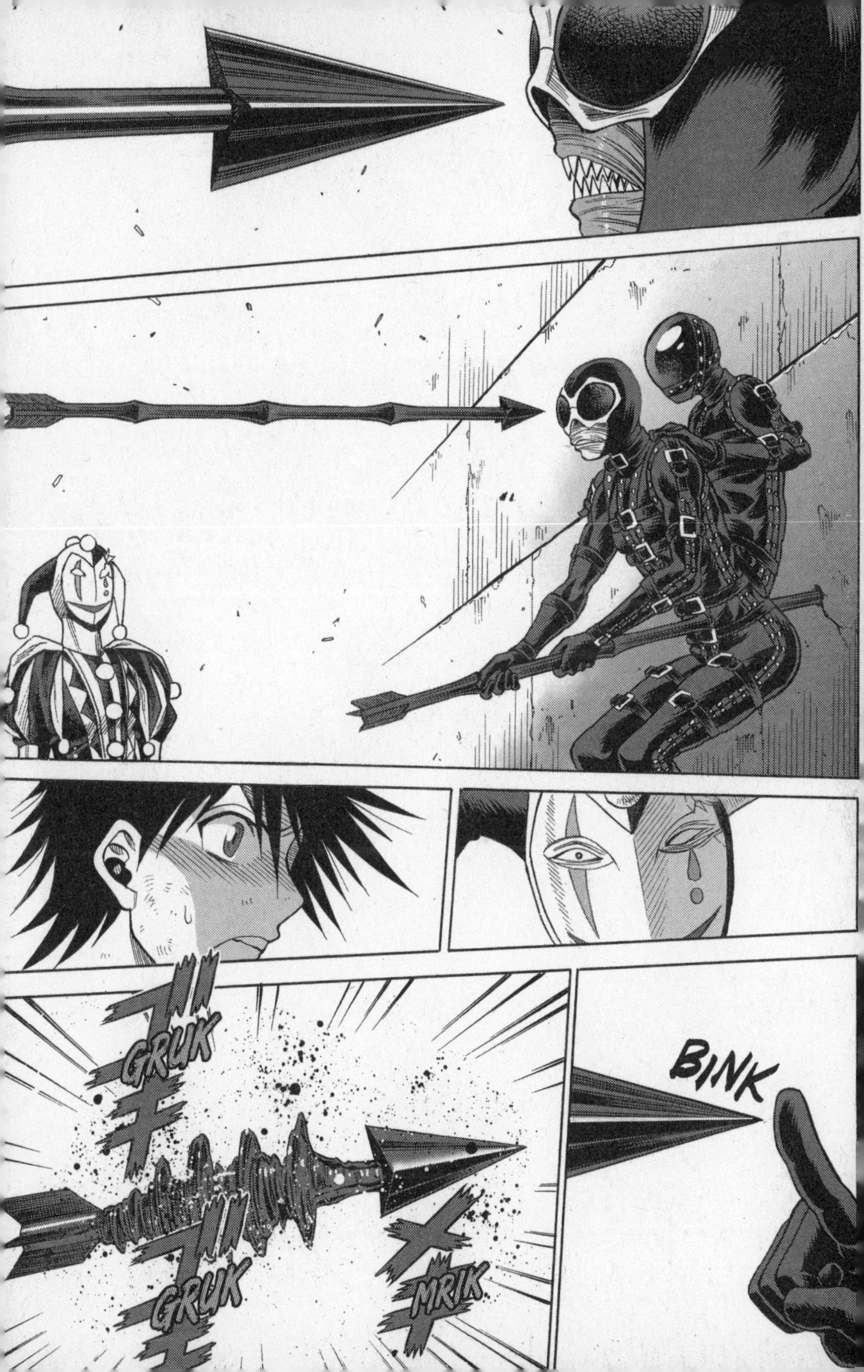
BINK
GRUK
MRIK
GRUK

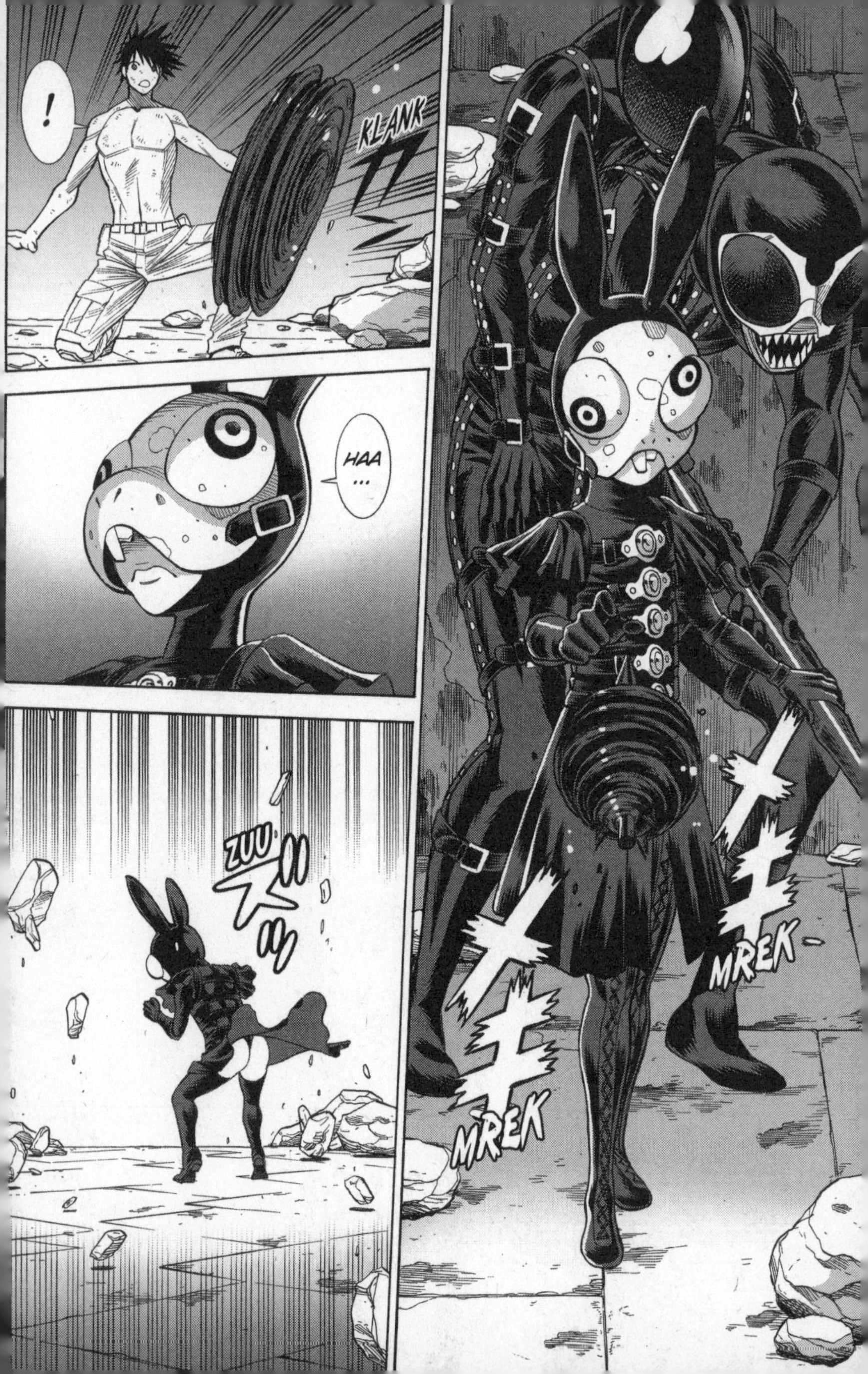
MREK
MREK
KLANK
!
HAA ...
ZUU

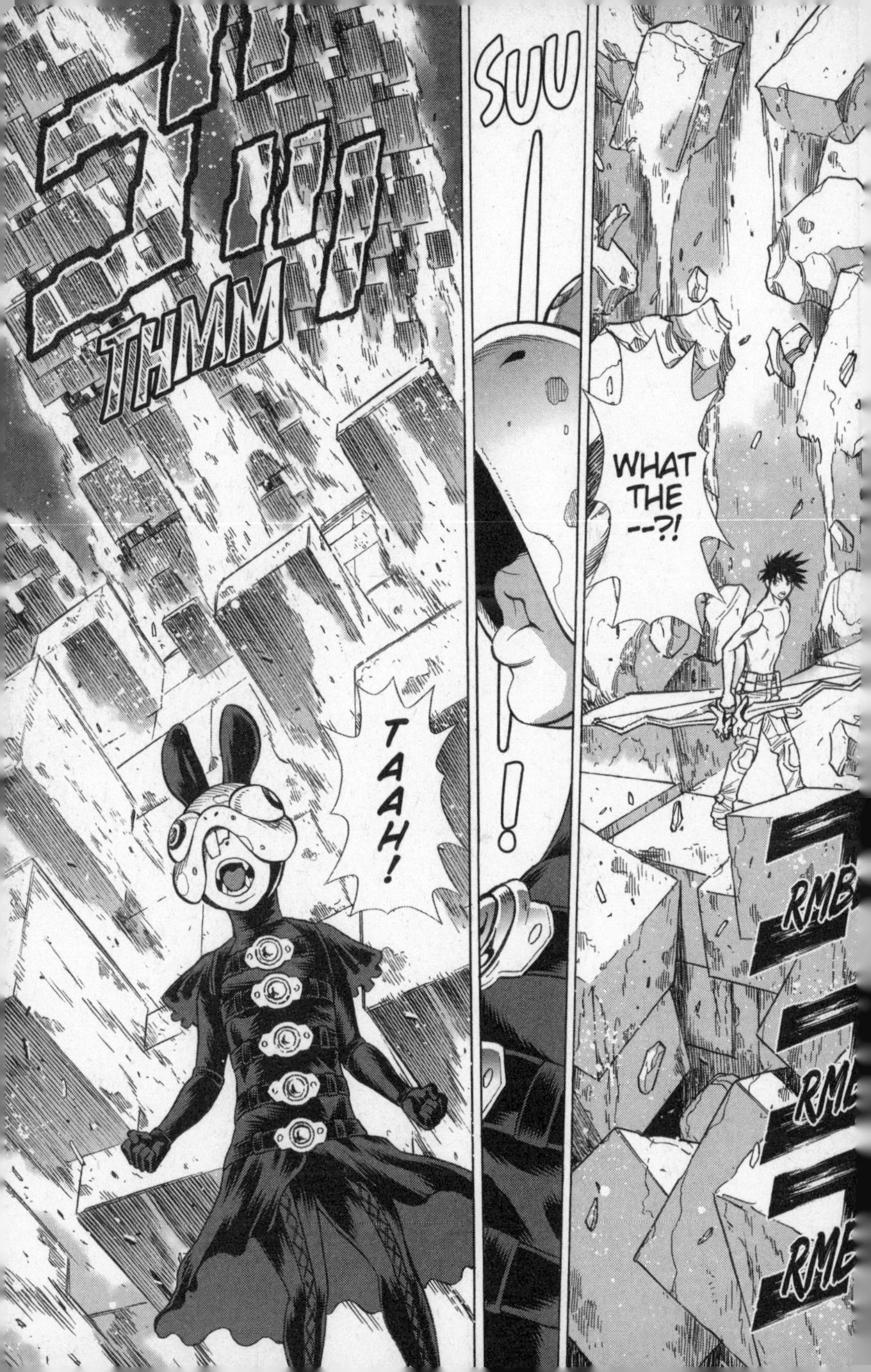
WHAT THE --?!
RMB
RM
RM
SUU
!
THMM
TAAH!

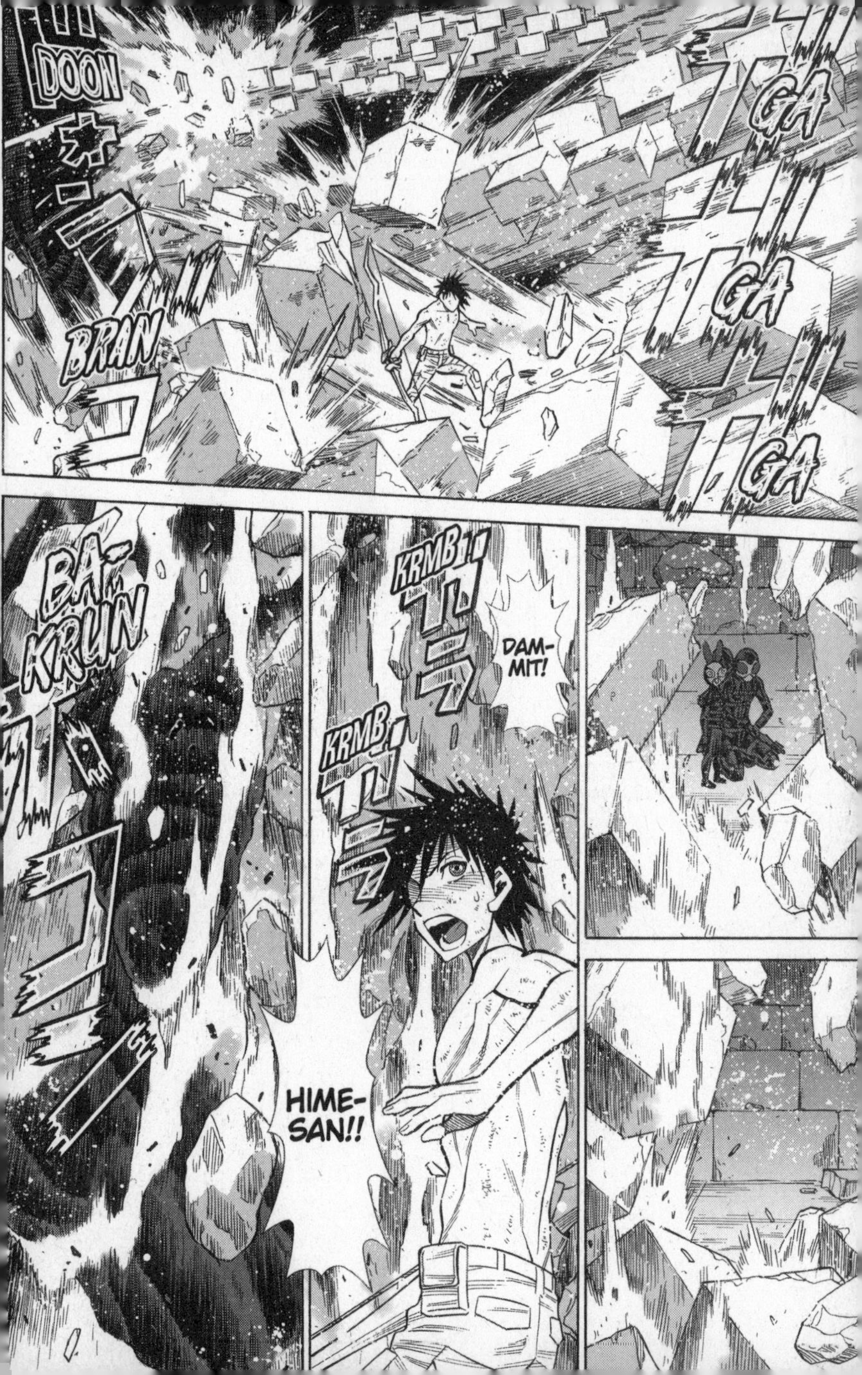
GA
GA
GA
DOON
BRAN
KRMB
DAM-
MIT!
KRMB
HIME-
SAN!!
BA-
KRUN

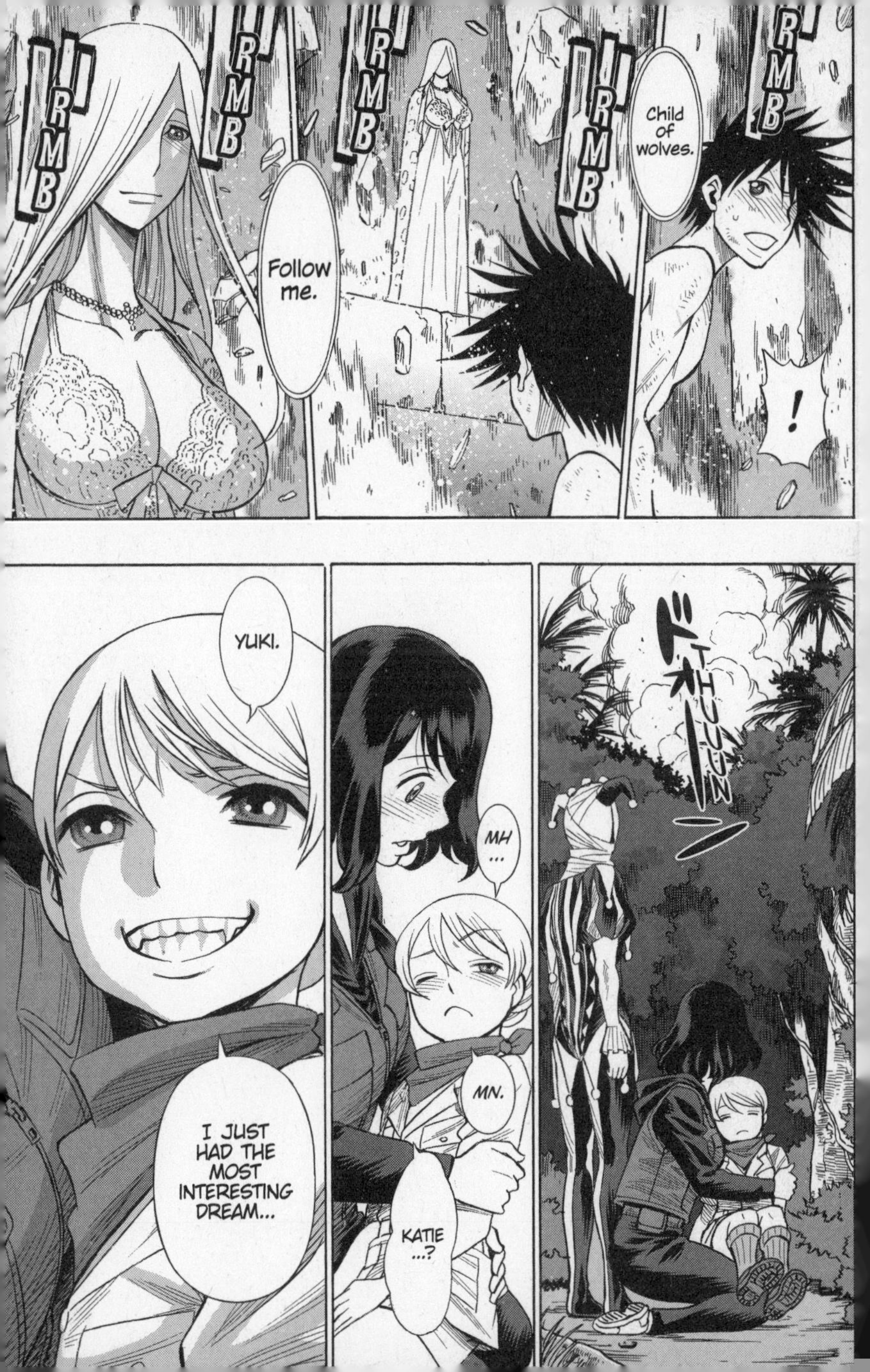
RMB
Child of wolves.
!
RMB
RMB
Follow me.
RMB
RMB
ドオーン
THUUUN
MH ...
MN.
KATIE ...?
YUKI.
I JUST HAD THE MOST INTERESTING DREAM...

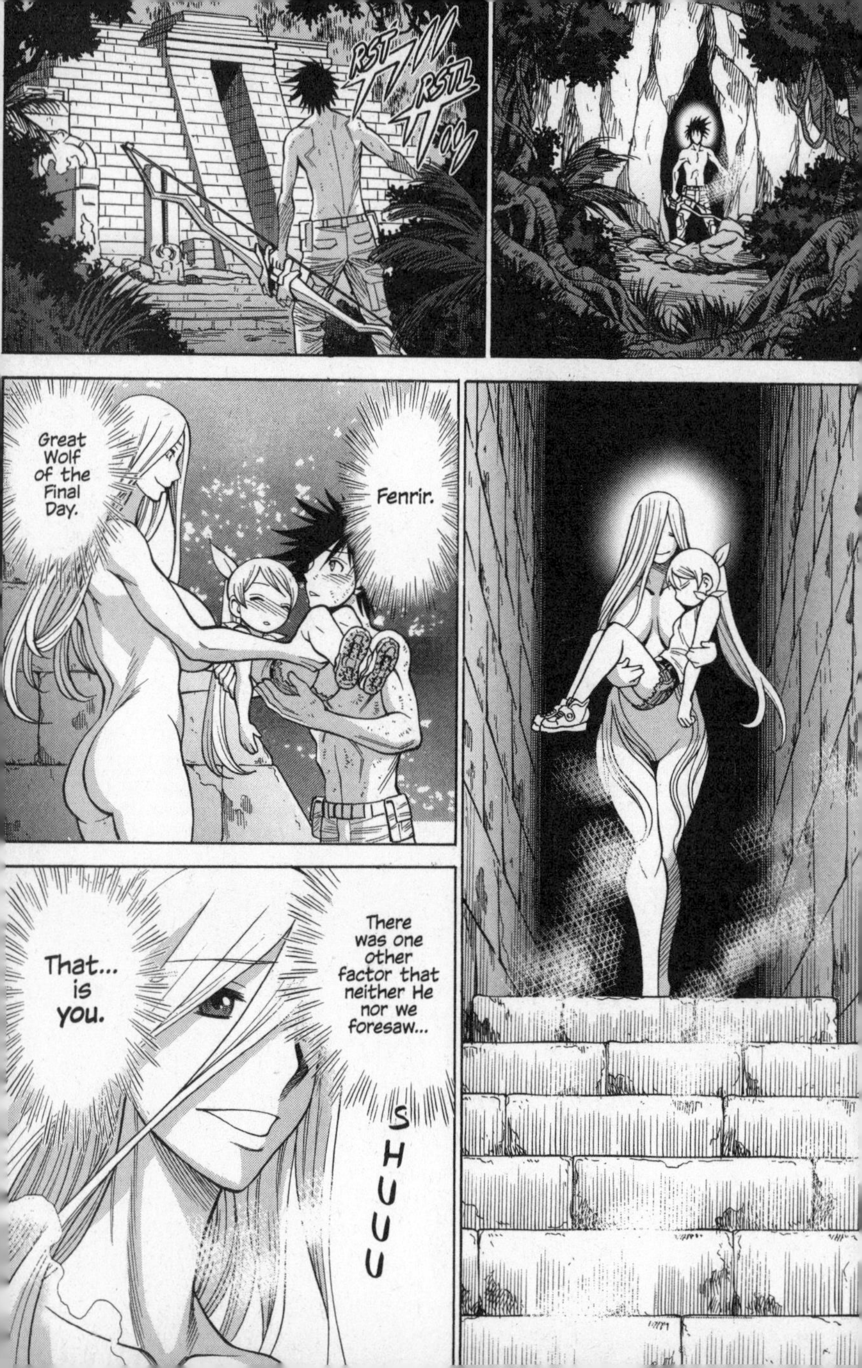
RST
RSTL
Fenrir.
Great Wolf of the Final Day.
There was one other factor that neither He nor we foresaw...
That... is you.
SHUUU

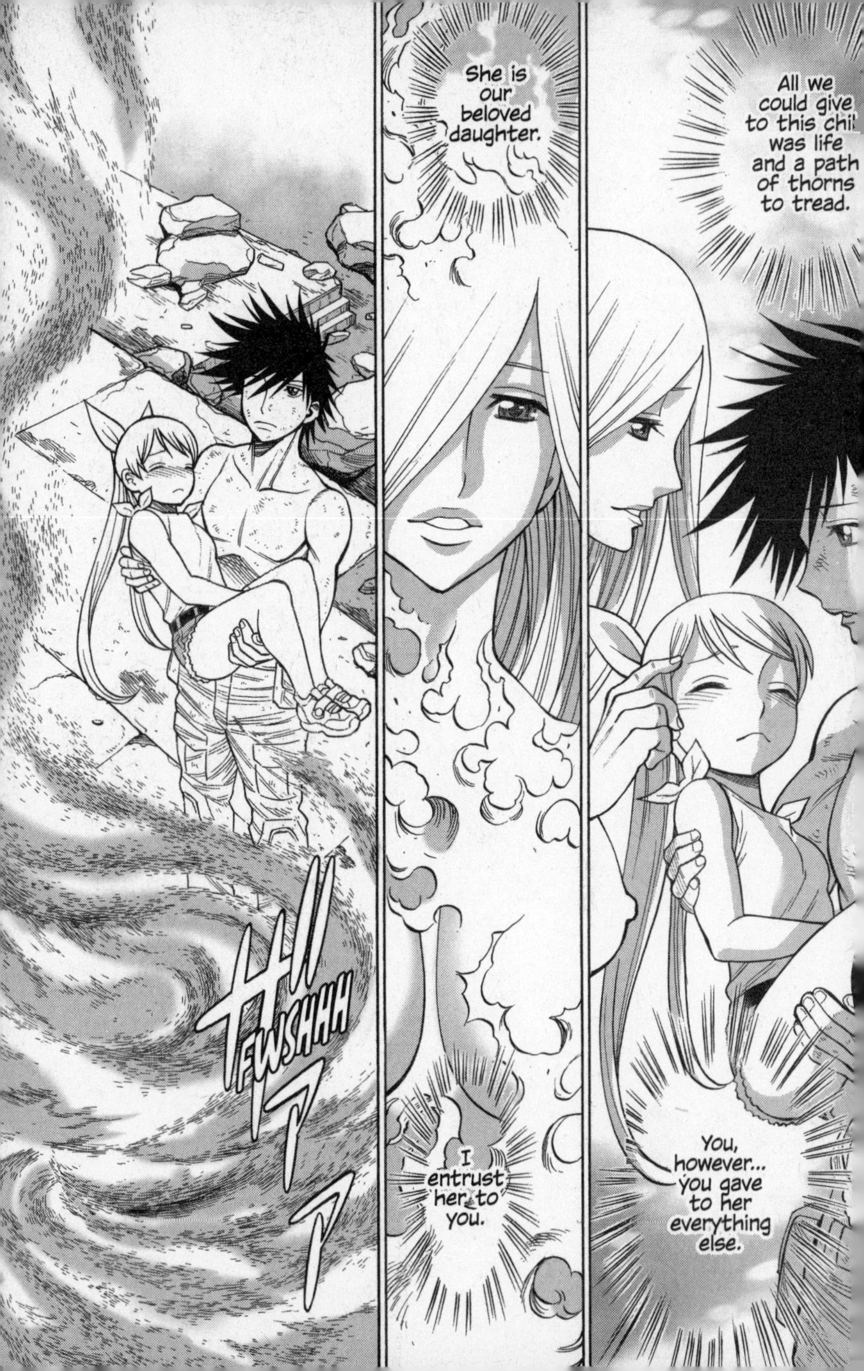
All we could give to this chil was life and a path of thorns to tread.
You, however... you gave to her everything else.
She is our beloved daughter.
I entrust her to you.
FWSHHH

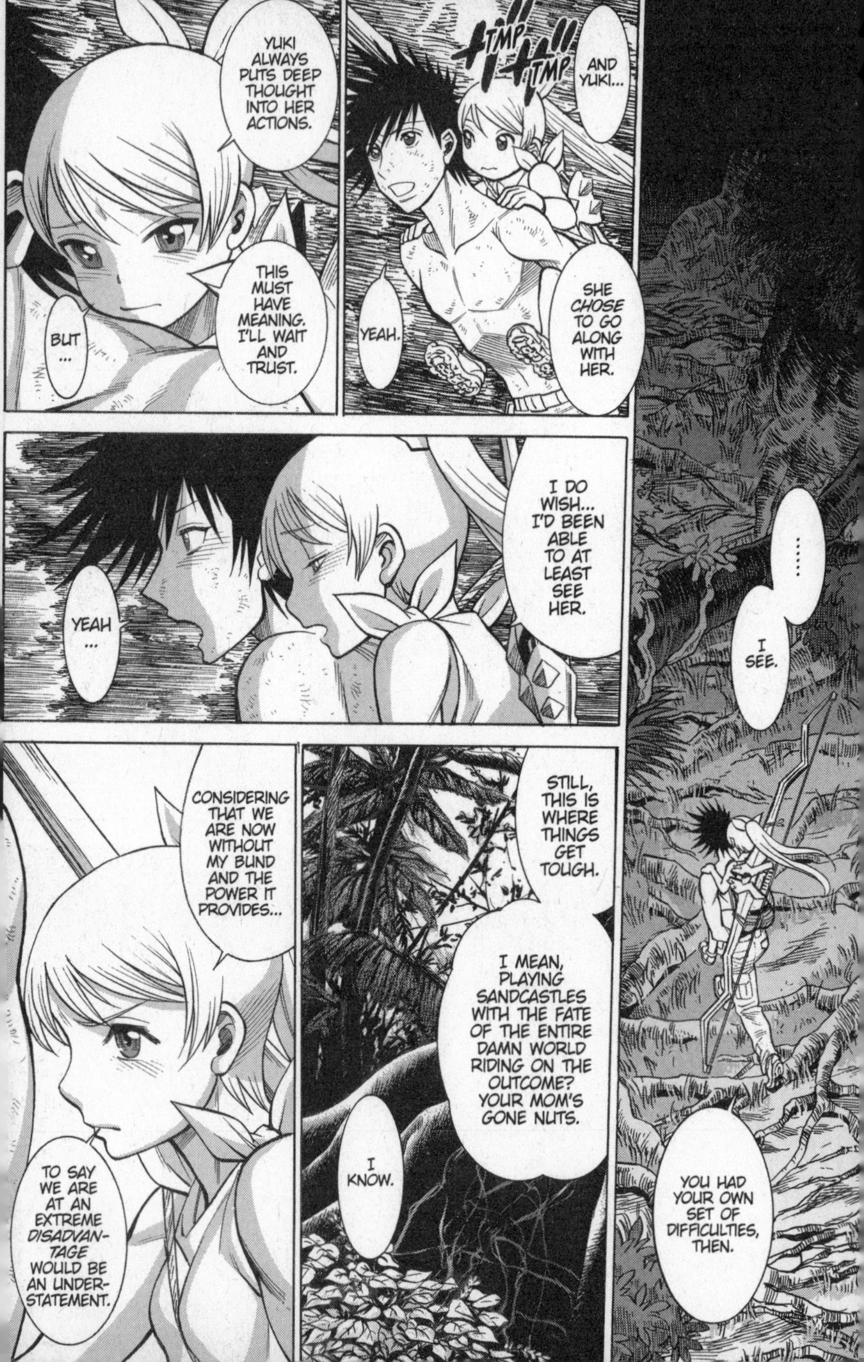
......
I SEE.
YOU HAD YOUR OWN SET OF DIFFICULTIES, THEN.
TMP TMP
AND YUKI...
SHE CHOSE TO GO ALONG WITH HER.
YEAH.
YUKI ALWAYS PUTS DEEP THOUGHT INTO HER ACTIONS.
THIS MUST HAVE MEANING. I'LL WAIT AND TRUST.
BUT ...
I DO WISH... I'D BEEN ABLE TO AT LEAST SEE HER.
YEAH ...
STILL, THIS IS WHERE THINGS GET TOUGH.
I MEAN, PLAYING SANDCASTLES WITH THE FATE OF THE ENTIRE DAMN WORLD RIDING ON THE OUTCOME? YOUR MOM'S GONE NUTS.
I KNOW.
CONSIDERING THAT WE ARE NOW WITHOUT MY BUND AND THE POWER IT PROVIDES...
TO SAY WE ARE AT AN EXTREME *DISADVANTAGE* WOULD BE AN UNDER-STATEMENT.

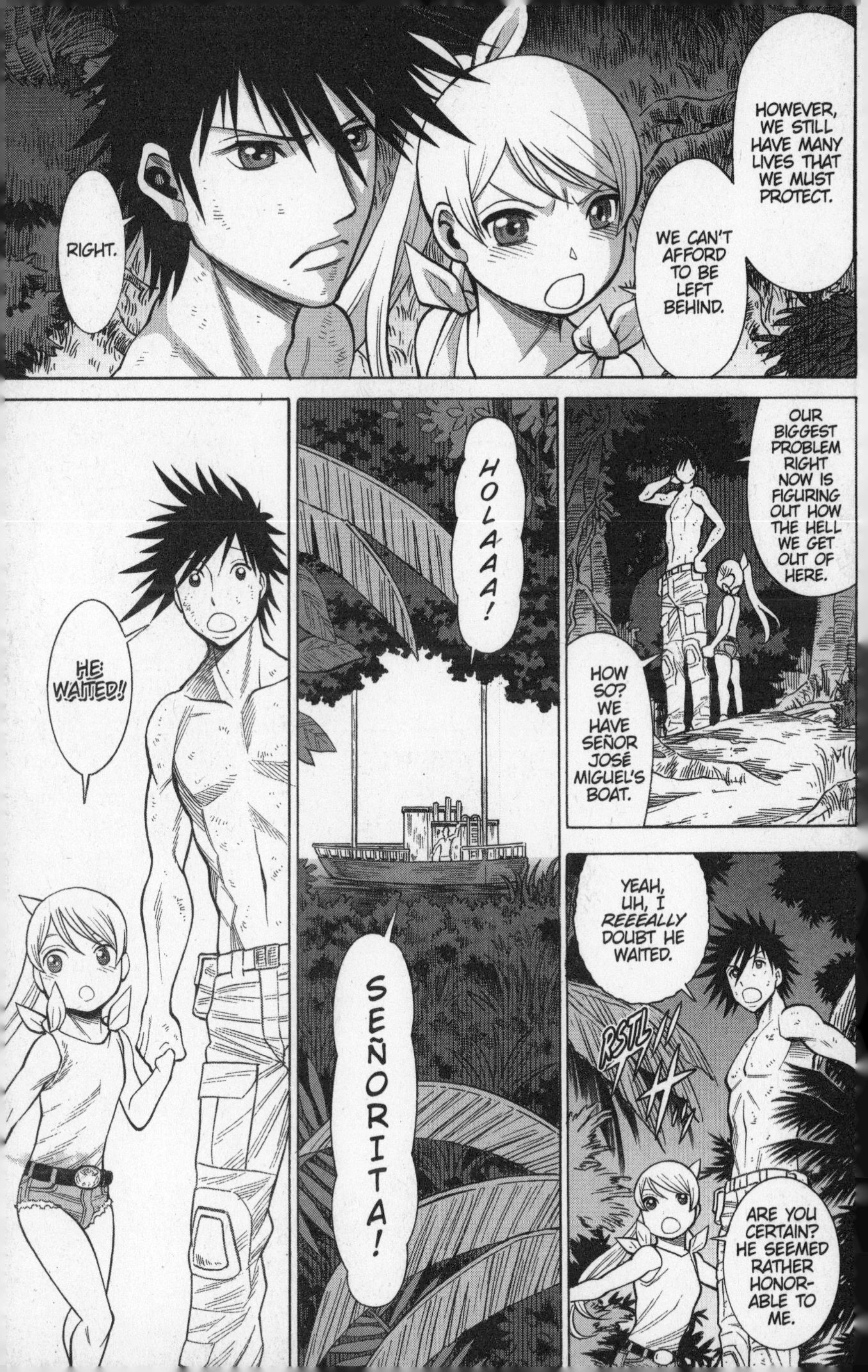
HOWEVER, WE STILL HAVE MANY LIVES THAT WE MUST PROTECT.
WE CAN'T AFFORD TO BE LEFT BEHIND.
RIGHT.
OUR BIGGEST PROBLEM RIGHT NOW IS FIGURING OUT HOW THE HELL WE GET OUT OF HERE.
HOW SO? WE HAVE SEÑOR JOSÉ MIGUEL'S BOAT.
YEAH, UH, I *REEEALLY* DOUBT HE WAITED.
RSTL
ARE YOU CERTAIN? HE SEEMED RATHER HONOR-ABLE TO ME.
HOLAAAA!
SEÑORITA!
HE WAITED!!

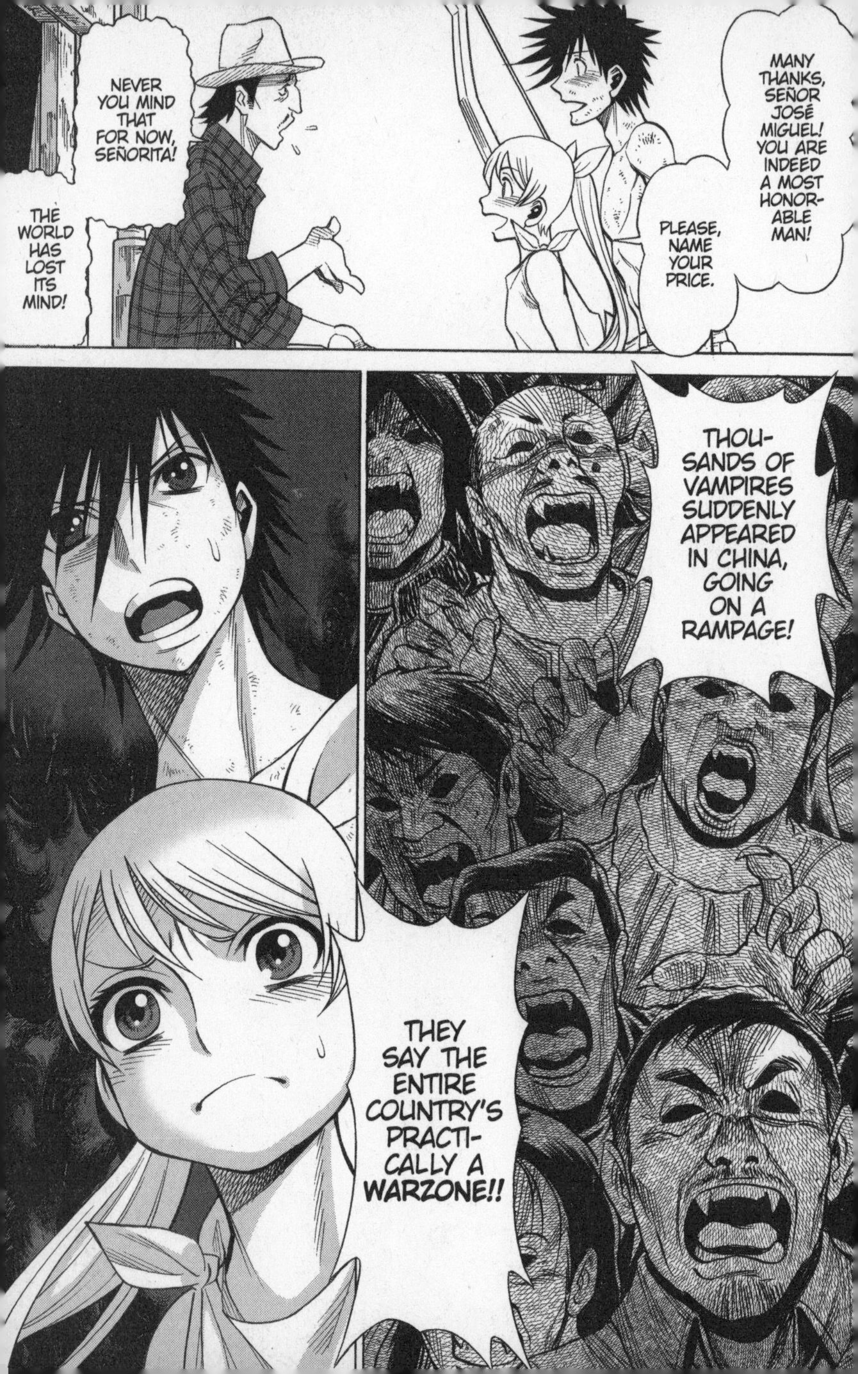
MANY THANKS, SEÑOR JOSÉ MIGUEL! YOU ARE INDEED A MOST HONORABLE MAN!
PLEASE, NAME YOUR PRICE.
NEVER YOU MIND THAT FOR NOW, SEÑORITA!
THE WORLD HAS LOST ITS MIND!
THOUSANDS OF VAMPIRES SUDDENLY APPEARED IN CHINA, GOING ON A RAMPAGE!
THEY SAY THE ENTIRE COUNTRY'S PRACTICALLY A WARZONE!!

Chapter 7: Fools' Game

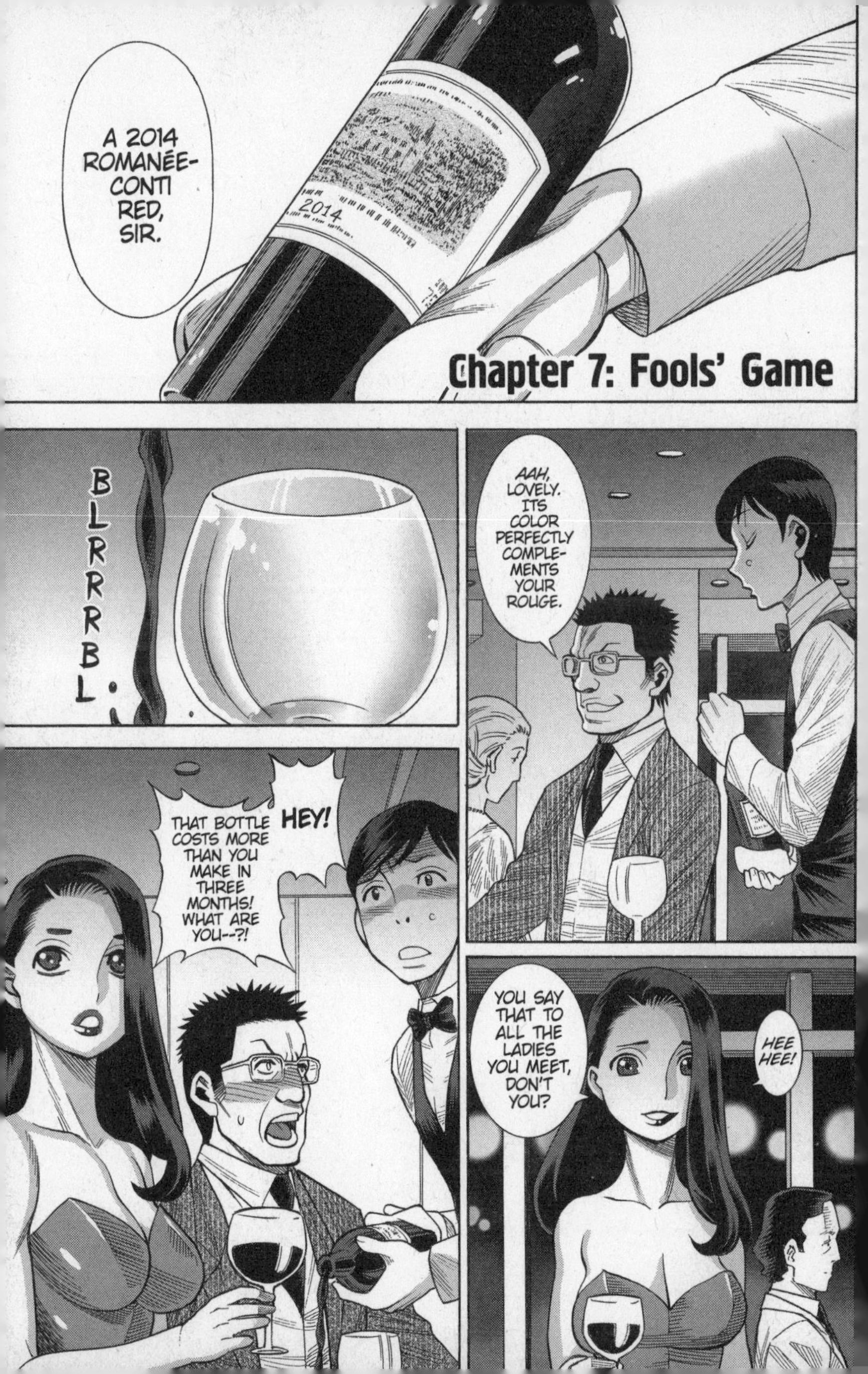
A 2014 ROMANÉE-CONTI RED, SIR.
2014
AAH, LOVELY. ITS COLOR PERFECTLY COMPLEMENTS YOUR ROUGE.
YOU SAY THAT TO ALL THE LADIES YOU MEET, DON'T YOU?
HEE HEE!
BLRRRBL
HEY!
THAT BOTTLE COSTS MORE THAN YOU MAKE IN THREE MONTHS! WHAT ARE YOU--?!

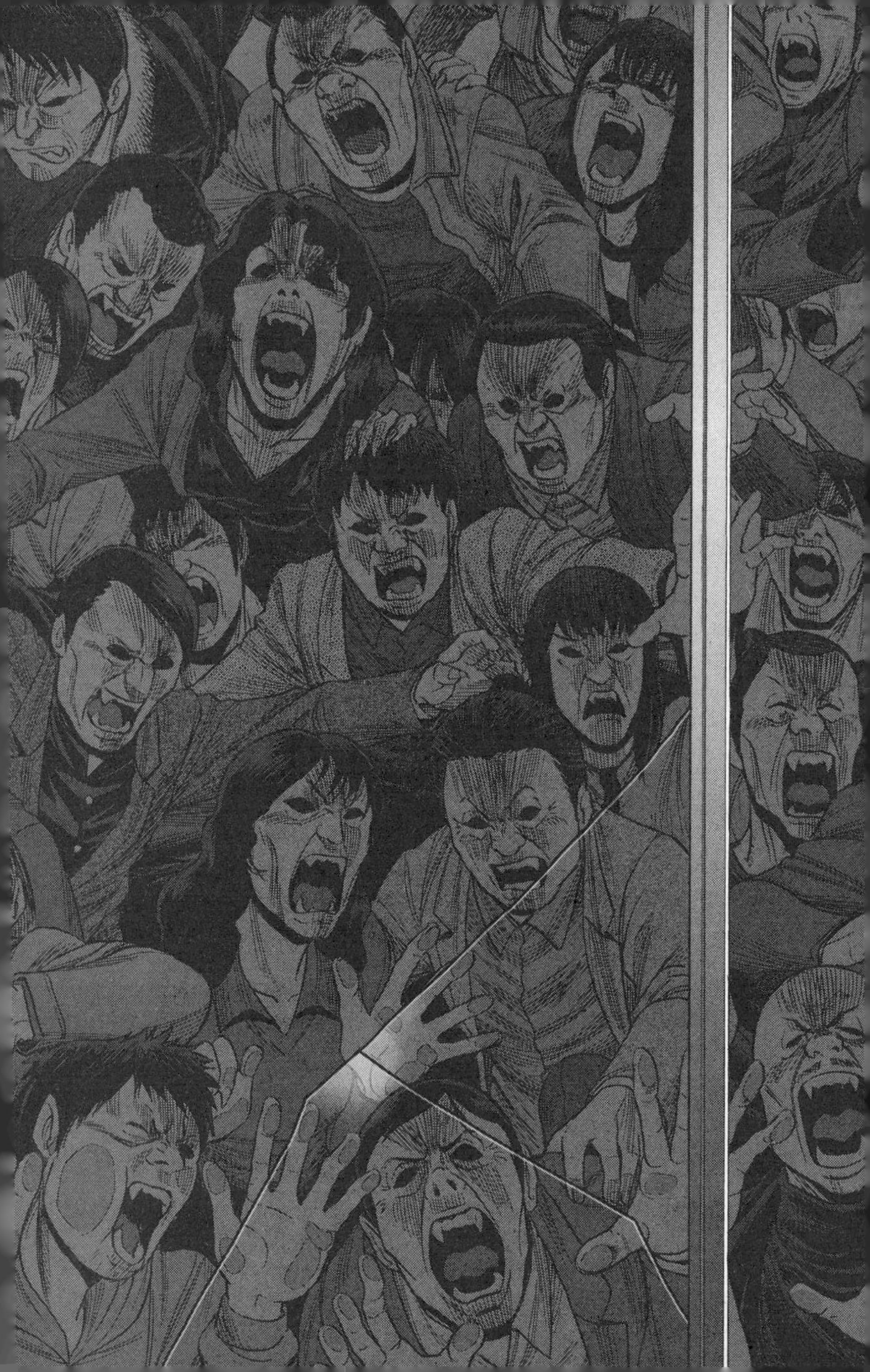

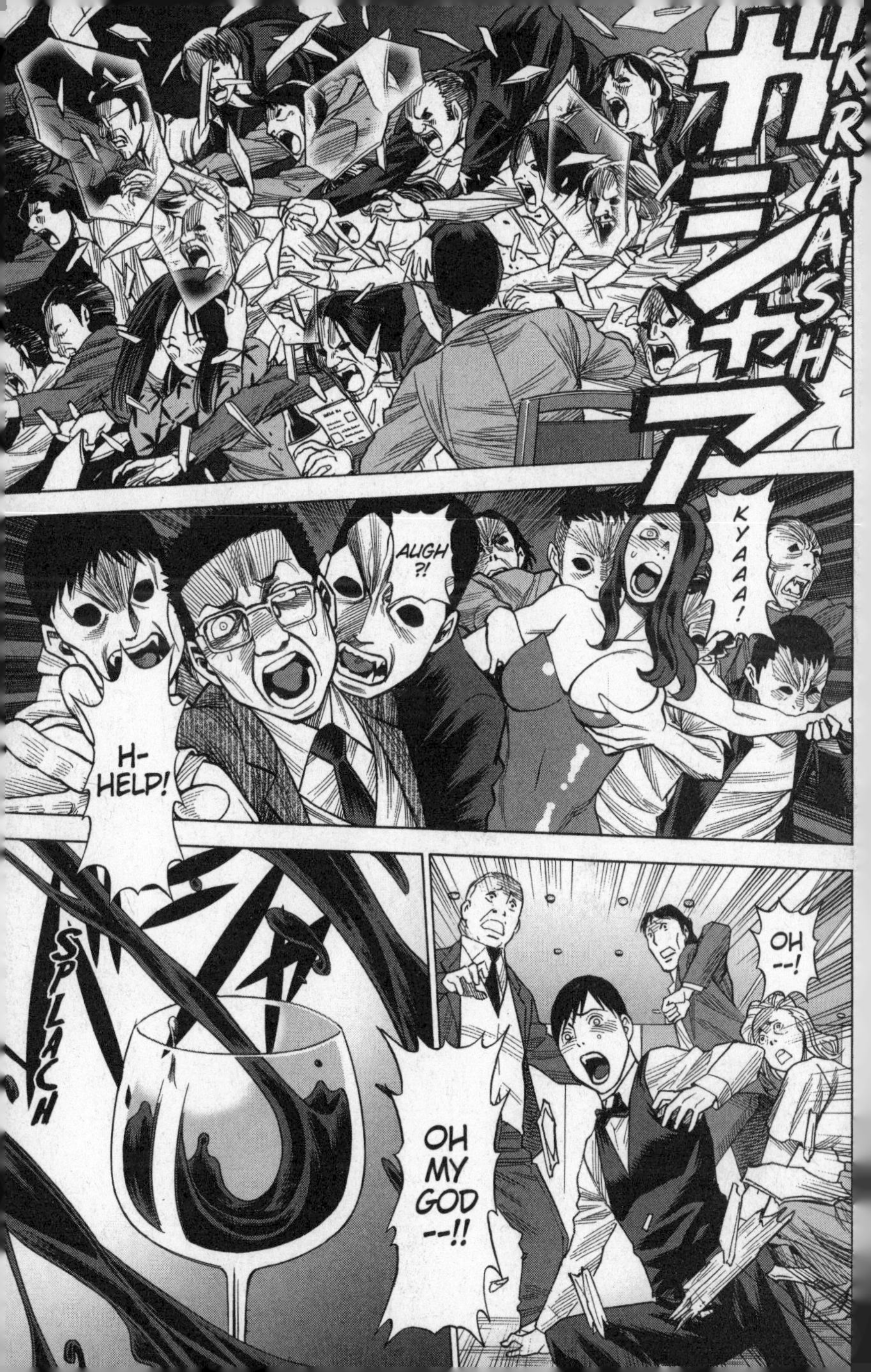
KRAASH
KYAAA!
AUGH ?!
H-HELP!
OH --!
OH MY GOD --!!
SPLACH

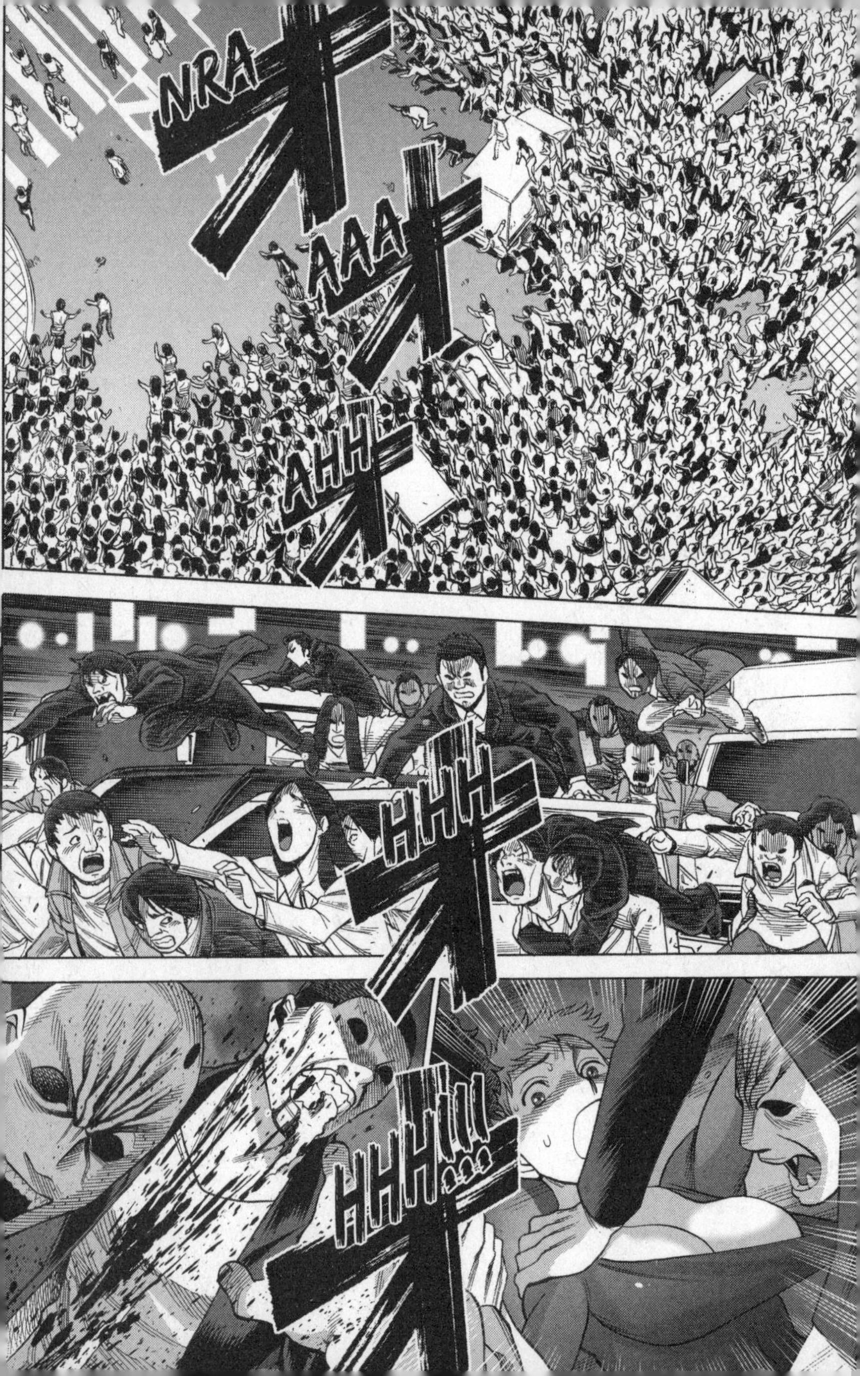
NRA
AAA
AHH
HHH
HHH!!!

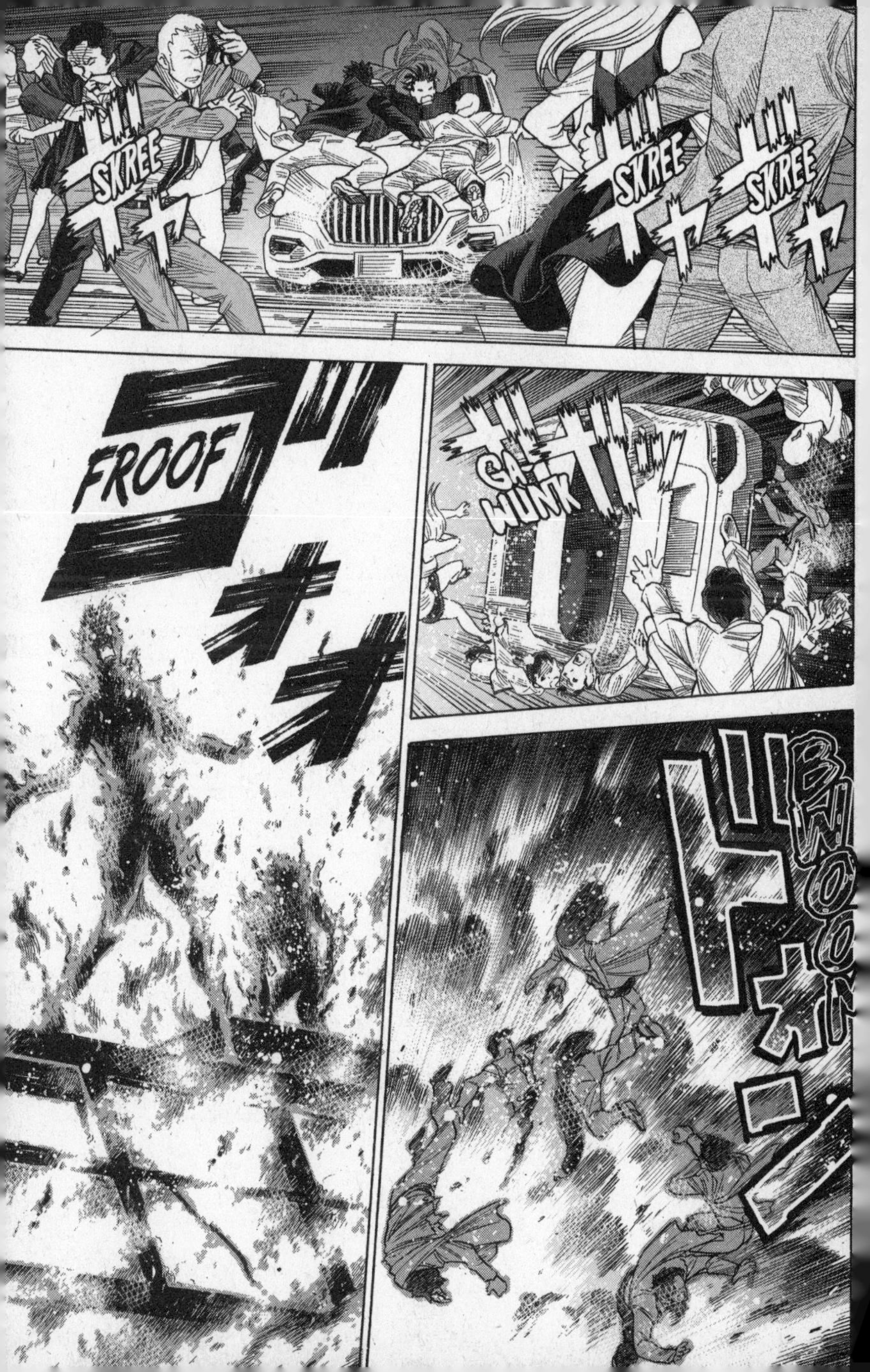
SKREE
SKREE
SKREE
GA-WUNK
BWOOM
FROOF

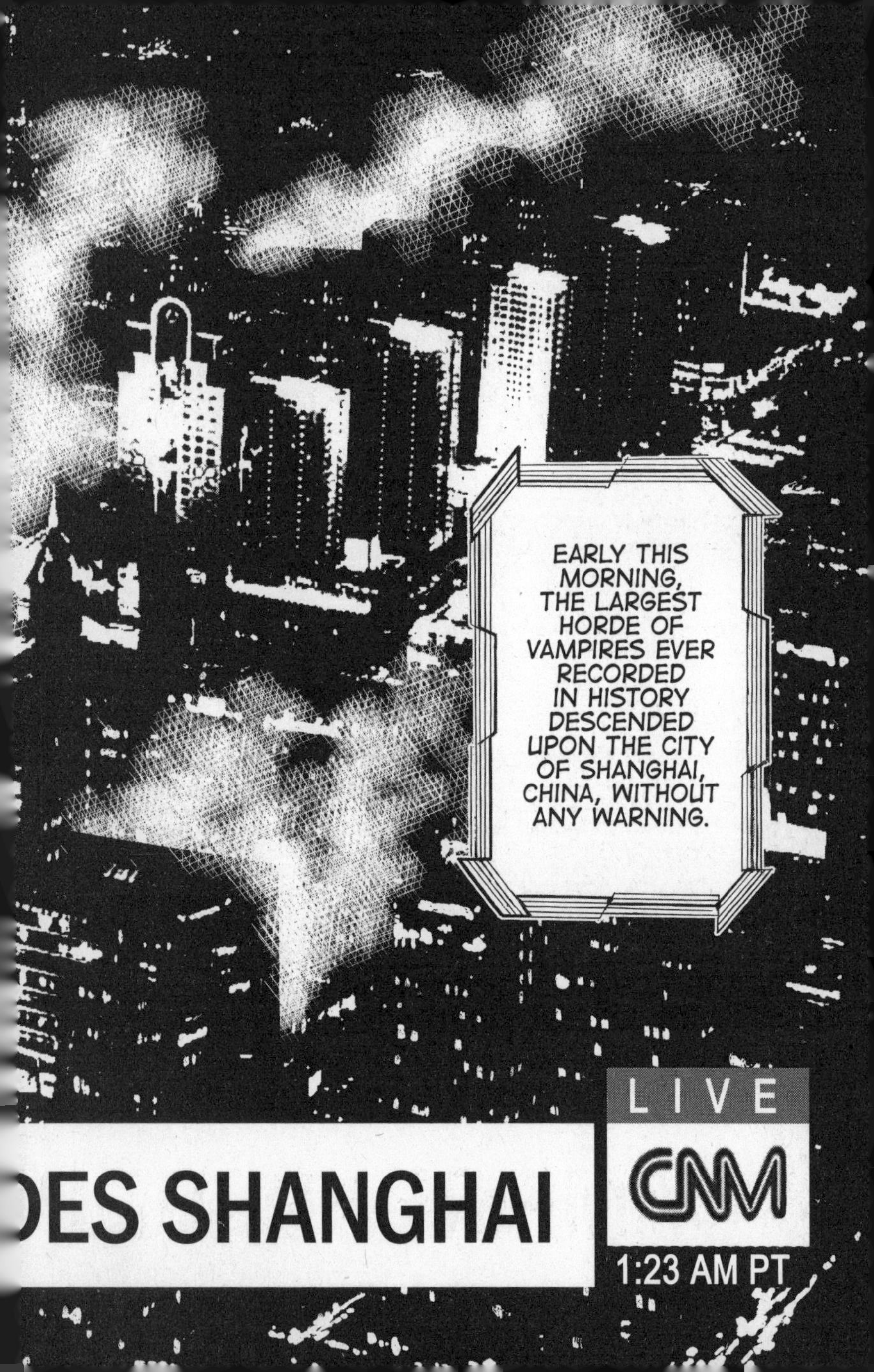

EARLY THIS MORNING, THE LARGEST HORDE OF VAMPIRES EVER RECORDED IN HISTORY DESCENDED UPON THE CITY OF SHANGHAI, CHINA, WITHOUT ANY WARNING.
LIVE
CNN
DES SHANGHAI
1:23 AM PT

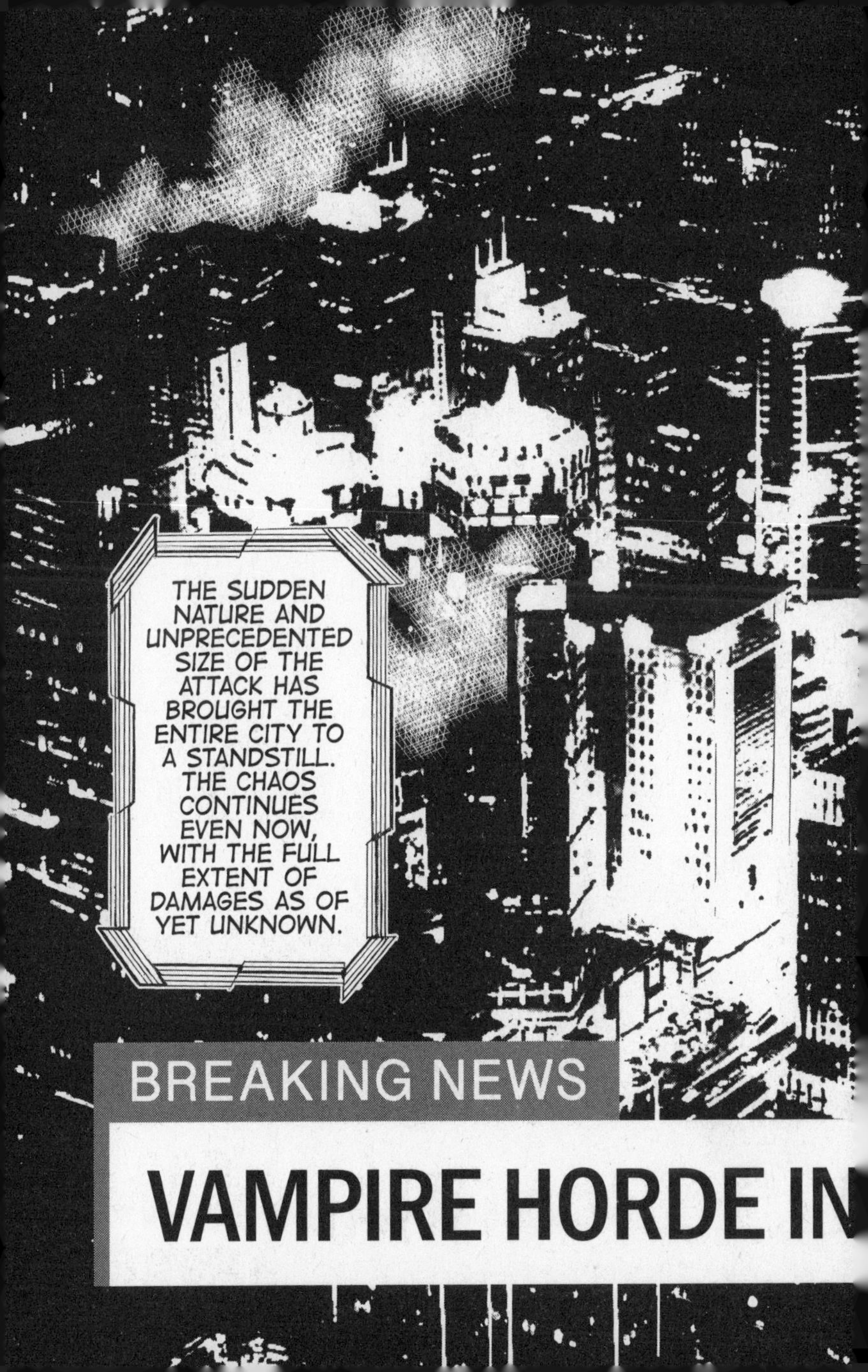
THE SUDDEN NATURE AND UNPRECEDENTED SIZE OF THE ATTACK HAS BROUGHT THE ENTIRE CITY TO A STANDSTILL. THE CHAOS CONTINUES EVEN NOW, WITH THE FULL EXTENT OF DAMAGES AS OF YET UNKNOWN.
BREAKING NEWS
VAMPIRE HORDE IN

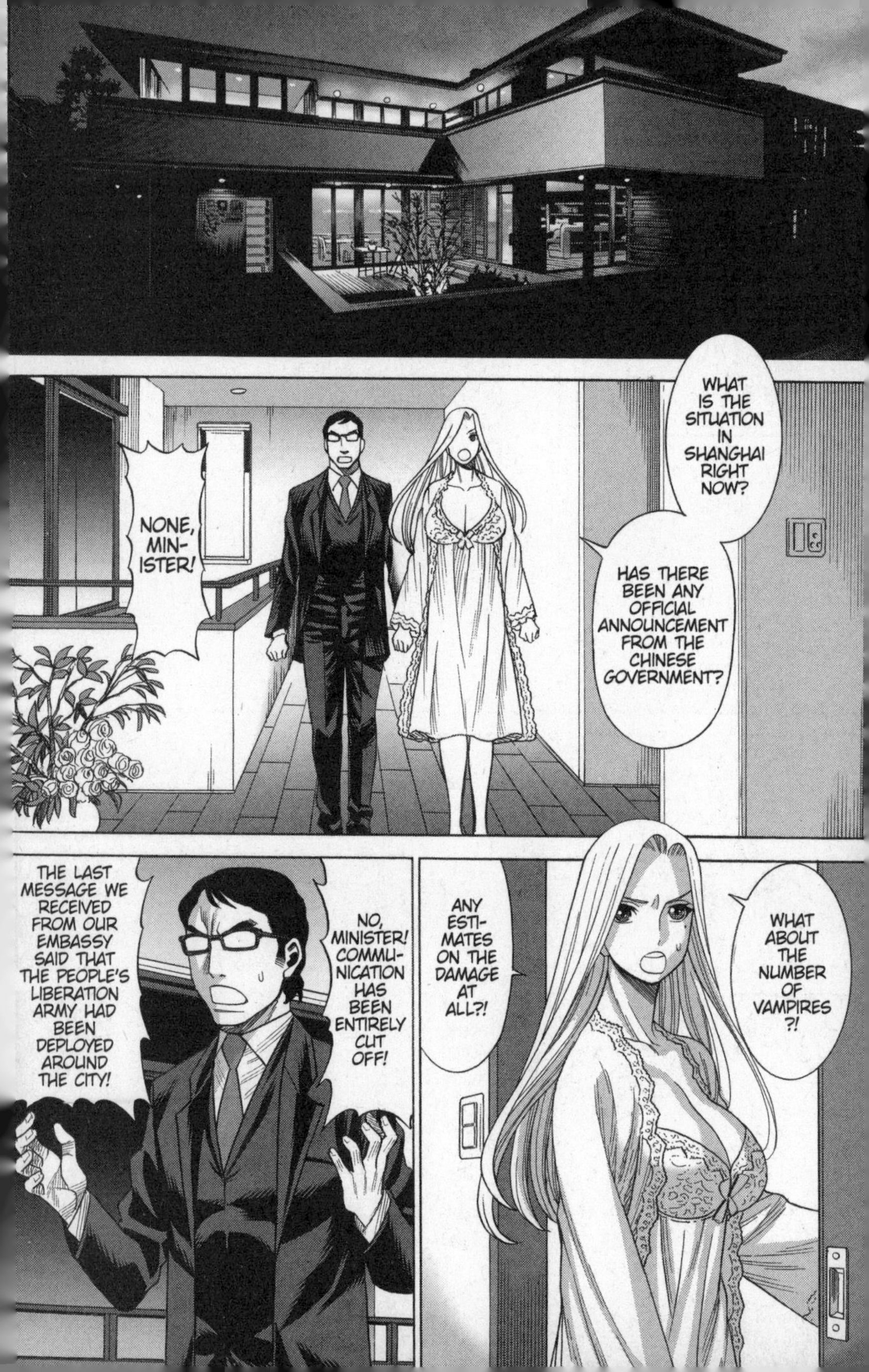

WHAT IS THE SITUATION IN SHANGHAI RIGHT NOW?
HAS THERE BEEN ANY OFFICIAL ANNOUNCEMENT FROM THE CHINESE GOVERNMENT?
NONE, MIN-ISTER!
WHAT ABOUT THE NUMBER OF VAMPIRES ?!
ANY ESTI-MATES ON THE DAMAGE AT ALL?!
NO, MINISTER! COMMU-NICATION HAS BEEN ENTIRELY CUT OFF!
THE LAST MESSAGE WE RECEIVED FROM OUR EMBASSY SAID THAT THE PEOPLE'S LIBERATION ARMY HAD BEEN DEPLOYED AROUND THE CITY!

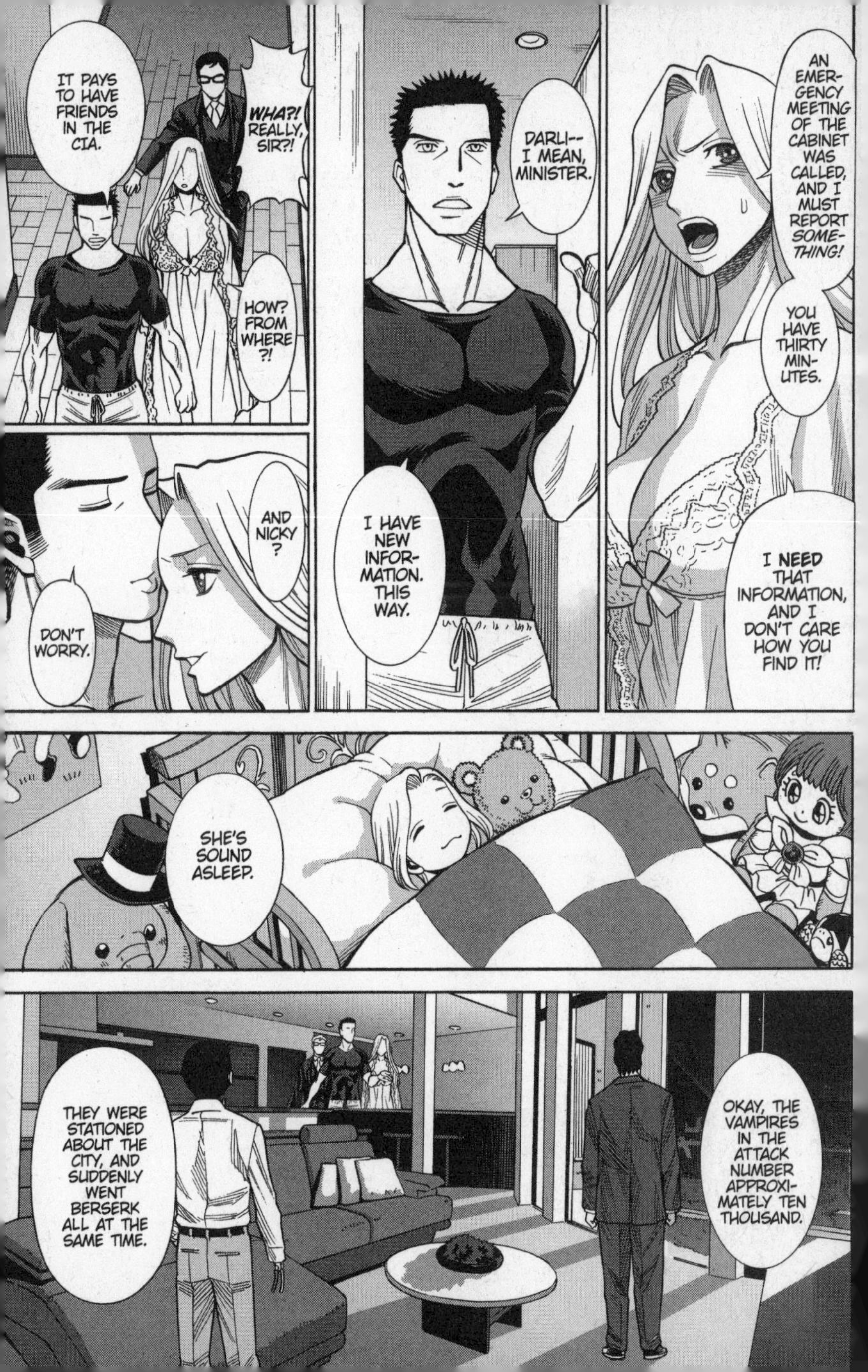
AN EMERGENCY MEETING OF THE CABINET WAS CALLED, AND I MUST REPORT SOMETHING!
YOU HAVE THIRTY MINUTES.
I NEED THAT INFORMATION, AND I DON'T CARE HOW YOU FIND IT!
DARLI-- I MEAN, MINISTER.
I HAVE NEW INFORMATION. THIS WAY.
WHA?! REALLY, SIR?!
HOW? FROM WHERE?!
IT PAYS TO HAVE FRIENDS IN THE CIA.
AND NICKY?
DON'T WORRY.
SHE'S SOUND ASLEEP.
OKAY, THE VAMPIRES IN THE ATTACK NUMBER APPROXIMATELY TEN THOUSAND.
THEY WERE STATIONED ABOUT THE CITY, AND SUDDENLY WENT BERSERK ALL AT THE SAME TIME.

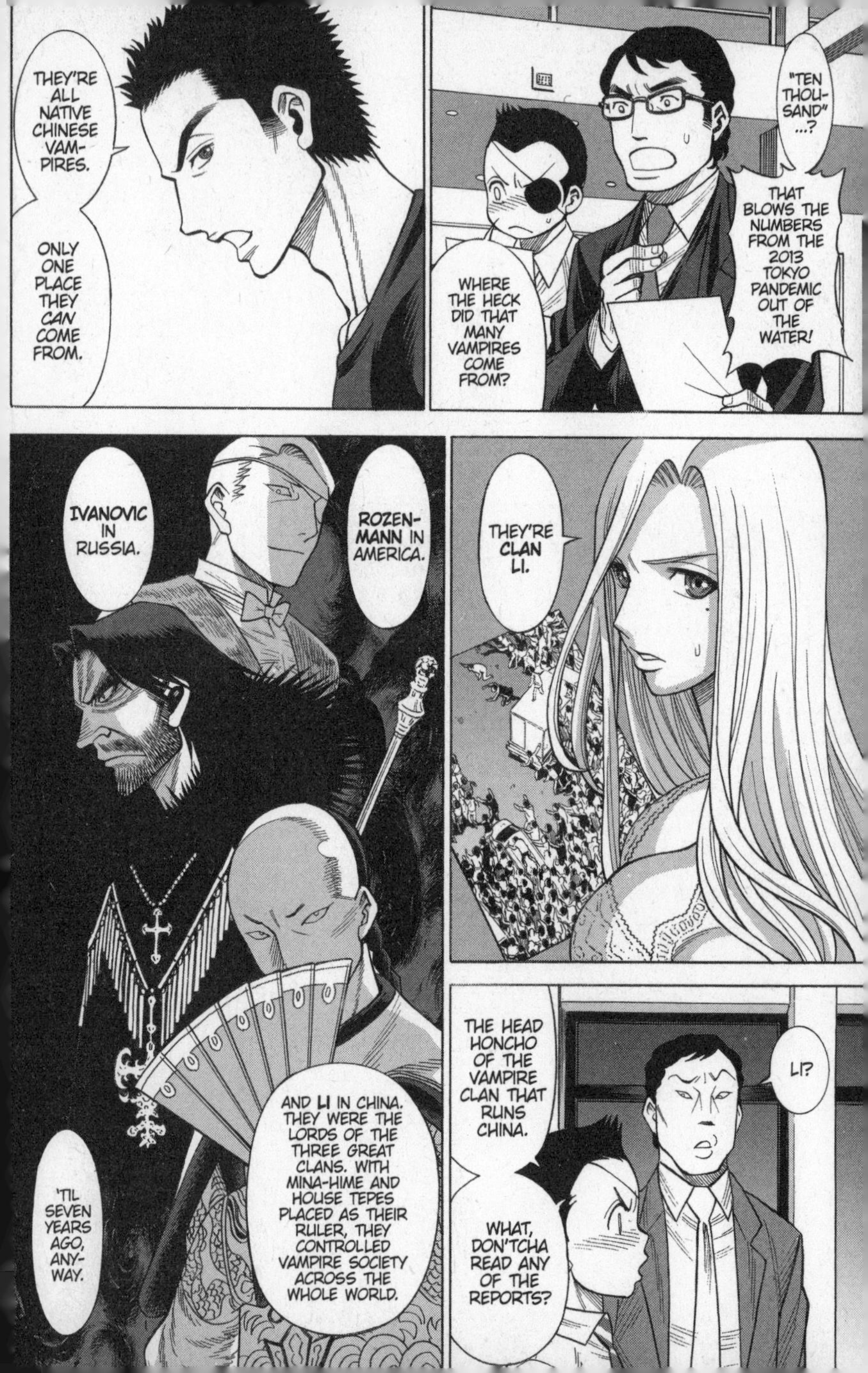
"TEN THOUSAND" ...?
THAT BLOWS THE NUMBERS FROM THE 2013 TOKYO PANDEMIC OUT OF THE WATER!
WHERE THE HECK DID THAT MANY VAMPIRES COME FROM?
THEY'RE ALL NATIVE CHINESE VAMPIRES.
ONLY ONE PLACE THEY *CAN* COME FROM.
THEY'RE **CLAN LI.**
LI?
THE HEAD HONCHO OF THE VAMPIRE CLAN THAT RUNS CHINA.
WHAT, DON'TCHA READ ANY OF THE REPORTS?
ROZENMANN IN AMERICA.
IVANOVIC IN RUSSIA.
AND **LI** IN CHINA. THEY WERE THE LORDS OF THE THREE GREAT CLANS. WITH MINA-HIME AND HOUSE TEPES PLACED AS THEIR RULER, THEY CONTROLLED VAMPIRE SOCIETY ACROSS THE WHOLE WORLD.
'TIL SEVEN YEARS AGO, ANYWAY.

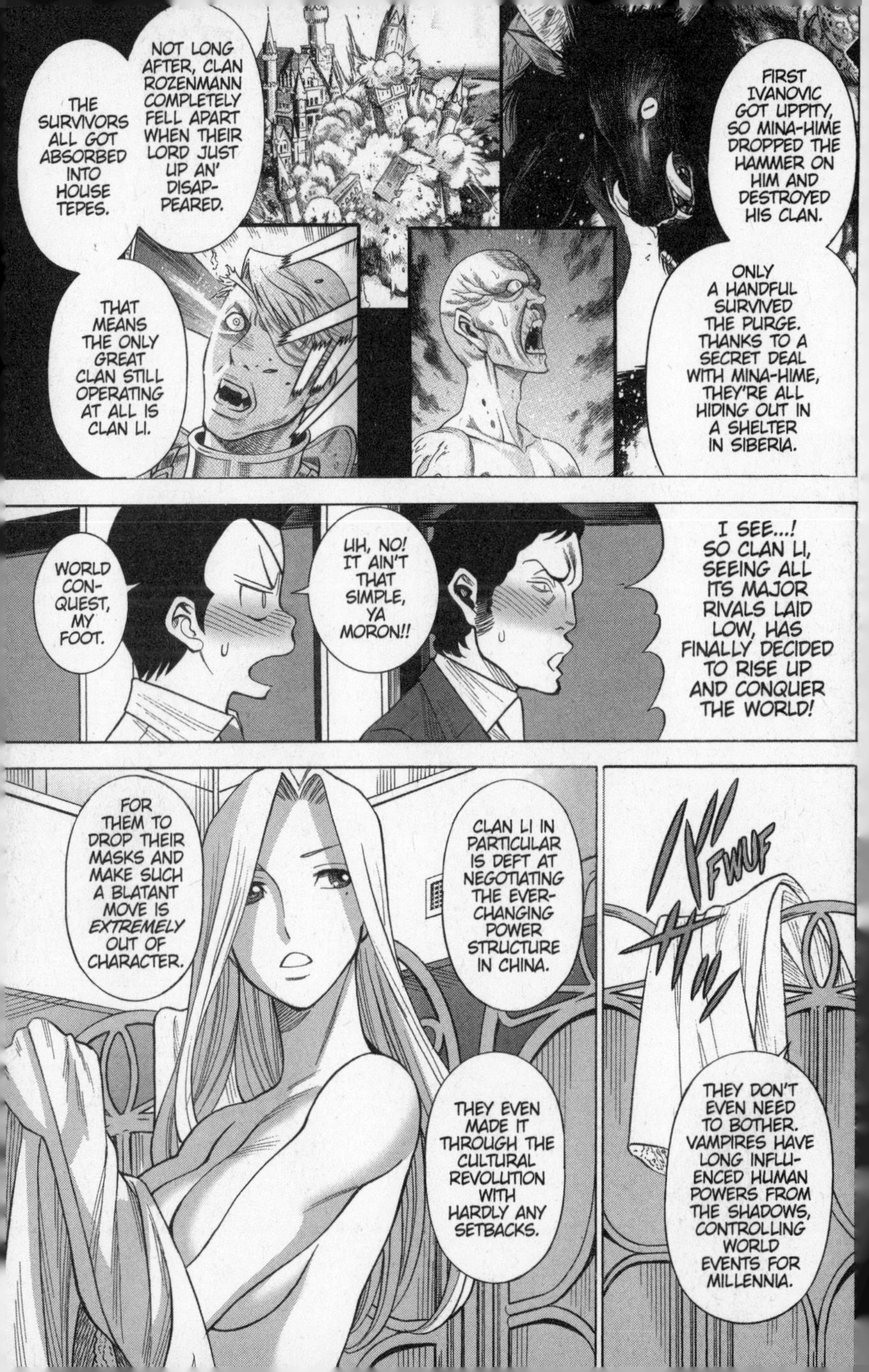
FIRST IVANOVIC GOT UPPITY, SO MINA-HIME DROPPED THE HAMMER ON HIM AND DESTROYED HIS CLAN.
ONLY A HANDFUL SURVIVED THE PURGE. THANKS TO A SECRET DEAL WITH MINA-HIME, THEY'RE ALL HIDING OUT IN A SHELTER IN SIBERIA.
NOT LONG AFTER, CLAN ROZENMANN COMPLETELY FELL APART WHEN THEIR LORD JUST UP AN' DISAP-PEARED.
THE SURVIVORS ALL GOT ABSORBED INTO HOUSE TEPES.
THAT MEANS THE ONLY GREAT CLAN STILL OPERATING AT ALL IS CLAN LI.
I SEE...! SO CLAN LI, SEEING ALL ITS MAJOR RIVALS LAID LOW, HAS FINALLY DECIDED TO RISE UP AND CONQUER THE WORLD!
UH, NO! IT AIN'T THAT SIMPLE, YA MORON!!
WORLD CON-QUEST, MY FOOT.
FWUF
THEY DON'T EVEN NEED TO BOTHER. VAMPIRES HAVE LONG INFLU-ENCED HUMAN POWERS FROM THE SHADOWS, CONTROLLING WORLD EVENTS FOR MILLENNIA.
FOR THEM TO DROP THEIR MASKS AND MAKE SUCH A BLATANT MOVE IS *EXTREMELY* OUT OF CHARACTER.
CLAN LI IN PARTICULAR IS DEFT AT NEGOTIATING THE EVER-CHANGING POWER STRUCTURE IN CHINA.
THEY EVEN MADE IT THROUGH THE CULTURAL REVOLUTION WITH HARDLY ANY SETBACKS.

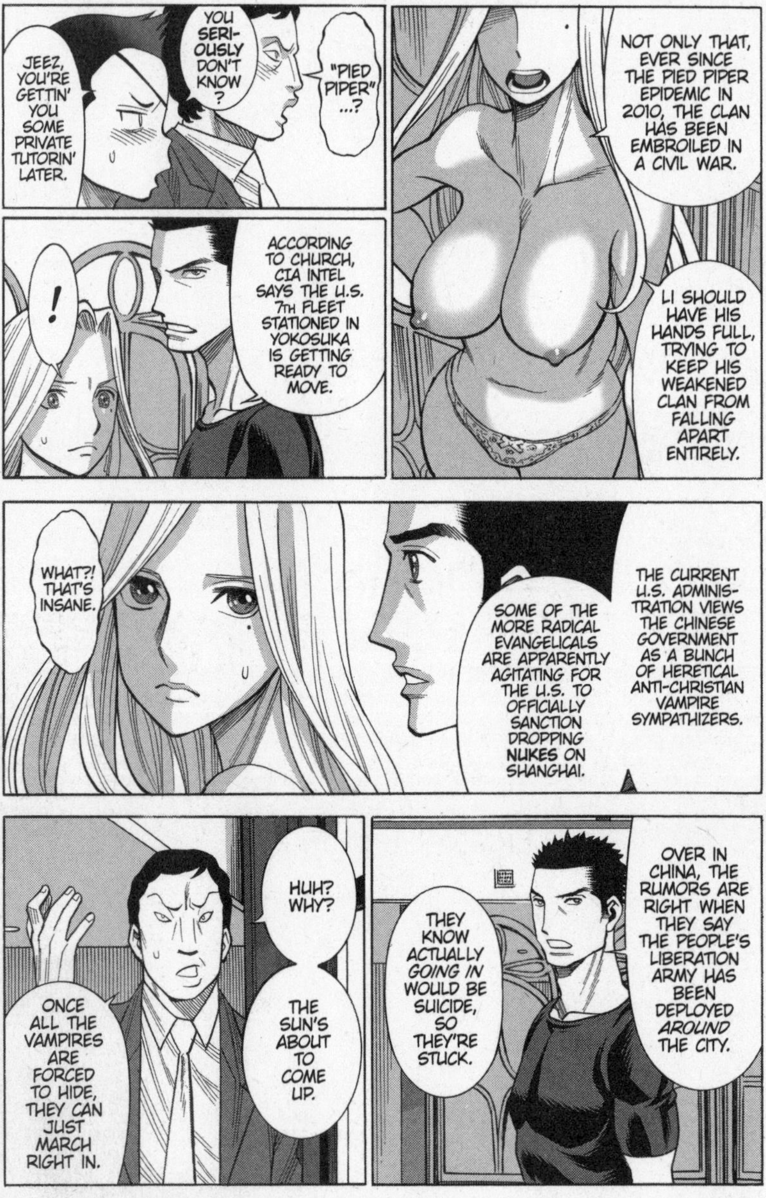
NOT ONLY THAT, EVER SINCE THE PIED PIPER EPIDEMIC IN 2010, THE CLAN HAS BEEN EMBROILED IN A CIVIL WAR.
LI SHOULD HAVE HIS HANDS FULL, TRYING TO KEEP HIS WEAKENED CLAN FROM FALLING APART ENTIRELY.
"PIED PIPER" ...?
YOU SERIOUSLY DON'T KNOW?
JEEZ, YOU'RE GETTIN' YOU SOME PRIVATE TUTORIN' LATER.
ACCORDING TO CHURCH, CIA INTEL SAYS THE U.S. 7TH FLEET STATIONED IN YOKOSUKA IS GETTING READY TO MOVE.
!
THE CURRENT U.S. ADMINISTRATION VIEWS THE CHINESE GOVERNMENT AS A BUNCH OF HERETICAL ANTI-CHRISTIAN VAMPIRE SYMPATHIZERS.
SOME OF THE MORE RADICAL EVANGELICALS ARE APPARENTLY AGITATING FOR THE U.S. TO OFFICIALLY SANCTION DROPPING NUKES ON SHANGHAI.
WHAT?! THAT'S INSANE.
OVER IN CHINA, THE RUMORS ARE RIGHT WHEN THEY SAY THE PEOPLE'S LIBERATION ARMY HAS BEEN DEPLOYED *AROUND* THE CITY.
THEY KNOW ACTUALLY *GOING IN* WOULD BE SUICIDE, SO THEY'RE STUCK.
HUH? WHY?
THE SUN'S ABOUT TO COME UP.
ONCE ALL THE VAMPIRES ARE FORCED TO HIDE, THEY CAN JUST MARCH RIGHT IN.

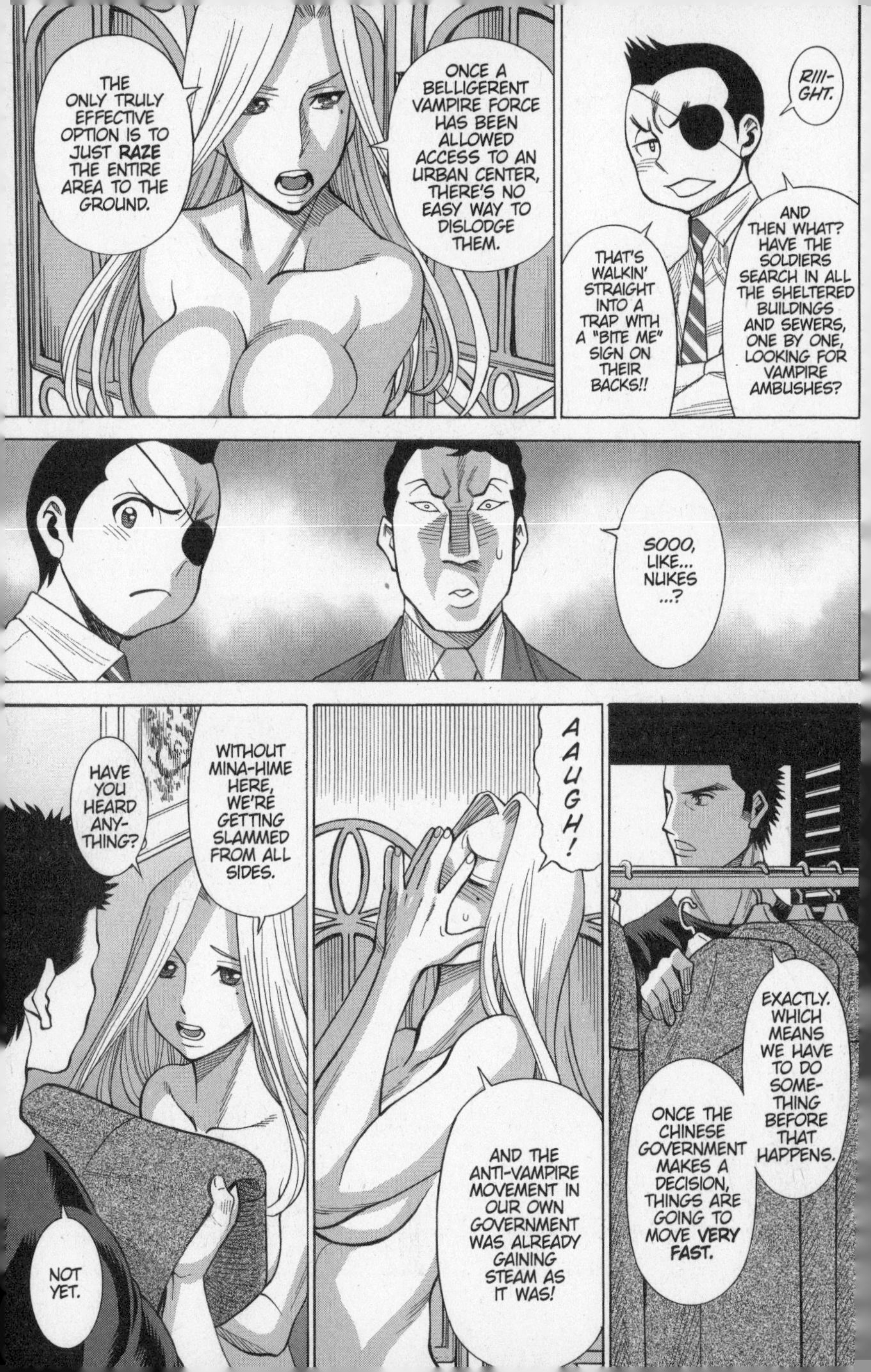
ONCE A BELLIGERENT VAMPIRE FORCE HAS BEEN ALLOWED ACCESS TO AN URBAN CENTER, THERE'S NO EASY WAY TO DISLODGE THEM.
THE ONLY TRULY EFFECTIVE OPTION IS TO JUST **RAZE** THE ENTIRE AREA TO THE GROUND.
RIII-GHT.
AND THEN WHAT? HAVE THE SOLDIERS SEARCH IN ALL THE SHELTERED BUILDINGS AND SEWERS, ONE BY ONE, LOOKING FOR VAMPIRE AMBUSHES?
THAT'S WALKIN' STRAIGHT INTO A TRAP WITH A "BITE ME" SIGN ON THEIR BACKS!!
SOOO, LIKE... NUKES ...?
WITHOUT MINA-HIME HERE, WE'RE GETTING SLAMMED FROM ALL SIDES.
HAVE YOU HEARD ANY-THING?
NOT YET.
AAUGH!
AND THE ANTI-VAMPIRE MOVEMENT IN OUR OWN GOVERNMENT WAS ALREADY GAINING STEAM AS IT WAS!
ONCE THE CHINESE GOVERNMENT MAKES A DECISION, THINGS ARE GOING TO MOVE **VERY FAST.**
EXACTLY. WHICH MEANS WE HAVE TO DO SOME-THING BEFORE THAT HAPPENS.

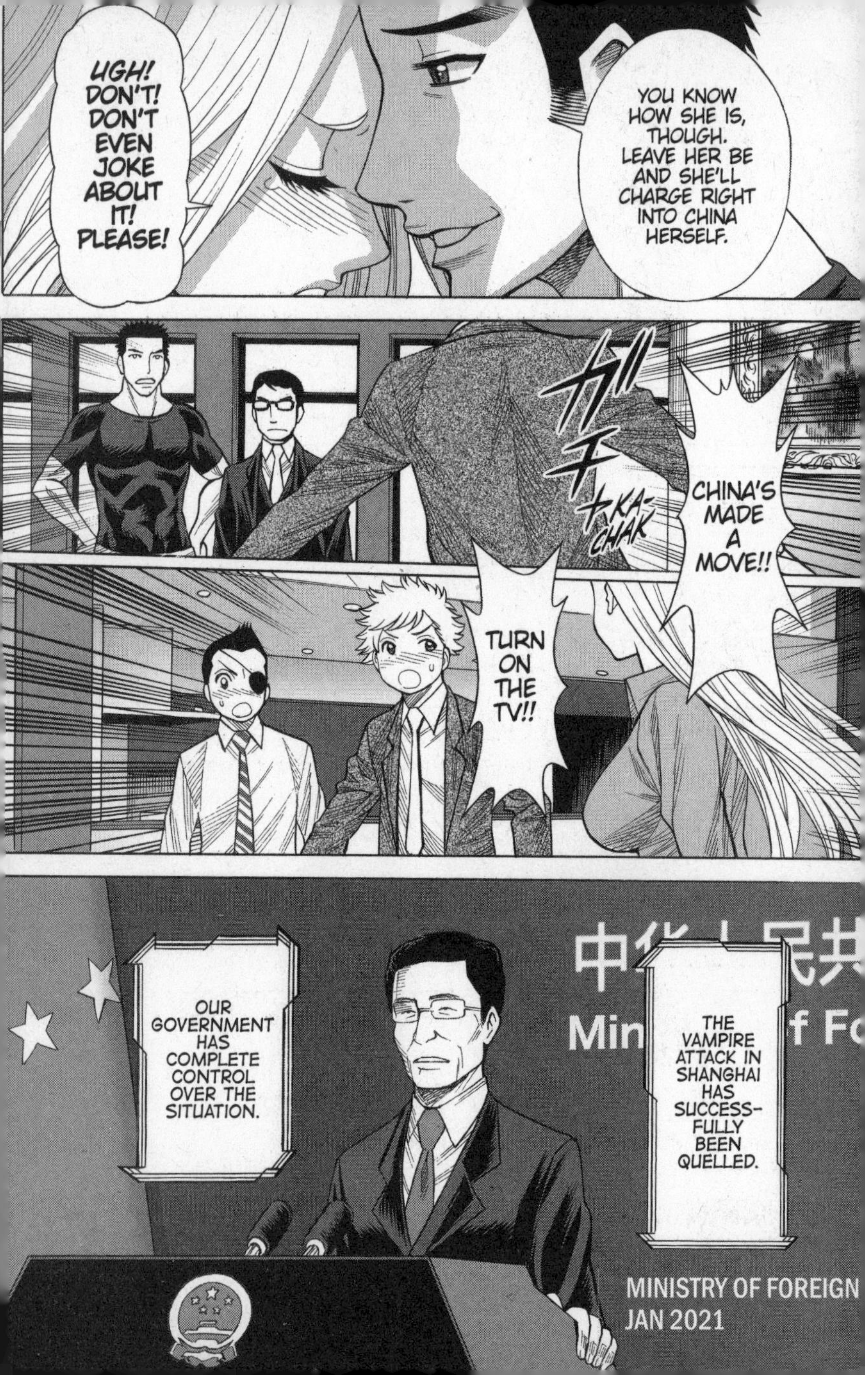

YOU KNOW HOW SHE IS, THOUGH. LEAVE HER BE AND SHE'LL CHARGE RIGHT INTO CHINA HERSELF.
UGH! DON'T! DON'T EVEN JOKE ABOUT IT! PLEASE!
KA-CHAK
CHINA'S MADE A MOVE!!
TURN ON THE TV!!
THE VAMPIRE ATTACK IN SHANGHAI HAS SUCCESSFULLY BEEN QUELLED.
OUR GOVERNMENT HAS COMPLETE CONTROL OVER THE SITUATION.
MINISTRY OF FOREIGN
JAN 2021

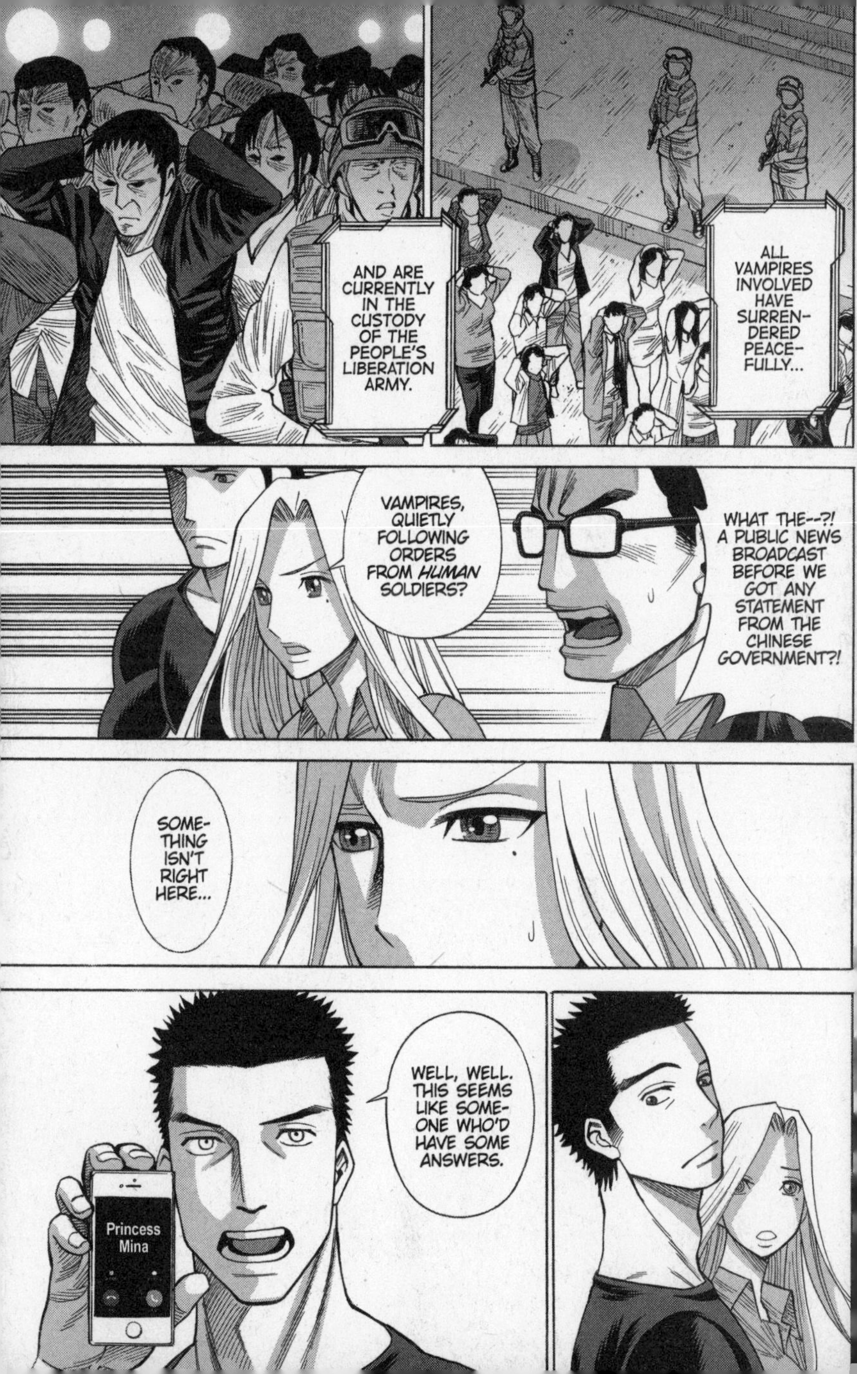
ALL VAMPIRES INVOLVED HAVE SURREN-DERED PEACE-FULLY...
AND ARE CURRENTLY IN THE CUSTODY OF THE PEOPLE'S LIBERATION ARMY.
WHAT THE--?! A PUBLIC NEWS BROADCAST BEFORE WE GOT ANY STATEMENT FROM THE CHINESE GOVERNMENT?!
VAMPIRES, QUIETLY FOLLOWING ORDERS FROM *HUMAN* SOLDIERS?
SOME-THING ISN'T RIGHT HERE...
WELL, WELL. THIS SEEMS LIKE SOME-ONE WHO'D HAVE SOME ANSWERS.
Princess Mina

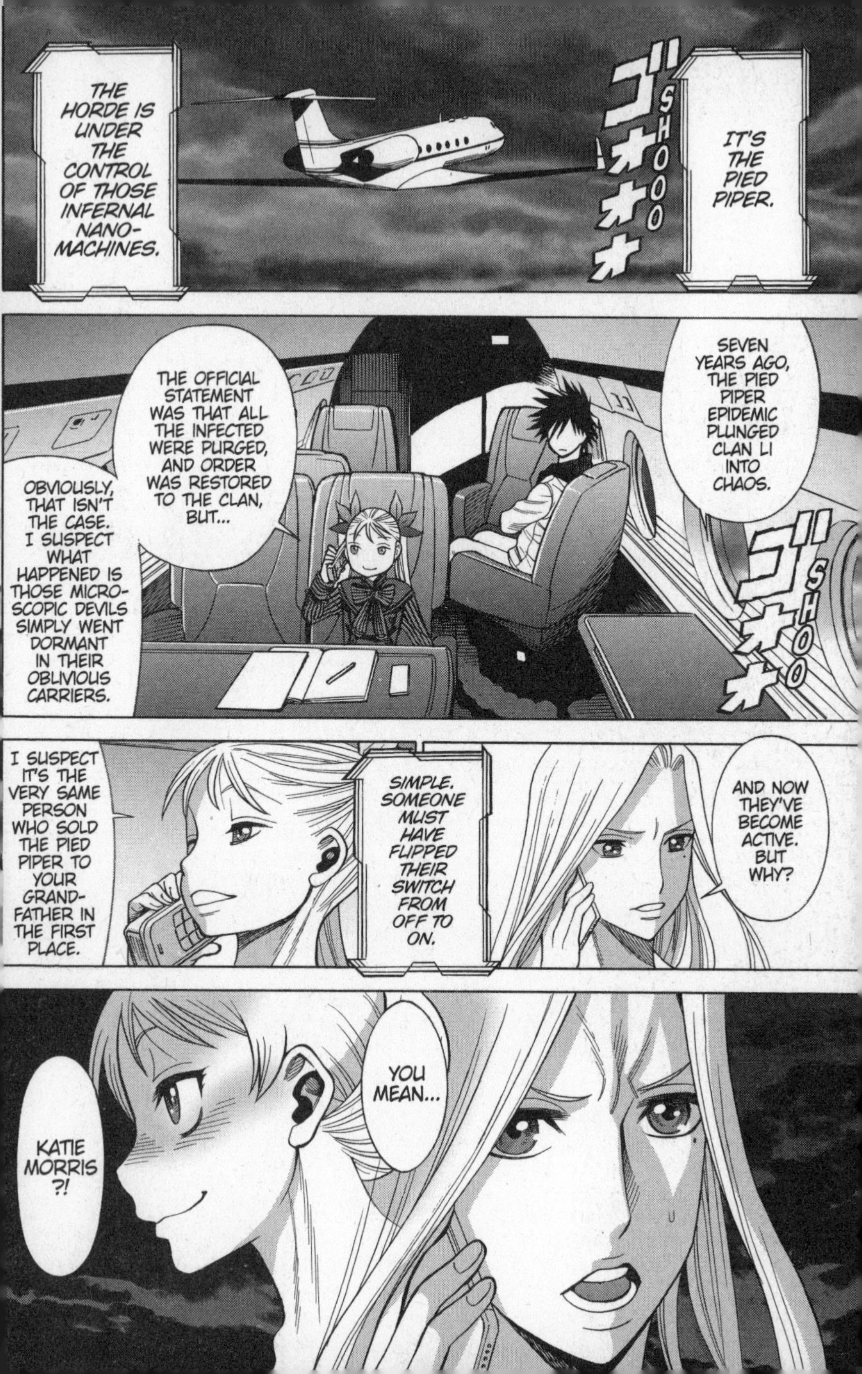
IT'S THE PIED PIPER.
ゴオオオ SHOOO
THE HORDE IS UNDER THE CONTROL OF THOSE INFERNAL NANO-MACHINES.
SEVEN YEARS AGO, THE PIED PIPER EPIDEMIC PLUNGED CLAN LI INTO CHAOS.
ゴオオ SHOOO
THE OFFICIAL STATEMENT WAS THAT ALL THE INFECTED WERE PURGED, AND ORDER WAS RESTORED TO THE CLAN, BUT...
OBVIOUSLY, THAT ISN'T THE CASE. I SUSPECT WHAT HAPPENED IS THOSE MICRO-SCOPIC DEVILS SIMPLY WENT DORMANT IN THEIR OBLIVIOUS CARRIERS.
AND NOW THEY'VE BECOME ACTIVE. BUT WHY?
SIMPLE. SOMEONE MUST HAVE FLIPPED THEIR SWITCH FROM OFF TO ON.
I SUSPECT IT'S THE VERY SAME PERSON WHO SOLD THE PIED PIPER TO YOUR GRAND-FATHER IN THE FIRST PLACE.
YOU MEAN...
KATIE MORRIS?!

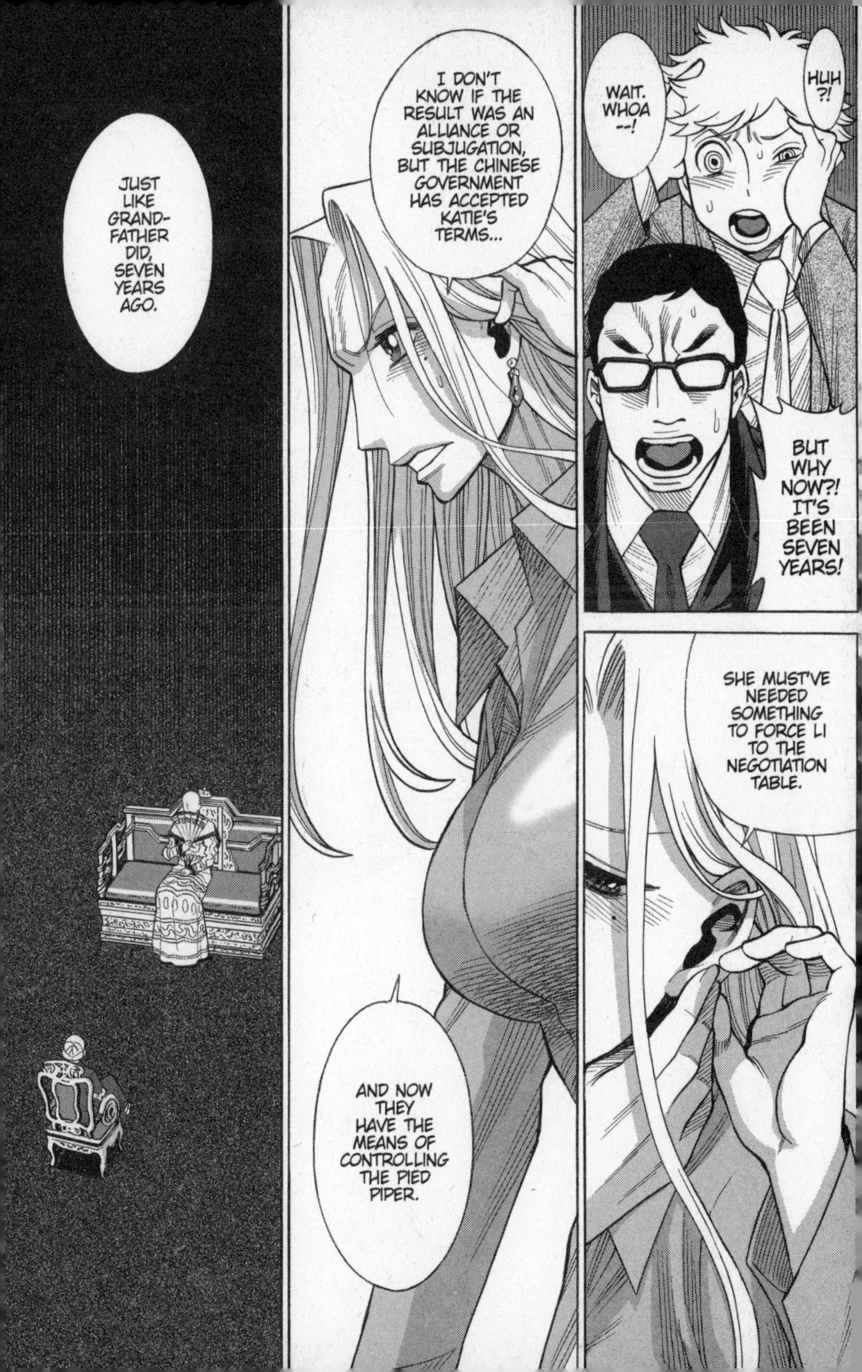
HUH?!
WAIT. WHOA--!
BUT WHY NOW?! IT'S BEEN SEVEN YEARS!
SHE MUST'VE NEEDED SOMETHING TO FORCE LI TO THE NEGOTIATION TABLE.
I DON'T KNOW IF THE RESULT WAS AN ALLIANCE OR SUBJUGATION, BUT THE CHINESE GOVERNMENT HAS ACCEPTED KATIE'S TERMS...
AND NOW THEY HAVE THE MEANS OF CONTROLLING THE PIED PIPER.
JUST LIKE GRAND-FATHER DID, SEVEN YEARS AGO.

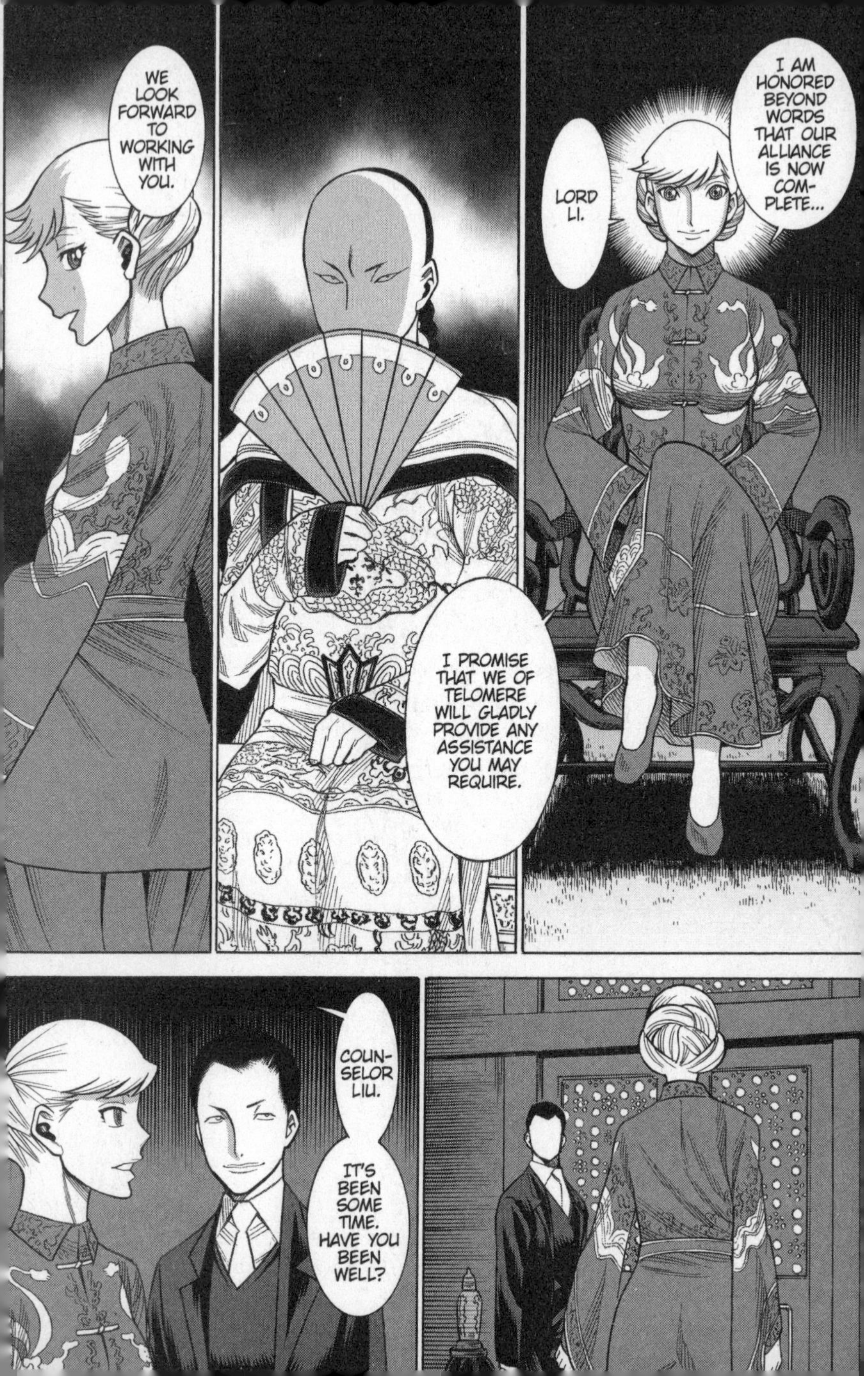
I AM HONORED BEYOND WORDS THAT OUR ALLIANCE IS NOW COM-PLETE...
LORD LI.
I PROMISE THAT WE OF TELOMERE WILL GLADLY PROVIDE ANY ASSISTANCE YOU MAY REQUIRE.
WE LOOK FORWARD TO WORKING WITH YOU.
COUN-SELOR LIU.
IT'S BEEN SOME TIME. HAVE YOU BEEN WELL?

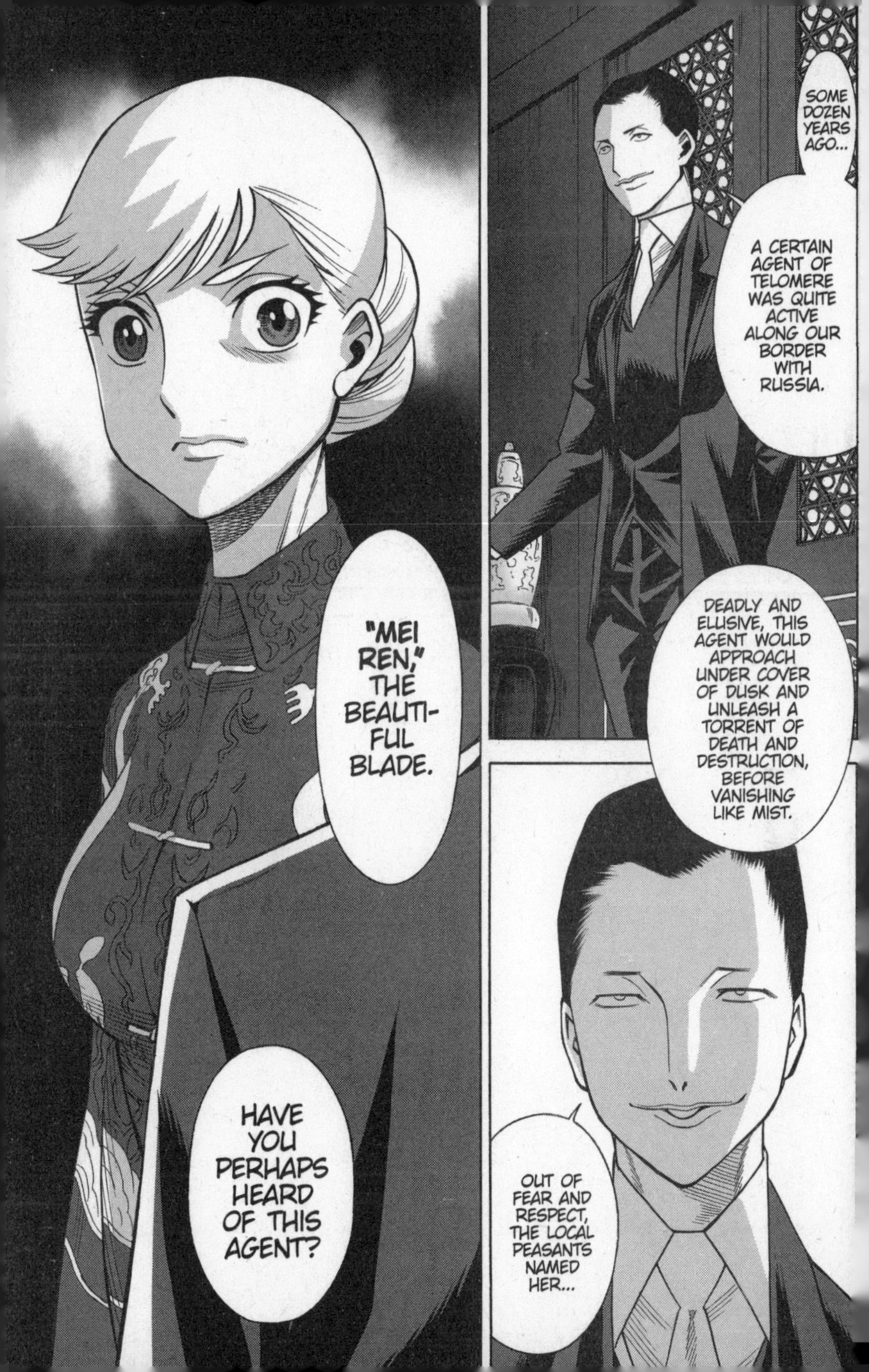
SOME DOZEN YEARS AGO...
A CERTAIN AGENT OF TELOMERE WAS QUITE ACTIVE ALONG OUR BORDER WITH RUSSIA.
DEADLY AND ELUSIVE, THIS AGENT WOULD APPROACH UNDER COVER OF DUSK AND UNLEASH A TORRENT OF DEATH AND DESTRUCTION, BEFORE VANISHING LIKE MIST.
OUT OF FEAR AND RESPECT, THE LOCAL PEASANTS NAMED HER...
"MEI REN," THE BEAUTI-FUL BLADE.
HAVE YOU PERHAPS HEARD OF THIS AGENT?

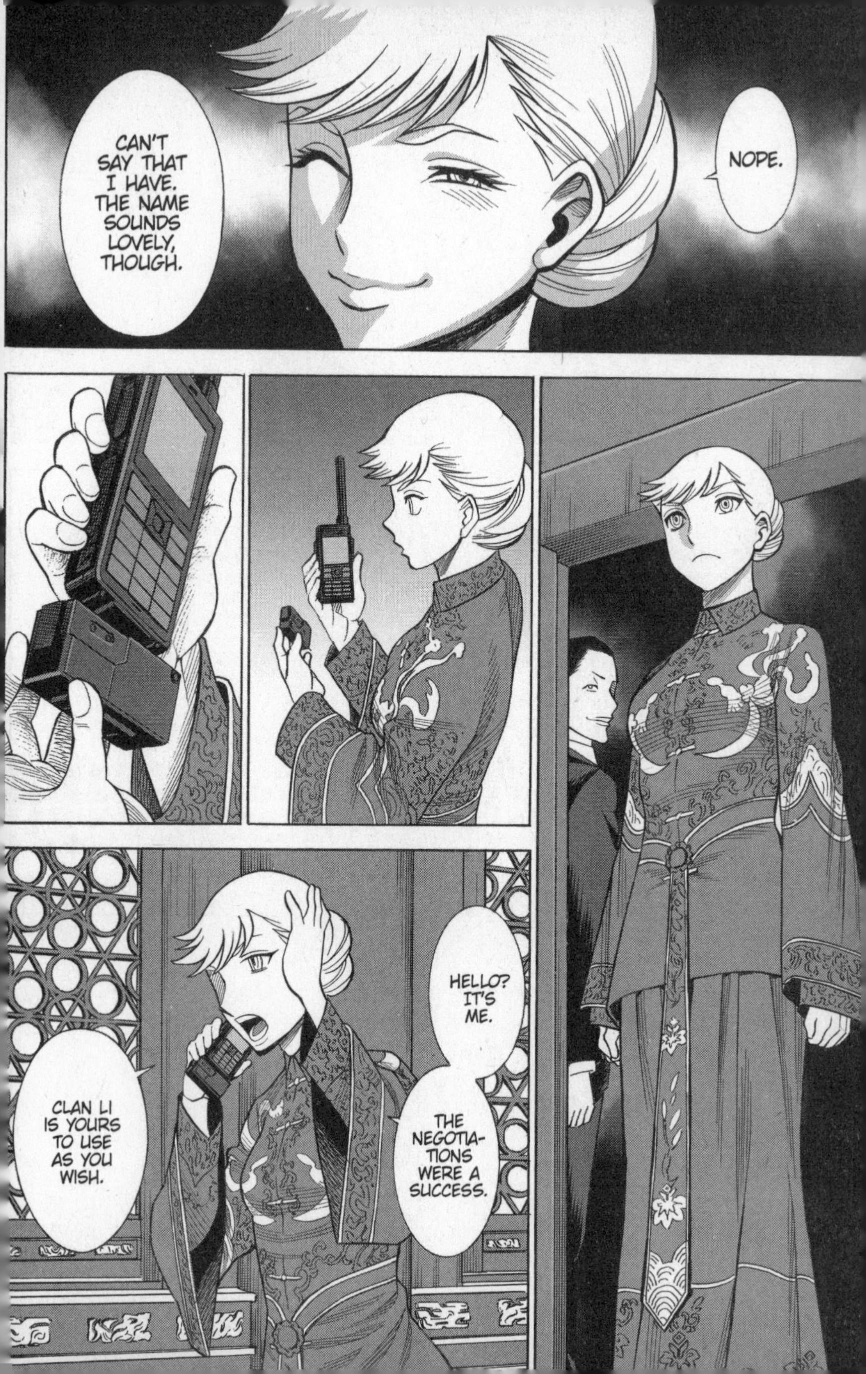
NOPE.
CAN'T SAY THAT I HAVE. THE NAME SOUNDS LOVELY, THOUGH.
HELLO? IT'S ME.
THE NEGOTIA-TIONS WERE A SUCCESS.
CLAN LI IS YOURS TO USE AS YOU WISH.

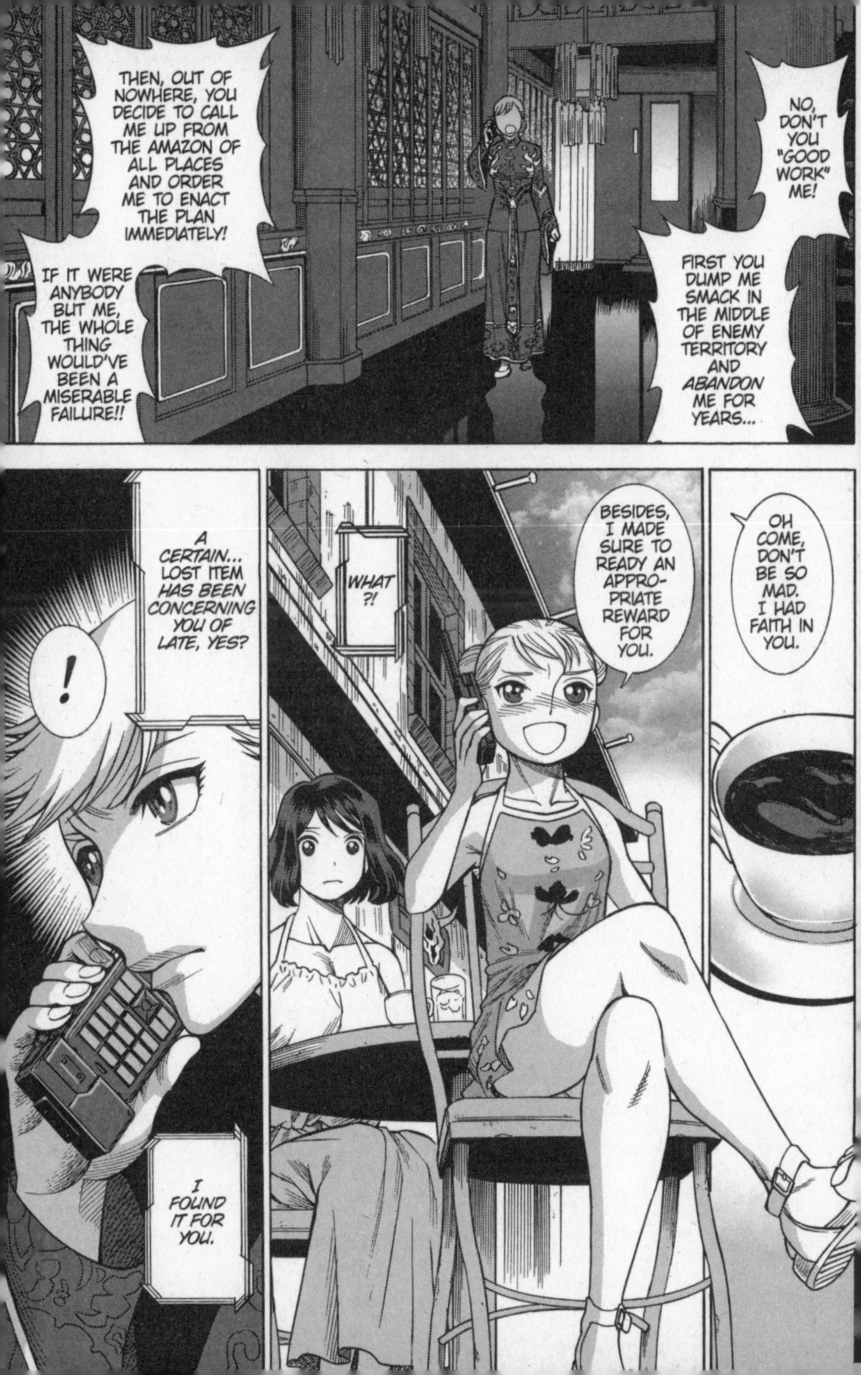
NO, DON'T YOU "GOOD WORK" ME!
FIRST YOU DUMP ME SMACK IN THE MIDDLE OF ENEMY TERRITORY AND *ABANDON* ME FOR YEARS...
THEN, OUT OF NOWHERE, YOU DECIDE TO CALL ME UP FROM THE AMAZON OF ALL PLACES AND ORDER ME TO ENACT THE PLAN IMMEDIATELY!
IF IT WERE ANYBODY BUT ME, THE WHOLE THING WOULD'VE BEEN A MISERABLE FAILURE!!
OH COME, DON'T BE SO MAD. I HAD FAITH IN YOU.
BESIDES, I MADE SURE TO READY AN APPRO-PRIATE REWARD FOR YOU.
WHAT ?!
A CERTAIN... LOST ITEM HAS BEEN CONCERNING YOU OF LATE, YES?
!
I FOUND IT FOR YOU.

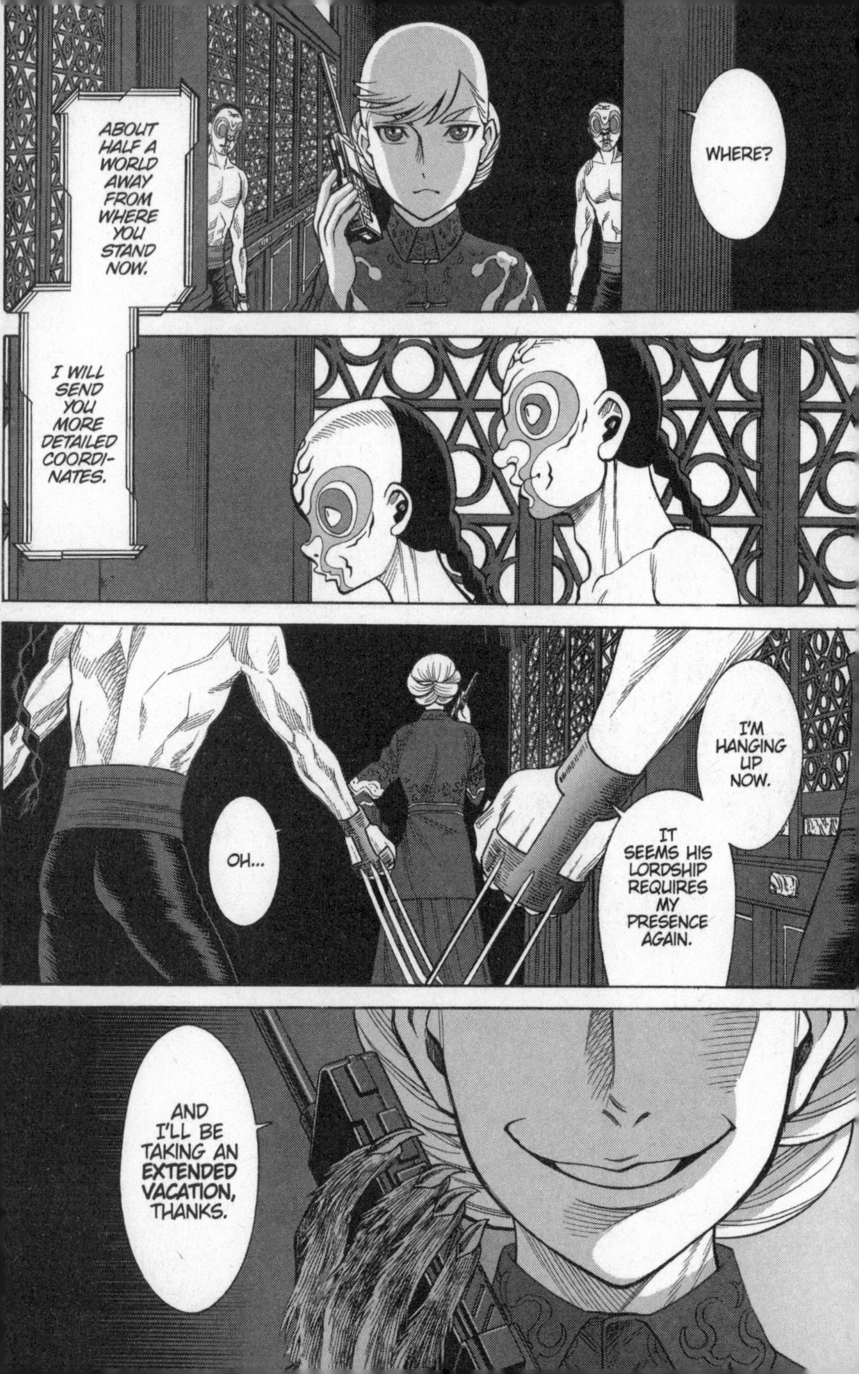
WHERE?
ABOUT HALF A WORLD AWAY FROM WHERE YOU STAND NOW.
I WILL SEND YOU MORE DETAILED COORDINATES.
I'M HANGING UP NOW.
IT SEEMS HIS LORDSHIP REQUIRES MY PRESENCE AGAIN.
OH...
AND I'LL BE TAKING AN EXTENDED VACATION, THANKS.

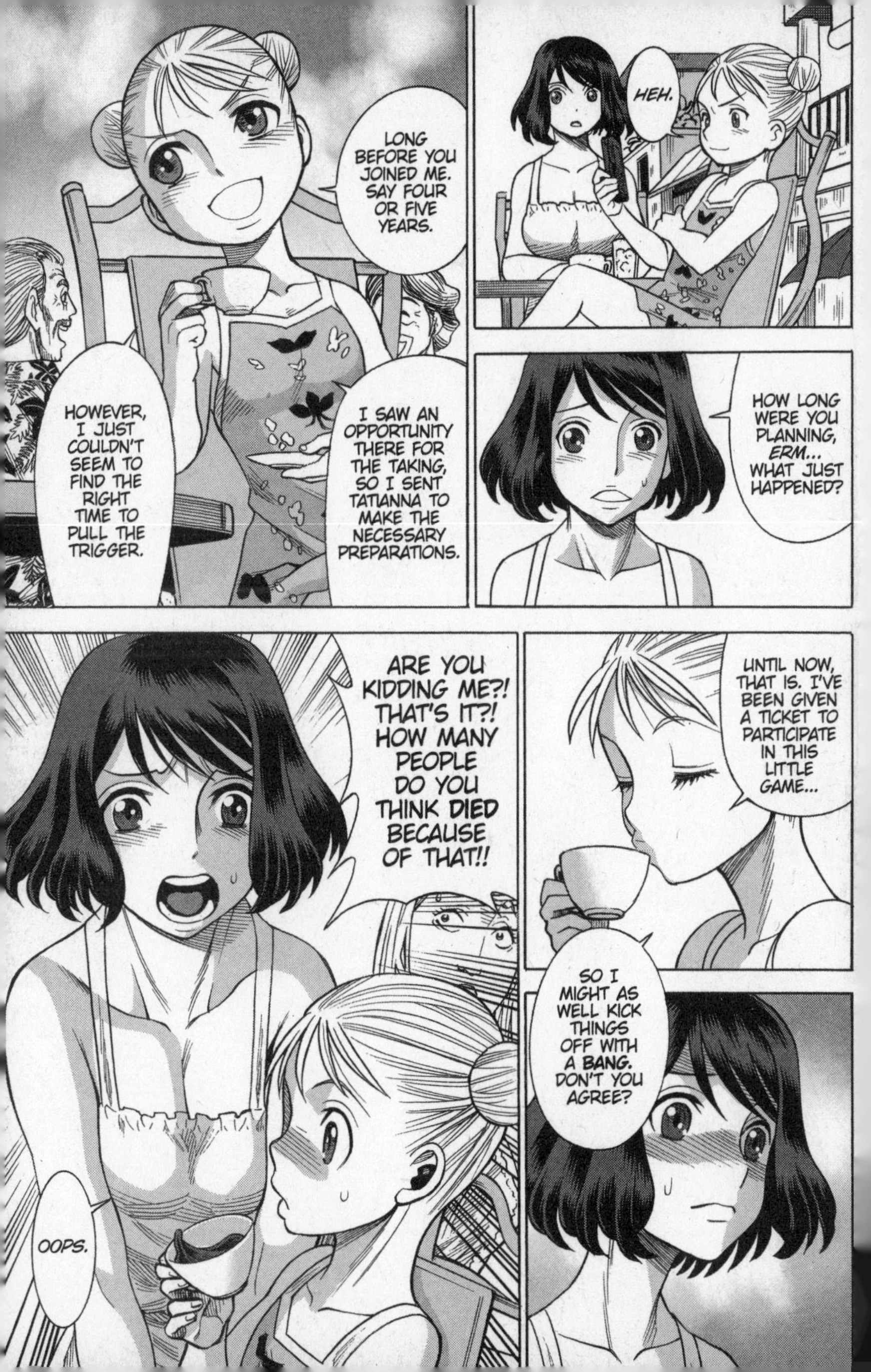
HEH.
HOW LONG WERE YOU PLANNING, *ERM*... WHAT JUST HAPPENED?
LONG BEFORE YOU JOINED ME. SAY FOUR OR FIVE YEARS.
I SAW AN OPPORTUNITY THERE FOR THE TAKING, SO I SENT TATIANNA TO MAKE THE NECESSARY PREPARATIONS.
HOWEVER, I JUST COULDN'T SEEM TO FIND THE RIGHT TIME TO PULL THE TRIGGER.
UNTIL NOW, THAT IS. I'VE BEEN GIVEN A TICKET TO PARTICIPATE IN THIS LITTLE GAME...
SO I MIGHT AS WELL KICK THINGS OFF WITH A **BANG**. DON'T YOU AGREE?
ARE YOU KIDDING ME?! THAT'S IT?! HOW MANY PEOPLE DO YOU THINK **DIED** BECAUSE OF THAT!!
OOPS.

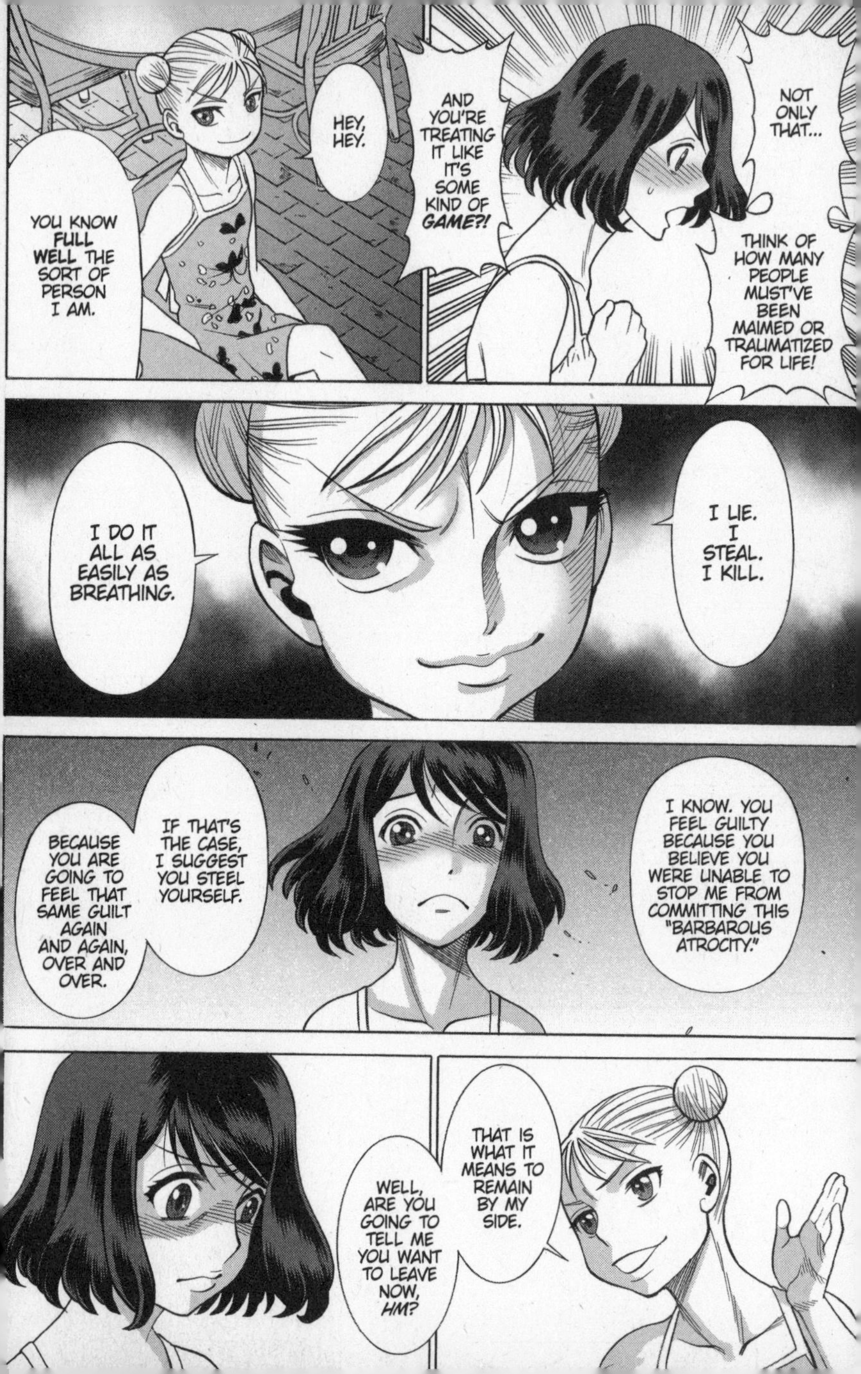
NOT ONLY THAT...
THINK OF HOW MANY PEOPLE MUST'VE BEEN MAIMED OR TRAUMATIZED FOR LIFE!
AND YOU'RE TREATING IT LIKE IT'S SOME KIND OF *GAME?!*
HEY, HEY.
YOU KNOW **FULL WELL** THE SORT OF PERSON I AM.
I LIE. I STEAL. I KILL.
I DO IT ALL AS EASILY AS BREATHING.
I KNOW. YOU FEEL GUILTY BECAUSE YOU BELIEVE YOU WERE UNABLE TO STOP ME FROM COMMITTING THIS "BARBAROUS ATROCITY."
IF THAT'S THE CASE, I SUGGEST YOU STEEL YOURSELF.
BECAUSE YOU ARE GOING TO FEEL THAT SAME GUILT AGAIN AND AGAIN, OVER AND OVER.
THAT IS WHAT IT MEANS TO REMAIN BY MY SIDE.
WELL, ARE YOU GOING TO TELL ME YOU WANT TO LEAVE NOW, *HM?*

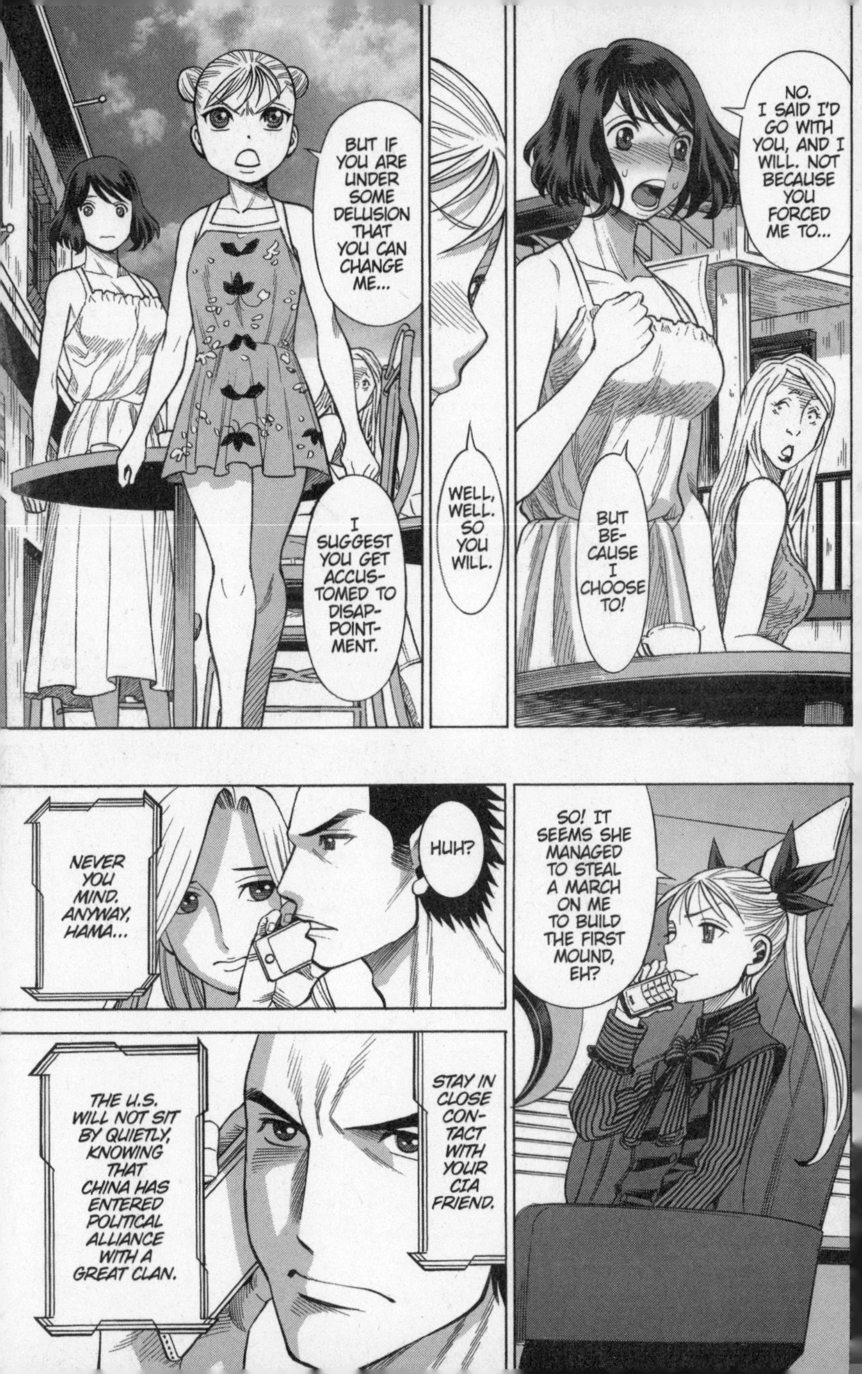
NO. I SAID I'D GO WITH YOU, AND I WILL. NOT BECAUSE YOU FORCED ME TO...
BUT BE-CAUSE I CHOOSE TO!
WELL, WELL. SO YOU WILL.
BUT IF YOU ARE UNDER SOME DELUSION THAT YOU CAN CHANGE ME...
I SUGGEST YOU GET ACCUS-TOMED TO DISAP-POINT-MENT.
SO! IT SEEMS SHE MANAGED TO STEAL A MARCH ON ME TO BUILD THE FIRST MOUND, EH?
HUH?
NEVER YOU MIND. ANYWAY, HAMA...
STAY IN CLOSE CON-TACT WITH YOUR CIA FRIEND.
THE U.S. WILL NOT SIT BY QUIETLY, KNOWING THAT CHINA HAS ENTERED POLITICAL ALLIANCE WITH A GREAT CLAN.

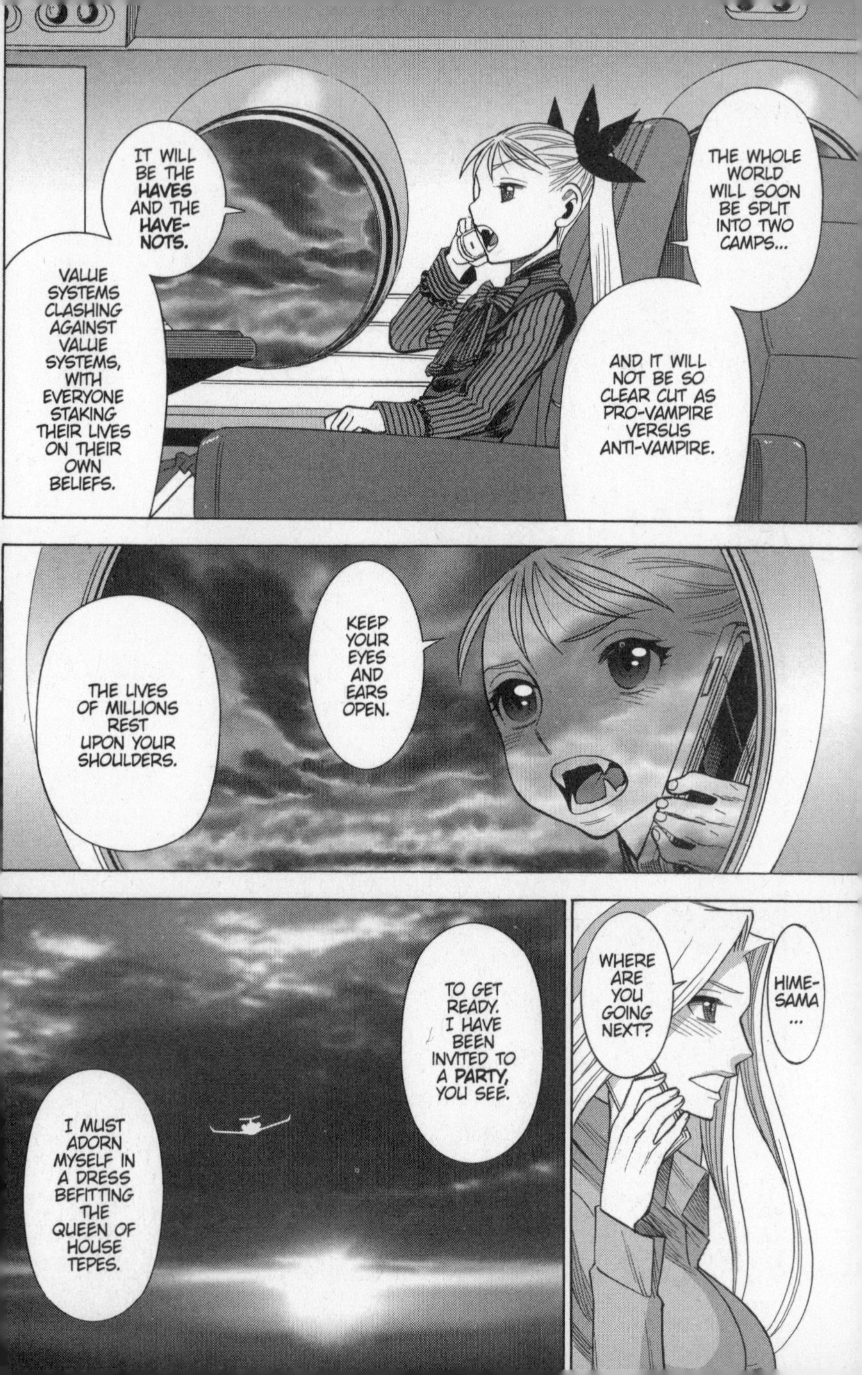
THE WHOLE WORLD WILL SOON BE SPLIT INTO TWO CAMPS...
AND IT WILL NOT BE SO CLEAR CUT AS PRO-VAMPIRE VERSUS ANTI-VAMPIRE.
IT WILL BE THE HAVES AND THE HAVE-NOTS.
VALUE SYSTEMS CLASHING AGAINST VALUE SYSTEMS, WITH EVERYONE STAKING THEIR LIVES ON THEIR OWN BELIEFS.
KEEP YOUR EYES AND EARS OPEN.
THE LIVES OF MILLIONS REST UPON YOUR SHOULDERS.
HIME-SAMA ...
WHERE ARE YOU GOING NEXT?
TO GET READY. I HAVE BEEN INVITED TO A PARTY, YOU SEE.
I MUST ADORN MYSELF IN A DRESS BEFITTING THE QUEEN OF HOUSE TEPES.

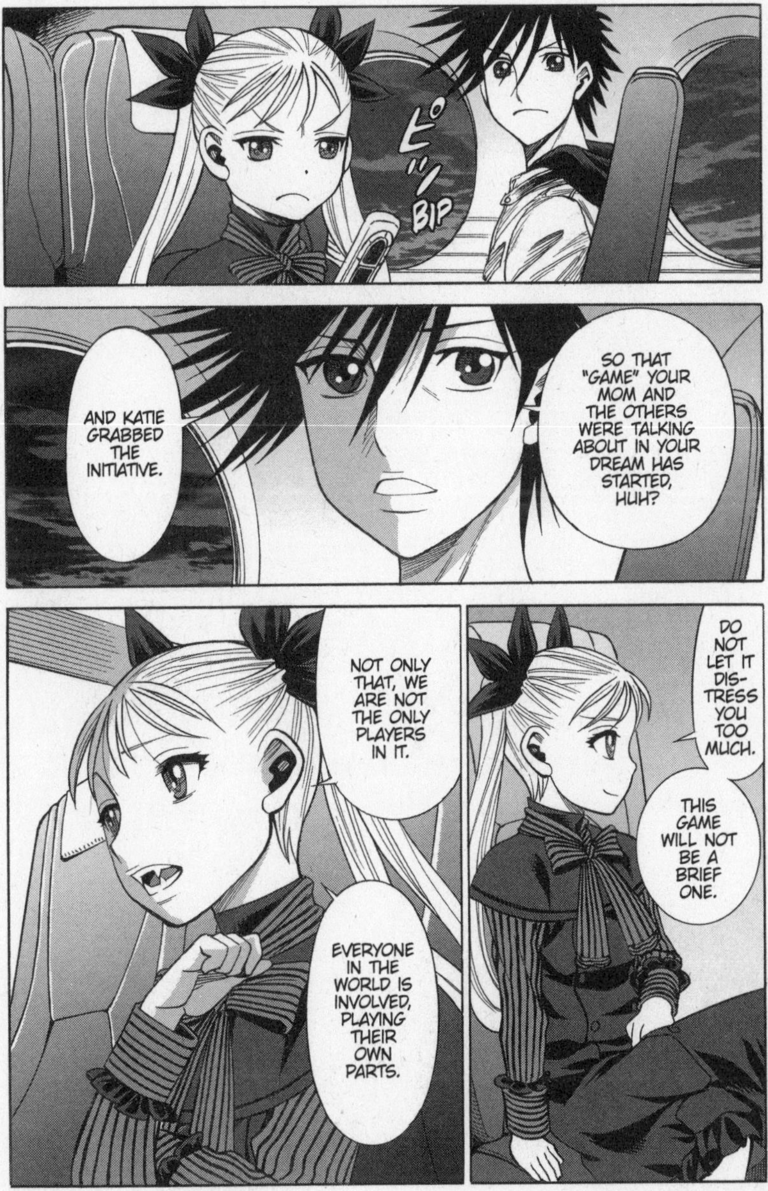
ピッ
BIP
SO THAT "GAME" YOUR MOM AND THE OTHERS WERE TALKING ABOUT IN YOUR DREAM HAS STARTED, HUH?
AND KATIE GRABBED THE INITIATIVE.
DO NOT LET IT DIS-TRESS YOU TOO MUCH.
THIS GAME WILL NOT BE A BRIEF ONE.
NOT ONLY THAT, WE ARE NOT THE ONLY PLAYERS IN IT.
EVERYONE IN THE WORLD IS INVOLVED, PLAYING THEIR OWN PARTS.

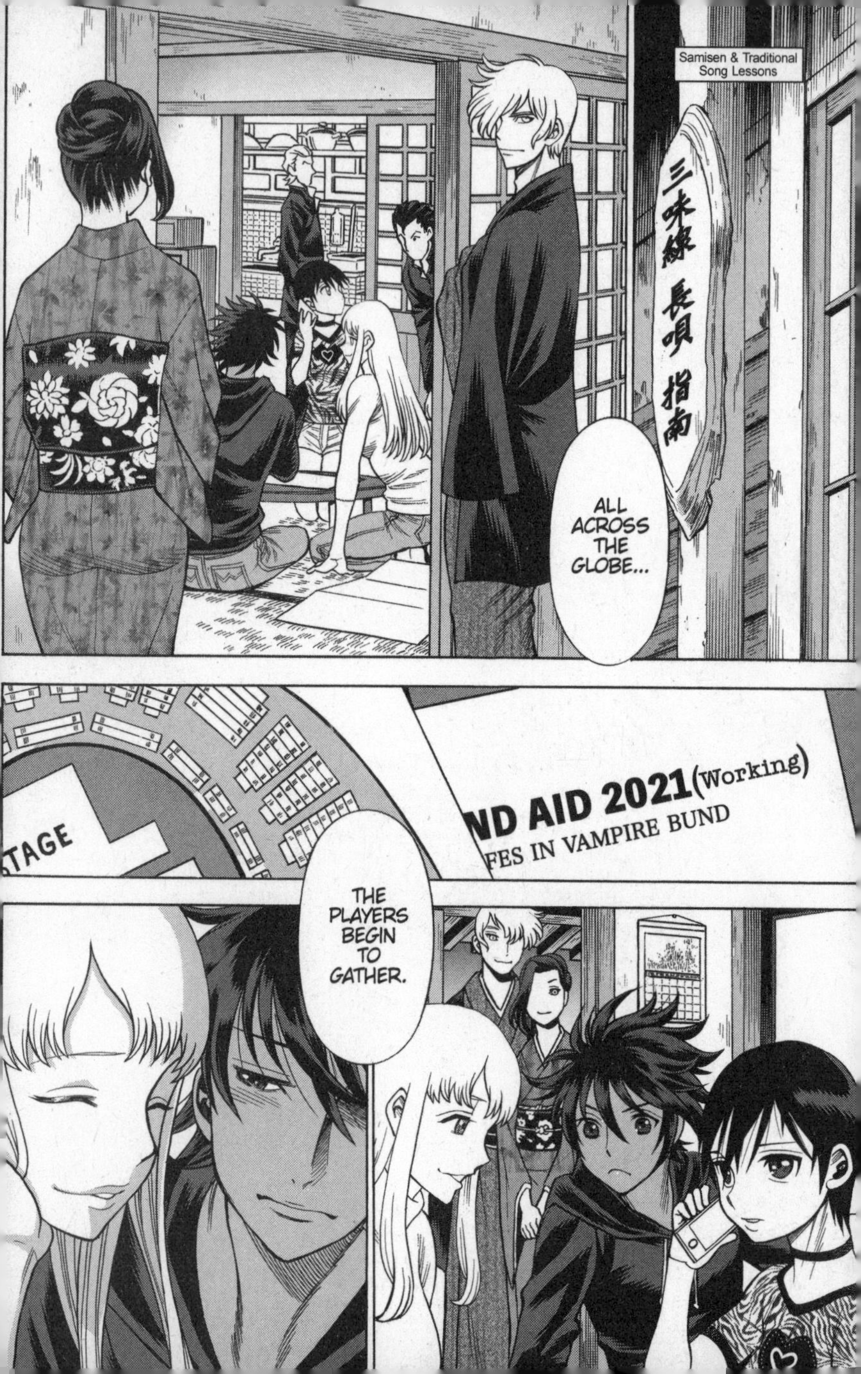
Samisen & Traditional Song Lessons
三味線 長唄 指南
ALL ACROSS THE GLOBE...
ND AID 2021(Working)
FES IN VAMPIRE BUND
TAGE
THE PLAYERS BEGIN TO GATHER.

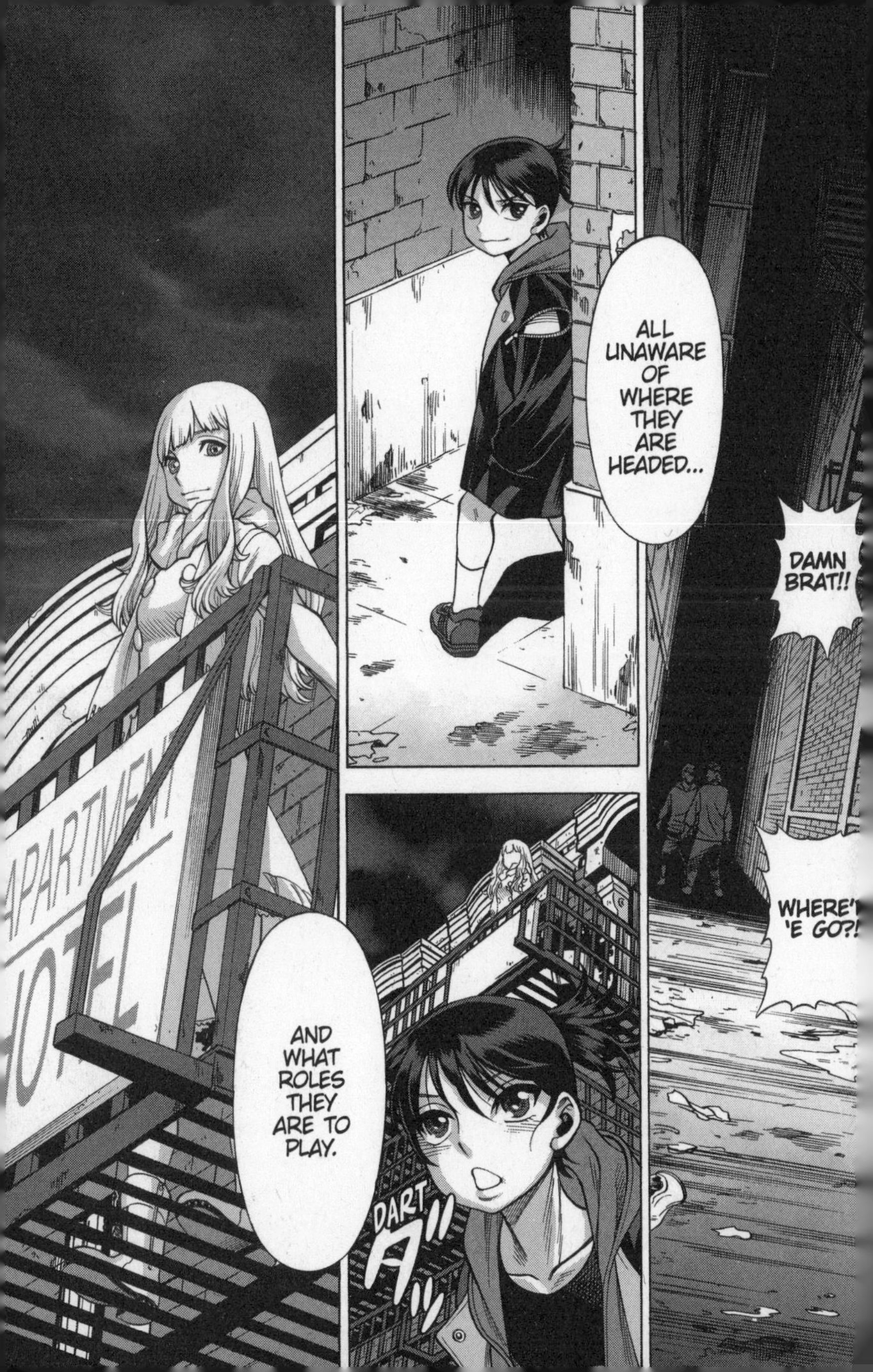
DAMN BRAT!!
WHERE' 'E GO?!
ALL UNAWARE OF WHERE THEY ARE HEADED...
AND WHAT ROLES THEY ARE TO PLAY.
DART
APARTMENT
HOTEL

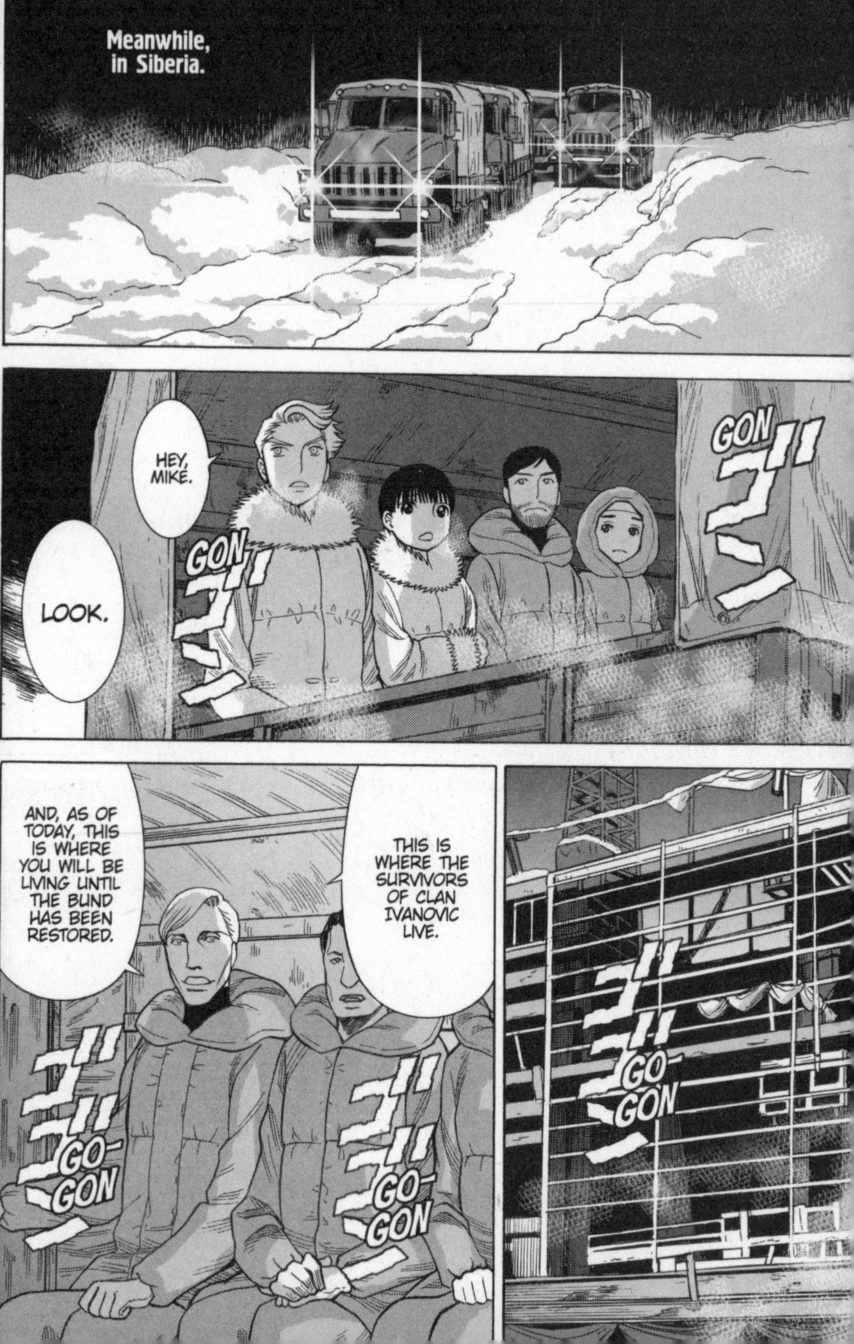
Meanwhile, in Siberia.
GON
HEY, MIKE.
LOOK.
GON
GO-GON
THIS IS WHERE THE SURVIVORS OF CLAN IVANOVIC LIVE.
AND, AS OF TODAY, THIS IS WHERE YOU WILL BE LIVING UNTIL THE BUND HAS BEEN RESTORED.
GO-GON
GO-GON

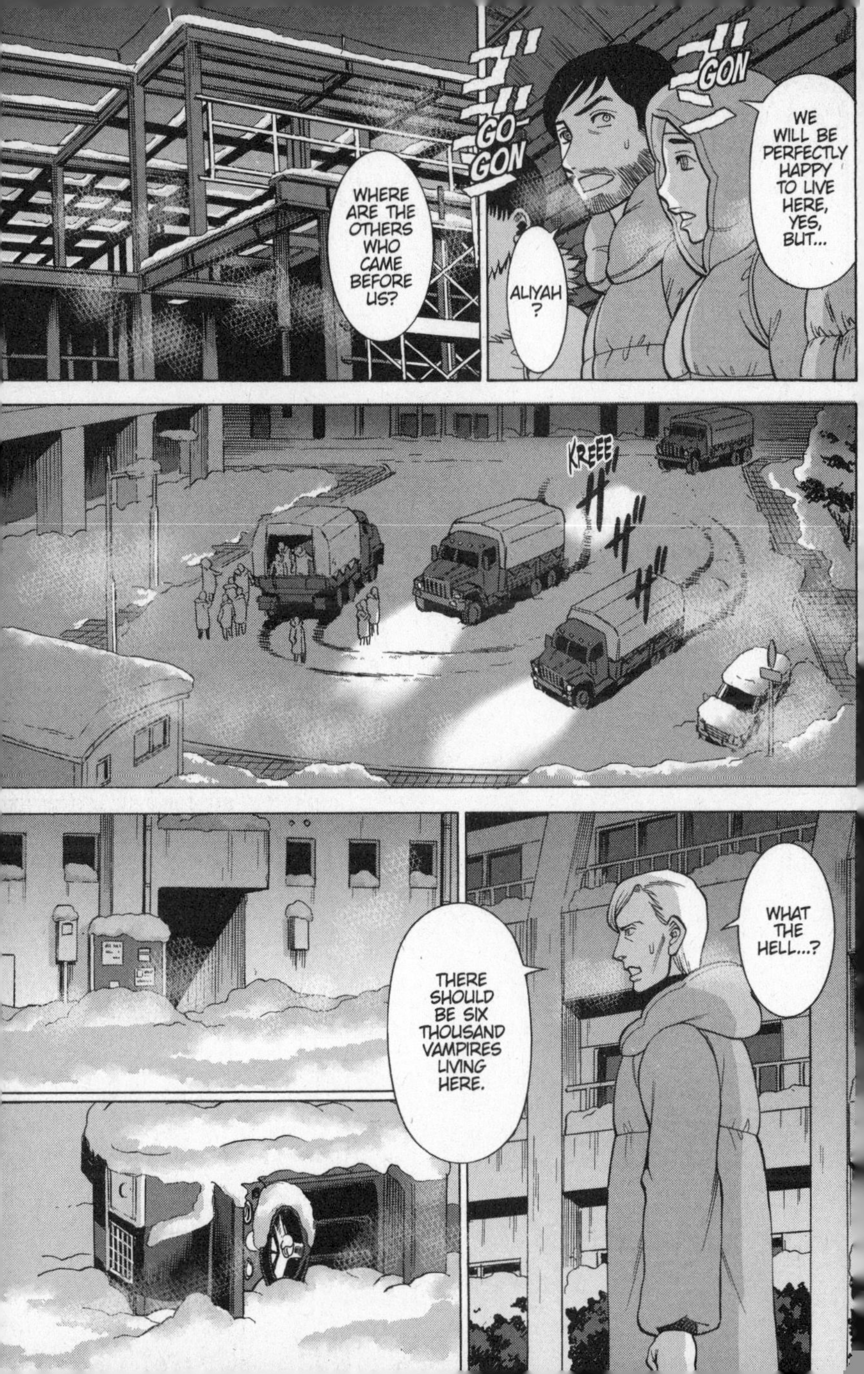
GON
WE WILL BE PERFECTLY HAPPY TO LIVE HERE, YES, BUT...
GO-GON
ALIYAH?
WHERE ARE THE OTHERS WHO CAME BEFORE US?
KREEE
WHAT THE HELL...?
THERE SHOULD BE SIX THOUSAND VAMPIRES LIVING HERE.

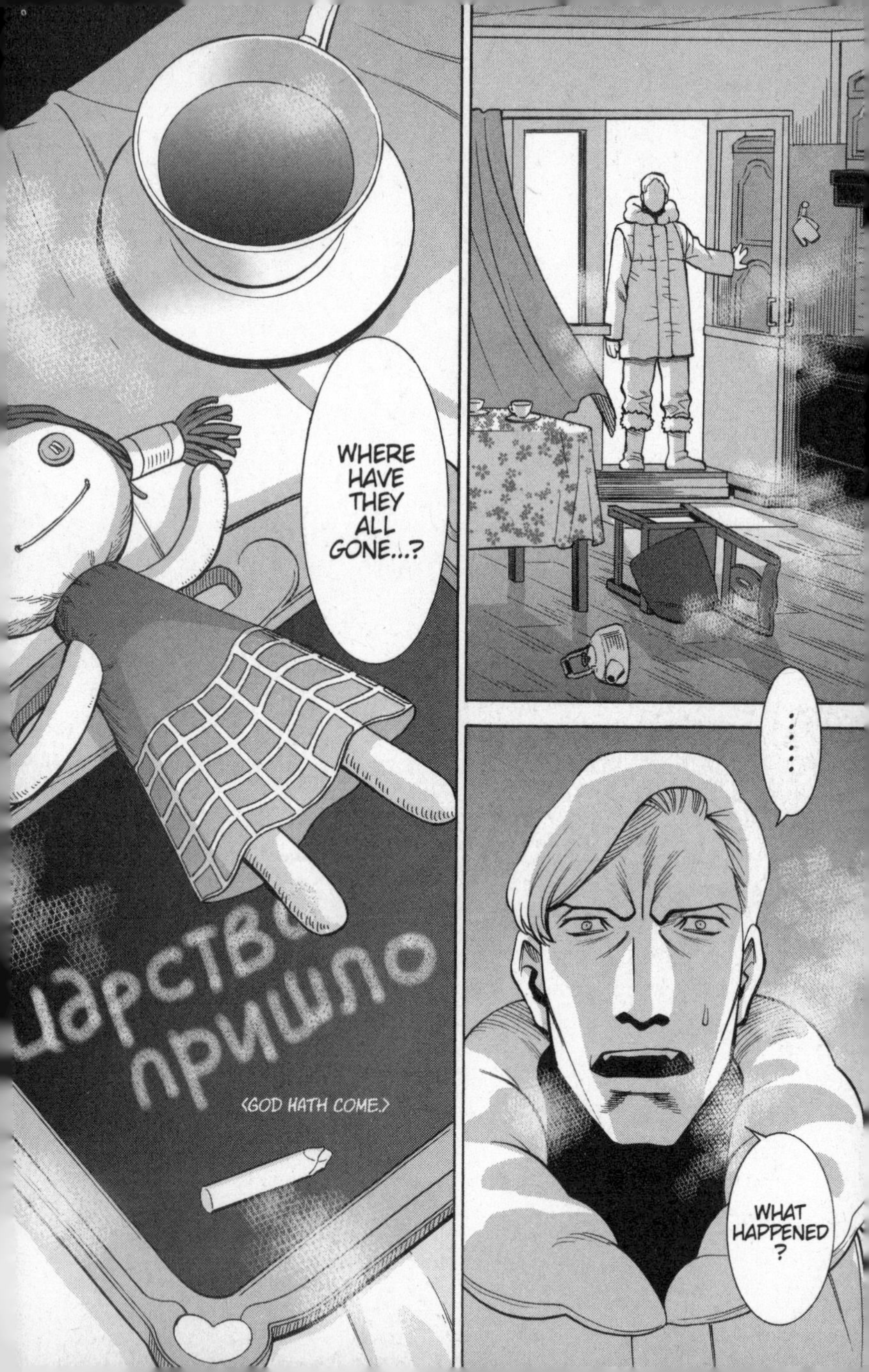
......
WHAT HAPPENED?
WHERE HAVE THEY ALL GONE...?
царство пришло
<GOD HATH COME.>

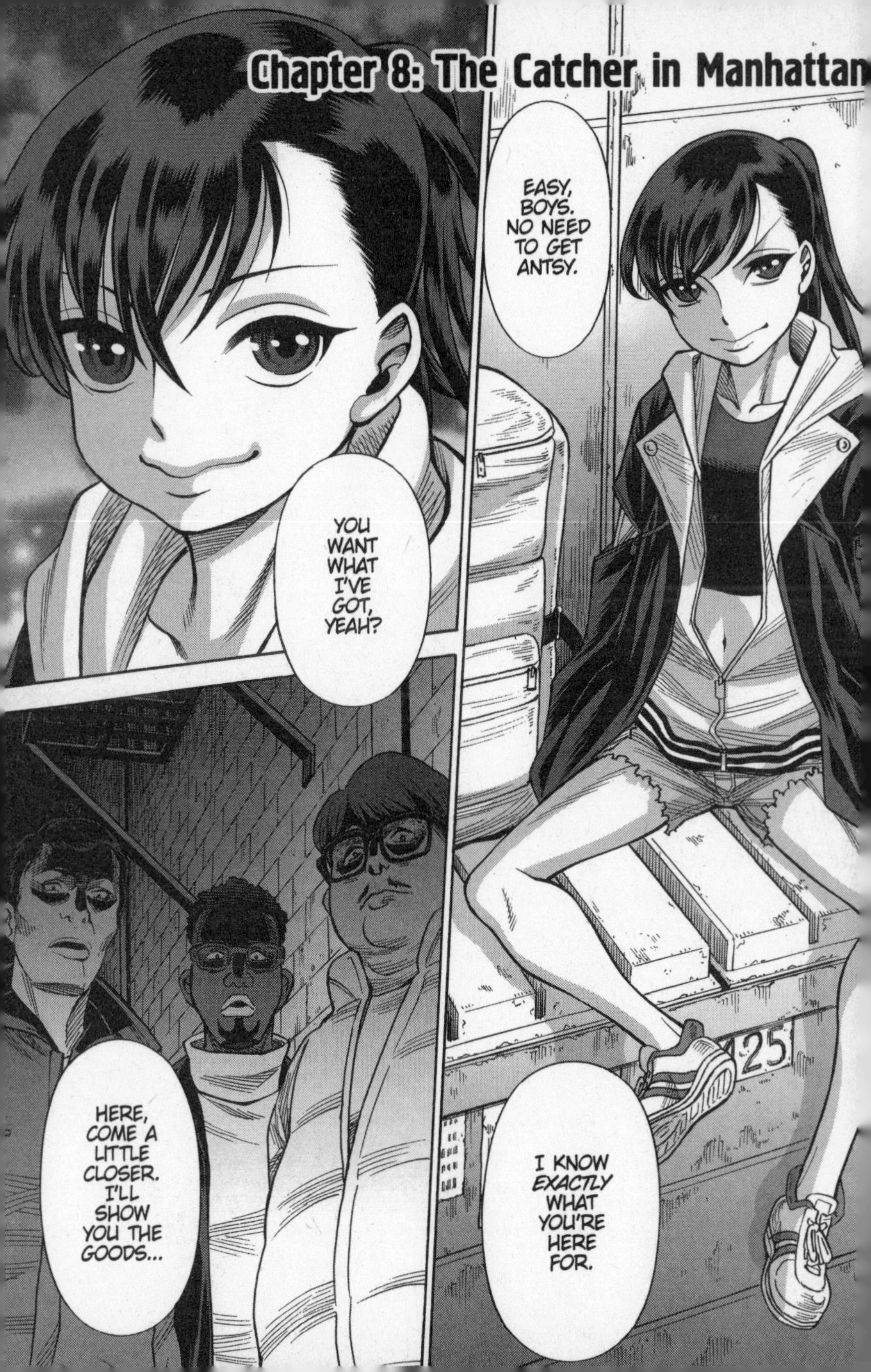
Chapter 8: The Catcher in Manhattan
EASY, BOYS. NO NEED TO GET ANTSY.
I KNOW *EXACTLY* WHAT YOU'RE HERE FOR.
YOU WANT WHAT I'VE GOT, YEAH?
HERE, COME A LITTLE CLOSER. I'LL SHOW YOU THE GOODS...
25

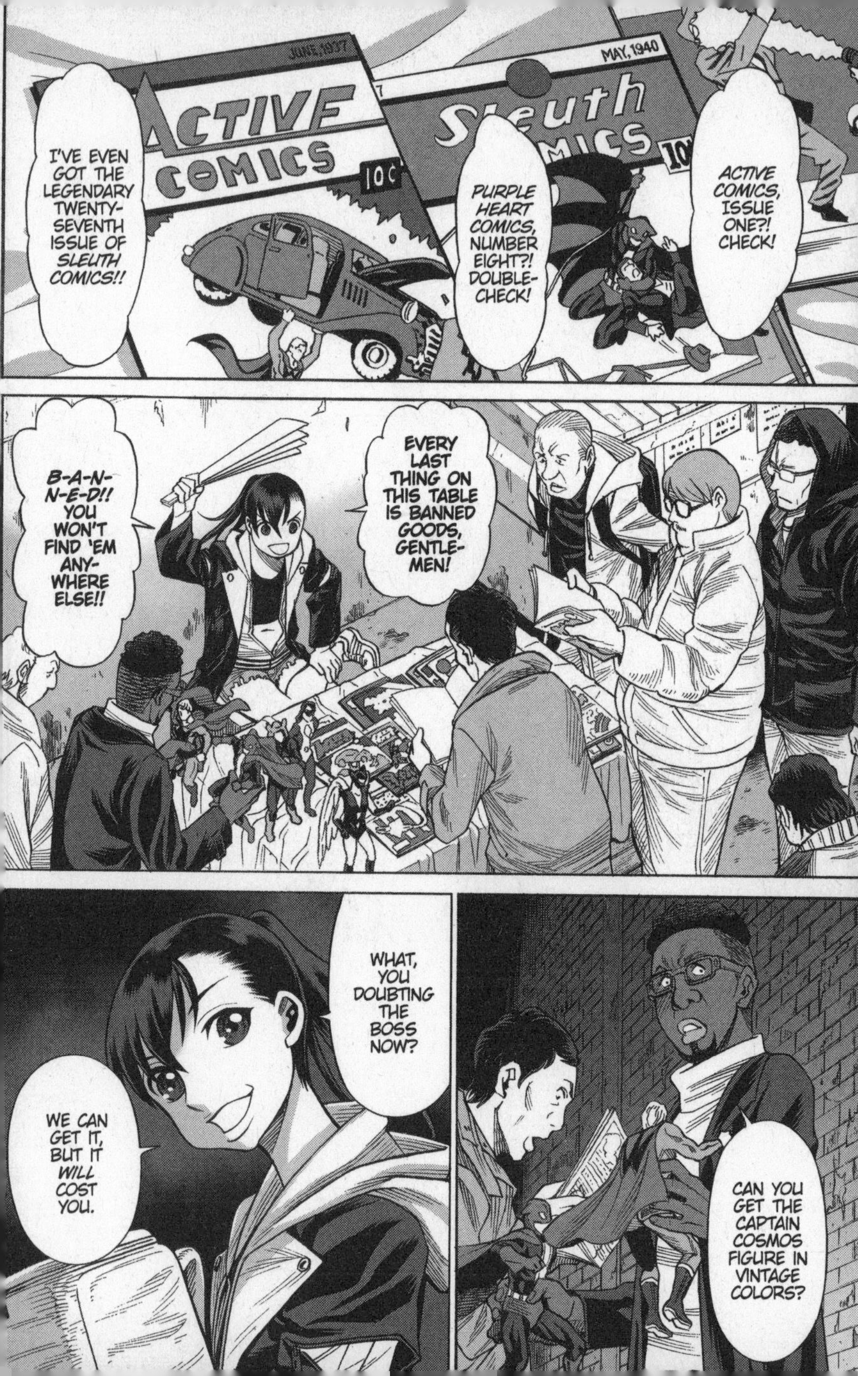
MAY, 1940
Sleuth COMICS
JUNE, 1937
ACTIVE COMICS
ACTIVE COMICS, ISSUE ONE?! CHECK!
PURPLE HEART COMICS, NUMBER EIGHT?! DOUBLE-CHECK!
I'VE EVEN GOT THE LEGENDARY TWENTY-SEVENTH ISSUE OF SLEUTH COMICS!!
EVERY LAST THING ON THIS TABLE IS BANNED GOODS, GENTLEMEN!
B-A-N-N-E-D!! YOU WON'T FIND 'EM ANYWHERE ELSE!!
CAN YOU GET THE CAPTAIN COSMOS FIGURE IN VINTAGE COLORS?
WHAT, YOU DOUBTING THE BOSS NOW?
WE CAN GET IT, BUT IT WILL COST YOU.

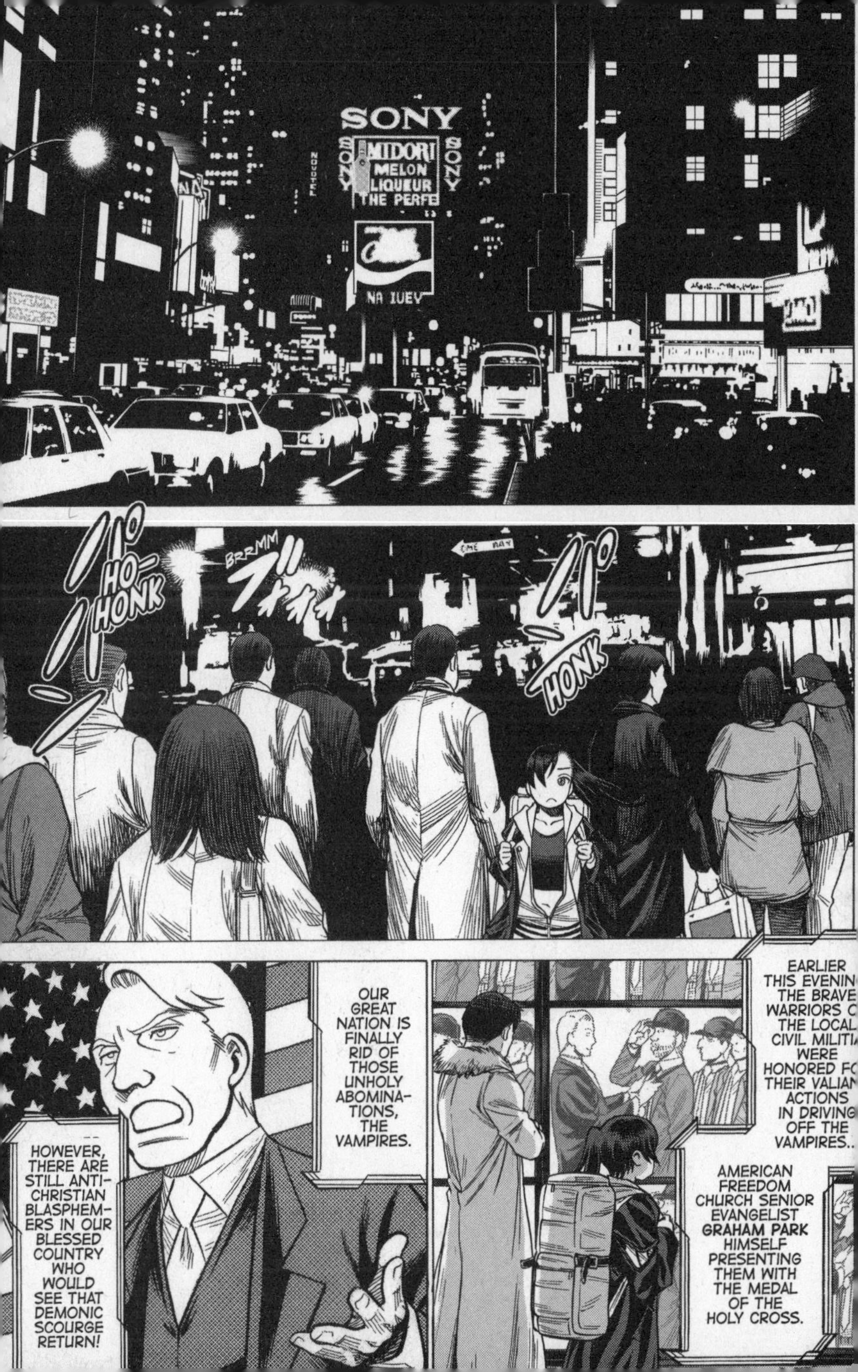
SONY
MIDORI MELON LIQUEUR THE PERFE
SONY
SONY
NOVOTEL
NA IUEY
HO-HONK
BRRMM
ONE WAY
HONK
EARLIER THIS EVENIN THE BRAVE WARRIORS O THE LOCAL CIVIL MILITI WERE HONORED FO THEIR VALIAN ACTIONS IN DRIVING OFF THE VAMPIRES..
AMERICAN FREEDOM CHURCH SENIOR EVANGELIST GRAHAM PARK HIMSELF PRESENTING THEM WITH THE MEDAL OF THE HOLY CROSS.
OUR GREAT NATION IS FINALLY RID OF THOSE UNHOLY ABOMINATIONS, THE VAMPIRES.
HOWEVER, THERE ARE STILL ANTI-CHRISTIAN BLASPHEMERS IN OUR BLESSED COUNTRY WHO WOULD SEE THAT DEMONIC SCOURGE RETURN!

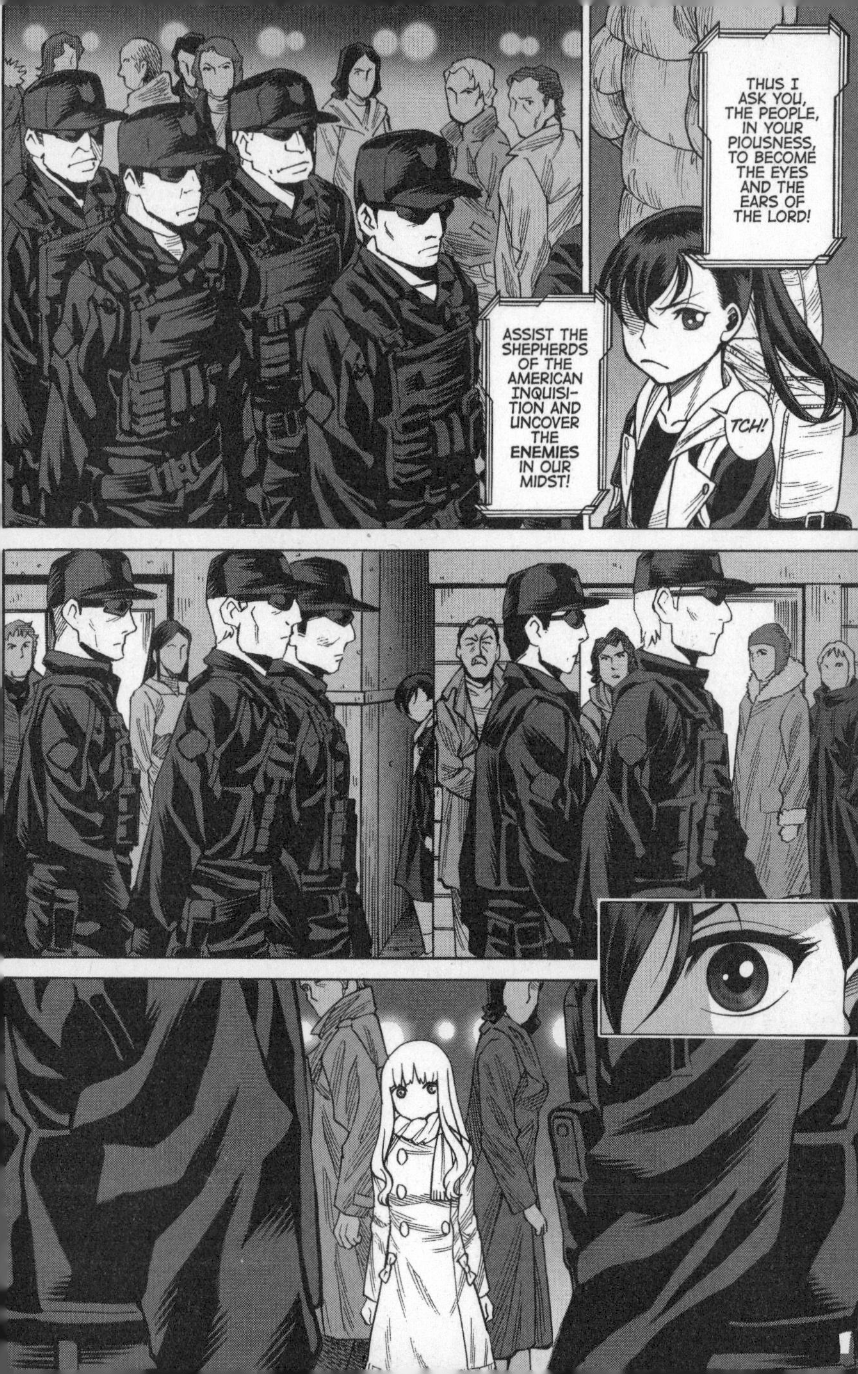
THUS I ASK YOU, THE PEOPLE, IN YOUR PIOUSNESS, TO BECOME THE EYES AND THE EARS OF THE LORD!
ASSIST THE SHEPHERDS OF THE AMERICAN INQUISI-TION AND UNCOVER THE ENEMIES IN OUR MIDST!
TCH!

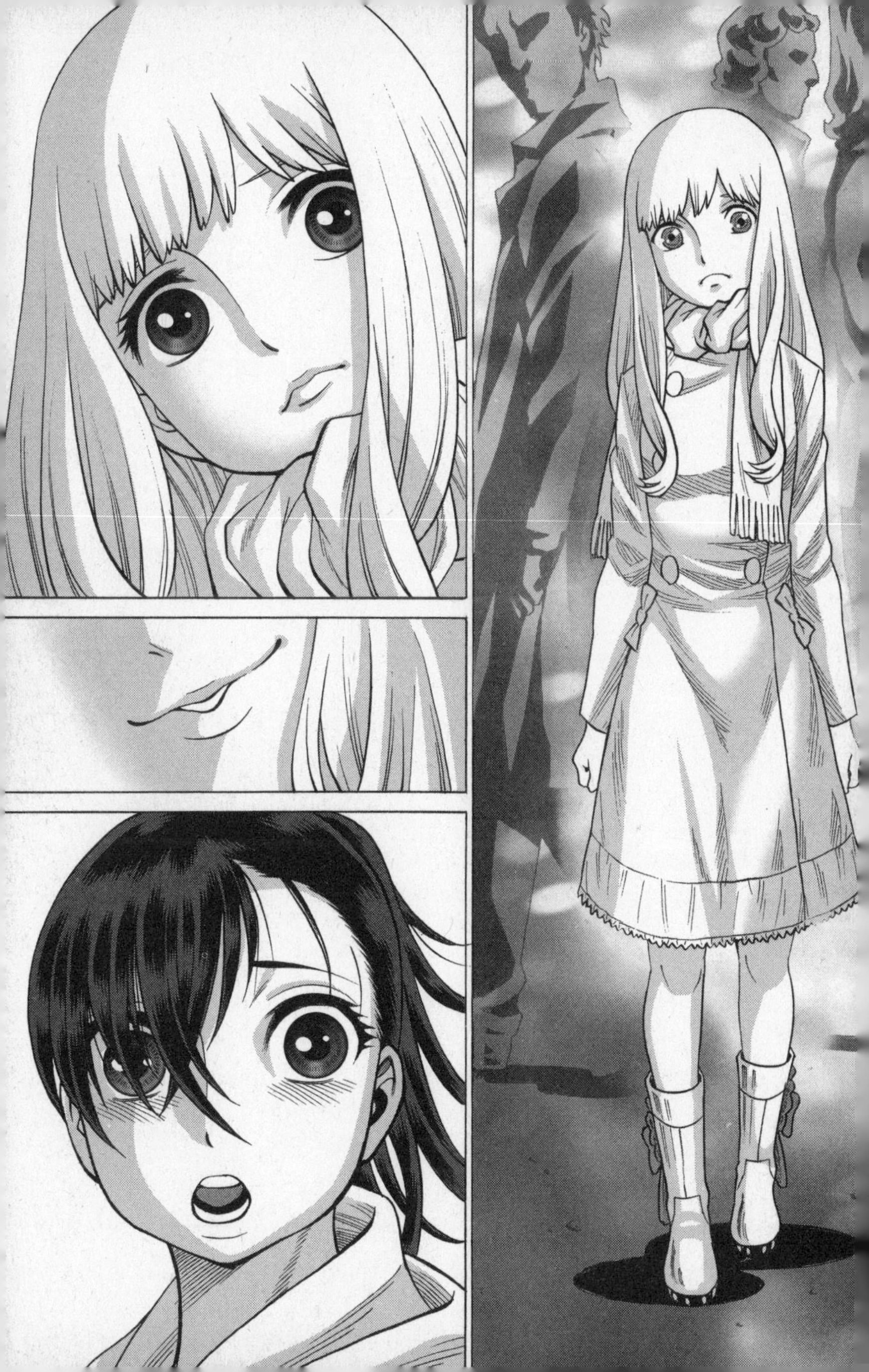

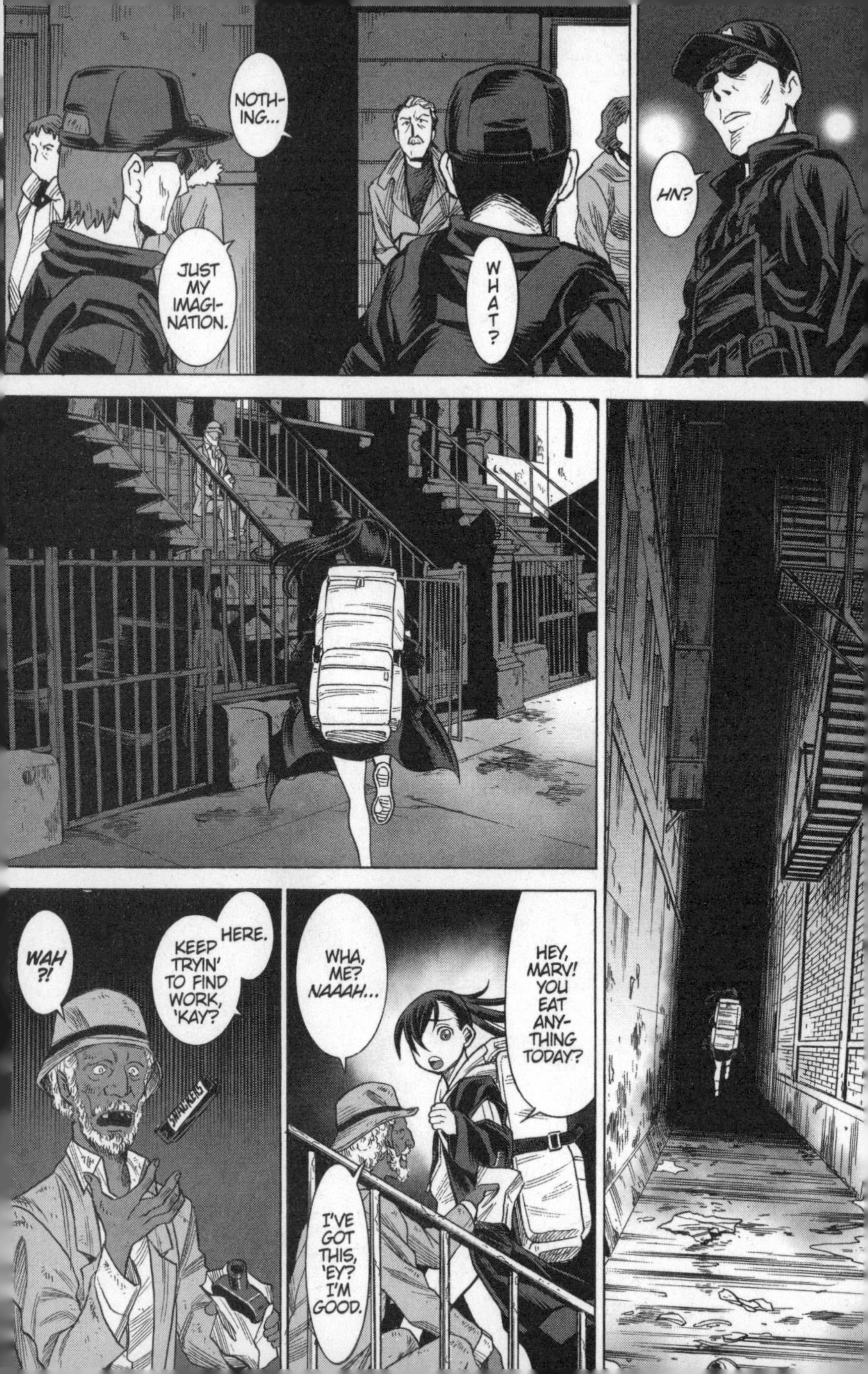
HN?
WHAT?
NOTHING...
JUST MY IMAGINATION.
HEY, MARV! YOU EAT ANYTHING TODAY?
WHA, ME? *NAAAH...*
I'VE GOT THIS, 'EY? I'M GOOD.
HERE. KEEP TRYIN' TO FIND WORK, 'KAY?
WAH ?!

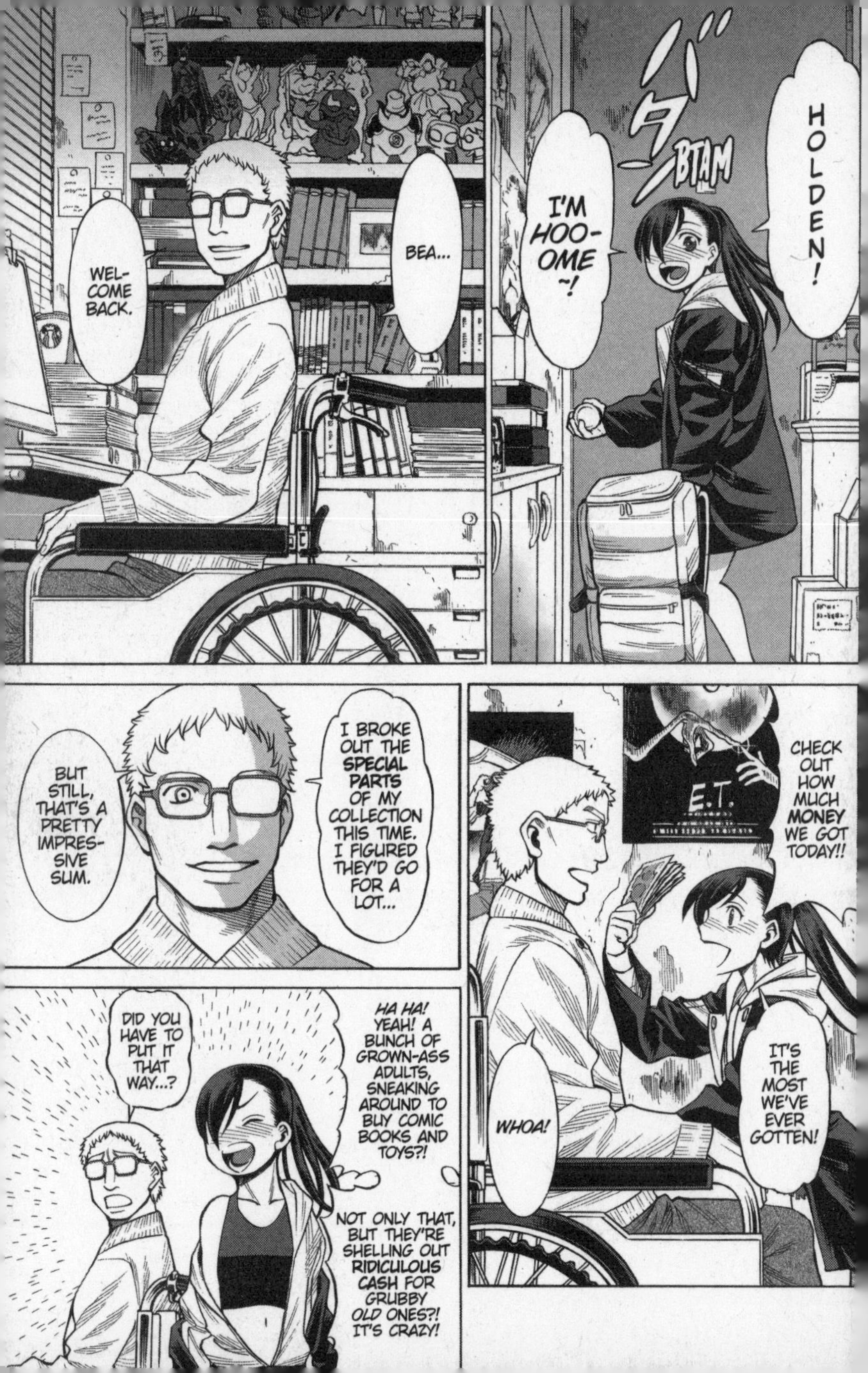
HOLDEN!
BTAM
I'M HOO-OME~!
BEA...
WEL-COME BACK.
CHECK OUT HOW MUCH MONEY WE GOT TODAY!!
IT'S THE MOST WE'VE EVER GOTTEN!
WHOA!
I BROKE OUT THE SPECIAL PARTS OF MY COLLECTION THIS TIME. I FIGURED THEY'D GO FOR A LOT...
BUT STILL, THAT'S A PRETTY IMPRESSIVE SUM.
HA HA! YEAH! A BUNCH OF GROWN-ASS ADULTS, SNEAKING AROUND TO BUY COMIC BOOKS AND TOYS?!
NOT ONLY THAT, BUT THEY'RE SHELLING OUT RIDICULOUS CASH FOR GRUBBY OLD ONES?! IT'S CRAZY!
DID YOU HAVE TO PUT IT THAT WAY...?

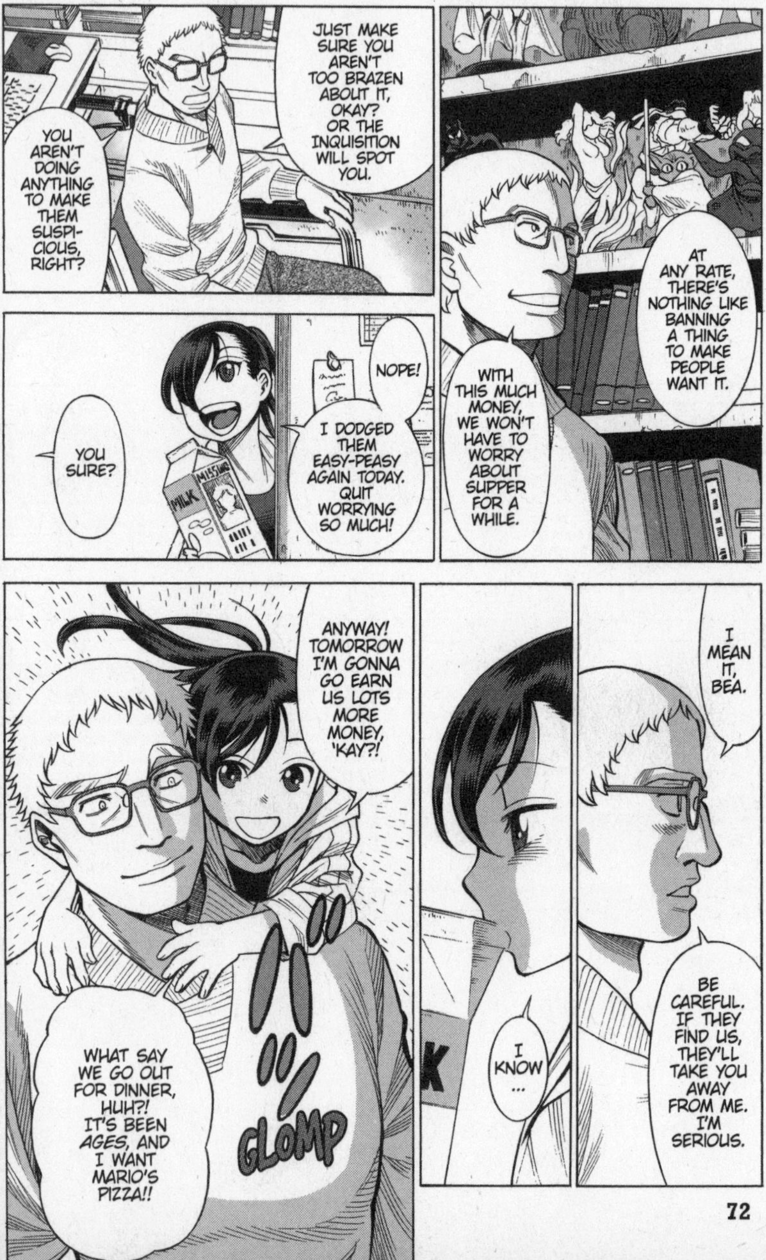
AT ANY RATE, THERE'S NOTHING LIKE BANNING A THING TO MAKE PEOPLE WANT IT.
WITH THIS MUCH MONEY, WE WON'T HAVE TO WORRY ABOUT SUPPER FOR A WHILE.
JUST MAKE SURE YOU AREN'T TOO BRAZEN ABOUT IT, OKAY? OR THE INQUISITION WILL SPOT YOU.
YOU AREN'T DOING ANYTHING TO MAKE THEM SUSPI-CIOUS, RIGHT?
NOPE!
I DODGED THEM EASY-PEASY AGAIN TODAY. QUIT WORRYING SO MUCH!
YOU SURE?
MILK
MISSING
I MEAN IT, BEA.
BE CAREFUL. IF THEY FIND US, THEY'LL TAKE YOU AWAY FROM ME. I'M SERIOUS.
I KNOW ...
ANYWAY! TOMORROW I'M GONNA GO EARN US LOTS MORE MONEY, 'KAY?!
GLOMP
WHAT SAY WE GO OUT FOR DINNER, HUH?! IT'S BEEN AGES, AND I WANT MARIO'S PIZZA!!

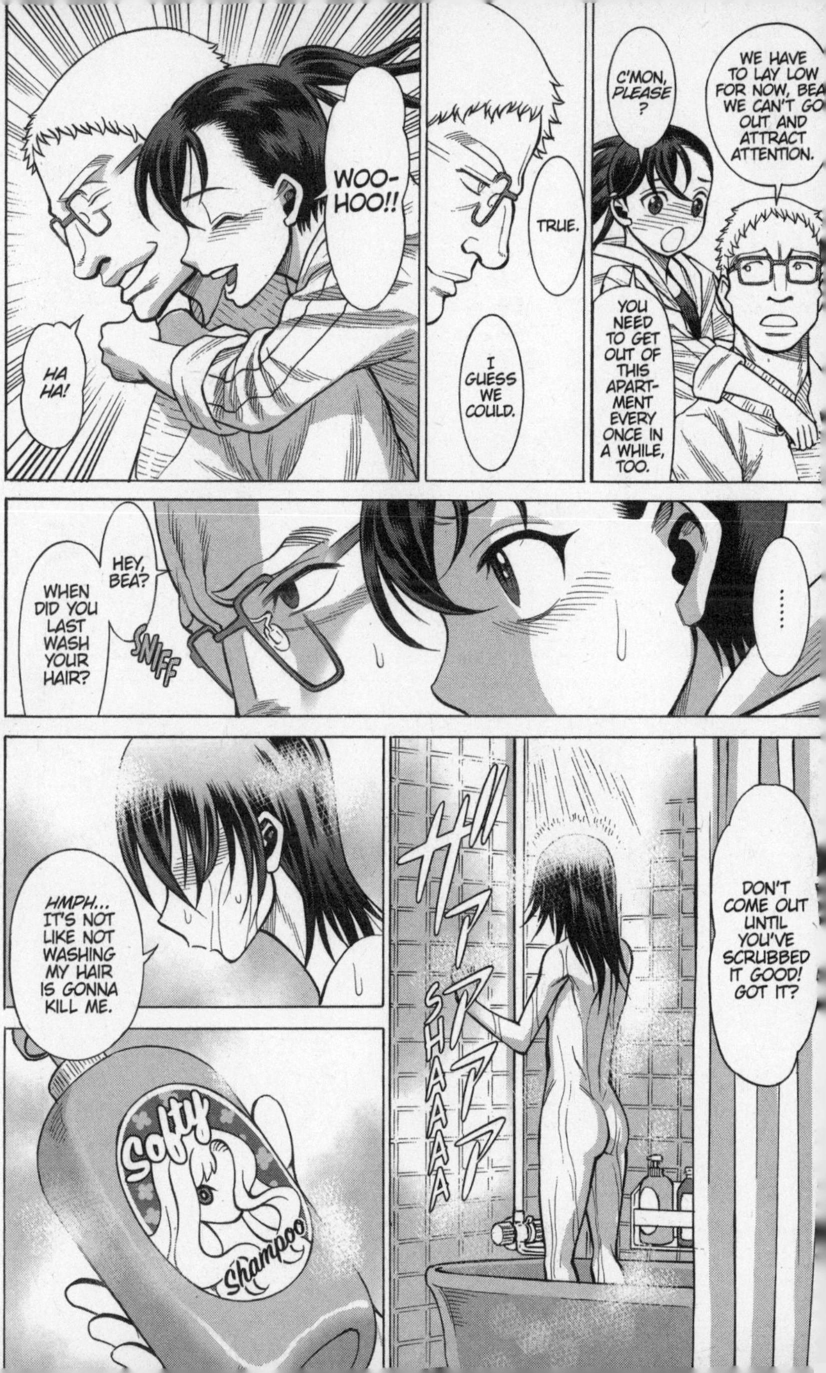
WE HAVE TO LAY LOW FOR NOW, BEA. WE CAN'T GO OUT AND ATTRACT ATTENTION.
C'MON, PLEASE?
YOU NEED TO GET OUT OF THIS APARTMENT EVERY ONCE IN A WHILE, TOO.
TRUE.
I GUESS WE COULD.
WOO-HOO!!
HA HA!
......
HEY, BEA?
SNIFF
WHEN DID YOU LAST WASH YOUR HAIR?
DON'T COME OUT UNTIL YOU'VE SCRUBBED IT GOOD! GOT IT?
SHAAAAA
HMPH... IT'S NOT LIKE NOT WASHING MY HAIR IS GONNA KILL ME.
Softy
Shampoo

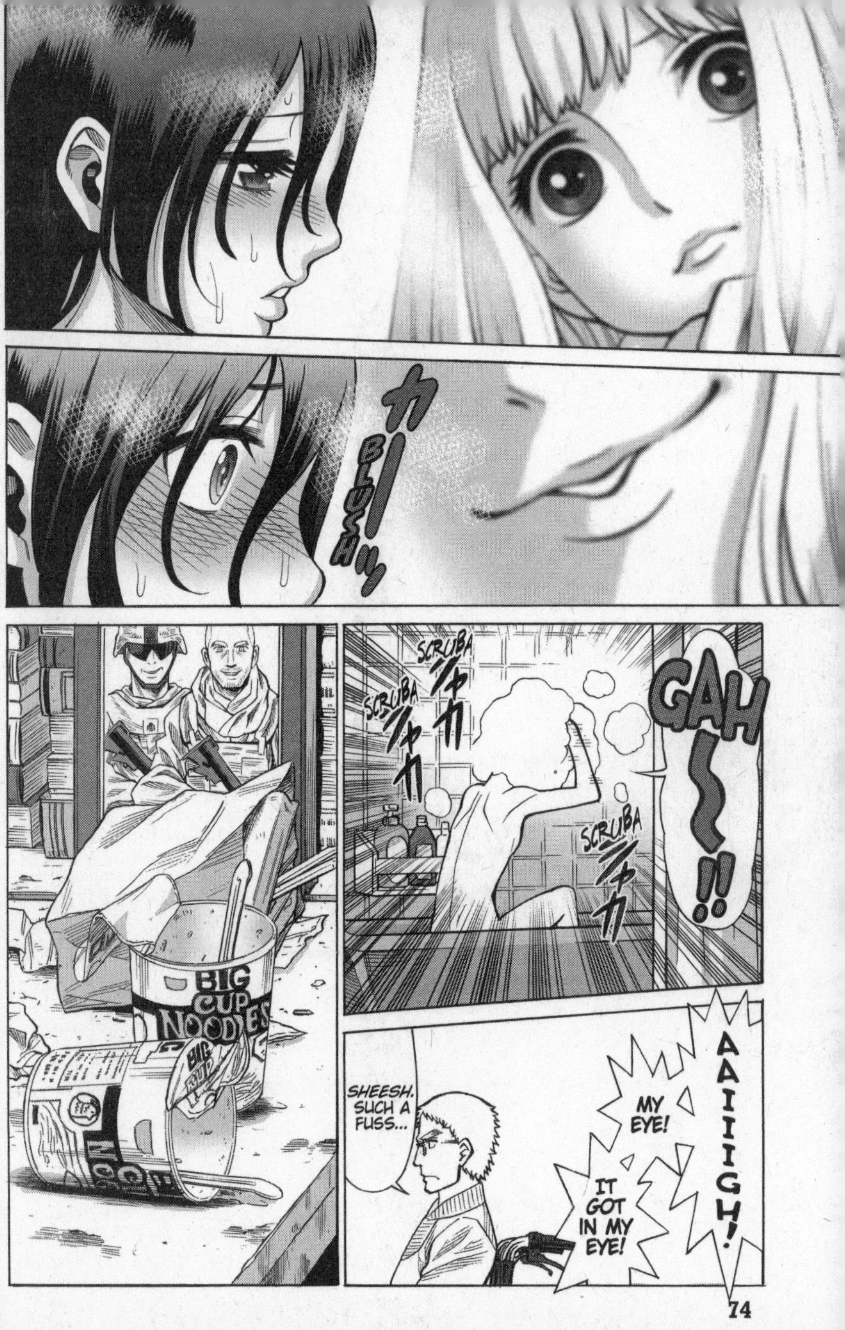
BLUSH
SCRUBA
SCRUBA
SCRUBA
GAH~!!
AAIIIGH!
MY EYE!
IT GOT IN MY EYE!
SHEESH. SUCH A FUSS...
BIG CUP NOODLES

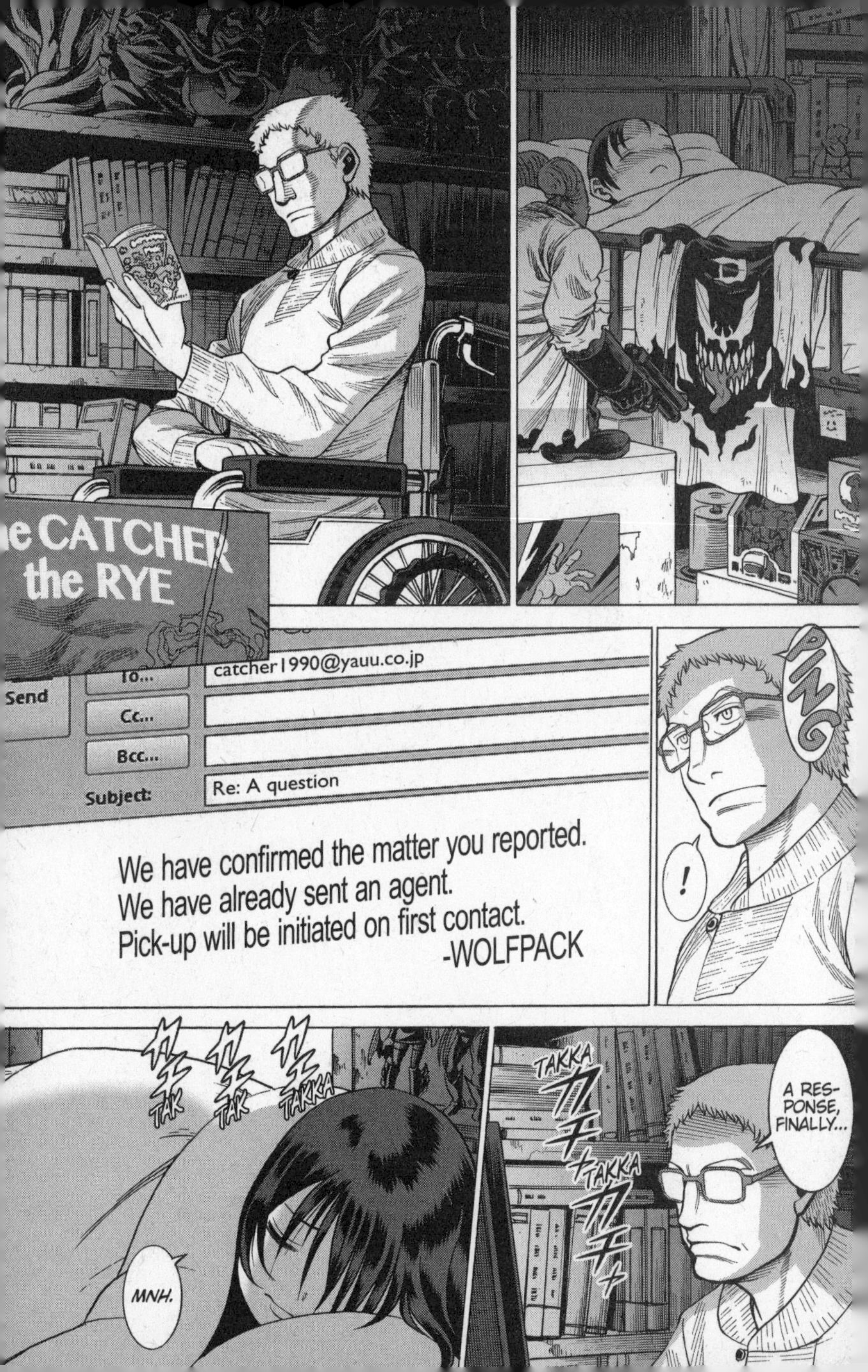
e CATCHER
the RYE
PING
!
To...
Send
Cc...
Bcc...
Subject:
catcher1990@yauu.co.jp
Re: A question
We have confirmed the matter you reported.
We have already sent an agent.
Pick-up will be initiated on first contact.
-WOLFPACK
TAKKA
TAKKA
A RES-PONSE, FINALLY...
TAK
TAK
TAKKA
MNH.

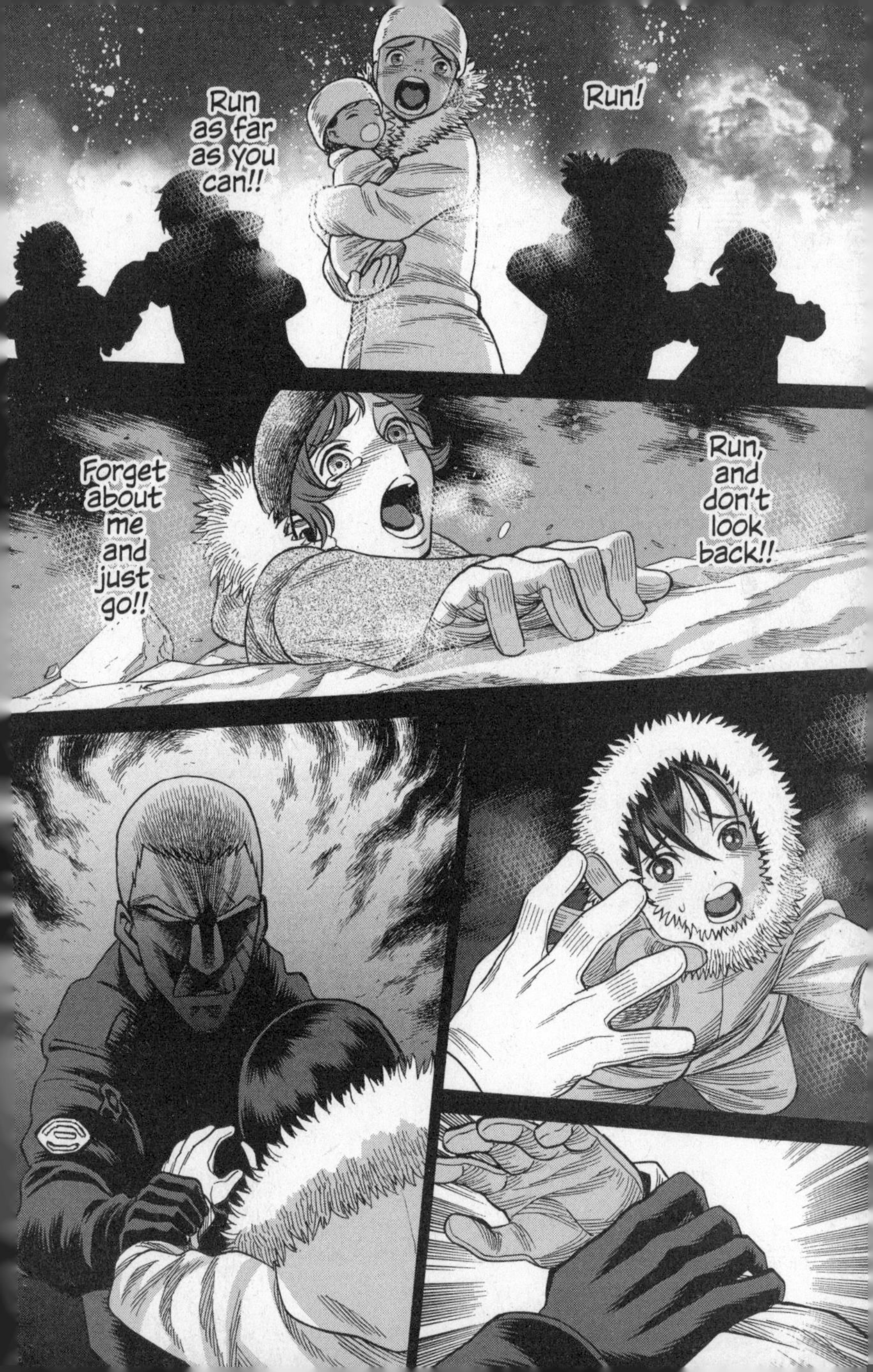
Run!
Run as far as you can!!
Run, and don't look back!!
Forget about me and just go!!

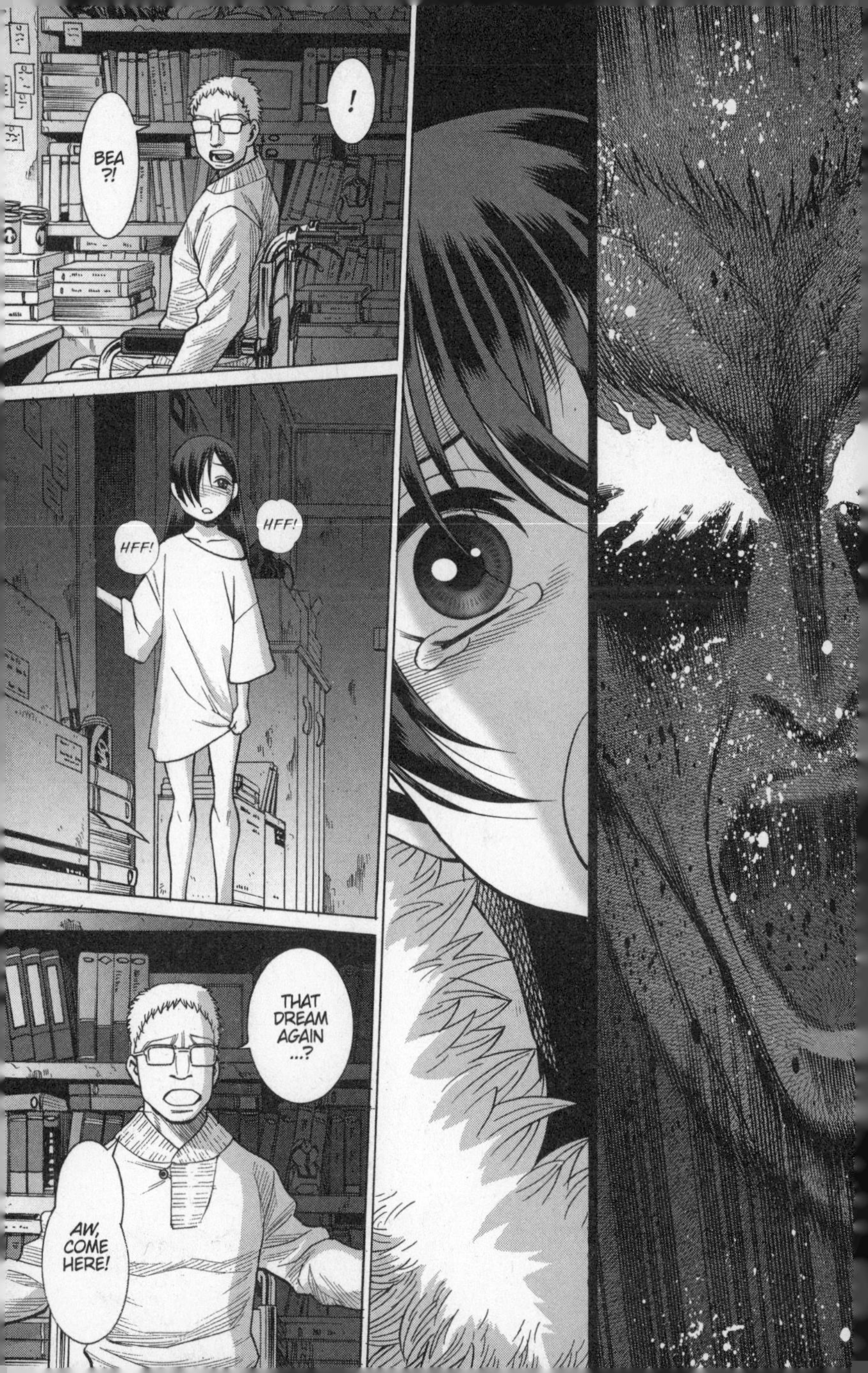
!
BEA ?!
HFF!
HFF!
THAT DREAM AGAIN ...?
AW, COME HERE!

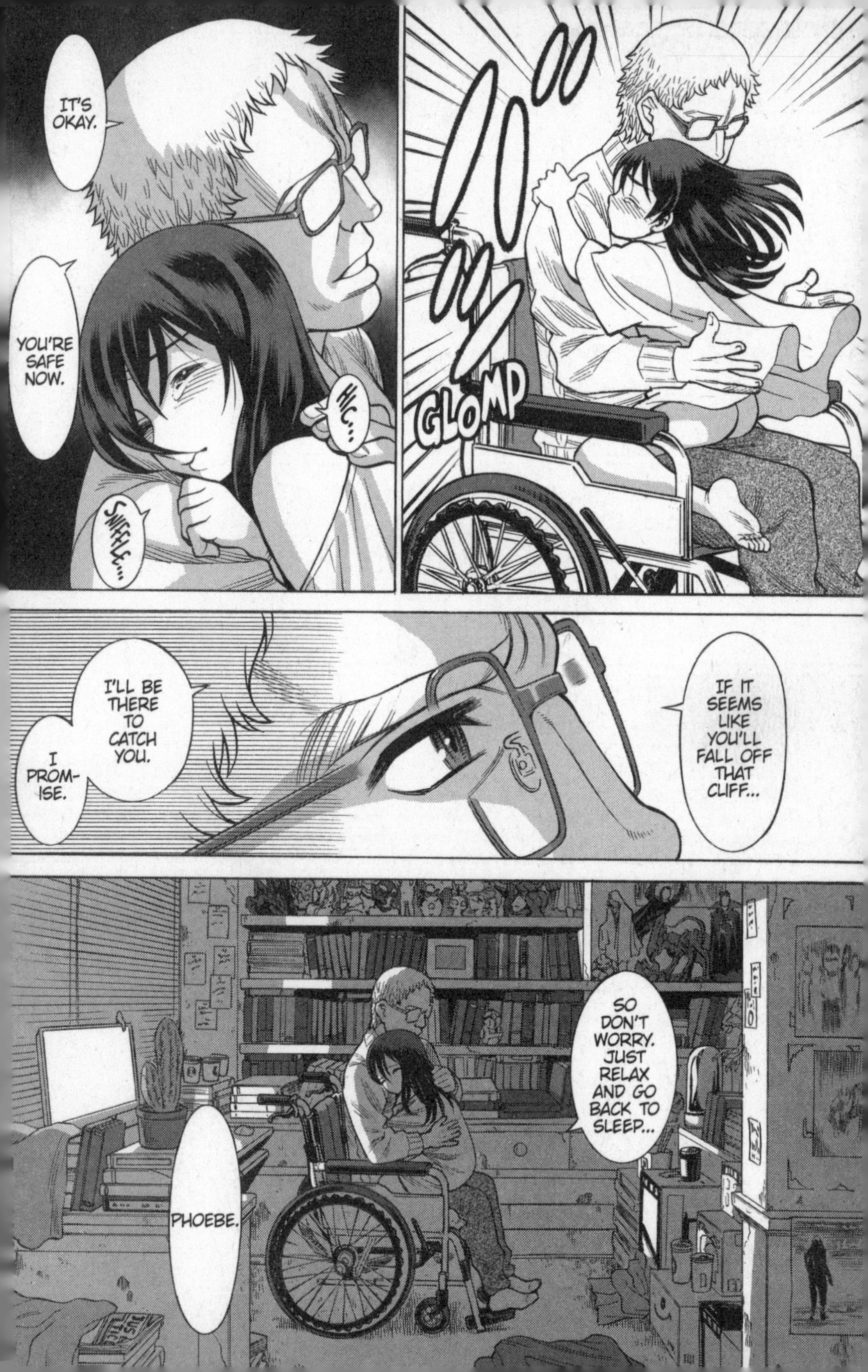
GLOMP
IT'S OKAY.
YOU'RE SAFE NOW.
HIC...
SNIFFLE...
IF IT SEEMS LIKE YOU'LL FALL OFF THAT CLIFF...
I'LL BE THERE TO CATCH YOU.
I PROMISE.
SO DON'T WORRY. JUST RELAX AND GO BACK TO SLEEP...
PHOEBE.

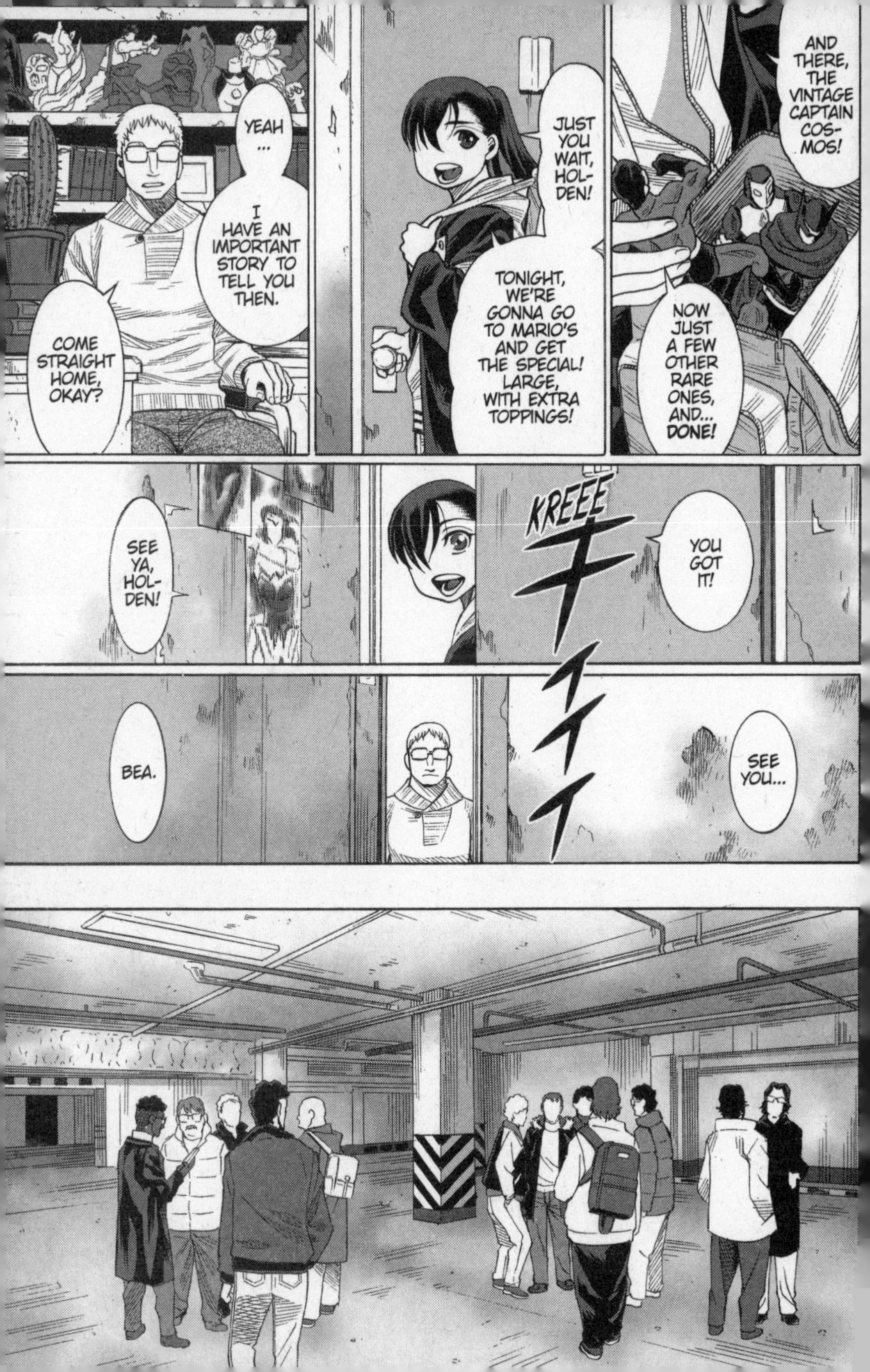
AND THERE, THE VINTAGE CAPTAIN COS-MOS!
NOW JUST A FEW OTHER RARE ONES, AND... DONE!
JUST YOU WAIT, HOL-DEN!
TONIGHT, WE'RE GONNA GO TO MARIO'S AND GET THE SPECIAL! LARGE, WITH EXTRA TOPPINGS!
YEAH ...
I HAVE AN IMPORTANT STORY TO TELL YOU THEN.
COME STRAIGHT HOME, OKAY?
YOU GOT IT!
KREEE
SEE YA, HOL-DEN!
SEE YOU...
BEA.

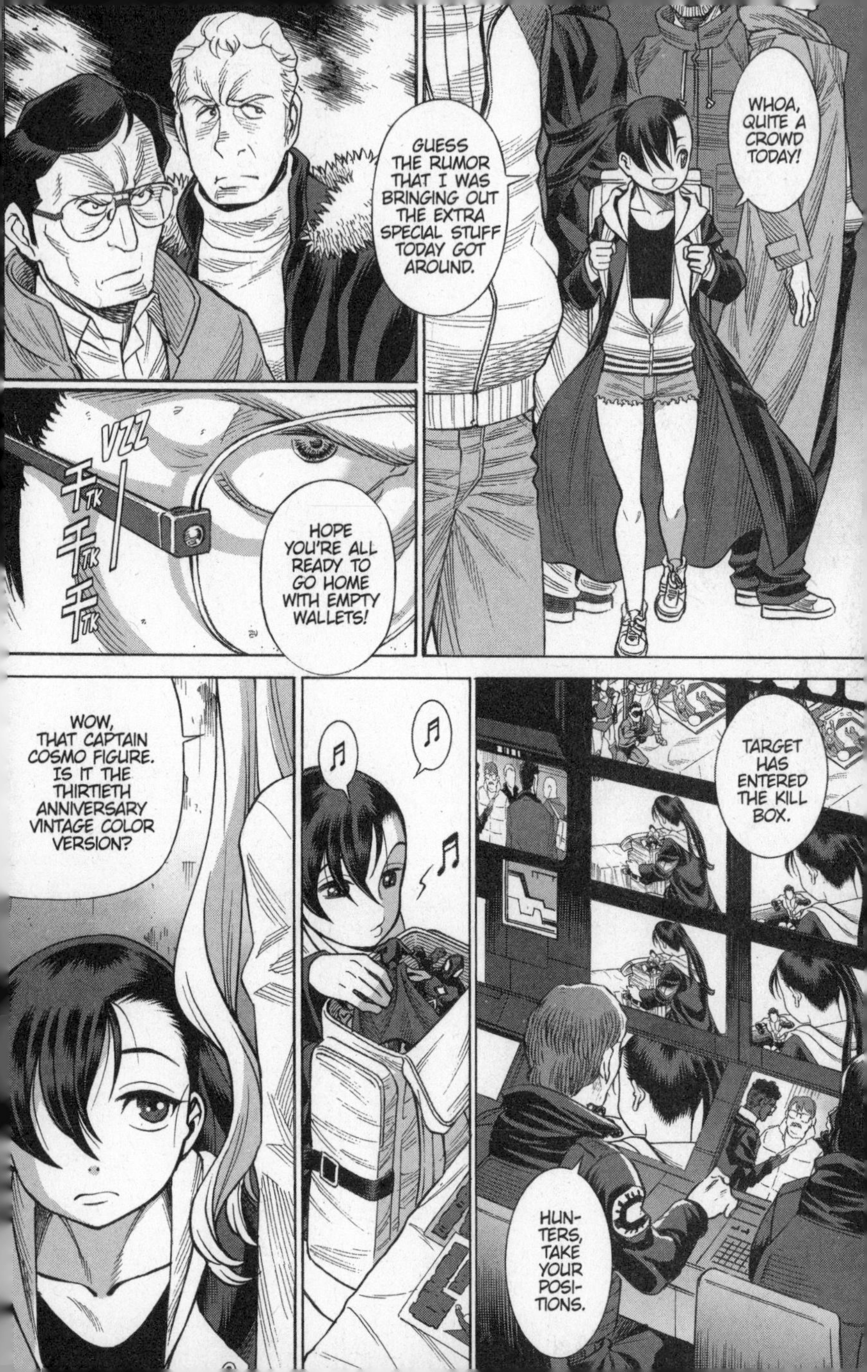
WHOA, QUITE A CROWD TODAY!
GUESS THE RUMOR THAT I WAS BRINGING OUT THE EXTRA SPECIAL STUFF TODAY GOT AROUND.
HOPE YOU'RE ALL READY TO GO HOME WITH EMPTY WALLETS!
VZZ
TK
TK
TK
TARGET HAS ENTERED THE KILL BOX.
HUNTERS, TAKE YOUR POSI-TIONS.
♪
♪
♪
WOW, THAT CAPTAIN COSMO FIGURE. IS IT THE THIRTIETH ANNIVERSARY VINTAGE COLOR VERSION?

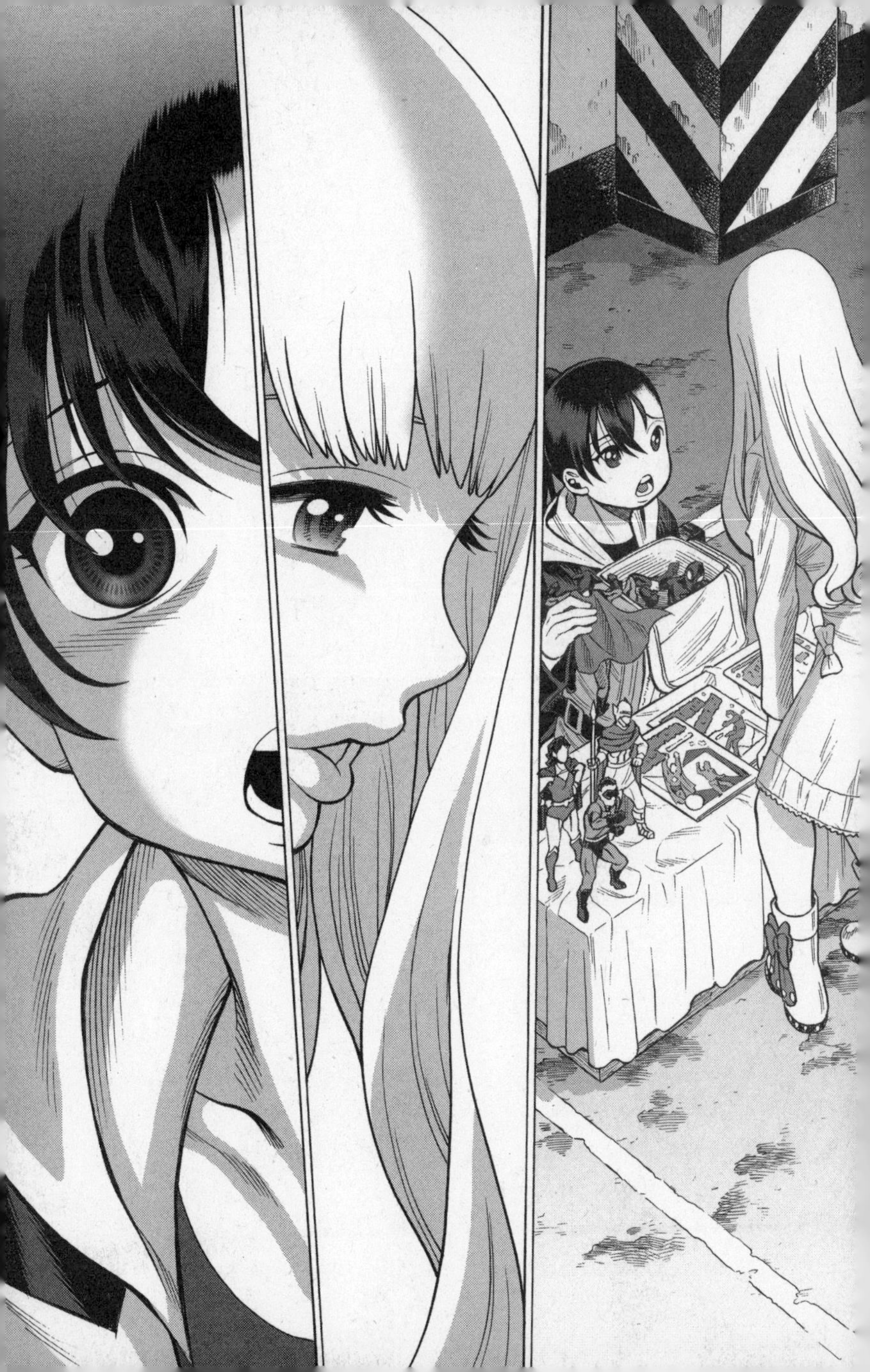

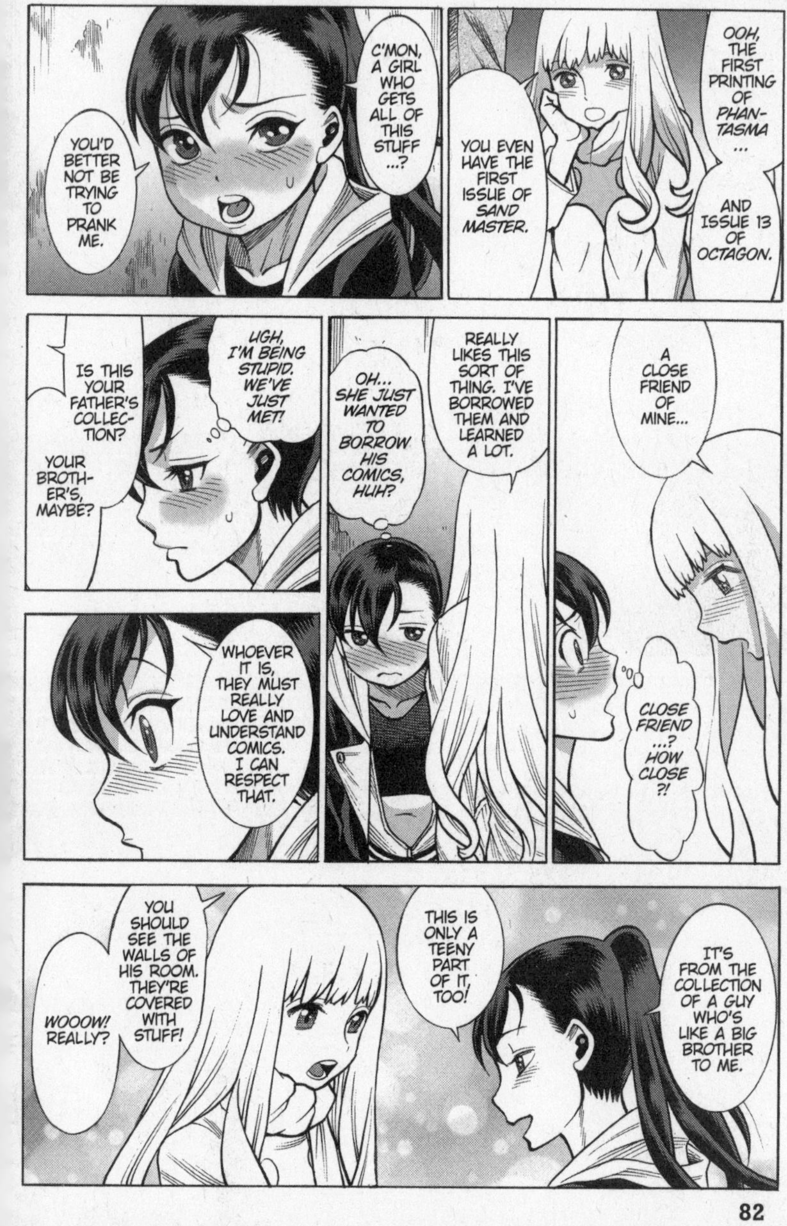
OOH, THE FIRST PRINTING OF PHANTASMA ...
AND ISSUE 13 OF OCTAGON.
YOU EVEN HAVE THE FIRST ISSUE OF SAND MASTER.
C'MON, A GIRL WHO GETS ALL OF THIS STUFF ...?
YOU'D BETTER NOT BE TRYING TO PRANK ME.
A CLOSE FRIEND OF MINE...
CLOSE FRIEND ...? HOW CLOSE ?!
REALLY LIKES THIS SORT OF THING. I'VE BORROWED THEM AND LEARNED A LOT.
OH... SHE JUST WANTED TO BORROW HIS COMICS, HUH?
UGH, I'M BEING STUPID. WE'VE JUST MET!
IS THIS YOUR FATHER'S COLLECTION?
YOUR BROTHER'S, MAYBE?
WHOEVER IT IS, THEY MUST REALLY LOVE AND UNDERSTAND COMICS. I CAN RESPECT THAT.
IT'S FROM THE COLLECTION OF A GUY WHO'S LIKE A BIG BROTHER TO ME.
THIS IS ONLY A TEENY PART OF IT, TOO!
YOU SHOULD SEE THE WALLS OF HIS ROOM. THEY'RE COVERED WITH STUFF!
WOOOW! REALLY?

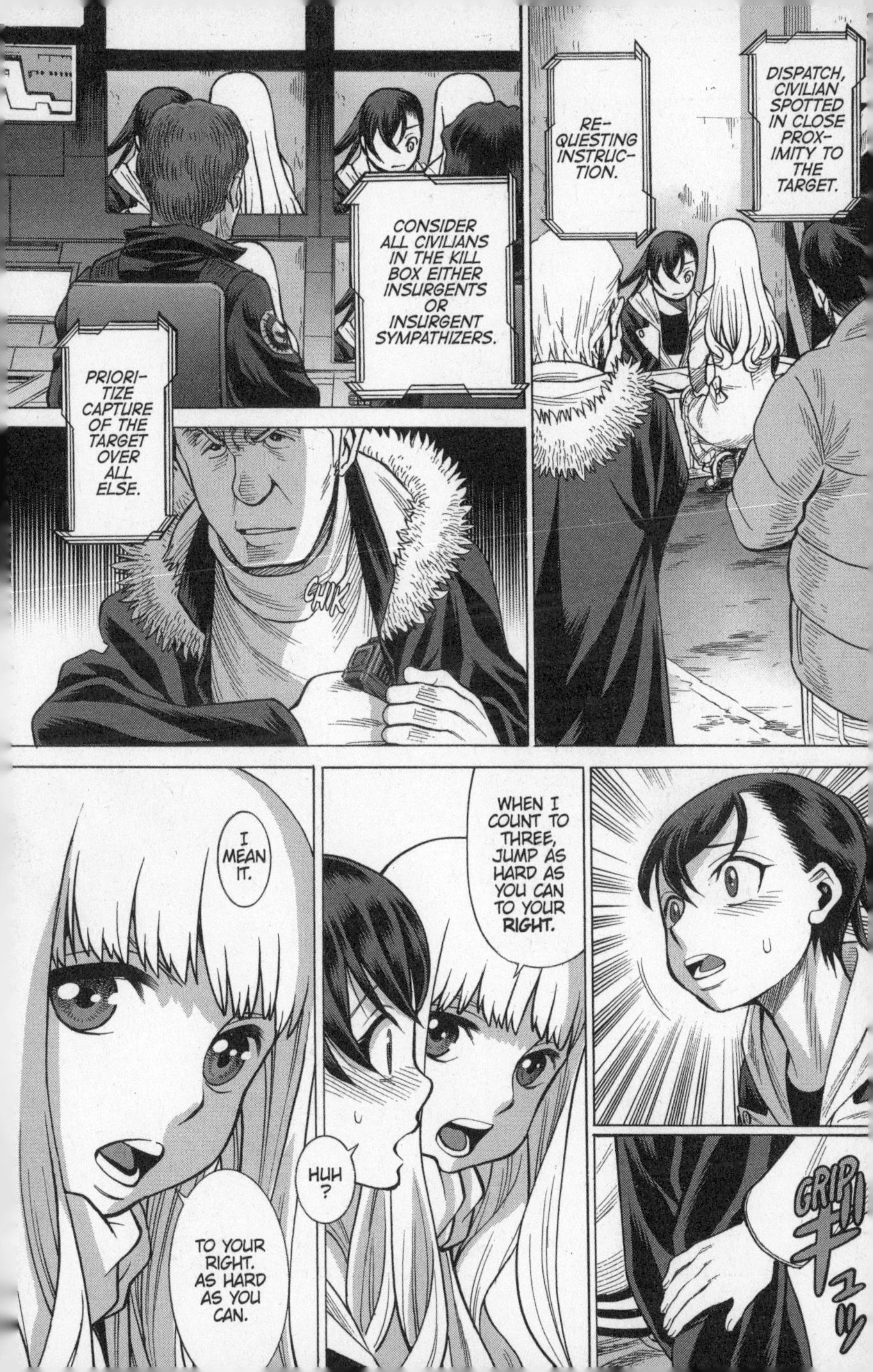
DISPATCH, CIVILIAN SPOTTED IN CLOSE PROXIMITY TO THE TARGET.
REQUESTING INSTRUCTION.
CONSIDER ALL CIVILIANS IN THE KILL BOX EITHER INSURGENTS OR INSURGENT SYMPATHIZERS.
PRIORITIZE CAPTURE OF THE TARGET OVER ALL ELSE.
CHIK
GRIP!!
ギュッ
WHEN I COUNT TO THREE, JUMP AS HARD AS YOU CAN TO YOUR RIGHT.
HUH?
I MEAN IT.
TO YOUR RIGHT. AS HARD AS YOU CAN.

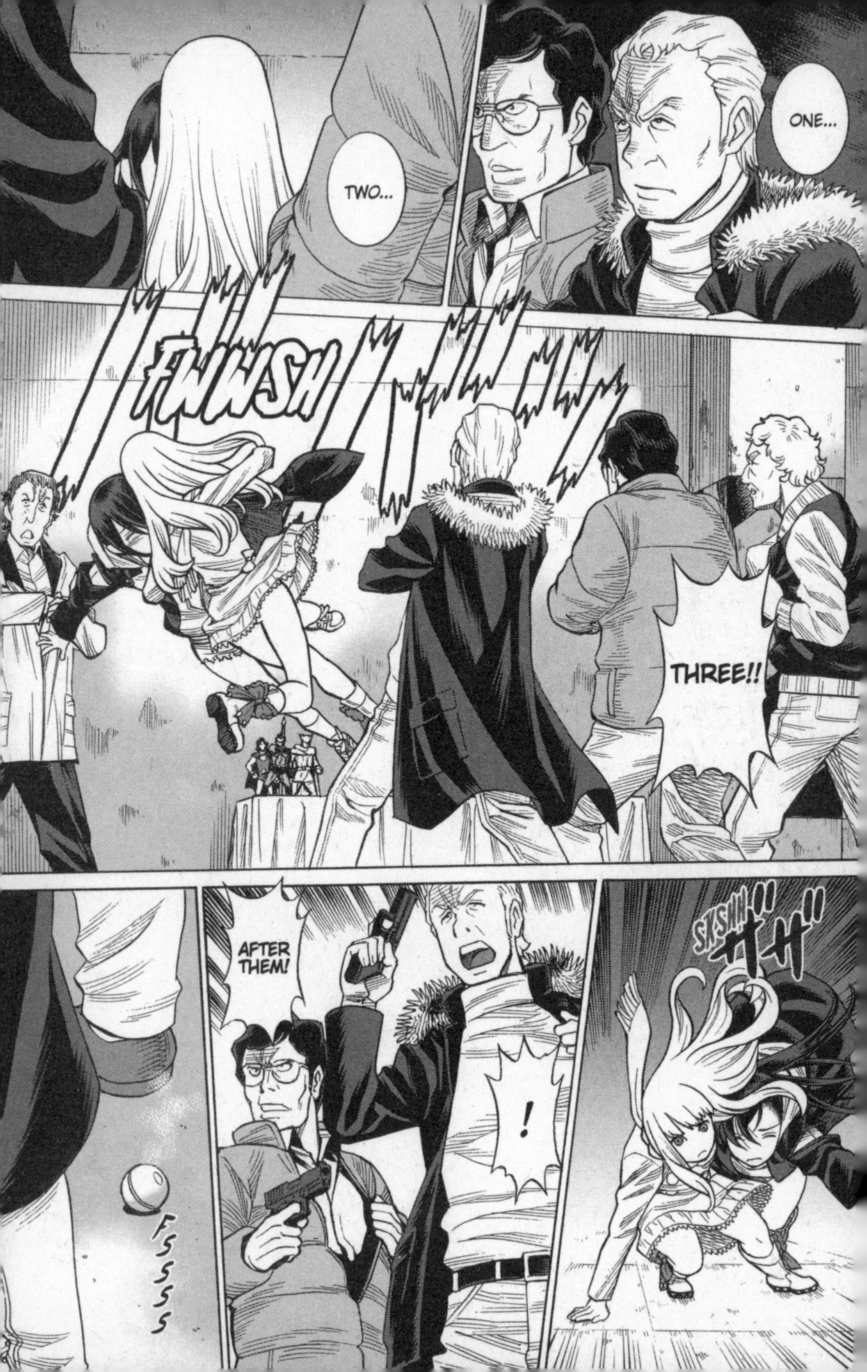
ONE...
TWO...
FWWSH
THREE!!
SKSHH!!
AFTER THEM!
!
FSSSS

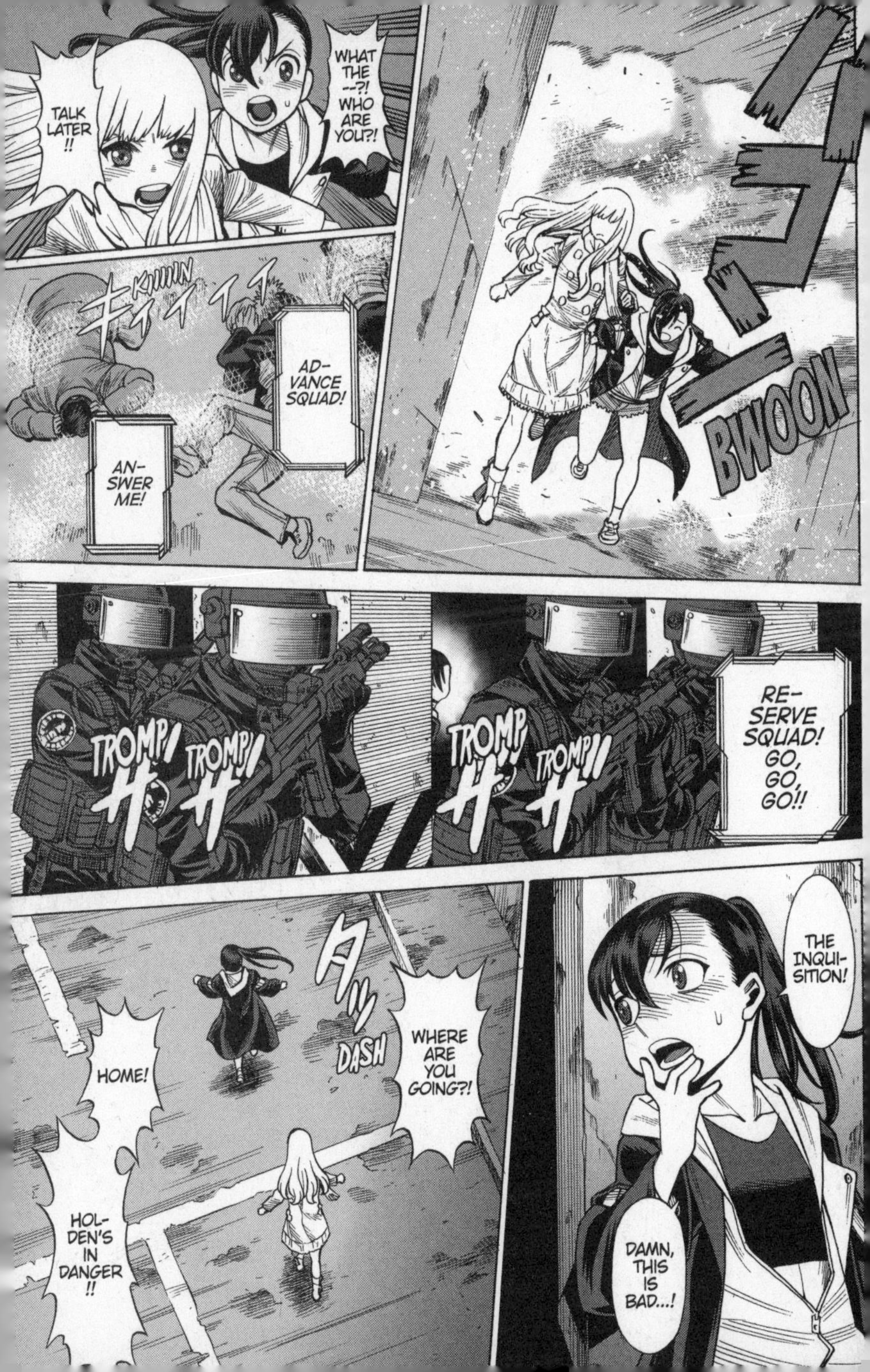
BWOON
WHAT THE --?! WHO ARE YOU?!
TALK LATER !!
KIIIIIN
ADVANCE SQUAD!
ANSWER ME!
RESERVE SQUAD! GO, GO, GO!!
TROMP!! TROMP!!
TROMP!! TROMP!!
THE INQUISITION!
DAMN, THIS IS BAD...!
DASH
WHERE ARE YOU GOING?!
HOME!
HOLDEN'S IN DANGER !!

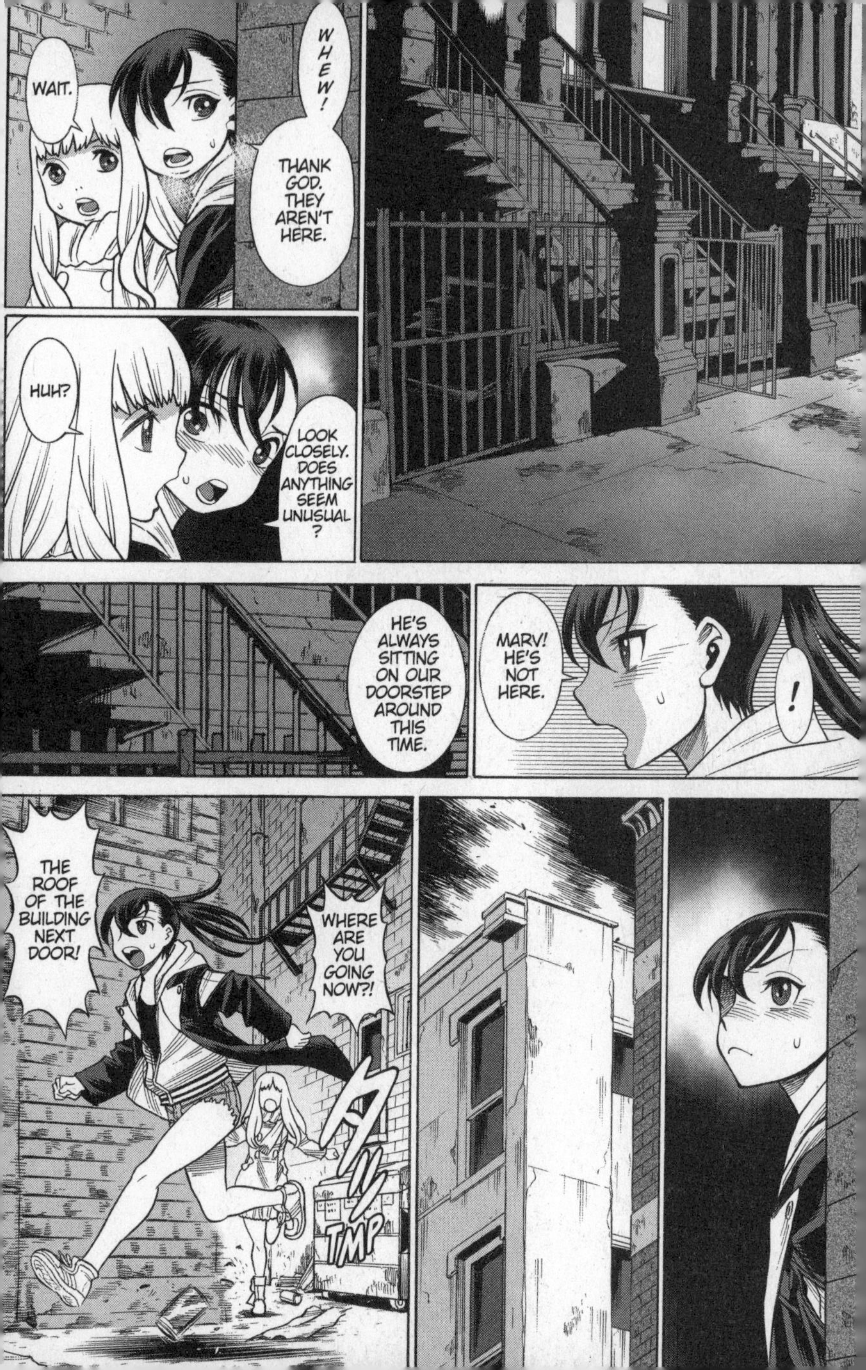
WHEW! THANK GOD. THEY AREN'T HERE.
WAIT.
LOOK CLOSELY. DOES ANYTHING SEEM UNUSUAL?
HUH?
!
MARV! HE'S NOT HERE.
HE'S ALWAYS SITTING ON OUR DOORSTEP AROUND THIS TIME.
WHERE ARE YOU GOING NOW?!
THE ROOF OF THE BUILDING NEXT DOOR!
TMP

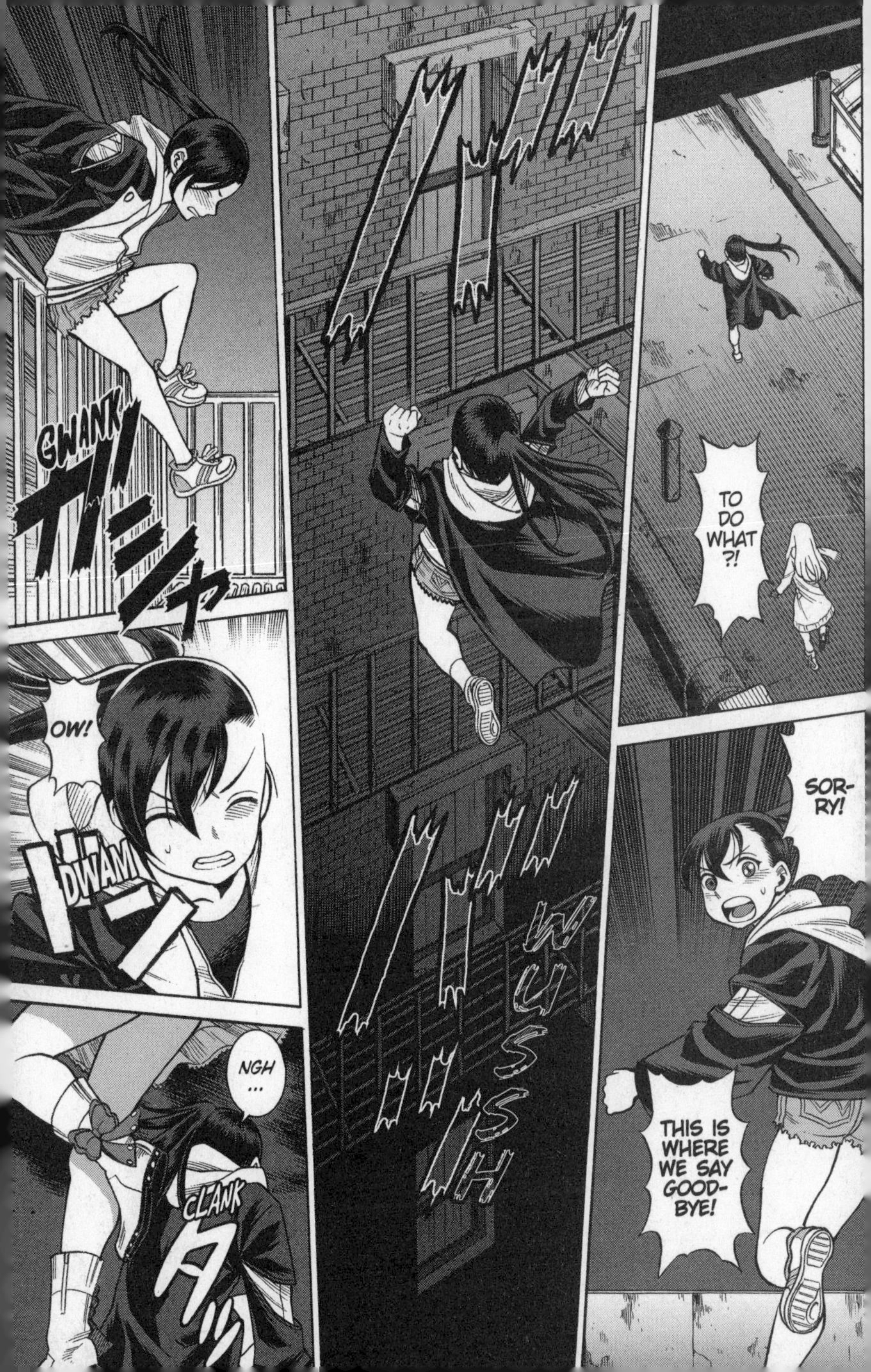
TO DO WHAT?!
SORRY!
THIS IS WHERE WE SAY GOOD-BYE!
WHUSSH
GWANK
OW!
DWAM
NGH...
CLANK

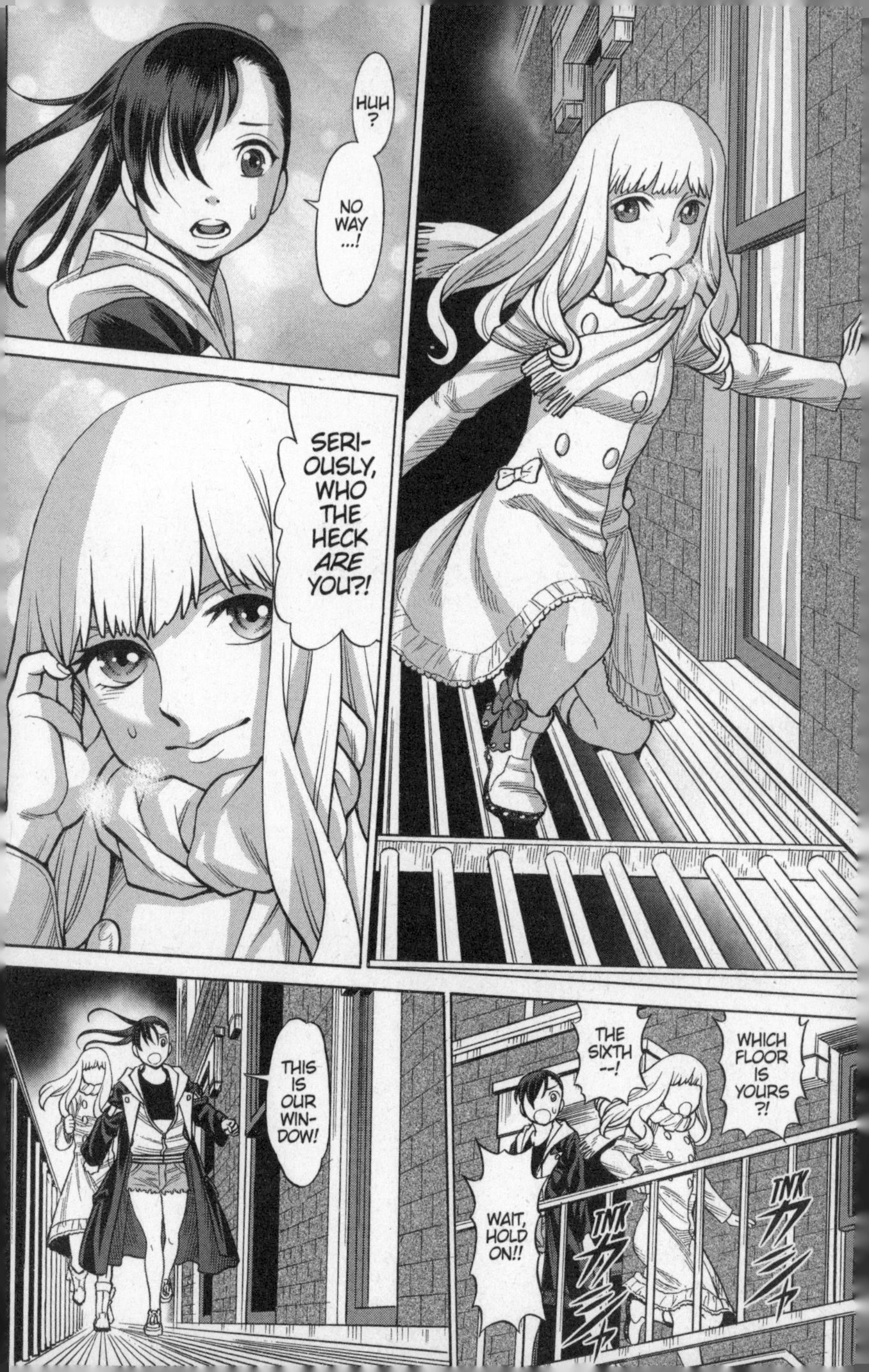
HUH?
NO WAY...!
SERIOUSLY, WHO THE HECK ARE YOU?!
WHICH FLOOR IS YOURS?!
THE SIXTH--!
WAIT, HOLD ON!!
TINK
TINK
THIS IS OUR WINDOW!

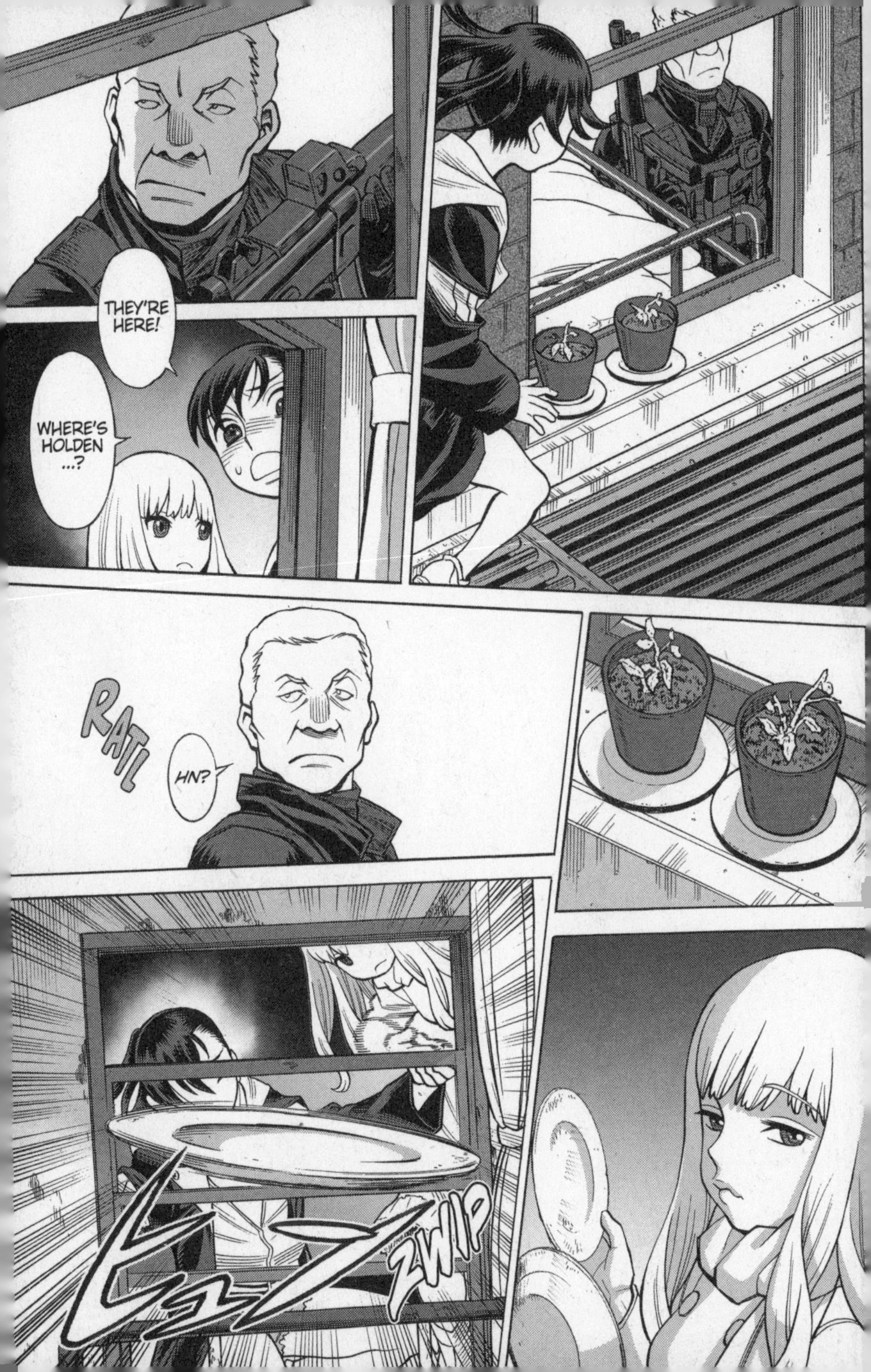
THEY'RE HERE!
WHERE'S HOLDEN ...?
RATTL
HN?
ZWIP

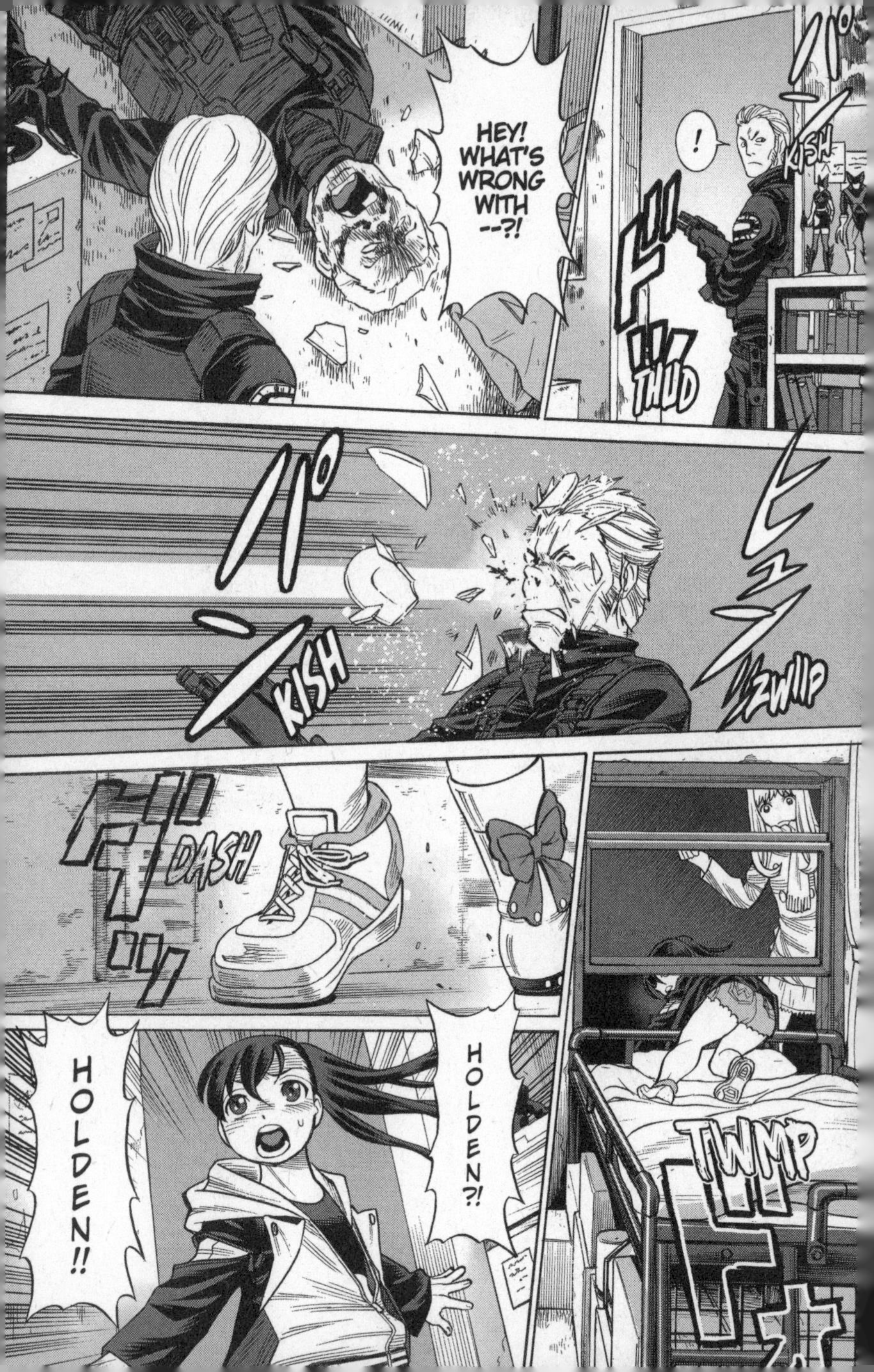
!
KISH
THUD
HEY! WHAT'S WRONG WITH --?!
ZWIIP
KISH
TWMP
DASH
HOLDEN?!
HOLDEN!!

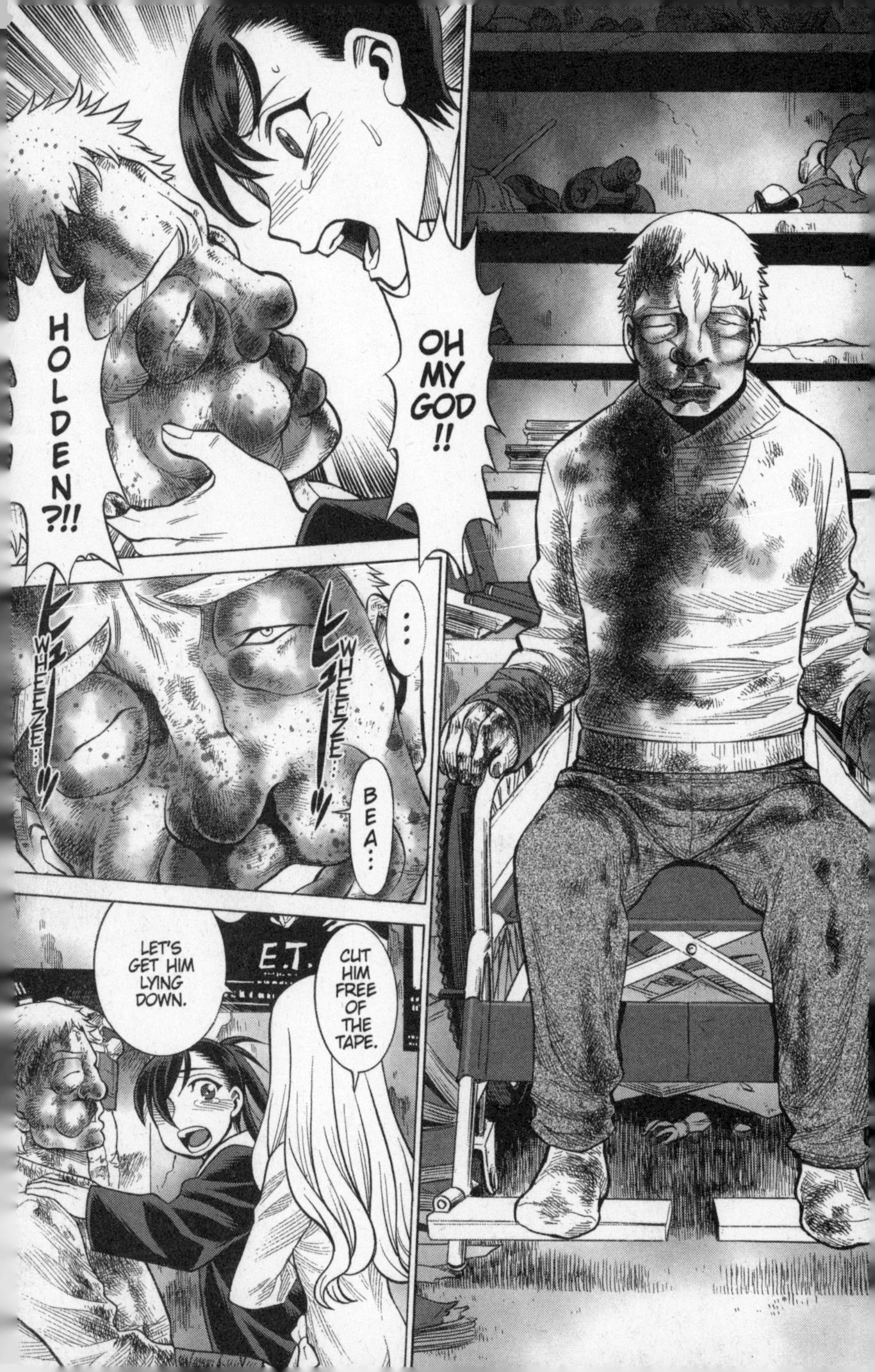
OH MY GOD!!
HOLDEN?!!
...
WHEEZE...
BEA...
WHEEZE...
E.T.
CUT HIM FREE OF THE TAPE.
LET'S GET HIM LYING DOWN.

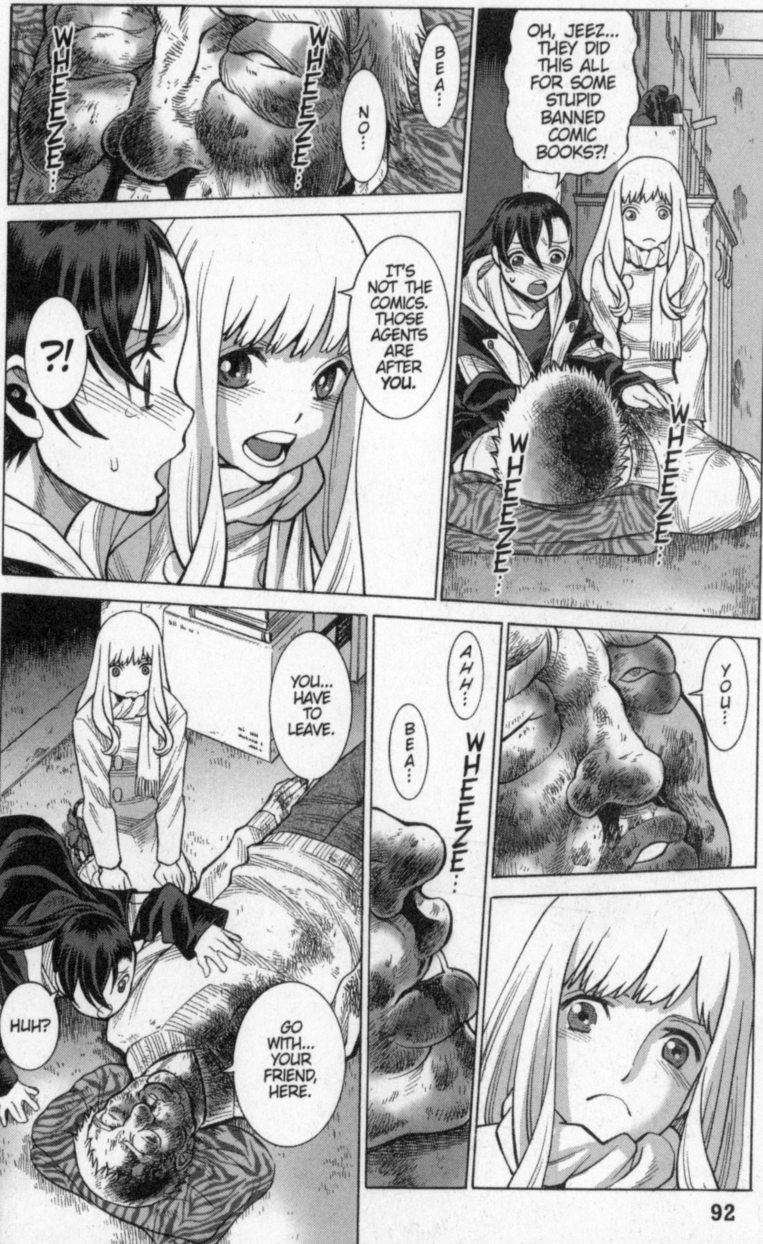
OH, JEEZ... THEY DID THIS ALL FOR SOME STUPID BANNED COMIC BOOKS?!
WHEEZE...
WHEEZE...
BEA...
NO...
WHEEZE...
WHEEZE...
IT'S NOT THE COMICS. THOSE AGENTS ARE AFTER YOU.
?!
YOU...
AHH...
BEA...
WHEEZE...
YOU... HAVE TO LEAVE.
GO WITH... YOUR FRIEND, HERE.
HUH?

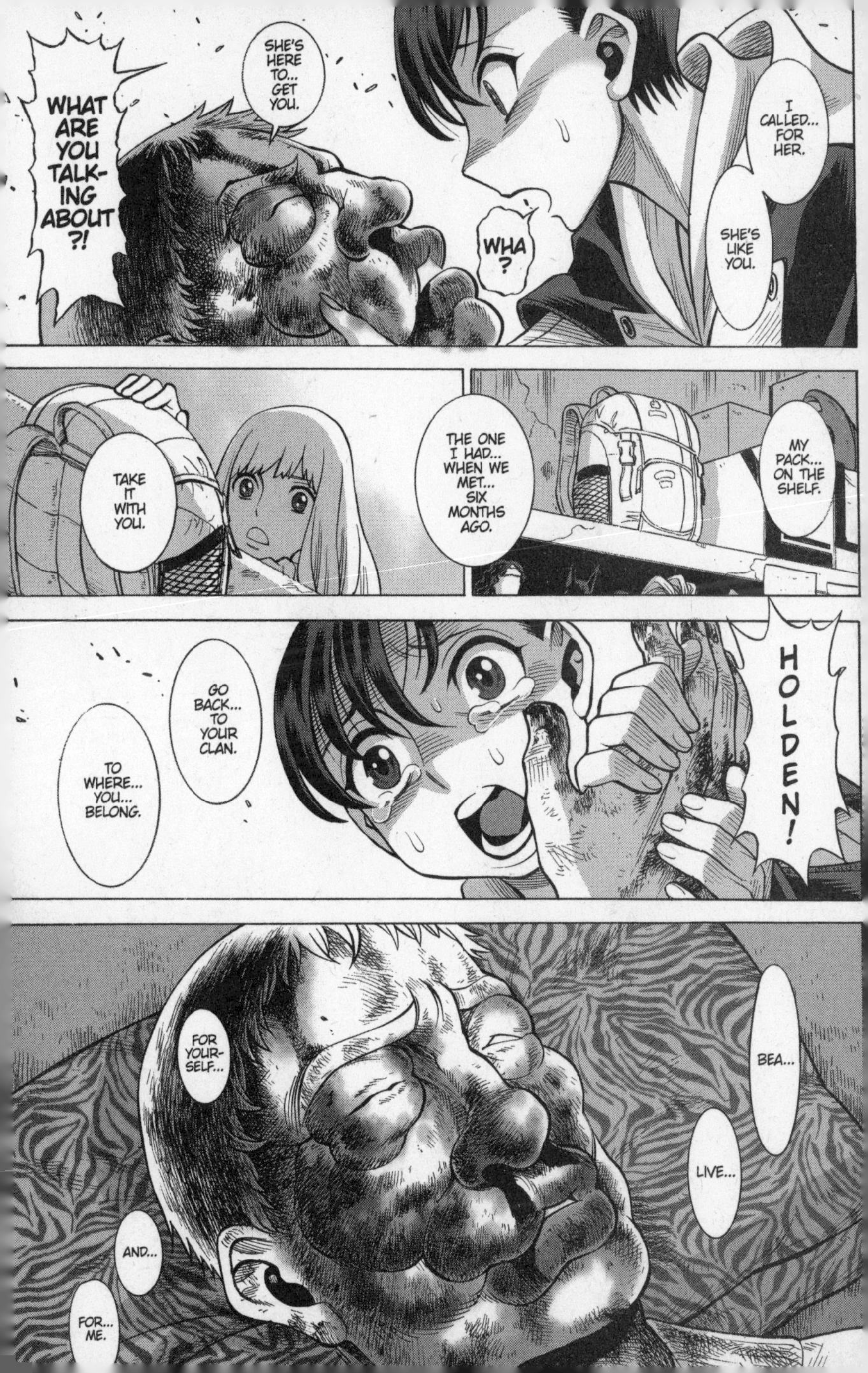
I CALLED... FOR HER.
SHE'S LIKE YOU.
WHA?
SHE'S HERE TO... GET YOU.
WHAT ARE YOU TALKING-ING ABOUT?!
MY PACK... ON THE SHELF.
THE ONE I HAD... WHEN WE MET... SIX MONTHS AGO.
TAKE IT WITH YOU.
HOLDEN!
GO BACK... TO YOUR CLAN.
TO WHERE... YOU... BELONG.
BEA...
LIVE...
FOR YOUR-SELF...
AND...
FOR... ME.

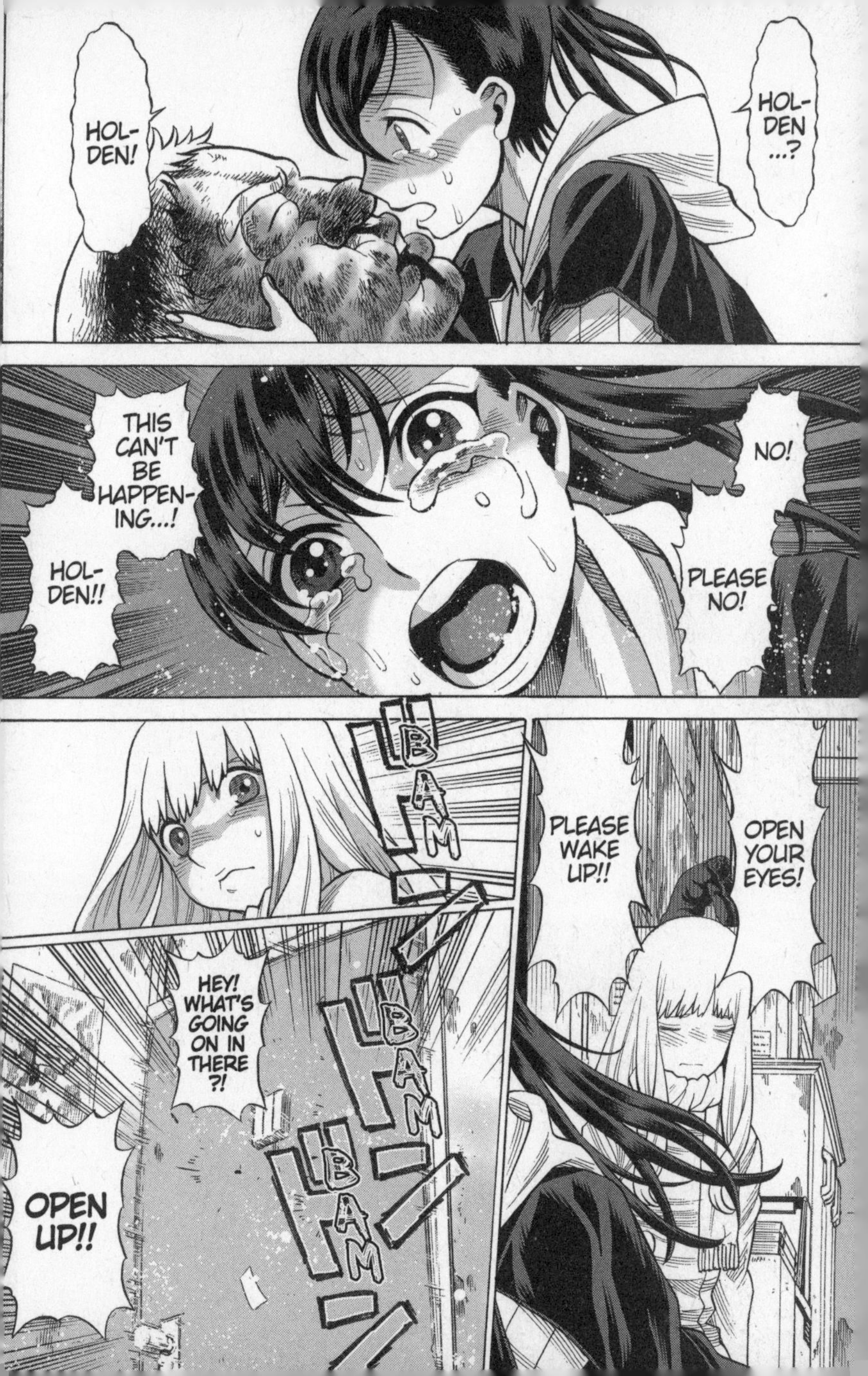
HOL-DEN...?
HOL-DEN!
NO!
PLEASE NO!
THIS CAN'T BE HAPPENING...!
HOL-DEN!!
OPEN YOUR EYES!
PLEASE WAKE UP!!
BAM
HEY! WHAT'S GOING ON IN THERE?!
BAM
BAM
OPEN UP!!

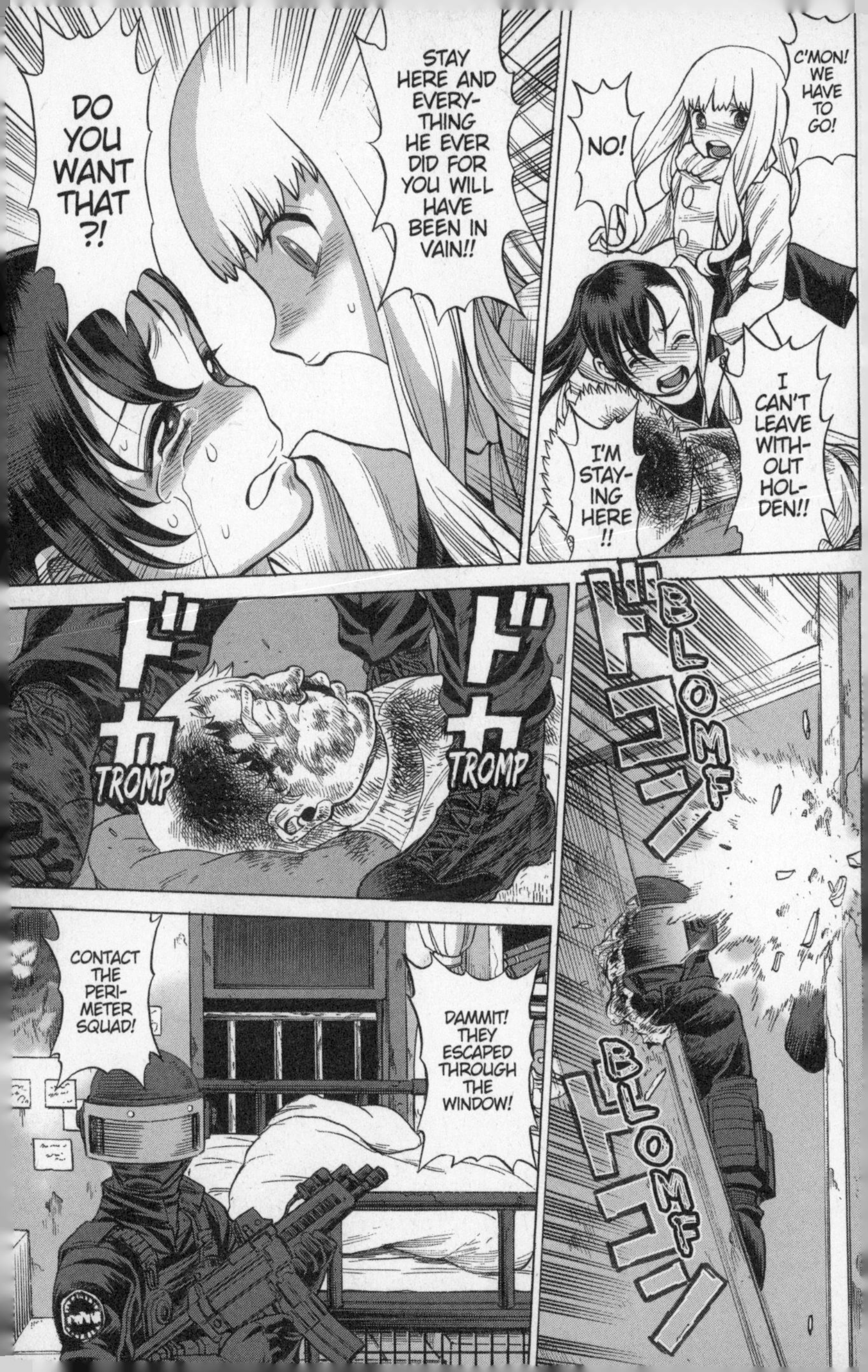
C'MON! WE HAVE TO GO!
NO!
I CAN'T LEAVE WITHOUT HOLDEN!!
I'M STAYING HERE!!
STAY HERE AND EVERYTHING HE EVER DID FOR YOU WILL HAVE BEEN IN VAIN!!
DO YOU WANT THAT?!
BLOMF
BLOMF
ドカ
TROMP
ドカ
TROMP
DAMMIT! THEY ESCAPED THROUGH THE WINDOW!
CONTACT THE PERIMETER SQUAD!

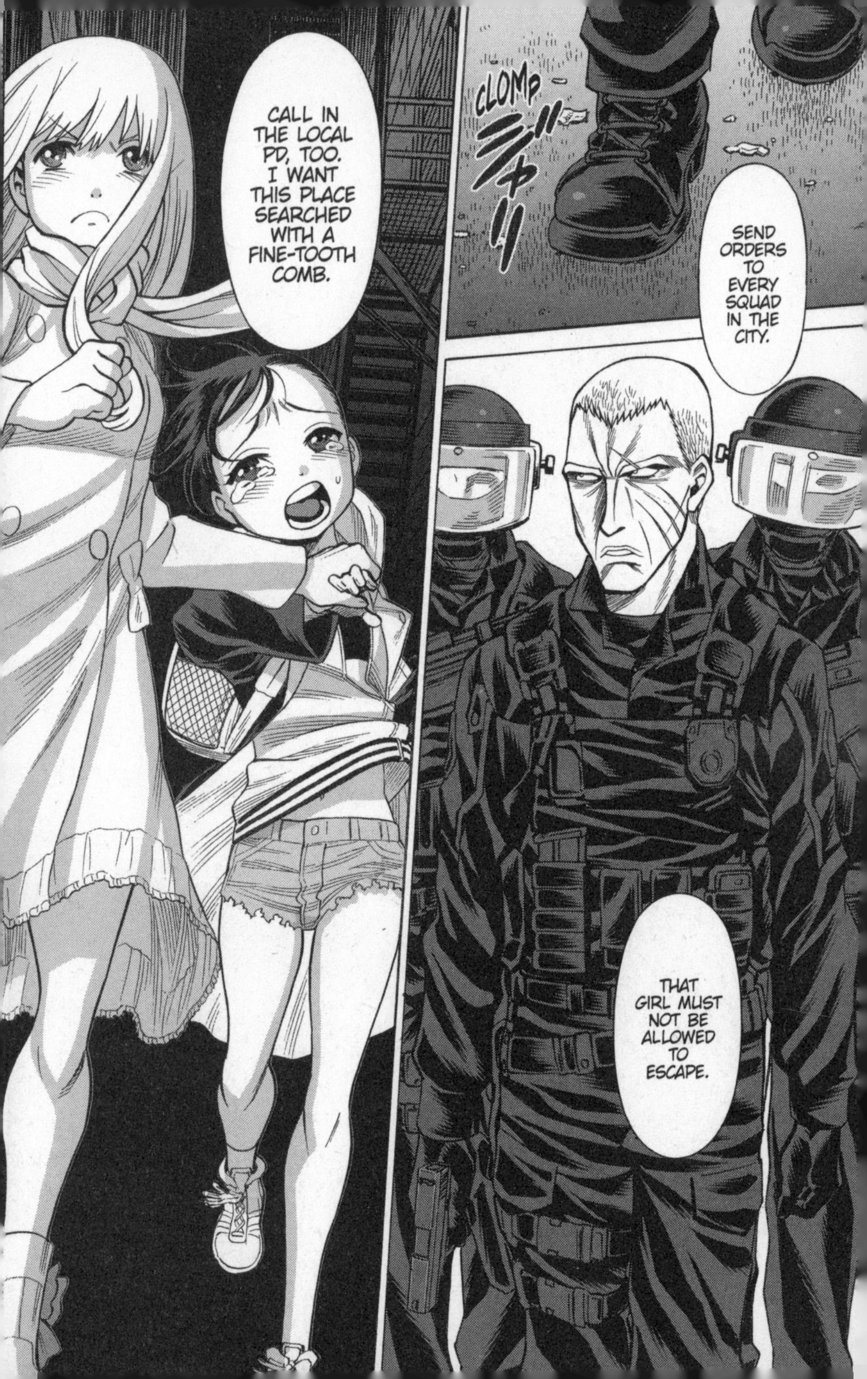
CLOMP
ジャリ
SEND ORDERS TO EVERY SQUAD IN THE CITY.
THAT GIRL MUST NOT BE ALLOWED TO ESCAPE.
CALL IN THE LOCAL PD, TOO. I WANT THIS PLACE SEARCHED WITH A FINE-TOOTH COMB.

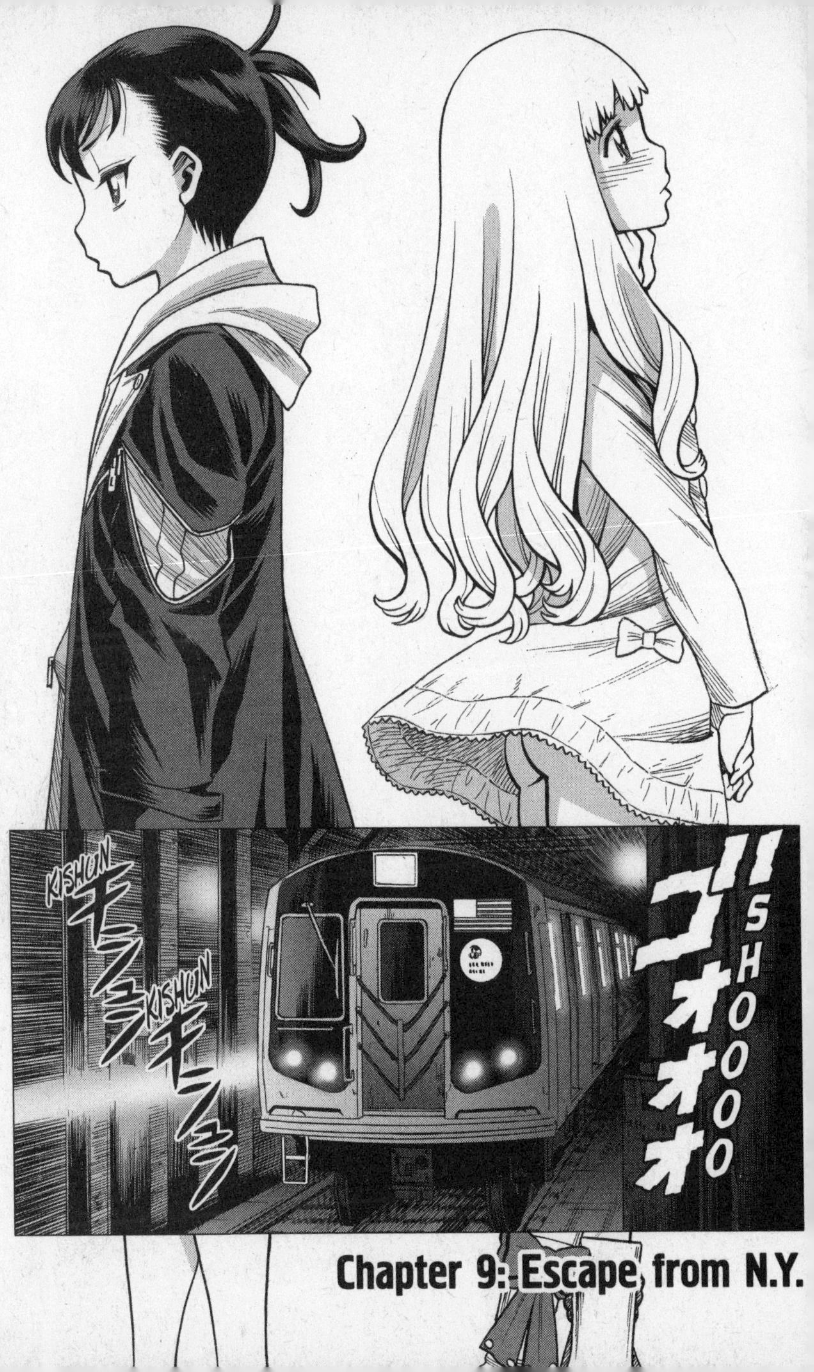
ゴオオオオ
SHOOOOO
キシュン
KISHUN
キシュン
KISHUN

Chapter 9: Escape from N.Y.

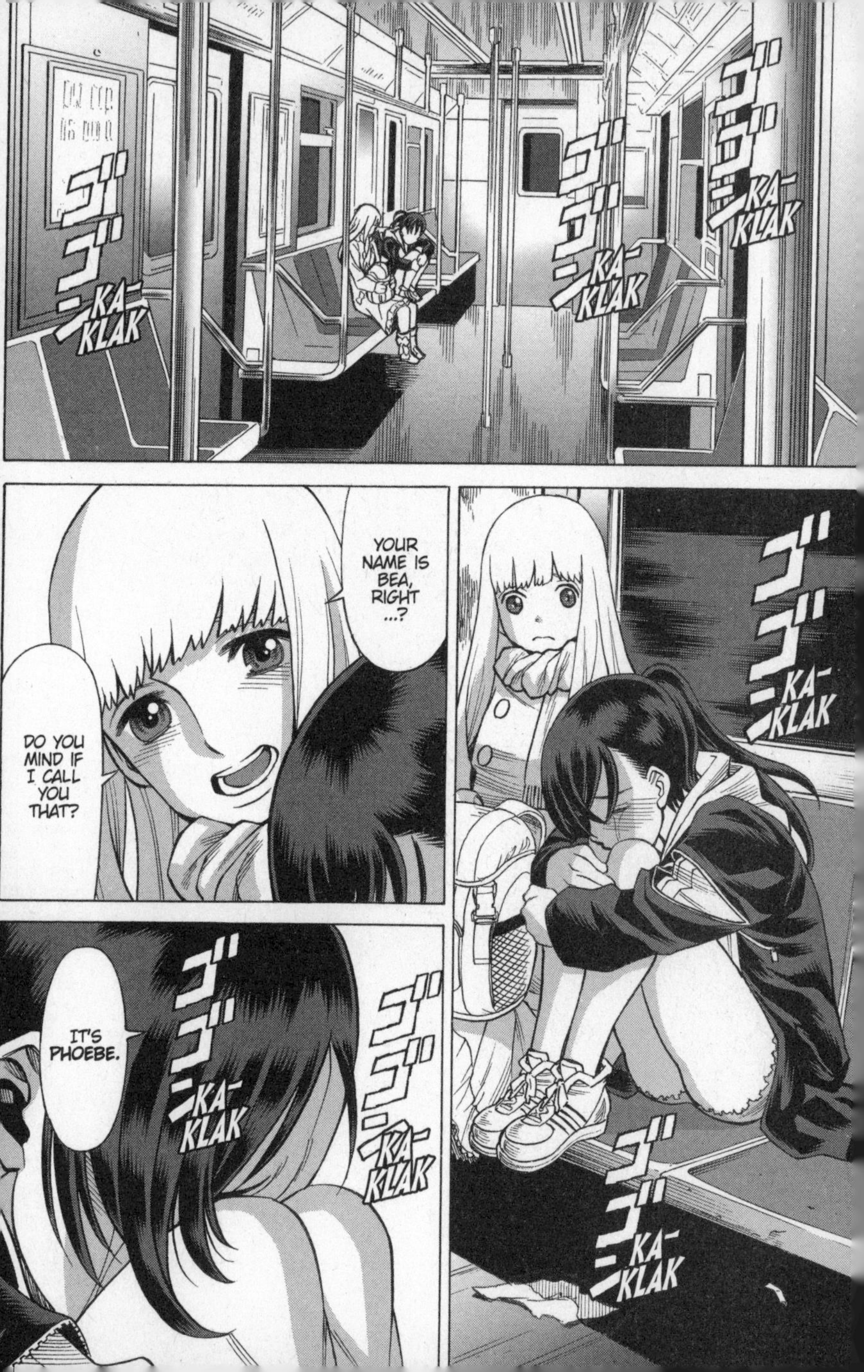
KA-KLAK
KA-KLAK
KA-KLAK
KA-KLAK
KA-KLAK
YOUR NAME IS BEA, RIGHT ...?
DO YOU MIND IF I CALL YOU THAT?
IT'S PHOEBE.
KA-KLAK
KA-KLAK

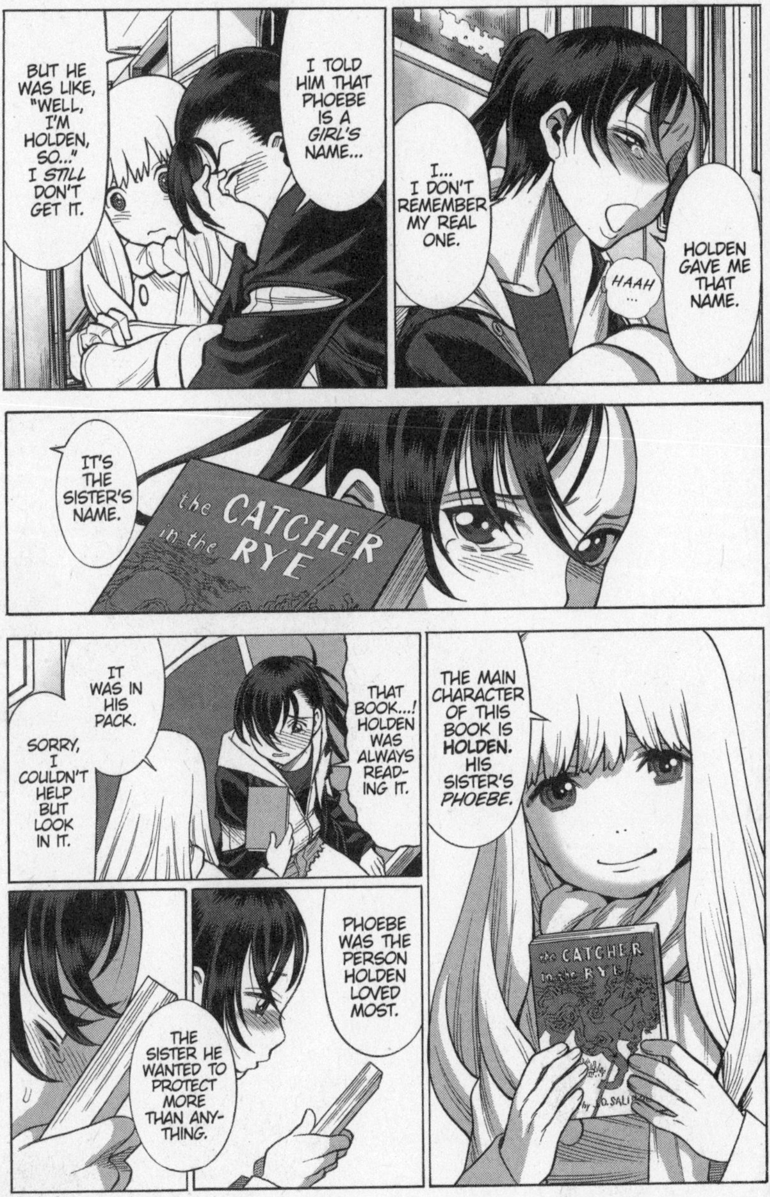
HOLDEN GAVE ME THAT NAME.
HAAH ...
I... I DON'T REMEMBER MY REAL ONE.
I TOLD HIM THAT PHOEBE IS A *GIRL'S* NAME...
BUT HE WAS LIKE, "WELL, I'M HOLDEN, SO..." I *STILL* DON'T GET IT.
IT'S THE SISTER'S NAME.
the CATCHER in the RYE
THE MAIN CHARACTER OF THIS BOOK IS **HOLDEN.** HIS SISTER'S *PHOEBE.*
the CATCHER in the RYE
THAT BOOK...! HOLDEN WAS ALWAYS READ-ING IT.
IT WAS IN HIS PACK.
SORRY, I COULDN'T HELP BUT LOOK IN IT.
PHOEBE WAS THE PERSON HOLDEN LOVED MOST.
THE SISTER HE WANTED TO PROTECT MORE THAN ANY-THING.

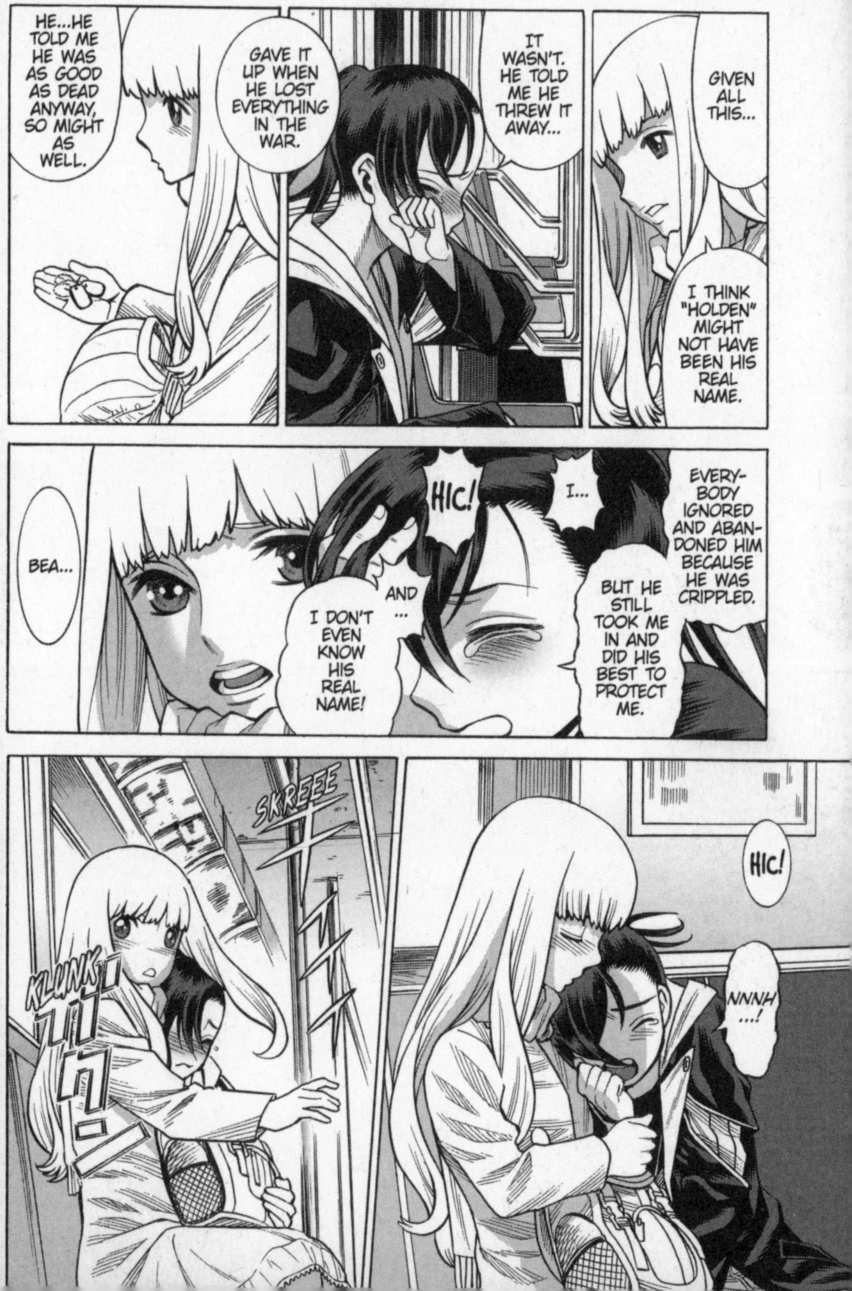
GIVEN ALL THIS...
I THINK "HOLDEN" MIGHT NOT HAVE BEEN HIS REAL NAME.
IT WASN'T. HE TOLD ME HE THREW IT AWAY...
GAVE IT UP WHEN HE LOST EVERYTHING IN THE WAR.
HE...HE TOLD ME HE WAS AS GOOD AS DEAD ANYWAY, SO MIGHT AS WELL.
EVERY-BODY IGNORED AND ABAN-DONED HIM BECAUSE HE WAS CRIPPLED.
BUT HE STILL TOOK ME IN AND DID HIS BEST TO PROTECT ME.
I...
HIC!
AND ...
I DON'T EVEN KNOW HIS REAL NAME!
BEA...
HIC!
NNNH ...!
SKREEE
KLUNK

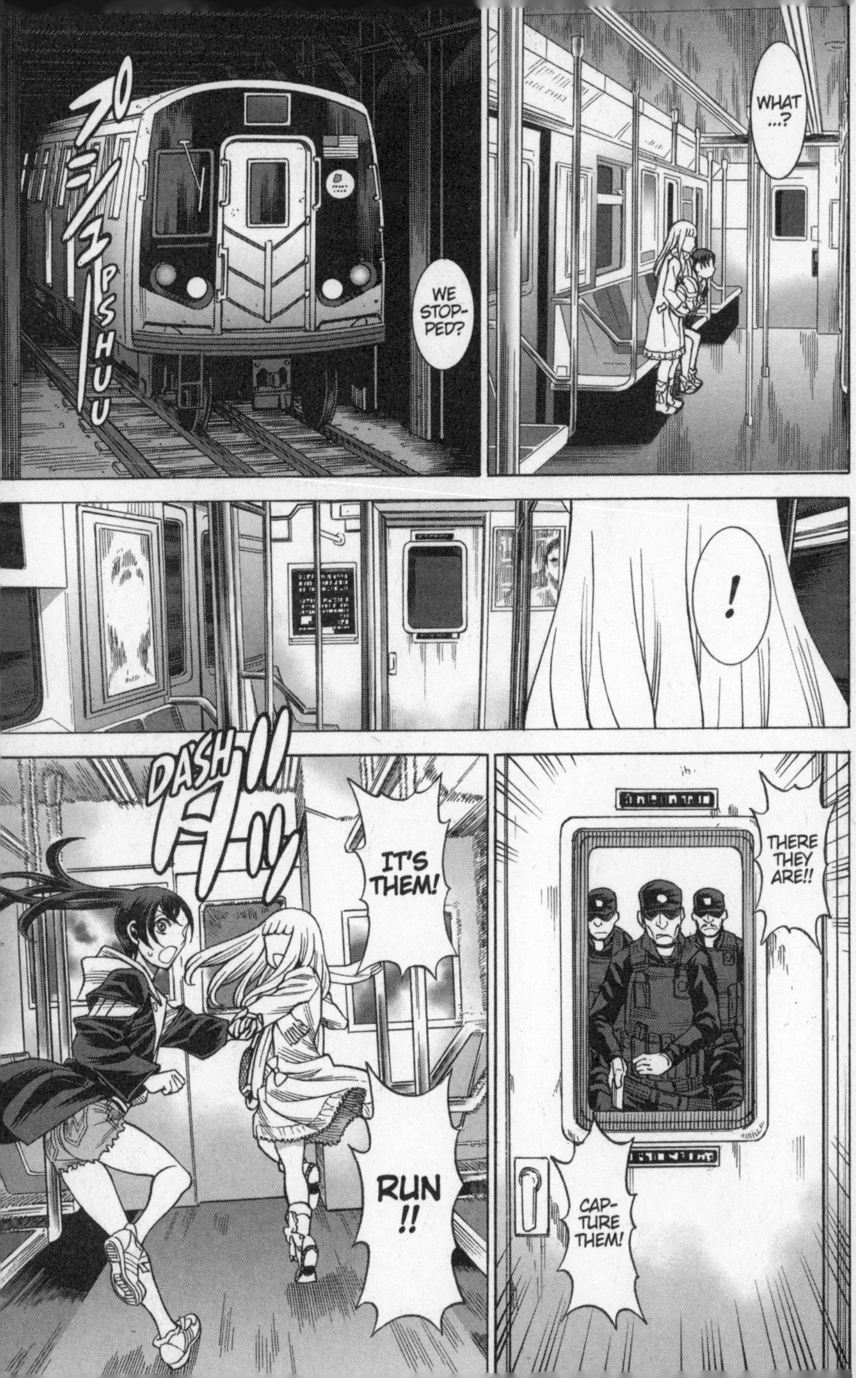
WHAT ...?
WE STOP-PED?
PSHUU
!
THERE THEY ARE!!
CAPTURE THEM!
DASH
IT'S THEM!
RUN !!

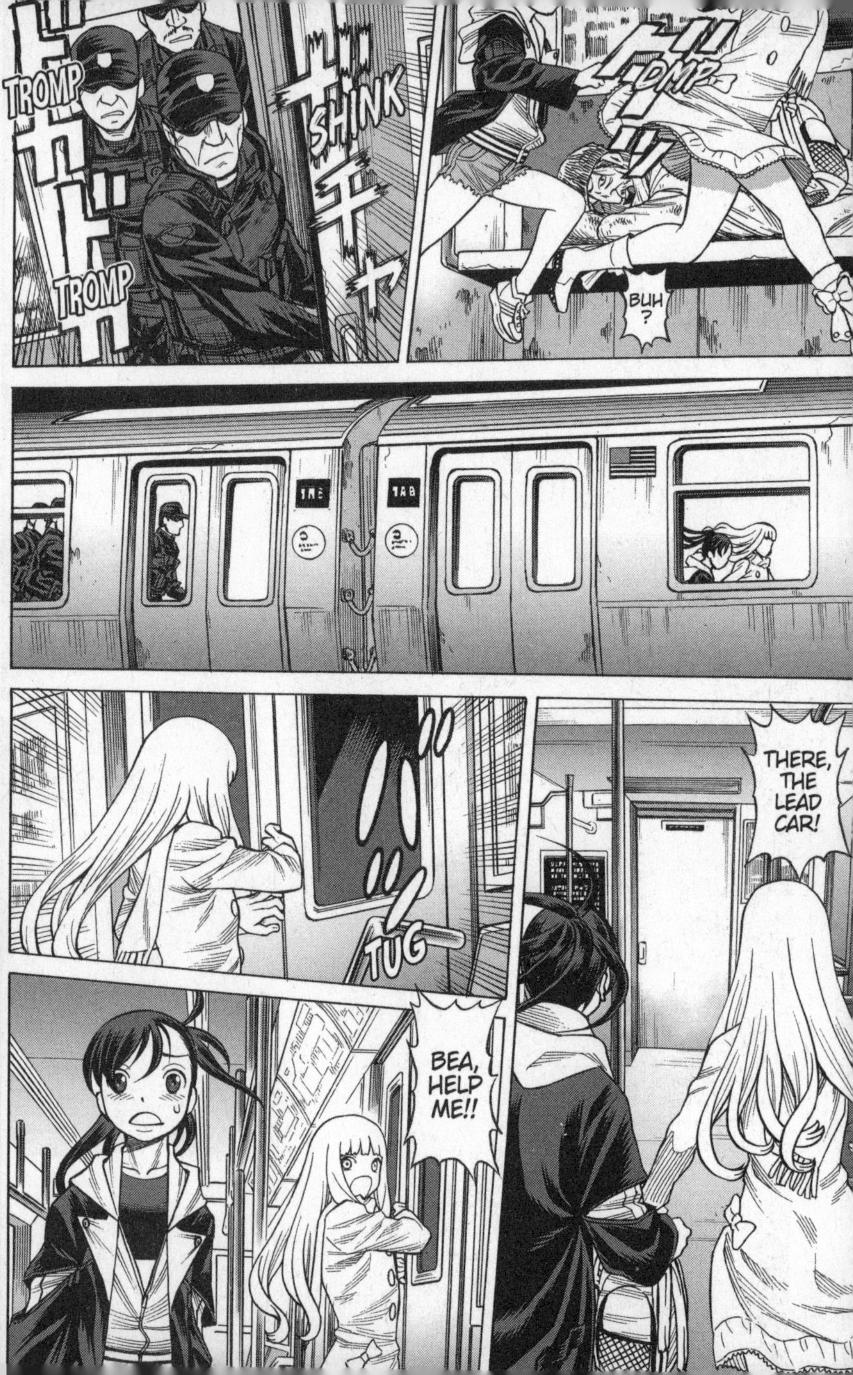
BUH?
SHINK
TROMP
TROMP
THERE, THE LEAD CAR!
TUG
BEA, HELP ME!!

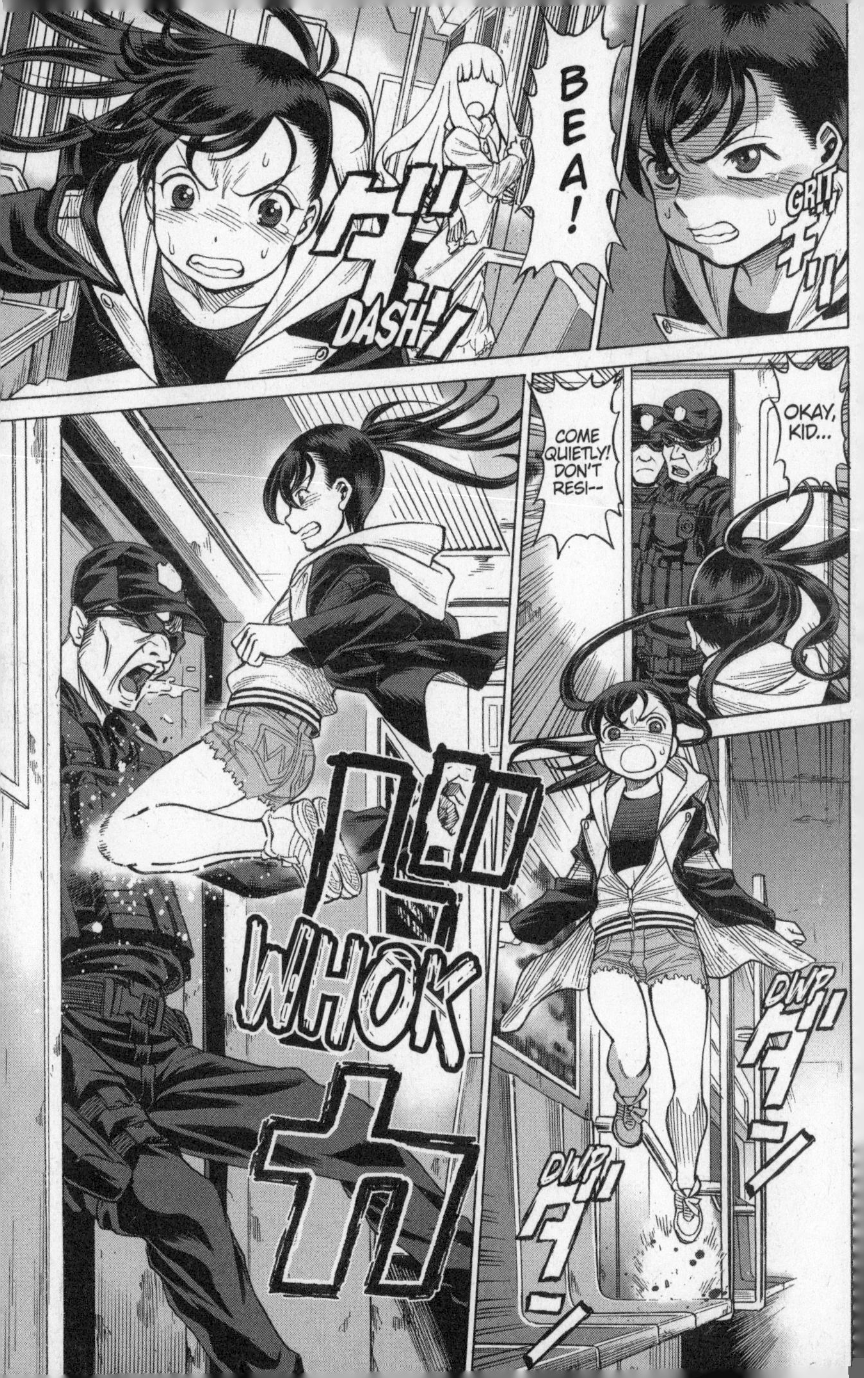
BEA!
GRIT
DASH
OKAY, KID...
COME QUIETLY! DON'T RESI--
DWP
DWP
WHOK

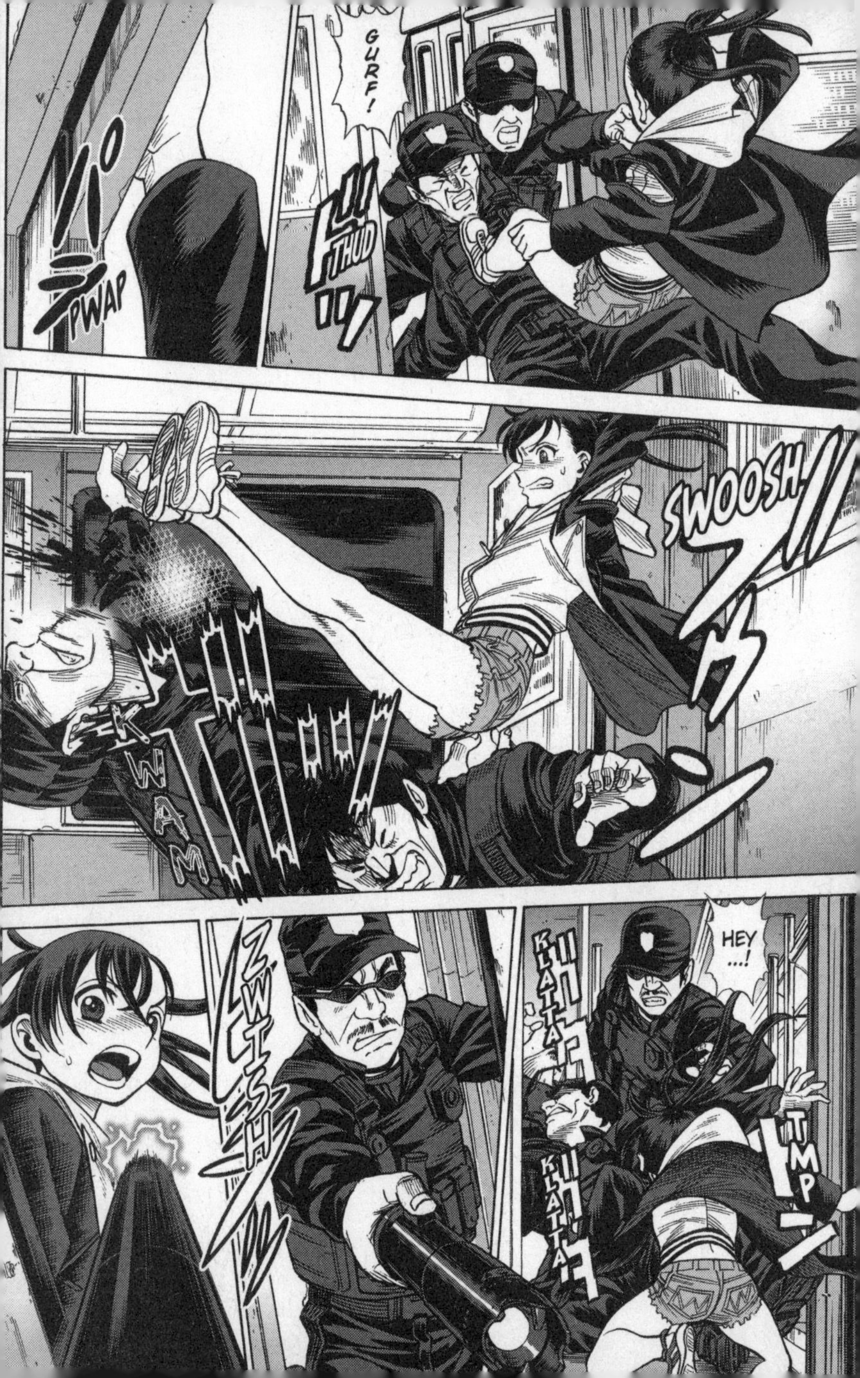
GURF!
THUD
PWAP
SWOOSH
WAM
HEY ...!
TMP
KLATTA
KLATTA
ZWISH

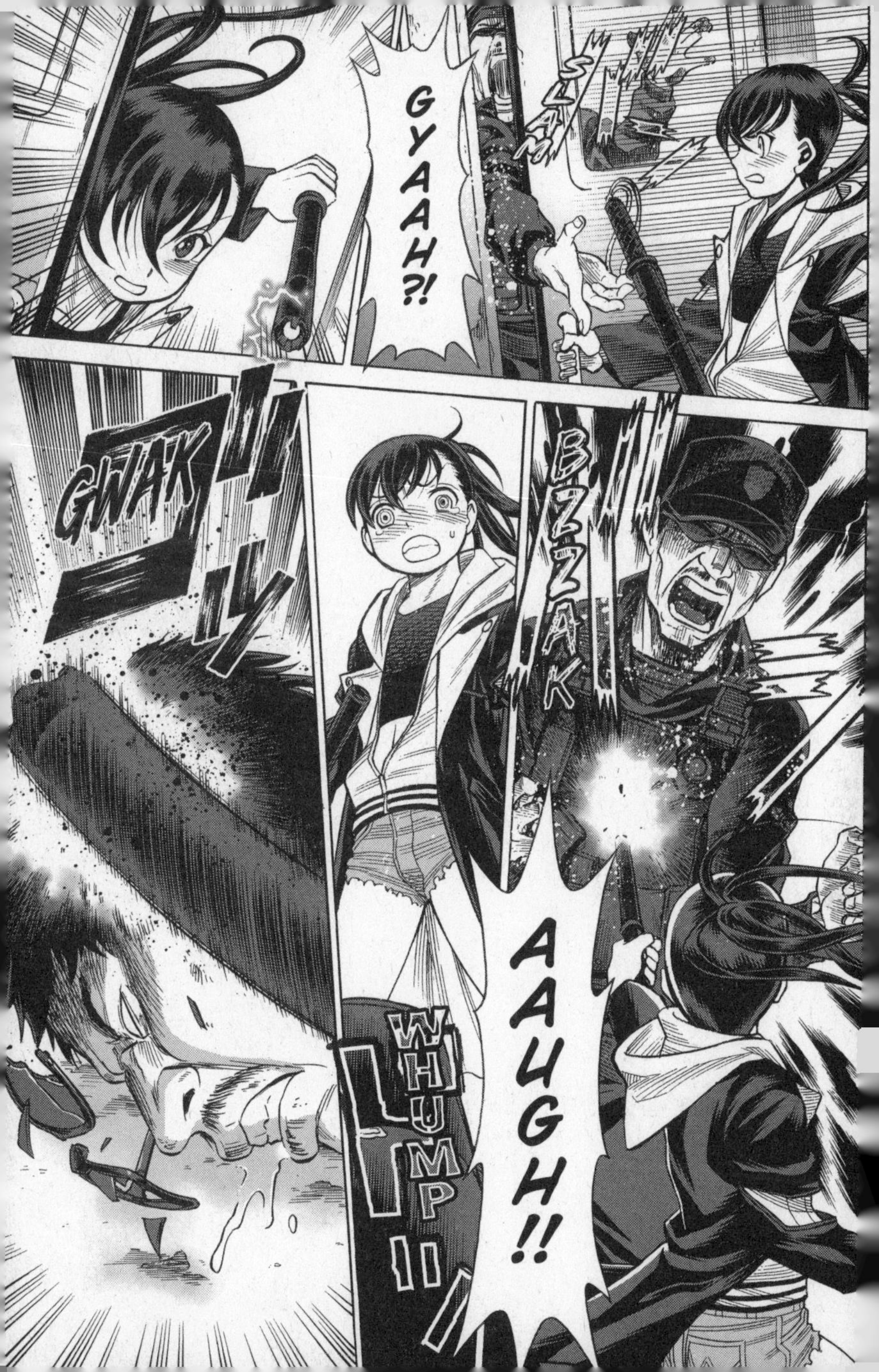
SLAM
GYAAAH?!
BZZZAK
AAUGH!!
WHUMP!!
GWAK

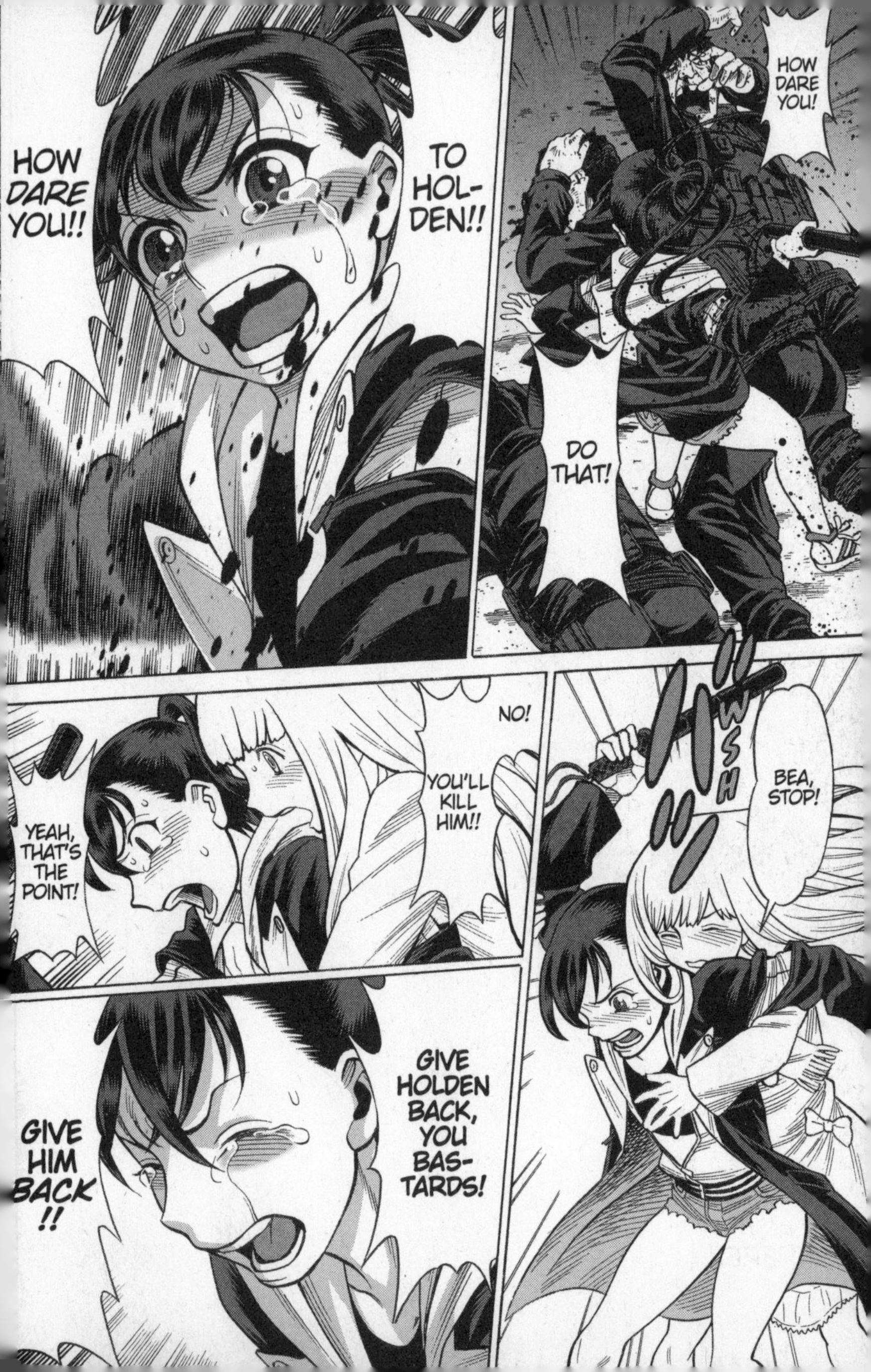
HOW DARE YOU!
DO THAT!
TO HOL-DEN!!
HOW DARE YOU!!
WSHH
BEA, STOP!
NO!
YOU'LL KILL HIM!!
YEAH, THAT'S THE POINT!
GIVE HOLDEN BACK, YOU BAS-TARDS!
GIVE HIM BACK!!

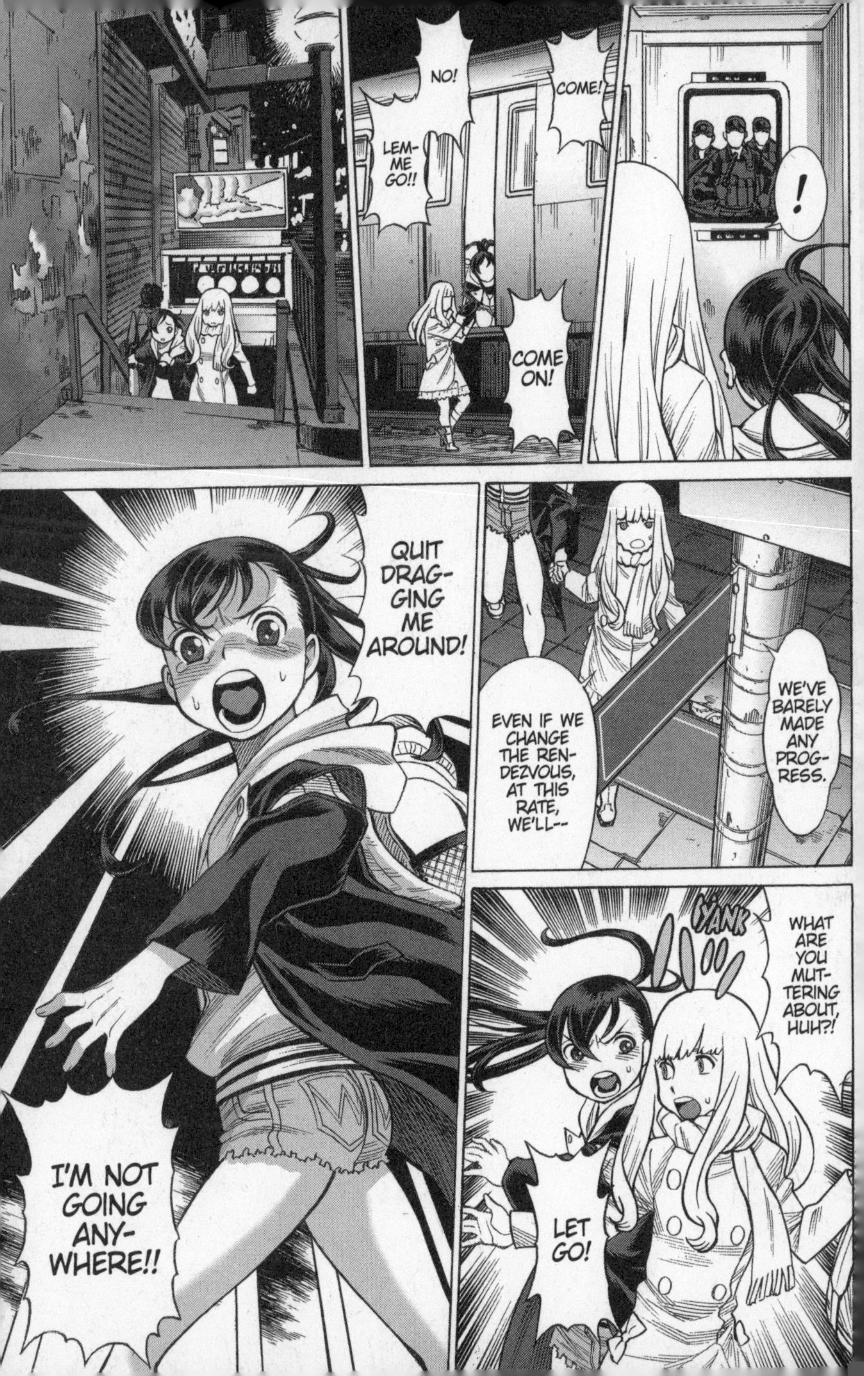
!
COME!
NO!
LEM-ME GO!!
COME ON!
WE'VE BARELY MADE ANY PROGRESS.
EVEN IF WE CHANGE THE RENDEZVOUS, AT THIS RATE, WE'LL--
WHAT ARE YOU MUTTERING ABOUT, HUH?!
YANK
LET GO!
QUIT DRAGGING ME AROUND!
I'M NOT GOING ANYWHERE!!

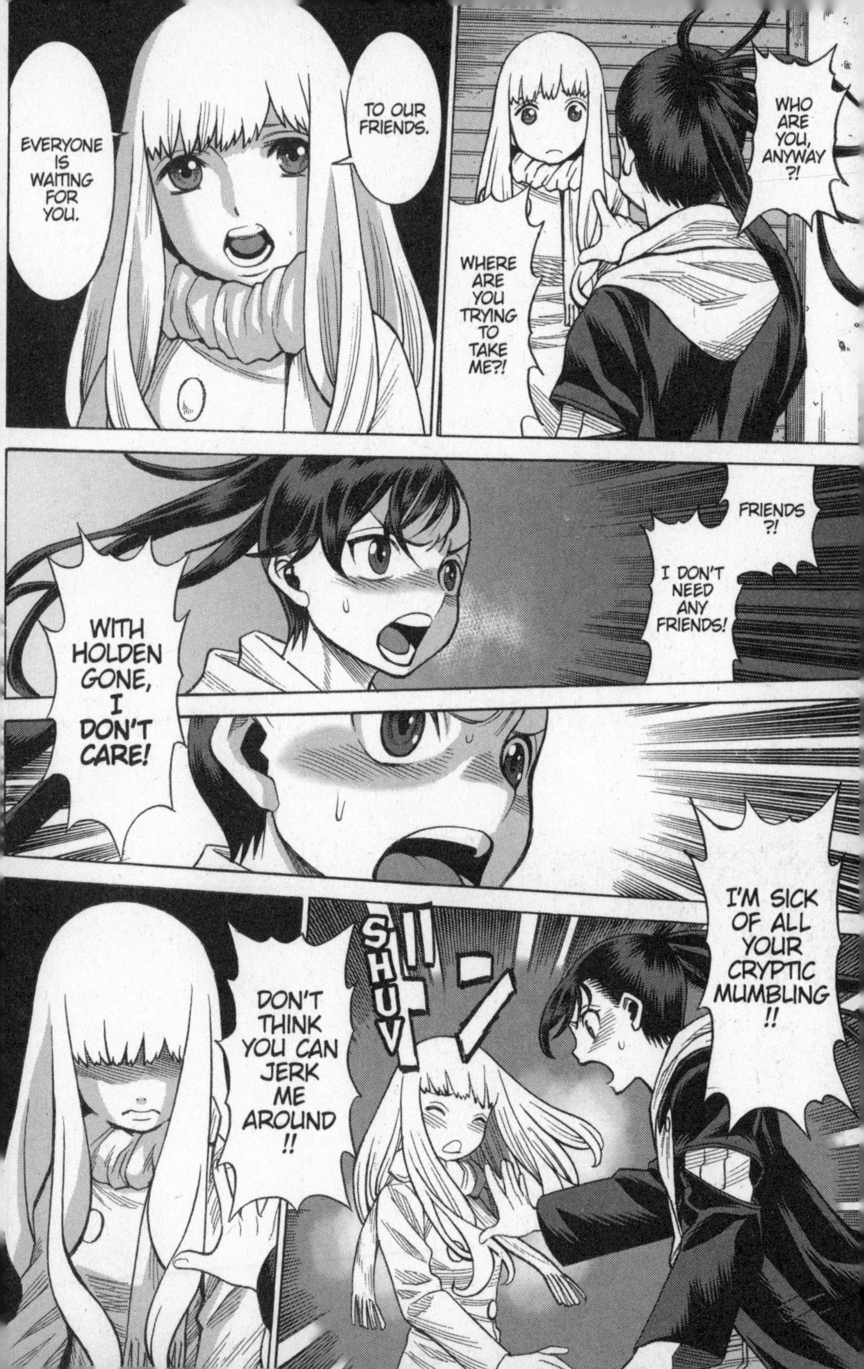
WHO ARE YOU, ANYWAY?!
WHERE ARE YOU TRYING TO TAKE ME?!
TO OUR FRIENDS.
EVERYONE IS WAITING FOR YOU.
FRIENDS?!
I DON'T NEED ANY FRIENDS!
WITH HOLDEN GONE, I DON'T CARE!
I'M SICK OF ALL YOUR CRYPTIC MUMBLING!!
SHUV
!!
DON'T THINK YOU CAN JERK ME AROUND!!

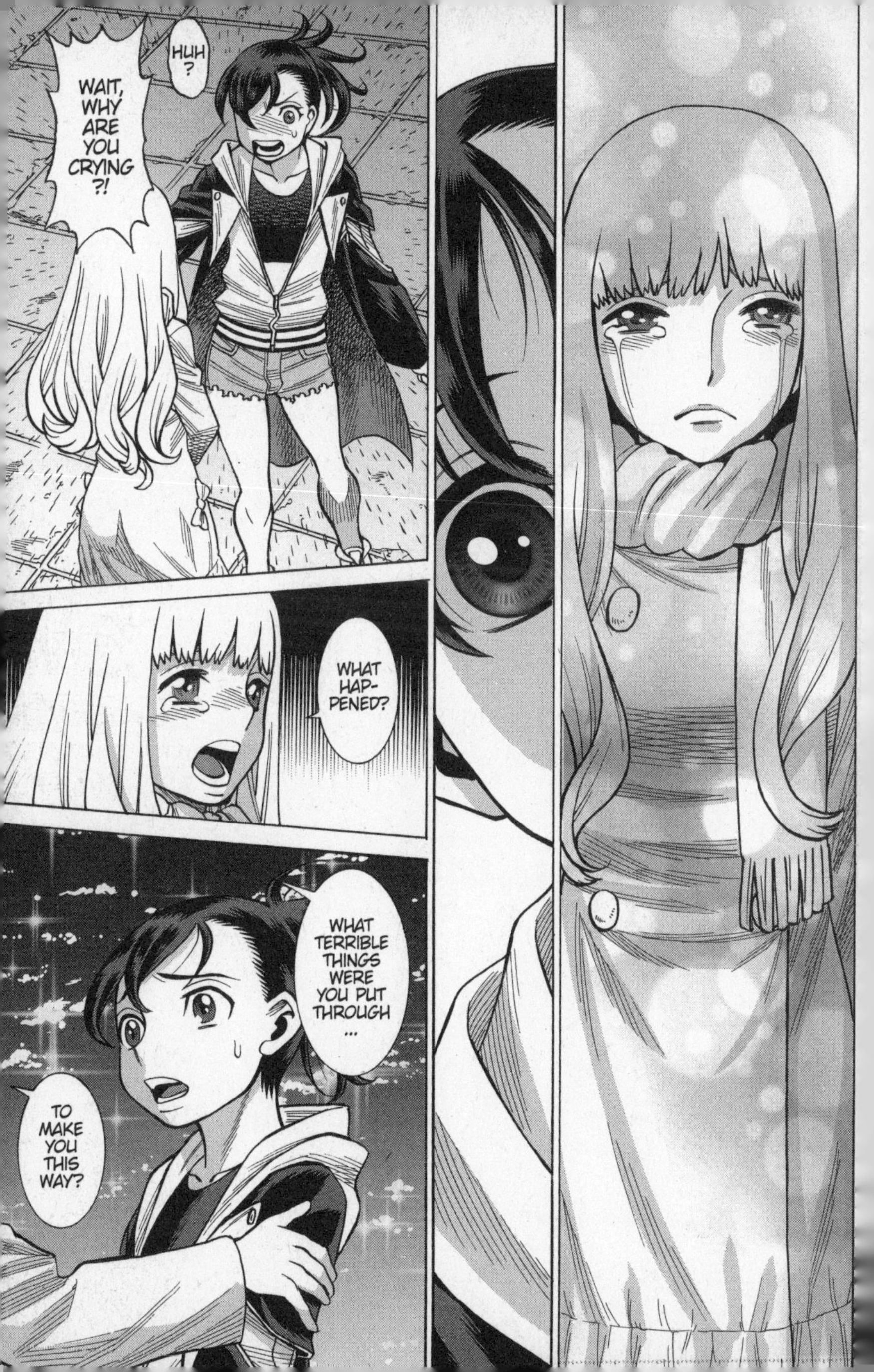
HUH?
WAIT, WHY ARE YOU CRYING?!
WHAT HAP-PENED?
WHAT TERRIBLE THINGS WERE YOU PUT THROUGH...
TO MAKE YOU THIS WAY?

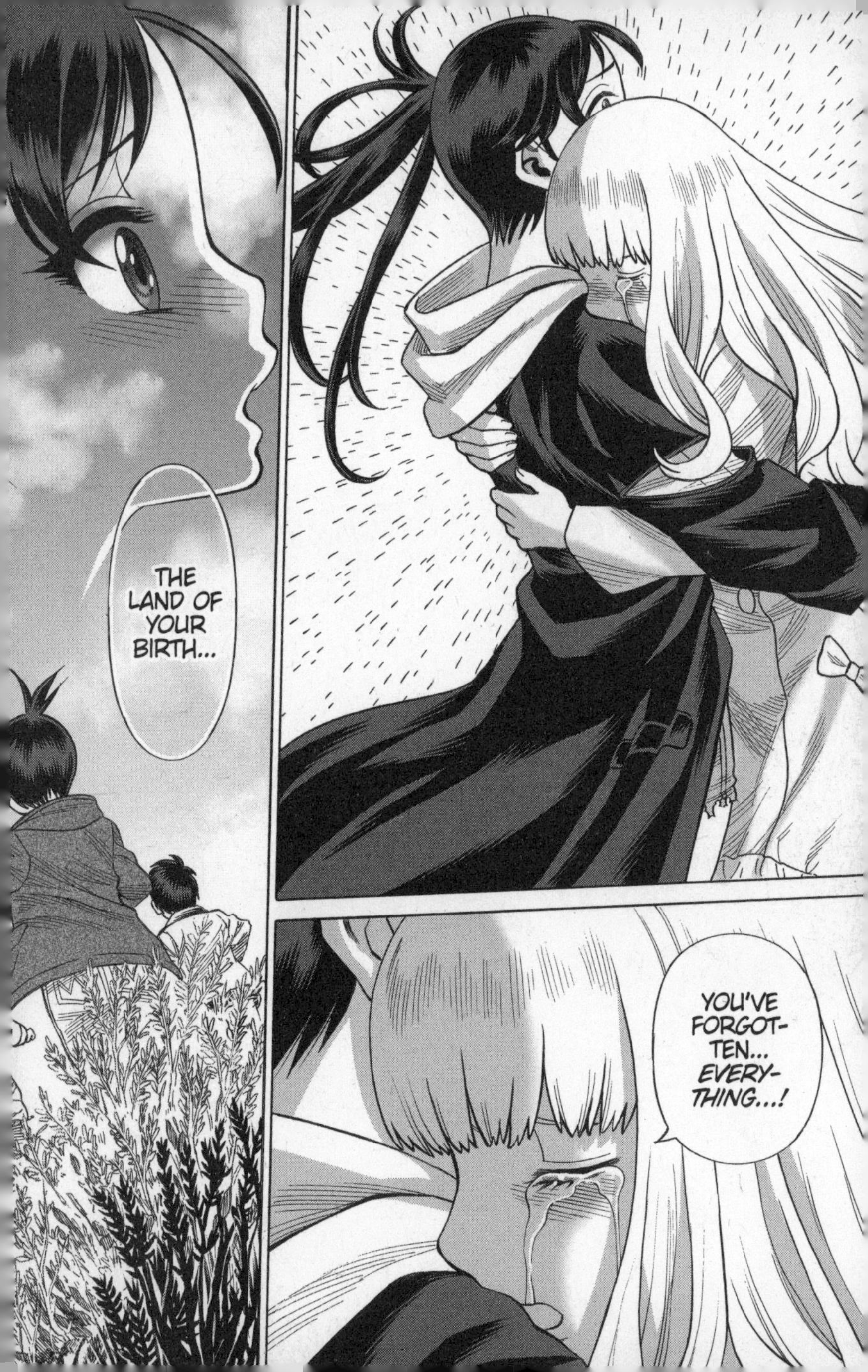
YOU'VE FORGOT-TEN... *EVERY-THING...!*
THE LAND OF YOUR BIRTH...

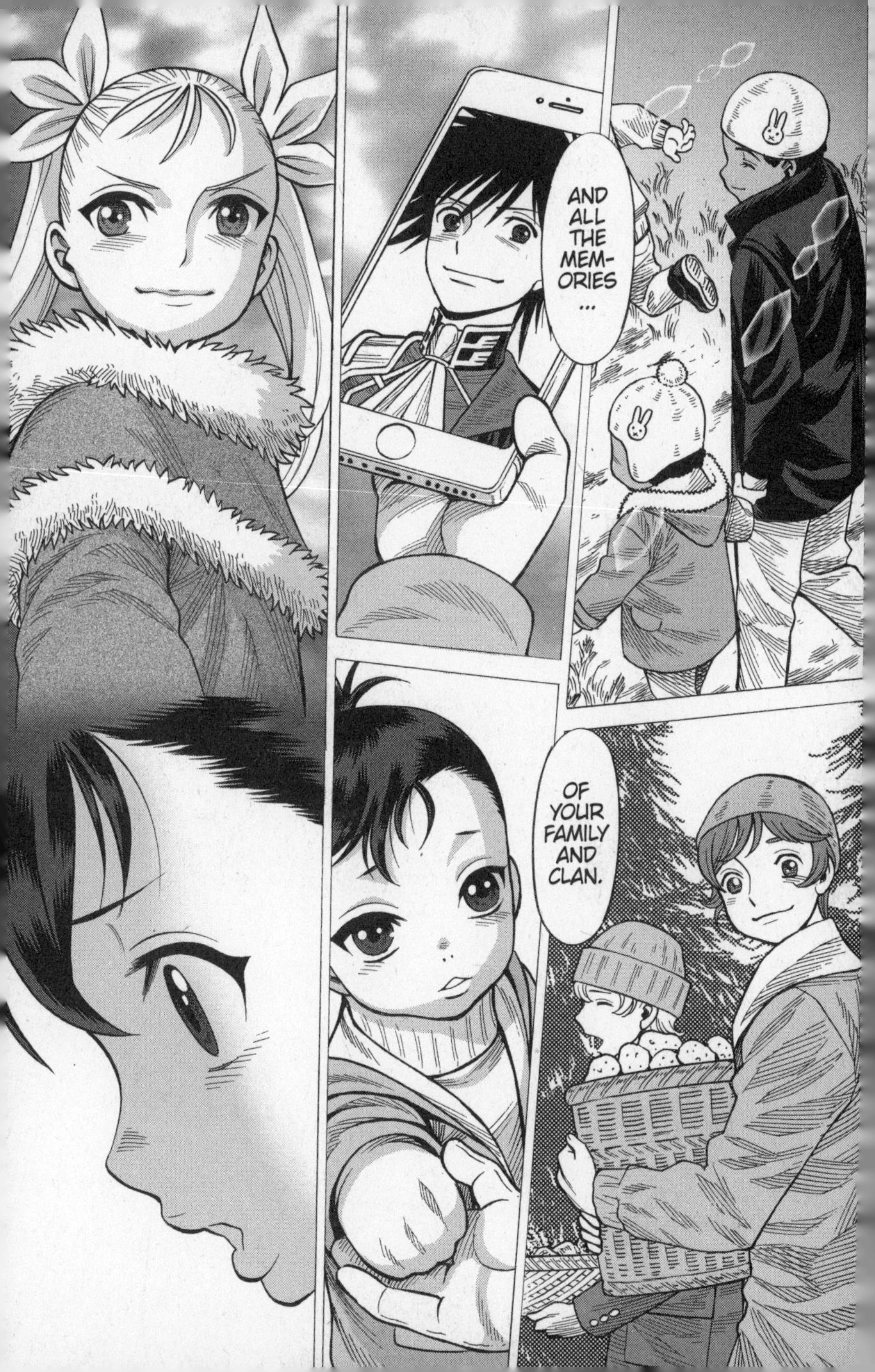
AND ALL THE MEMORIES ...
OF YOUR FAMILY AND CLAN.

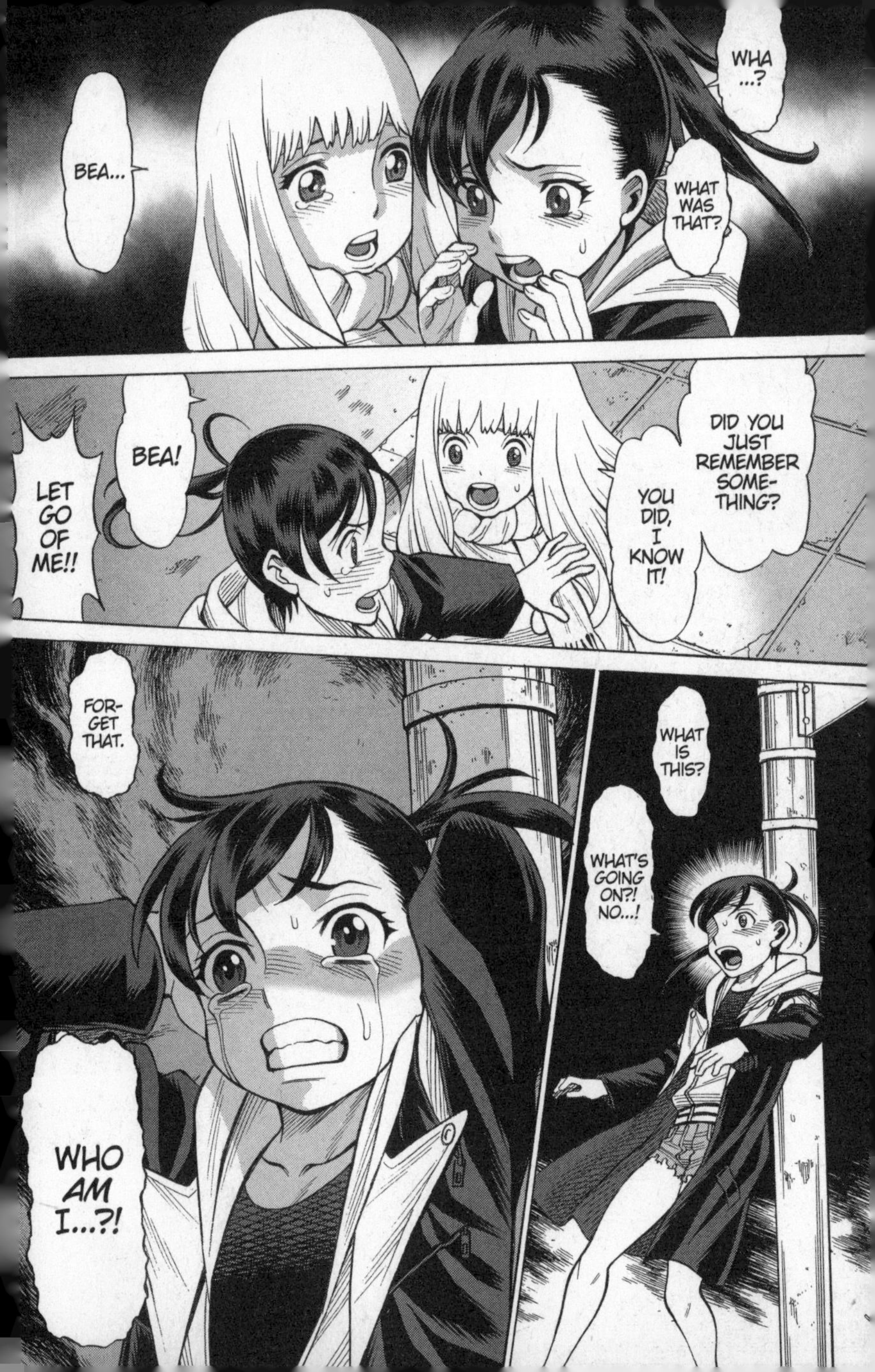
WHA...?
WHAT WAS THAT?
BEA...
DID YOU JUST REMEMBER SOME-THING?
YOU DID, I KNOW IT!
BEA!
LET GO OF ME!!
WHAT IS THIS?
WHAT'S GOING ON?! NO...!
FOR-GET THAT.
WHO AM I...?!

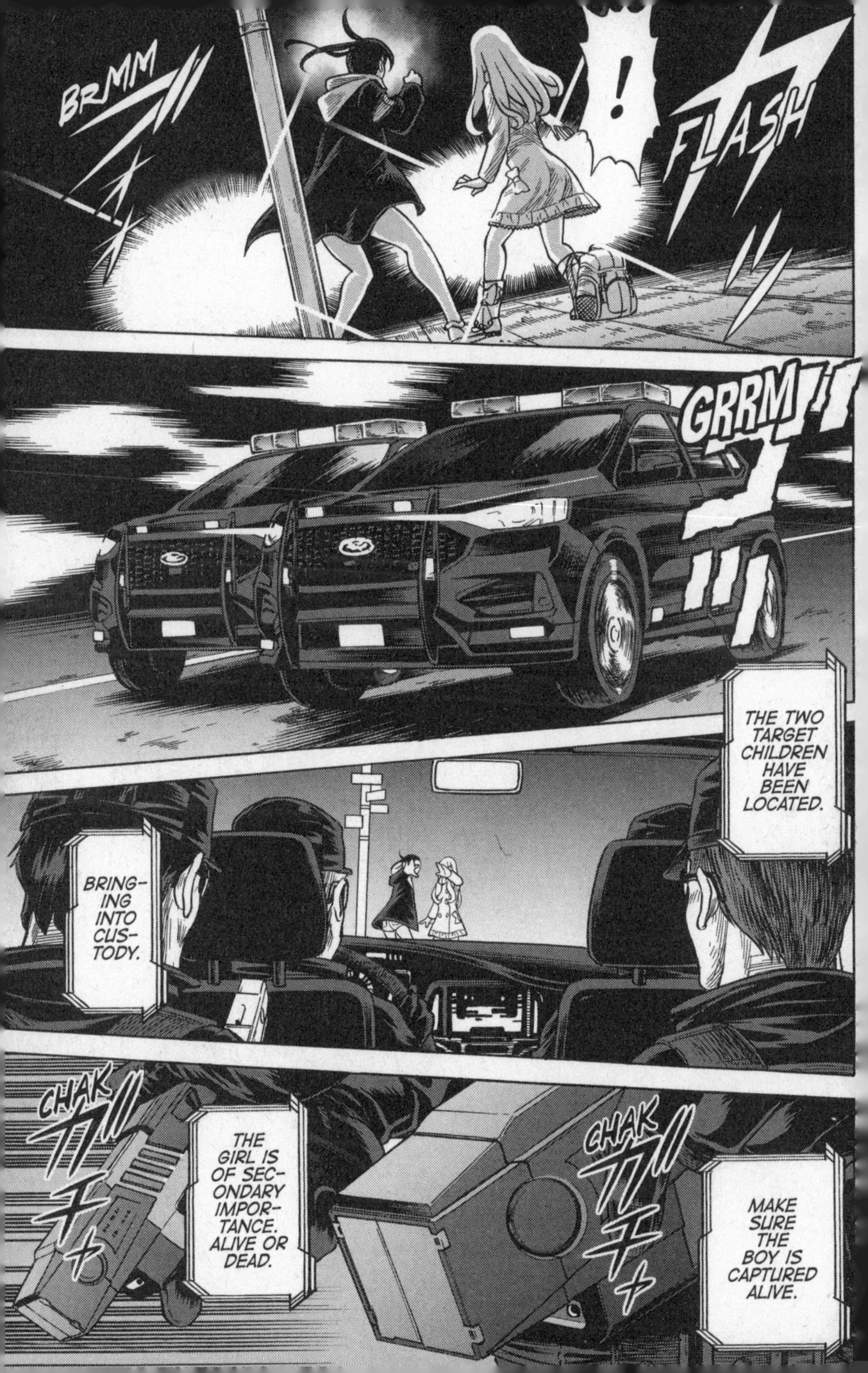
FLASH
!
BRMM
GRRM
THE TWO TARGET CHILDREN HAVE BEEN LOCATED.
BRING-ING INTO CUS-TODY.
CHAK
MAKE SURE THE BOY IS CAPTURED ALIVE.
THE GIRL IS OF SEC-ONDARY IMPOR-TANCE. ALIVE OR DEAD.
CHAK

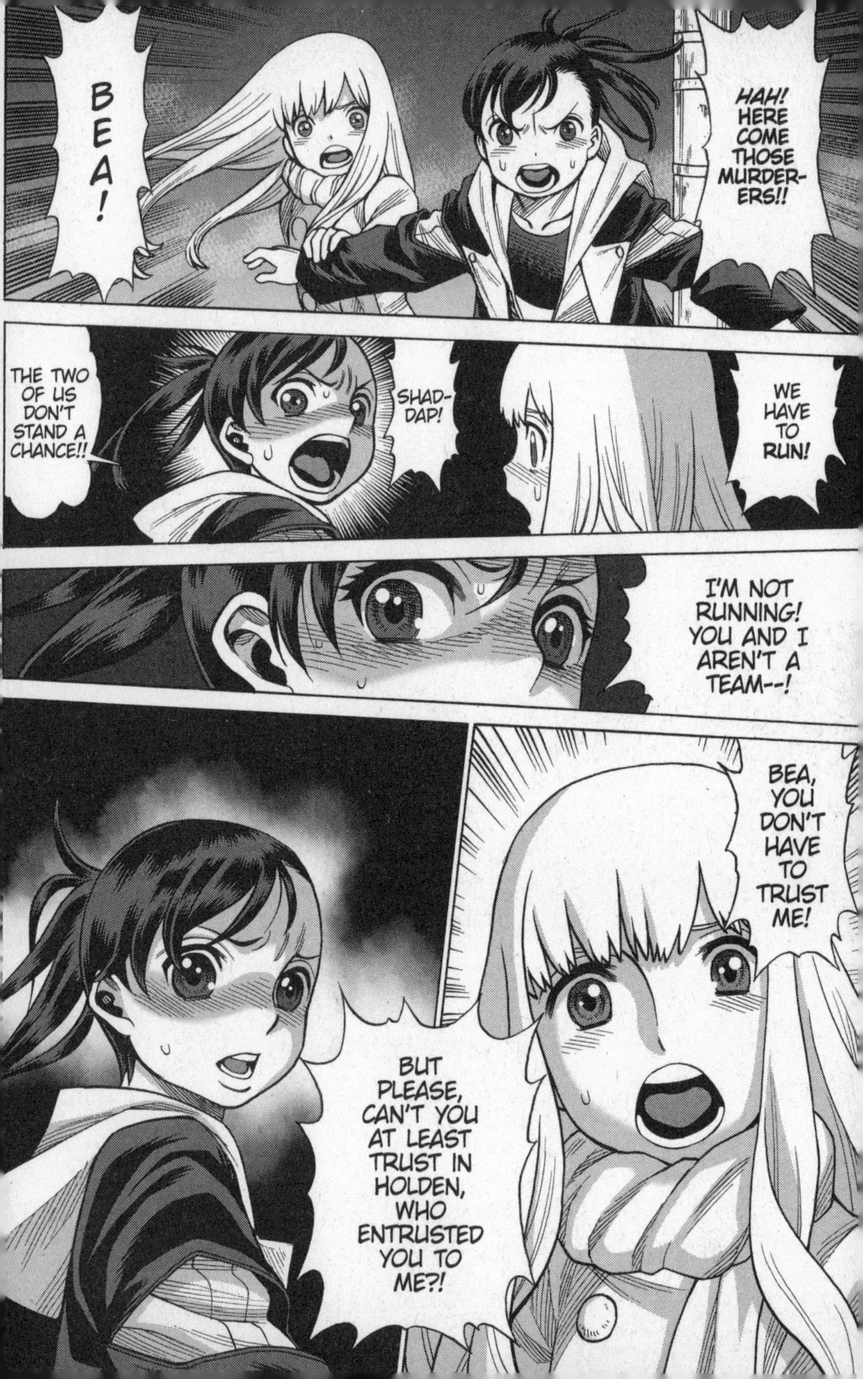
HAH! HERE COME THOSE MURDERERS!!
BEA!
WE HAVE TO RUN!
SHAD-DAP!
THE TWO OF US DON'T STAND A CHANCE!!
I'M NOT RUNNING! YOU AND I AREN'T A TEAM--!
BEA, YOU DON'T HAVE TO TRUST ME!
BUT PLEASE, CAN'T YOU AT LEAST TRUST IN HOLDEN, WHO ENTRUSTED YOU TO ME?!

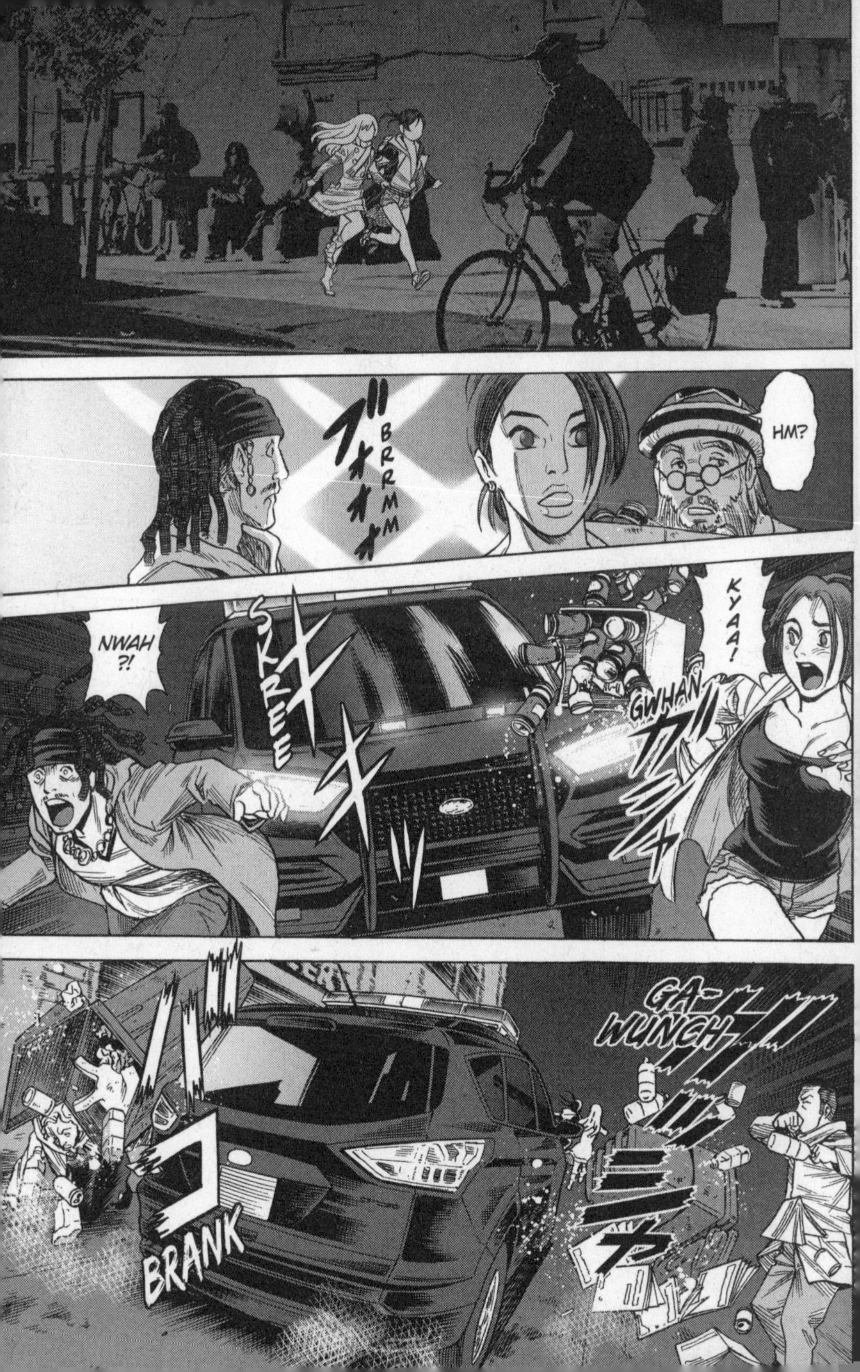
HM?
BRRMM
KYAA!
GWHAN
SKREE
NWAH ?!
GA-WUNCH
BRANK

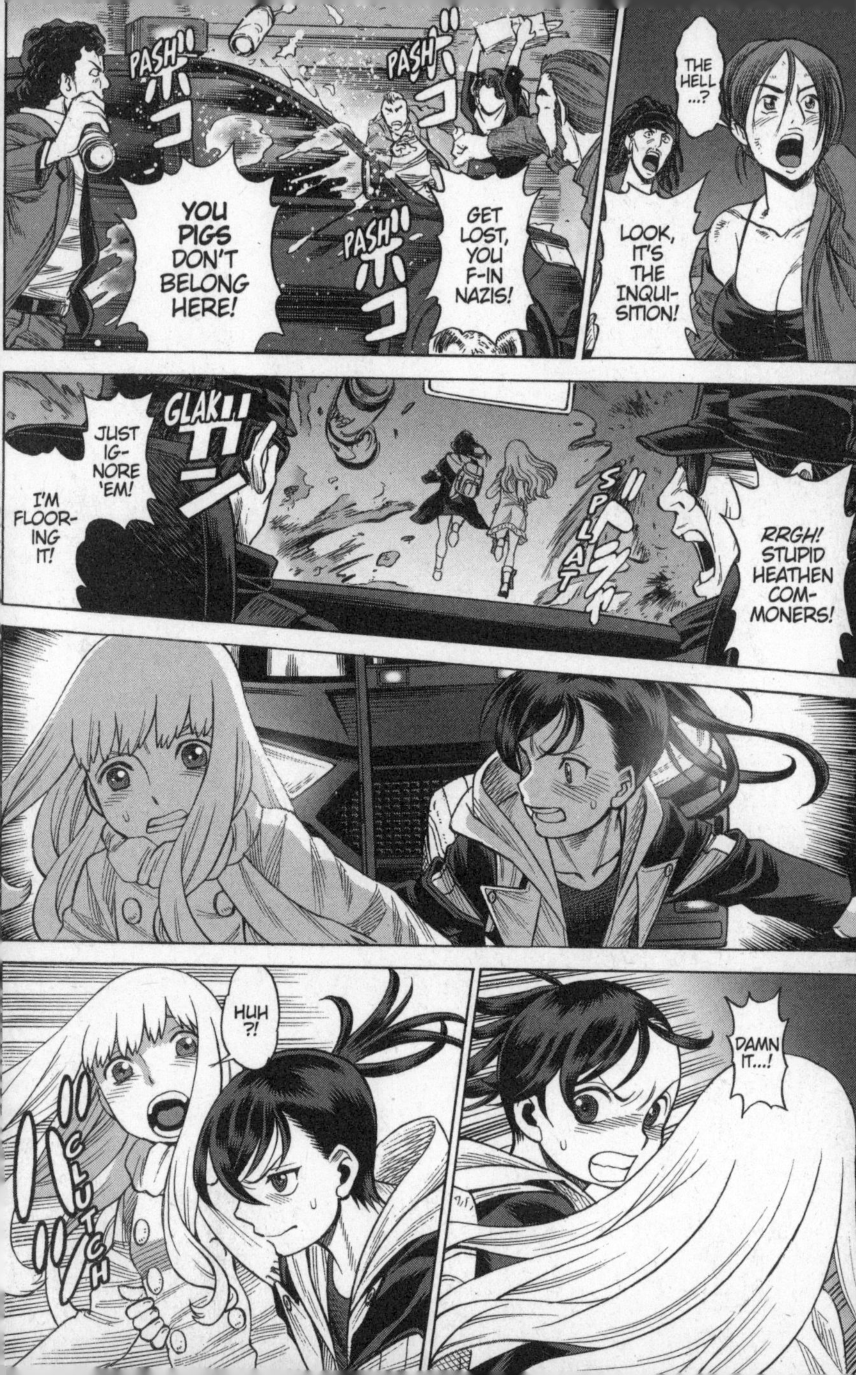
THE HELL ...?
LOOK, IT'S THE INQUISITION!
PASH!!
GET LOST, YOU F-IN NAZIS!
PASH!!
YOU PIGS DON'T BELONG HERE!
PASH!!
RRGH! STUPID HEATHEN COMMONERS!
SPLAT
GLAK!!
JUST IG-NORE 'EM!
I'M FLOOR-ING IT!
DAMN IT...!
HUH ?!
CLUTCH

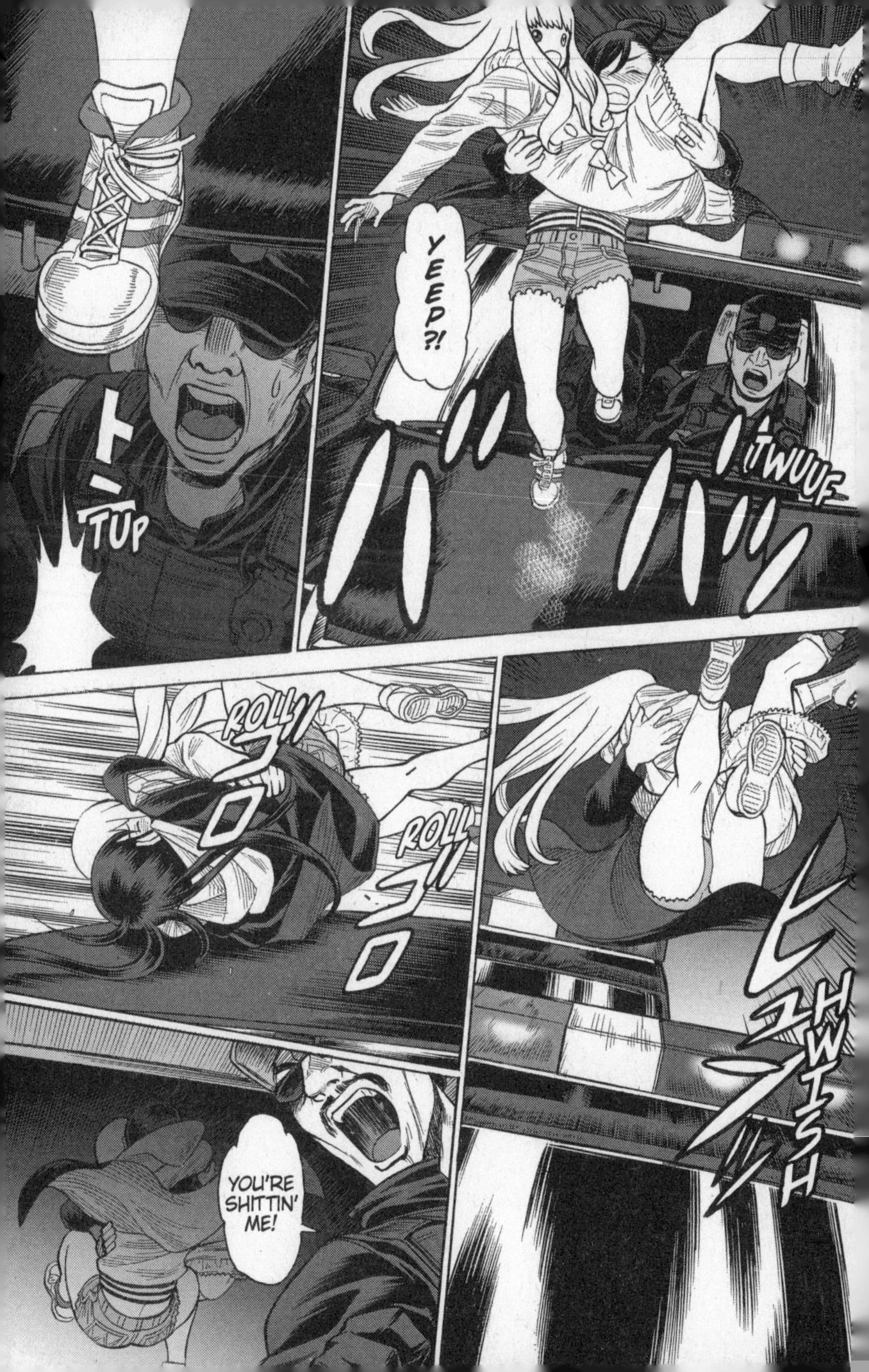
YEEP?!
TWUUF
TUP
HWISH
ROLL
ROLL
YOU'RE SHITTIN' ME!

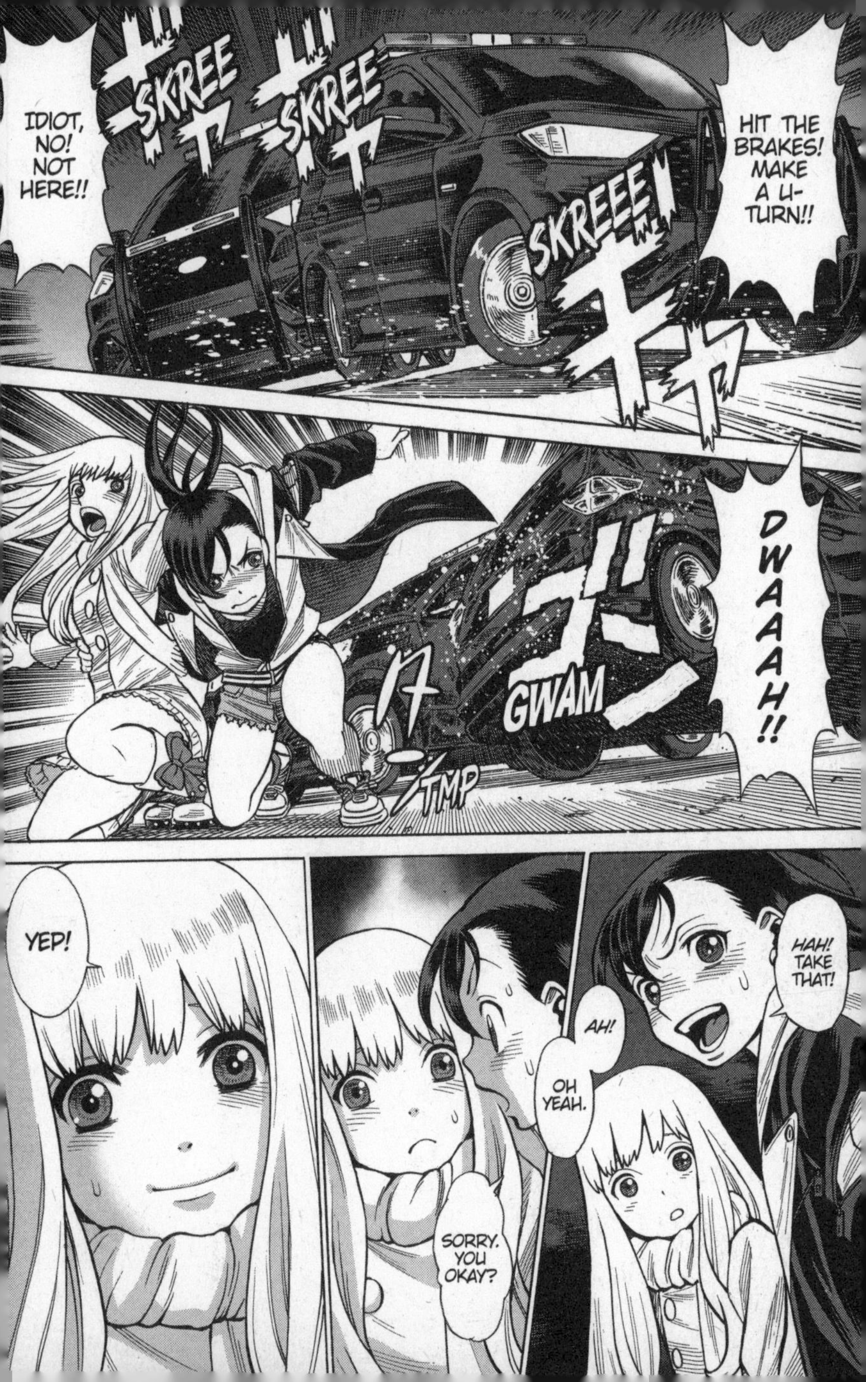
HIT THE BRAKES! MAKE A U-TURN!!
SKREEEE
SKREE
SKREE
IDIOT, NO! NOT HERE!!
DWAAAAH!!
GWAM
TMP
HAH! TAKE THAT!
AH!
OH YEAH.
SORRY. YOU OKAY?
YEP!

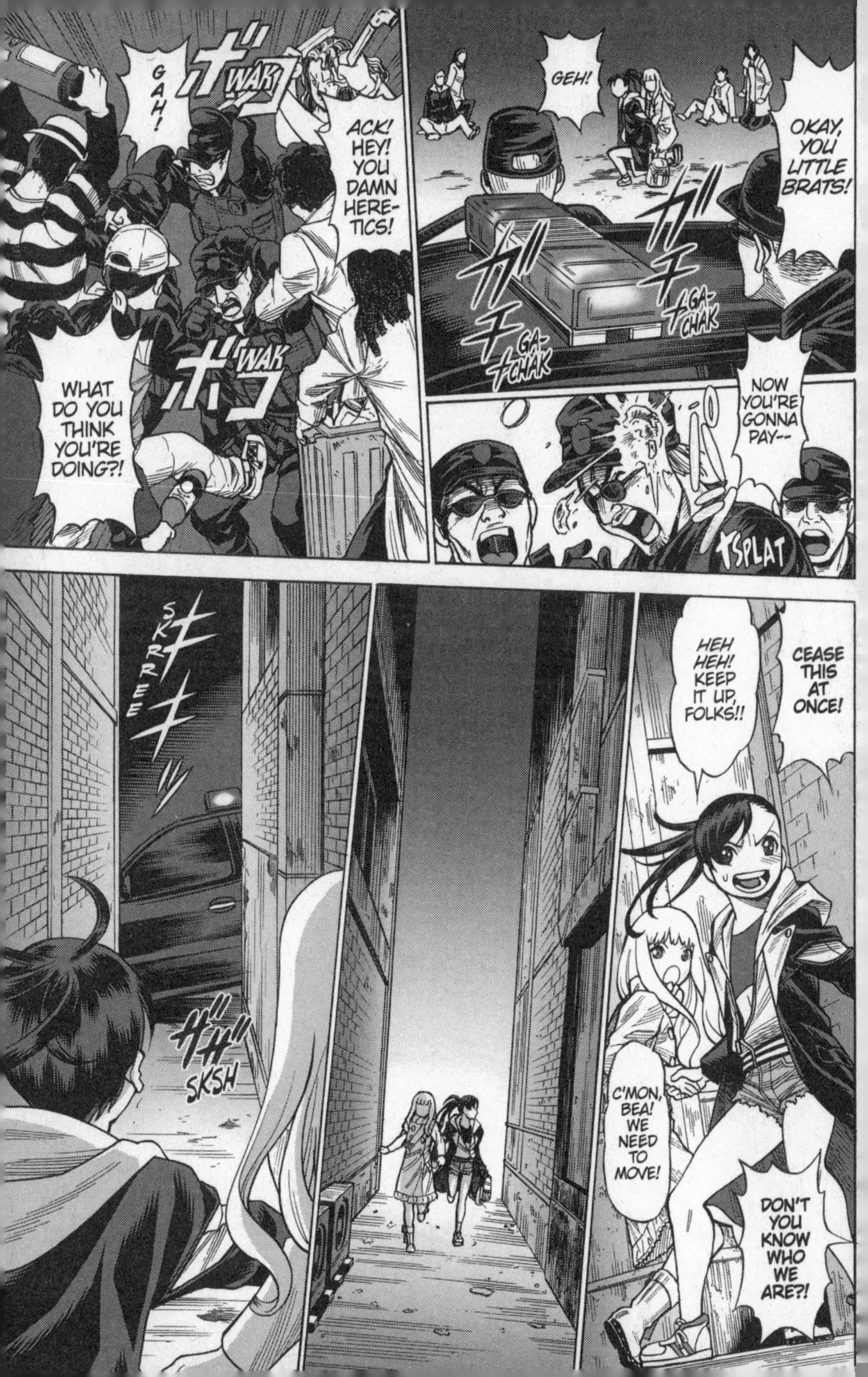
OKAY, YOU LITTLE BRATS!
GEH!
GA-CHAK
GA-CHAK
NOW YOU'RE GONNA PAY--
TSPLAT
GAH!
WAK
ACK! HEY! YOU DAMN HERETICS!
WAK
WHAT DO YOU THINK YOU'RE DOING?!
CEASE THIS AT ONCE!
HEH HEH! KEEP IT UP, FOLKS!!
C'MON, BEA! WE NEED TO MOVE!
DON'T YOU KNOW WHO WE ARE?!
SKRREE
SKSH

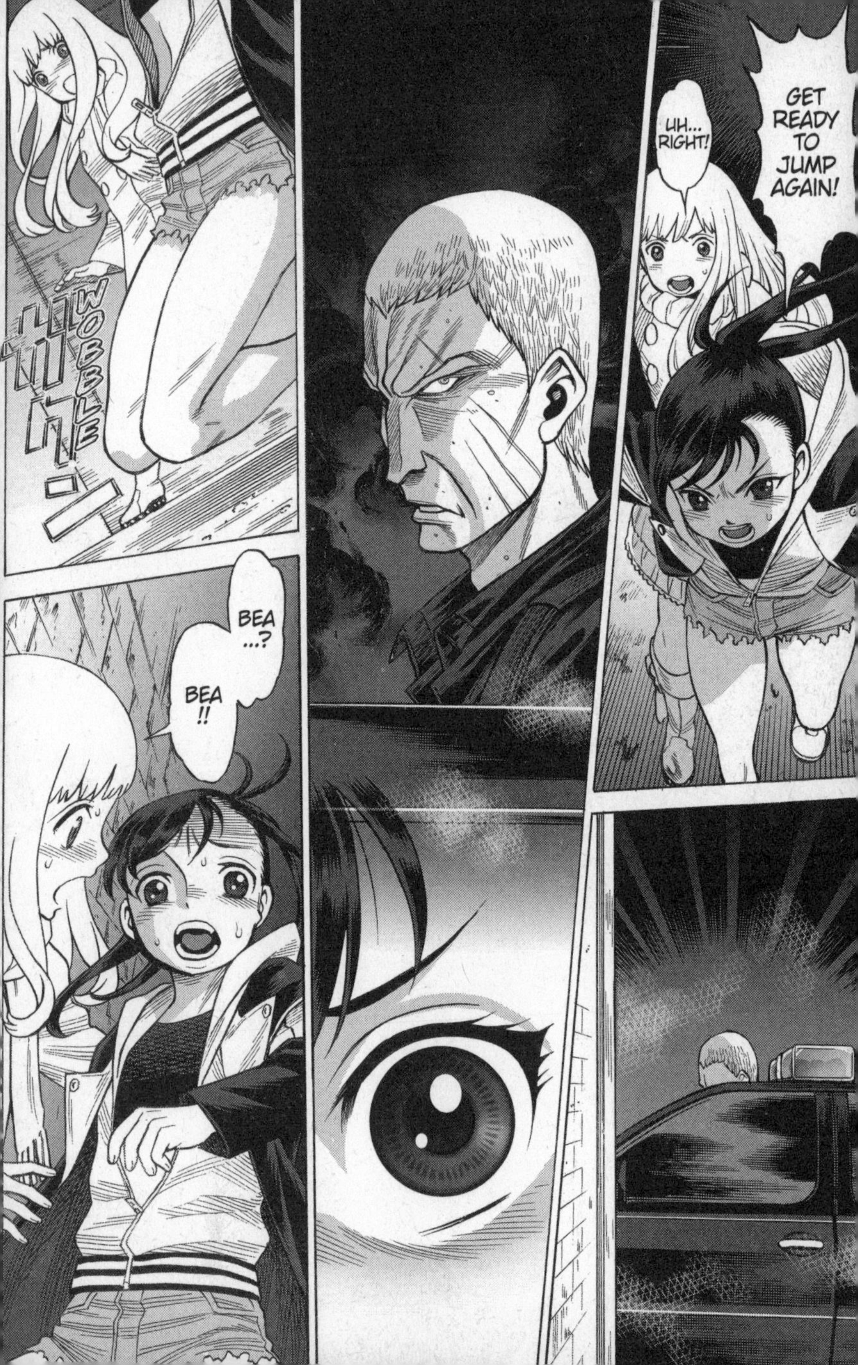
GET READY TO JUMP AGAIN!
UH... RIGHT!
WOBBLE
BEA ...?
BEA !!

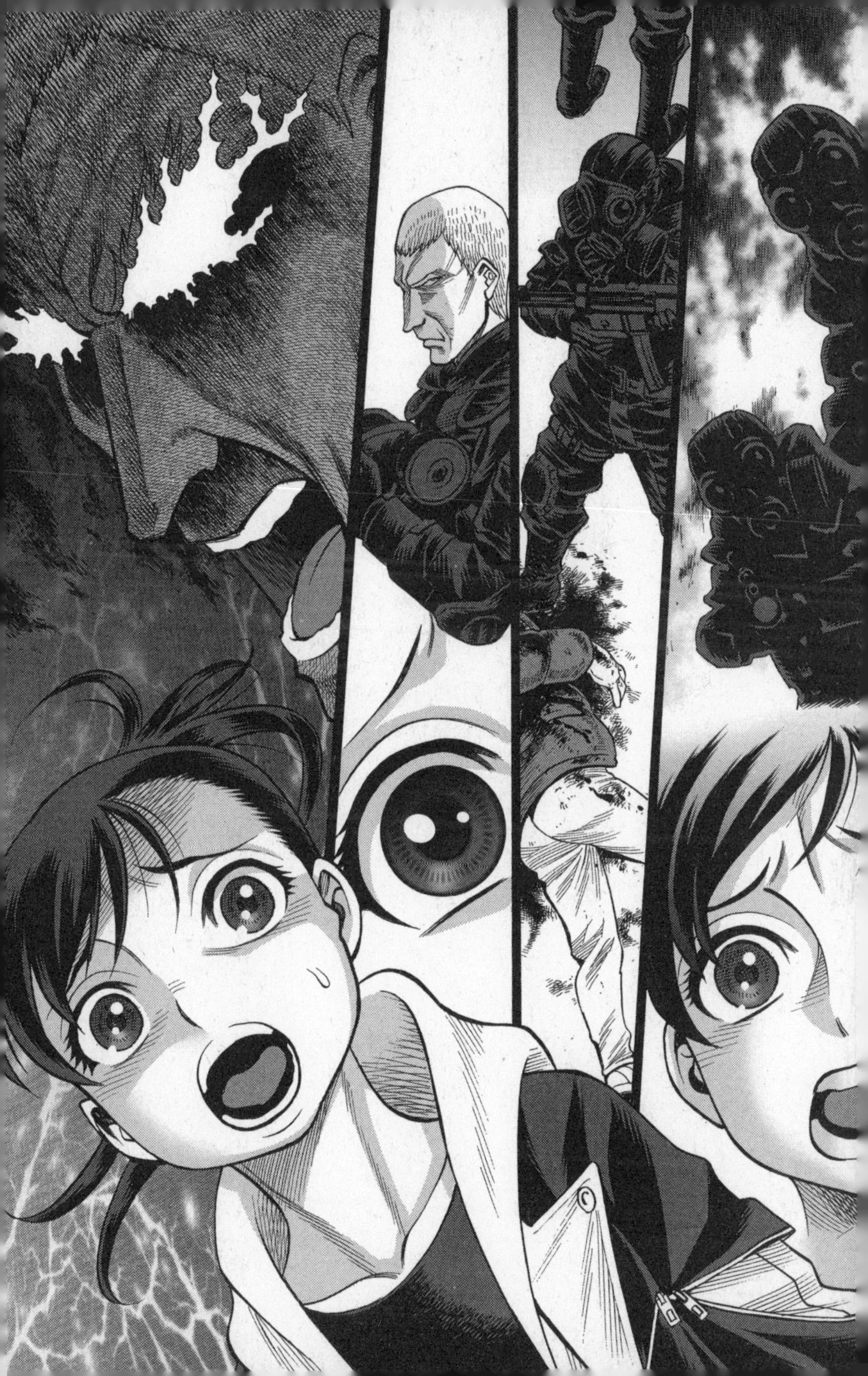

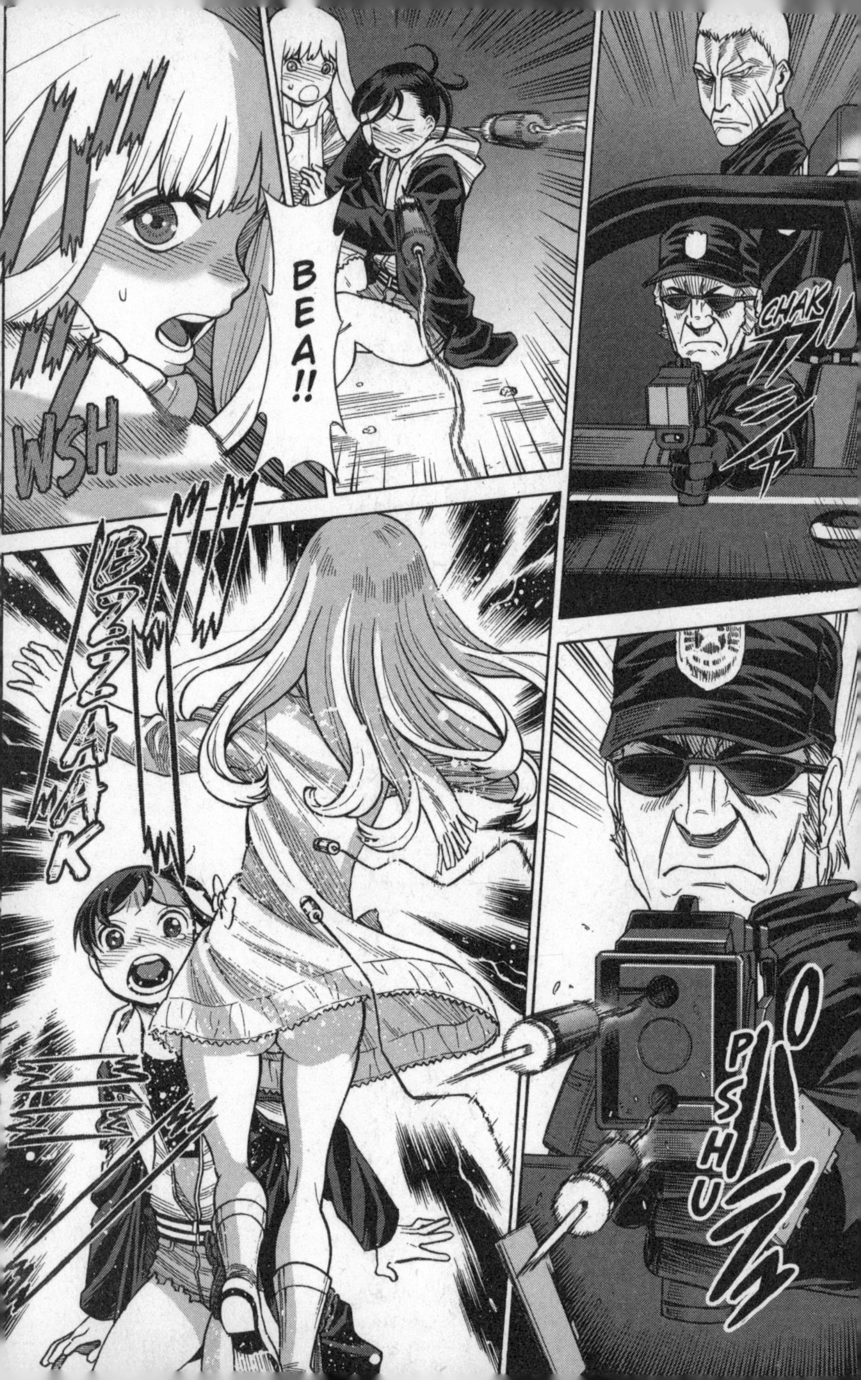
CHAK
BEA!!
WSH
PSHU
BZZZAAK

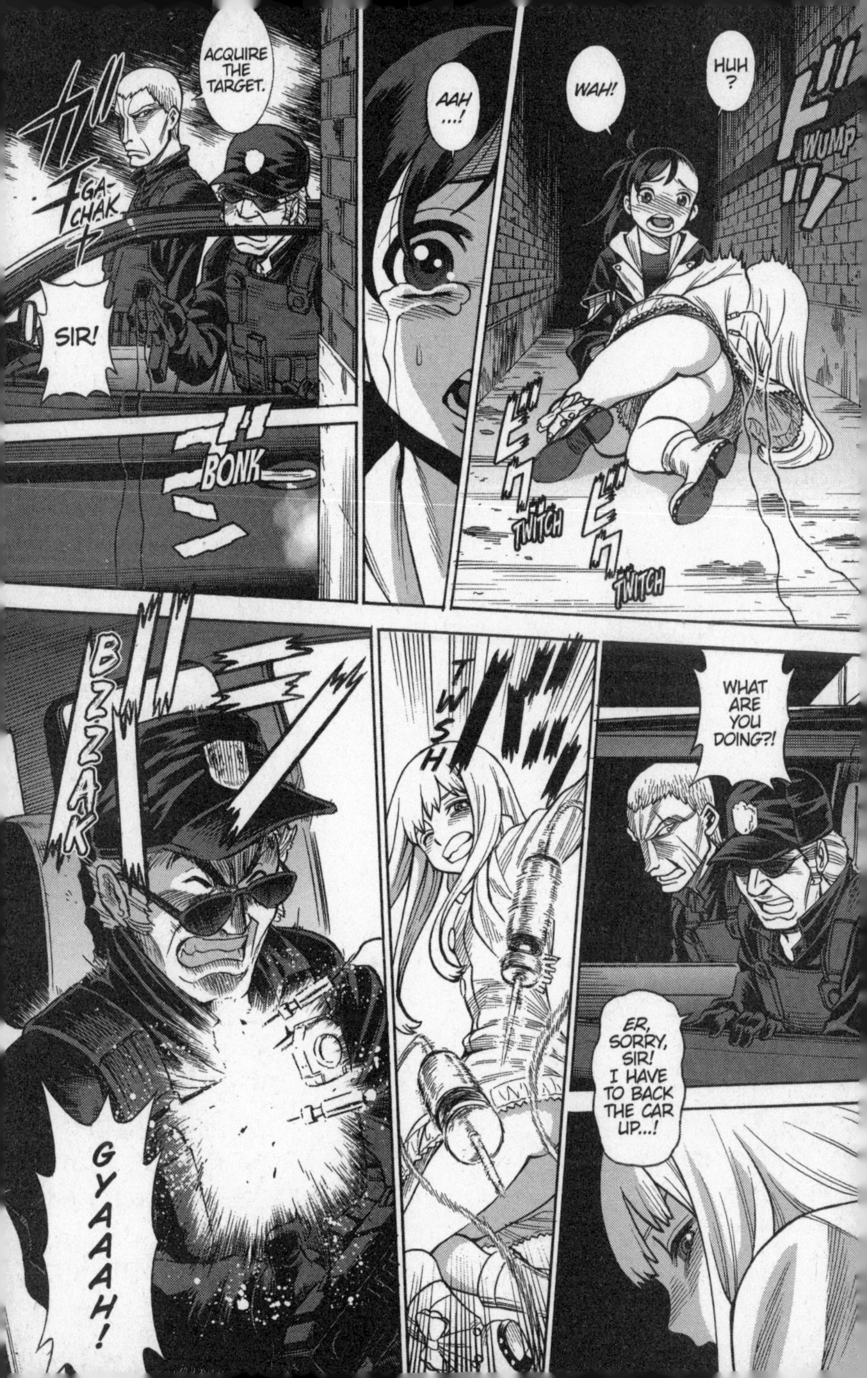
HUH?
WUMP
WAH!
TWITCH
TWITCH
AAH ...!
ACQUIRE THE TARGET.
GA-CHAK
SIR!
BONK
WHAT ARE YOU DOING?!
ER, SORRY, SIR! I HAVE TO BACK THE CAR UP...!
TWSH
BZZZAK
GYAAAAH!

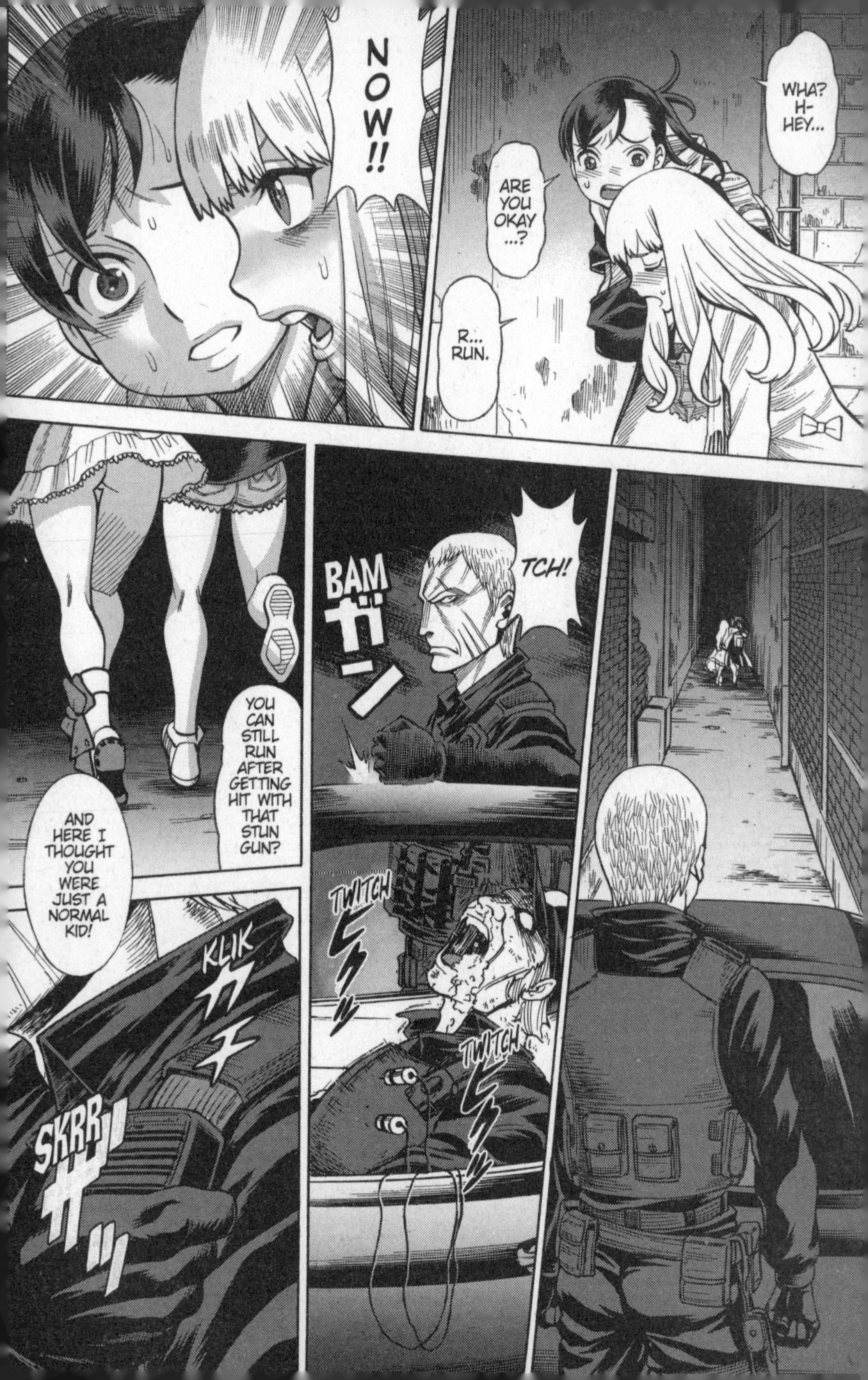
WHA? H- HEY...
ARE YOU OKAY ...?
R... RUN.
NOW!!
TCH!
BAM
YOU CAN STILL RUN AFTER GETTING HIT WITH THAT STUN GUN?
AND HERE I THOUGHT YOU WERE JUST A NORMAL KID!
TWITCH
TWITCH
KLIK
SKRR

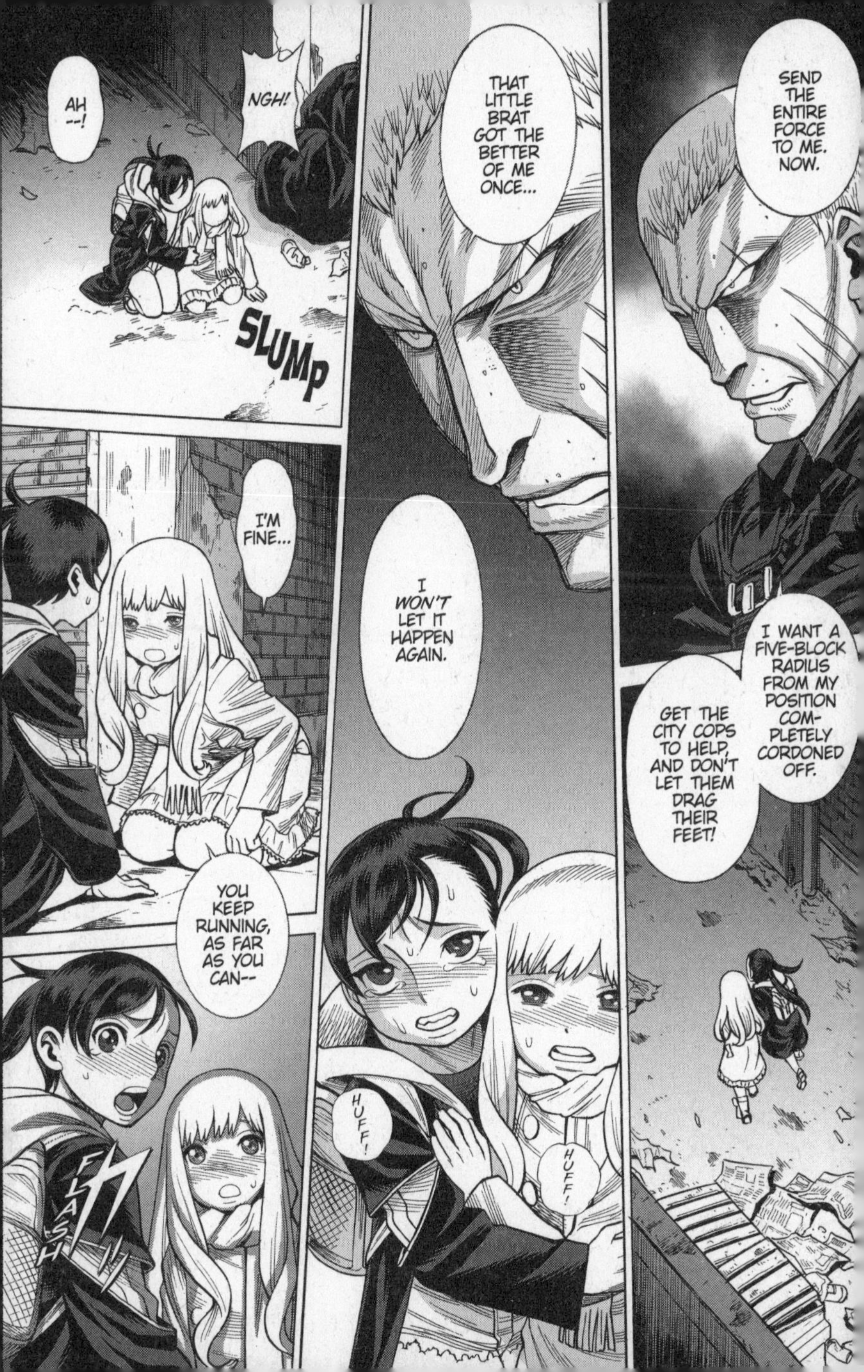
SEND THE ENTIRE FORCE TO ME. NOW.
I WANT A FIVE-BLOCK RADIUS FROM MY POSITION COM-PLETELY CORDONED OFF.
GET THE CITY COPS TO HELP, AND DON'T LET THEM DRAG THEIR FEET!
THAT LITTLE BRAT GOT THE BETTER OF ME ONCE...
I *WON'T* LET IT HAPPEN AGAIN.
HUFF!
HUFF!
NGH!
AH--!
SLUMP
I'M FINE...
YOU KEEP RUNNING, AS FAR AS YOU CAN--
FLASH

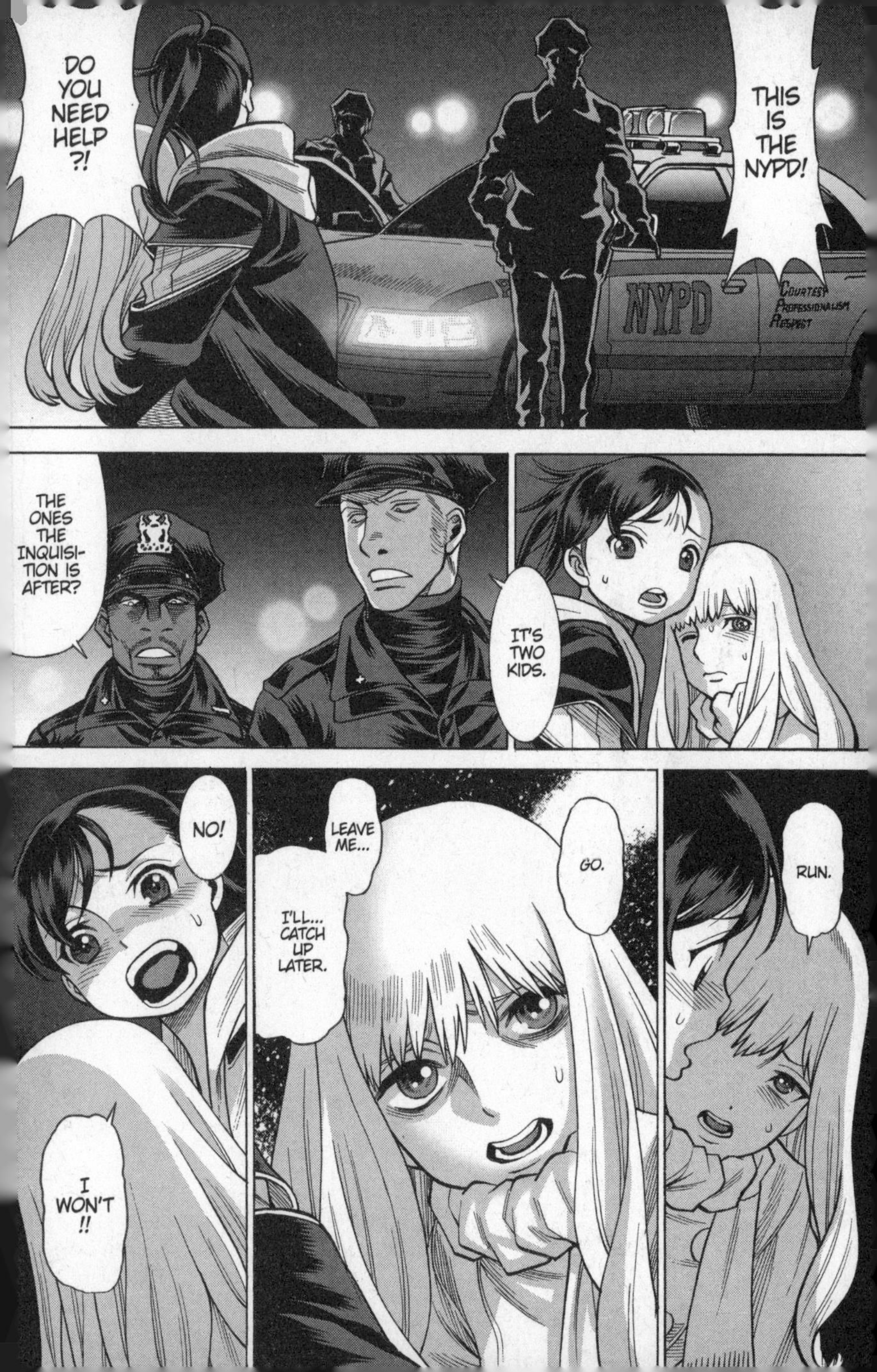
THIS IS THE NYPD!
NYPD
COURTESY PROFESSIONALISM RESPECT
DO YOU NEED HELP?!
IT'S TWO KIDS.
THE ONES THE INQUISITION IS AFTER?
RUN.
GO.
LEAVE ME...
I'LL... CATCH UP LATER.
NO!
I WON'T!!

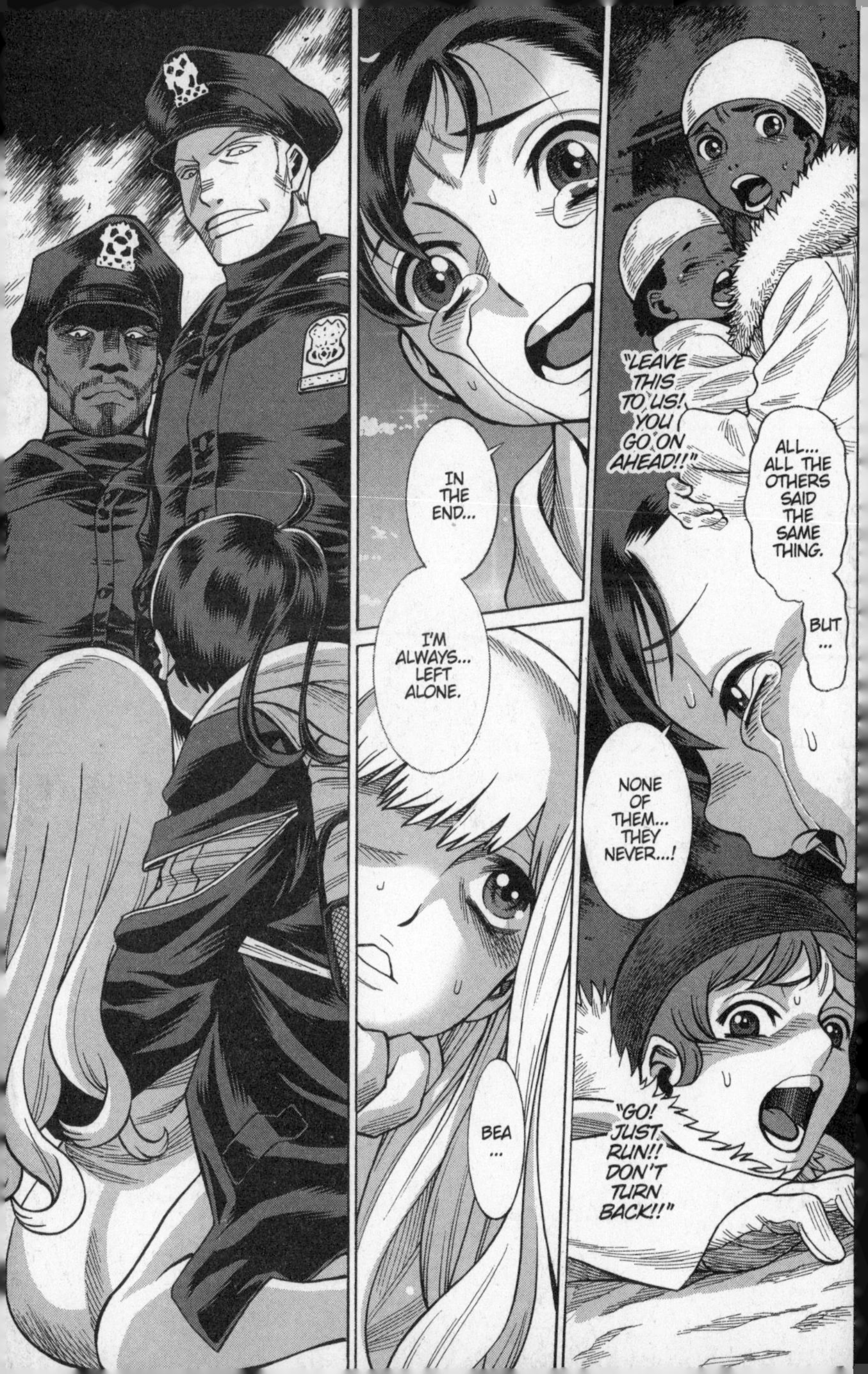
"LEAVE THIS TO US! YOU GO ON AHEAD!!"
ALL... ALL THE OTHERS SAID THE SAME THING.
BUT ...
NONE OF THEM... THEY NEVER...!
"GO! JUST RUN!! DON'T TURN BACK!!"
IN THE END...
I'M ALWAYS... LEFT ALONE.
BEA ...

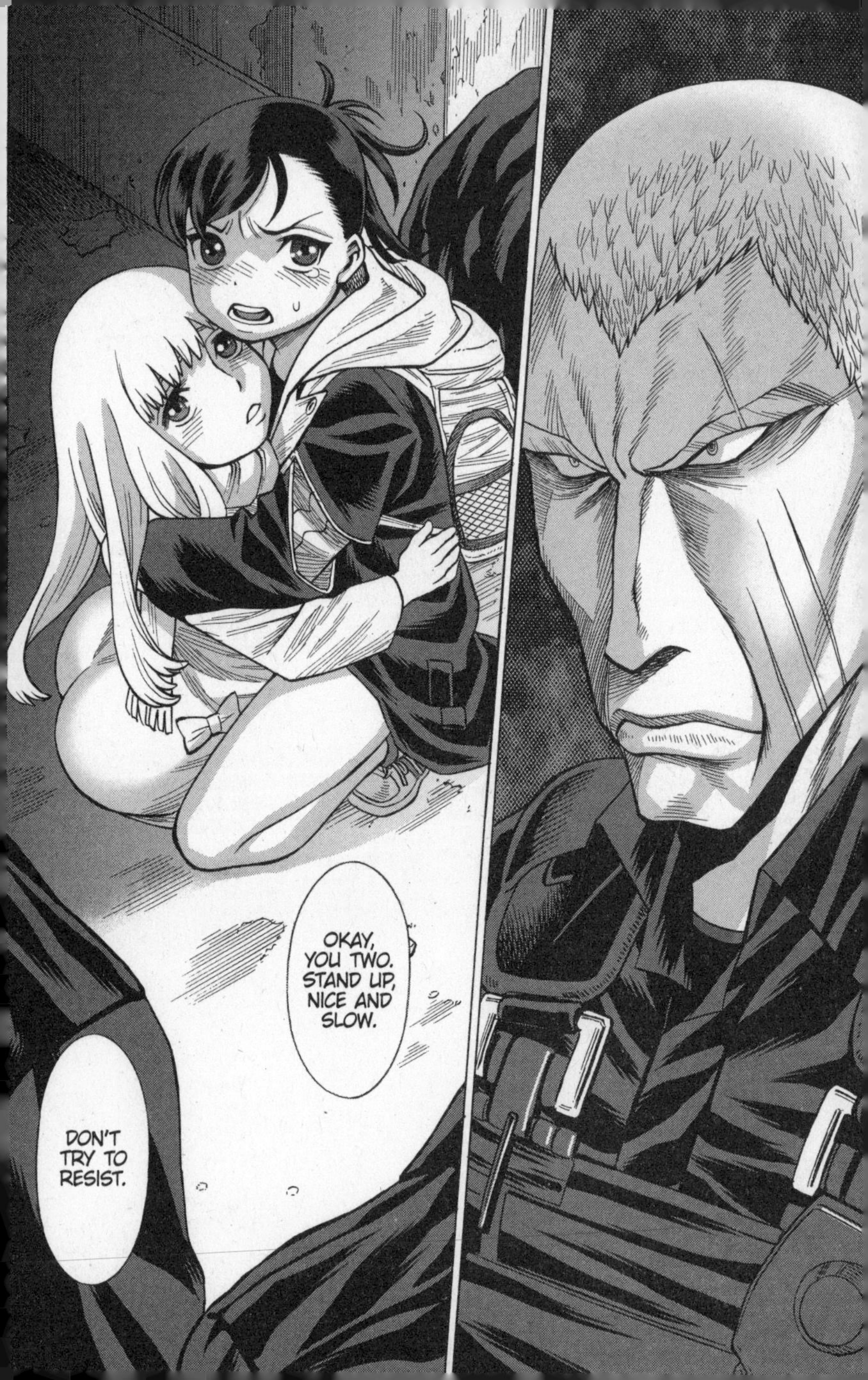
OKAY, YOU TWO. STAND UP, NICE AND SLOW.
DON'T TRY TO RESIST.

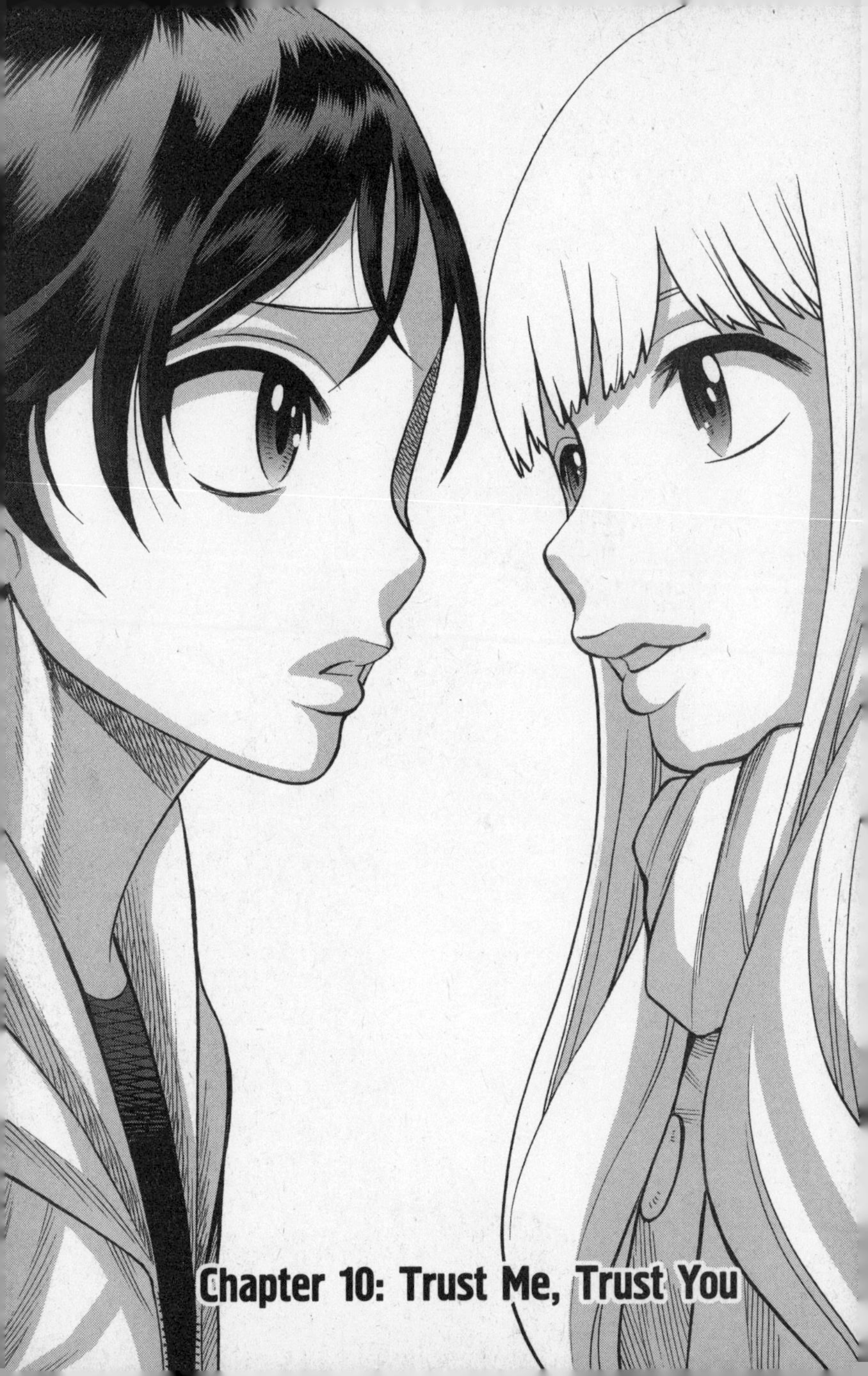
Chapter 10: Trust Me, Trust You

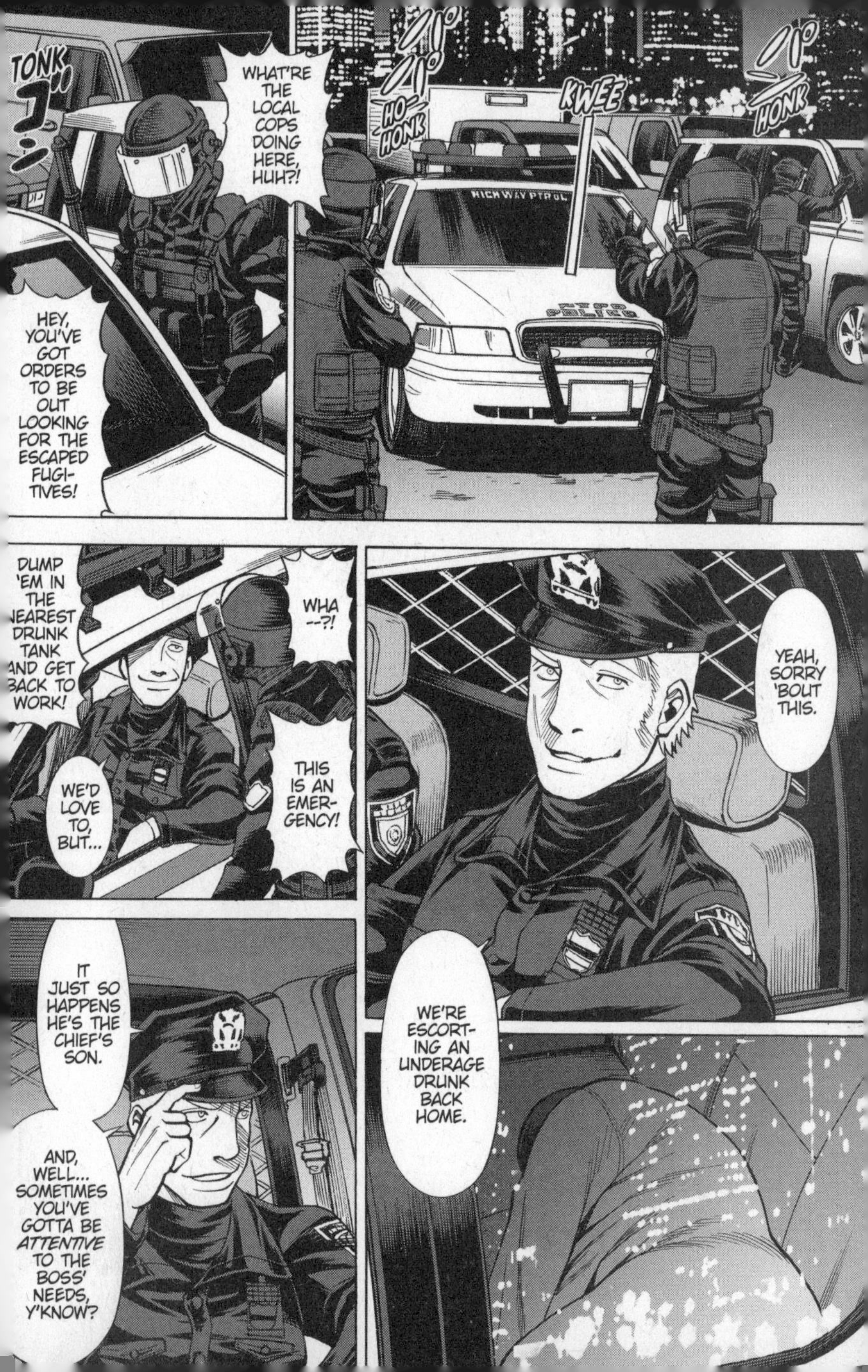
HO-HONK
KWEE
HONK
WHAT'RE THE LOCAL COPS DOING HERE, HUH?!
TONK
HEY, YOU'VE GOT ORDERS TO BE OUT LOOKING FOR THE ESCAPED FUGI-TIVES!
YEAH, SORRY 'BOUT THIS.
WE'RE ESCORT-ING AN UNDERAGE DRUNK BACK HOME.
WHA --?!
THIS IS AN EMER-GENCY!
DUMP 'EM IN THE NEAREST DRUNK TANK AND GET BACK TO WORK!
WE'D LOVE TO, BUT...
IT JUST SO HAPPENS HE'S THE CHIEF'S SON.
AND, WELL... SOMETIMES YOU'VE GOTTA BE *ATTENTIVE* TO THE BOSS' NEEDS, Y'KNOW?

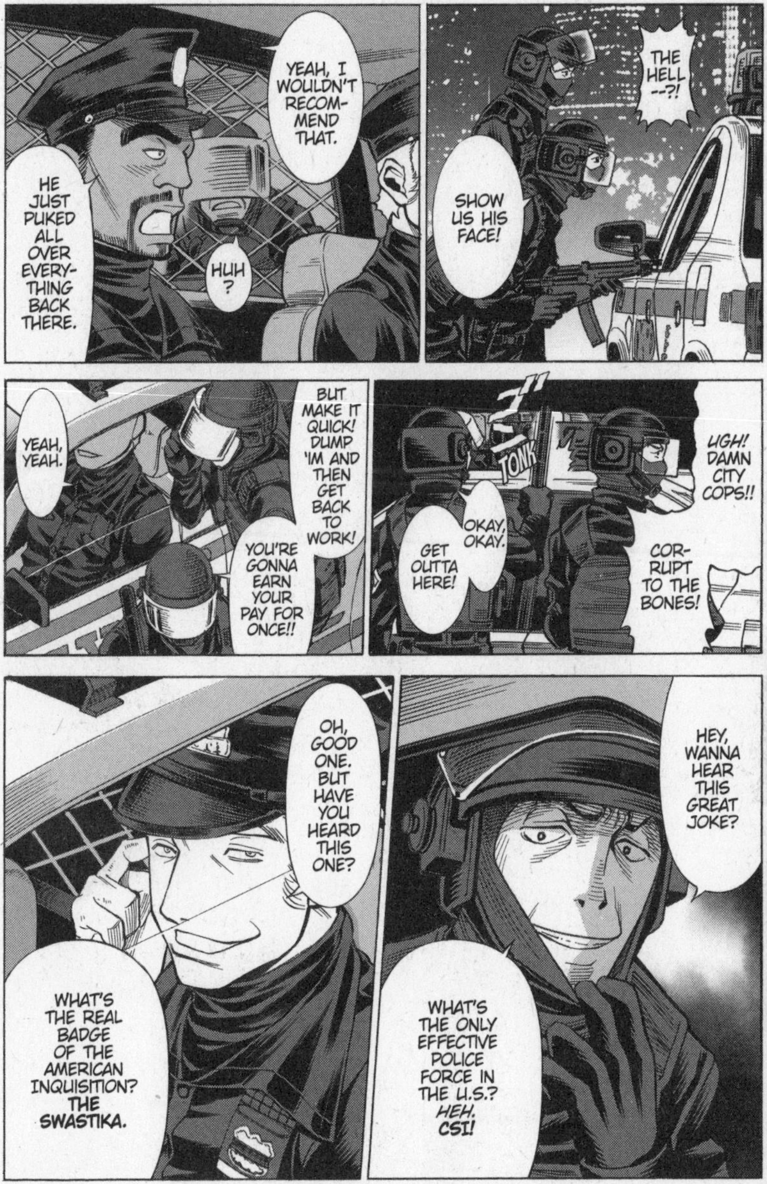
THE HELL --?!
SHOW US HIS FACE!
YEAH, I WOULDN'T RECOMMEND THAT.
HE JUST PUKED ALL OVER EVERYTHING BACK THERE.
HUH?
UGH! DAMN CITY COPS!!
CORRUPT TO THE BONES!
TONK
OKAY, OKAY.
GET OUTTA HERE!
BUT MAKE IT QUICK! DUMP 'IM AND THEN GET BACK TO WORK!
YEAH, YEAH.
YOU'RE GONNA EARN YOUR PAY FOR ONCE!!
HEY, WANNA HEAR THIS GREAT JOKE?
WHAT'S THE ONLY EFFECTIVE POLICE FORCE IN THE U.S.? HEH. CSI!
OH, GOOD ONE. BUT HAVE YOU HEARD THIS ONE?
WHAT'S THE REAL BADGE OF THE AMERICAN INQUISITION? THE SWASTIKA.

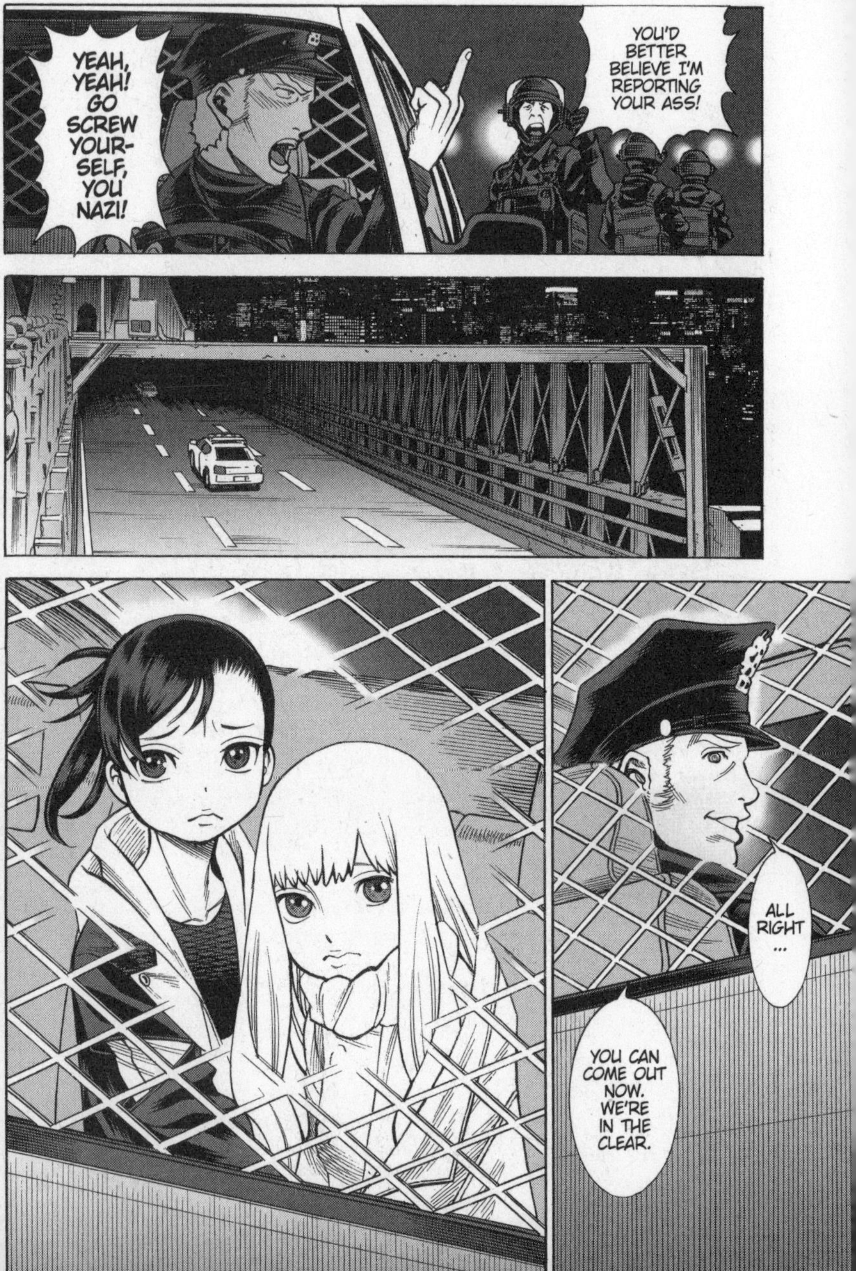
YOU'D BETTER BELIEVE I'M REPORTING YOUR ASS!
YEAH, YEAH! GO SCREW YOURSELF, YOU NAZI!
ALL RIGHT ...
YOU CAN COME OUT NOW. WE'RE IN THE CLEAR.

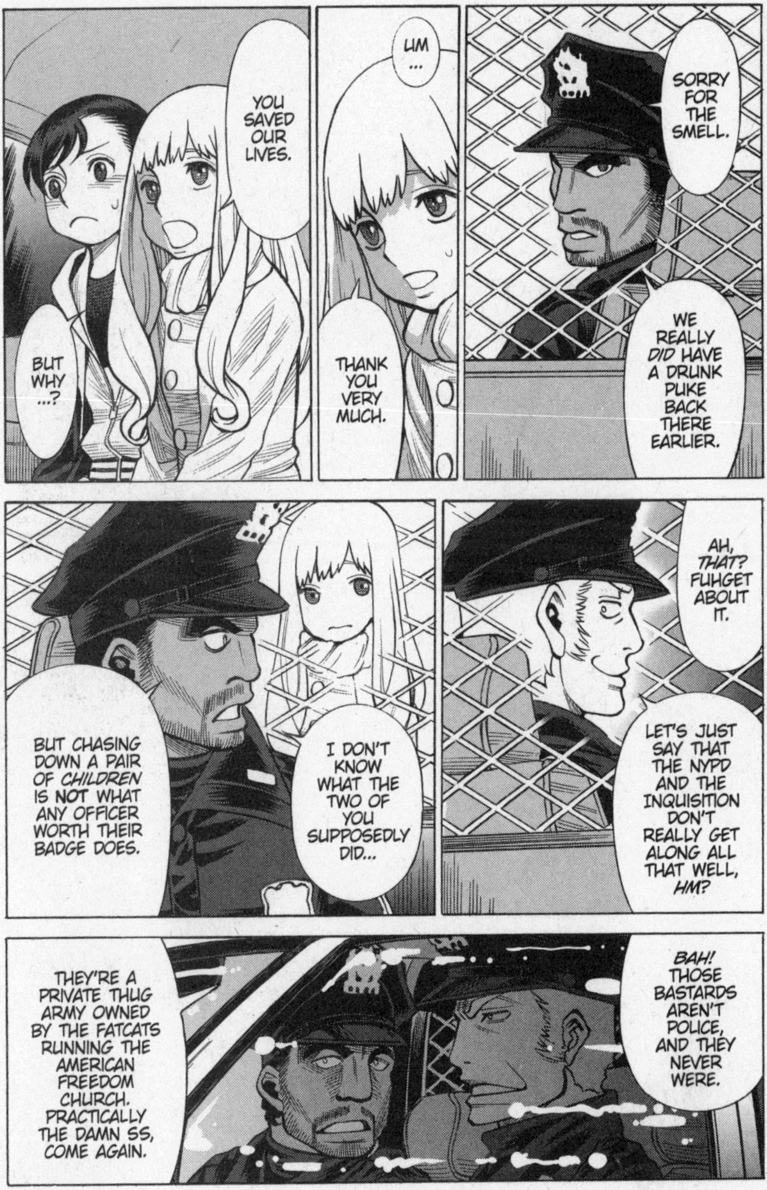
SORRY FOR THE SMELL.
WE REALLY *DID* HAVE A DRUNK PUKE BACK THERE EARLIER.
UM ...
THANK YOU VERY MUCH.
YOU SAVED OUR LIVES.
BUT WHY ...?
AH, *THAT?* FUHGET ABOUT IT.
LET'S JUST SAY THAT THE NYPD AND THE INQUISITION DON'T REALLY GET ALONG ALL THAT WELL, *HM?*
I DON'T KNOW WHAT THE TWO OF YOU SUPPOSEDLY DID...
BUT CHASING DOWN A PAIR OF *CHILDREN* IS **NOT** WHAT ANY OFFICER WORTH THEIR BADGE DOES.
BAH! THOSE BASTARDS AREN'T POLICE, AND THEY NEVER WERE.
THEY'RE A PRIVATE THUG ARMY OWNED BY THE FATCATS RUNNING THE AMERICAN FREEDOM CHURCH. PRACTICALLY THE DAMN SS, COME AGAIN.

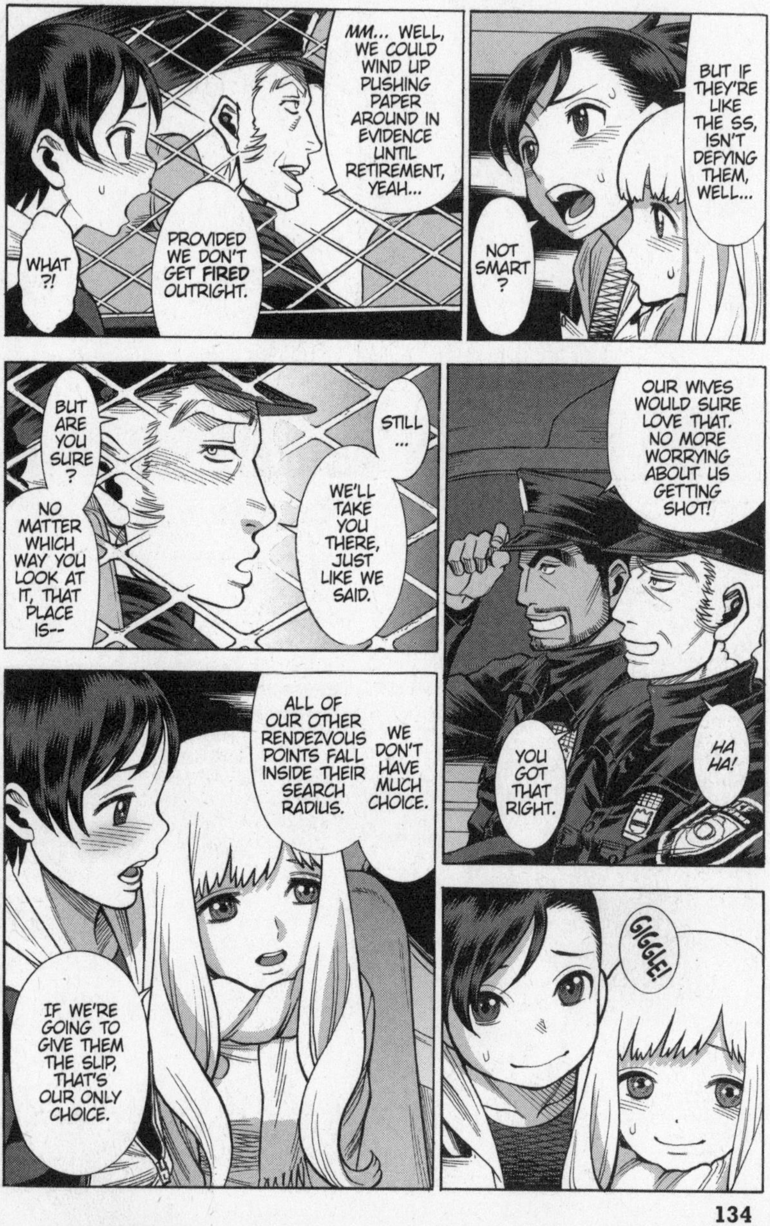
BUT IF THEY'RE LIKE THE SS, ISN'T DEFYING THEM, WELL...
NOT SMART?
MM... WELL, WE COULD WIND UP PUSHING PAPER AROUND IN EVIDENCE UNTIL RETIREMENT, YEAH...
PROVIDED WE DON'T GET **FIRED** OUTRIGHT.
WHAT?!
OUR WIVES WOULD SURE LOVE THAT. NO MORE WORRYING ABOUT US GETTING SHOT!
HA HA!
YOU GOT THAT RIGHT.
GIGGLE!
STILL...
WE'LL TAKE YOU THERE, JUST LIKE WE SAID.
BUT ARE YOU SURE?
NO MATTER WHICH WAY YOU LOOK AT IT, THAT PLACE IS--
WE DON'T HAVE MUCH CHOICE.
ALL OF OUR OTHER RENDEZVOUS POINTS FALL INSIDE THEIR SEARCH RADIUS.
IF WE'RE GOING TO GIVE THEM THE SLIP, THAT'S OUR ONLY CHOICE.

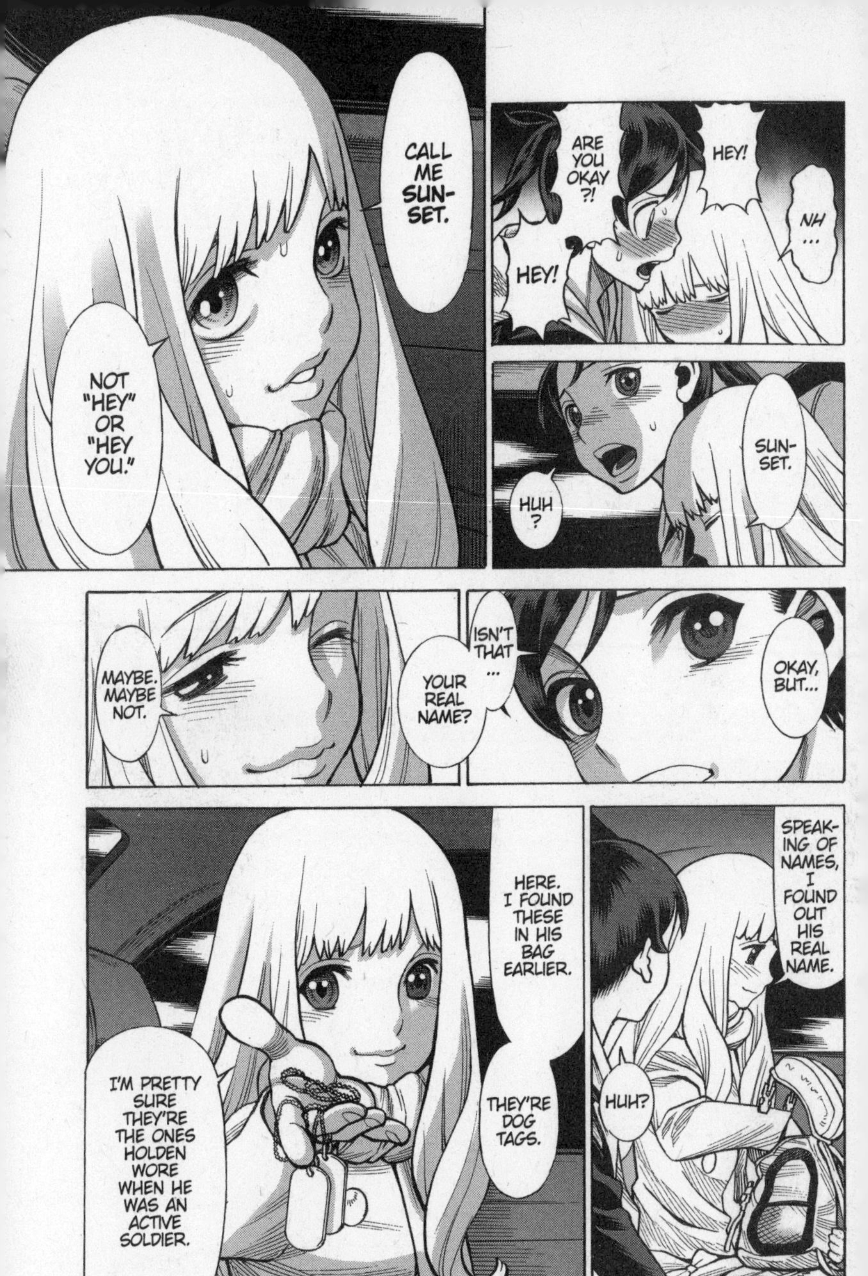
HEY!
NH...
ARE YOU OKAY?!
HEY!
SUN-SET.
HUH?
CALL ME SUN-SET.
NOT "HEY" OR "HEY YOU."
OKAY, BUT...
ISN'T THAT...
YOUR REAL NAME?
MAYBE. MAYBE NOT.
SPEAKING OF NAMES, I FOUND OUT HIS REAL NAME.
HUH?
HERE. I FOUND THESE IN HIS BAG EARLIER.
THEY'RE DOG TAGS.
I'M PRETTY SURE THEY'RE THE ONES HOLDEN WORE WHEN HE WAS AN ACTIVE SOLDIER.

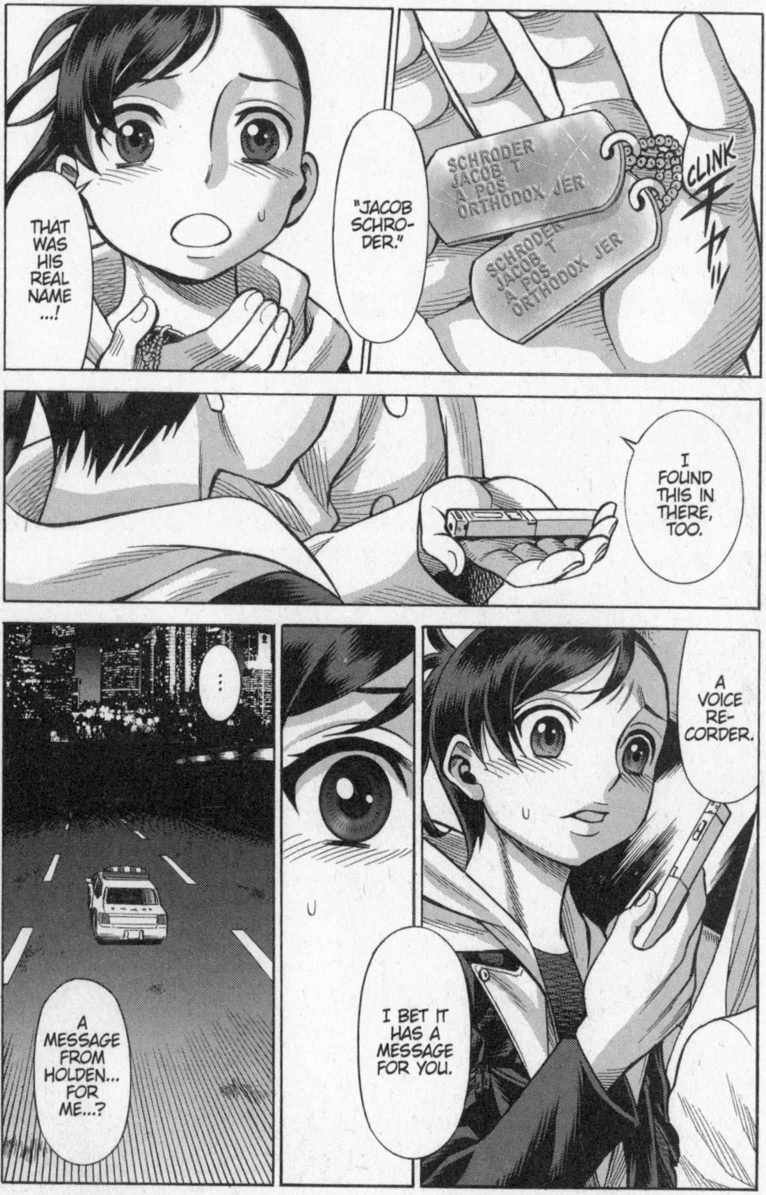
CLINK
SCHRODER JACOB T A POS ORTHODOX JER
SCHRODER JACOB T A POS ORTHODOX JER
"JACOB SCHRODER."
THAT WAS HIS REAL NAME ...!
I FOUND THIS IN THERE, TOO.
A VOICE RECORDER.
I BET IT HAS A MESSAGE FOR YOU.
...
A MESSAGE FROM HOLDEN... FOR ME...?

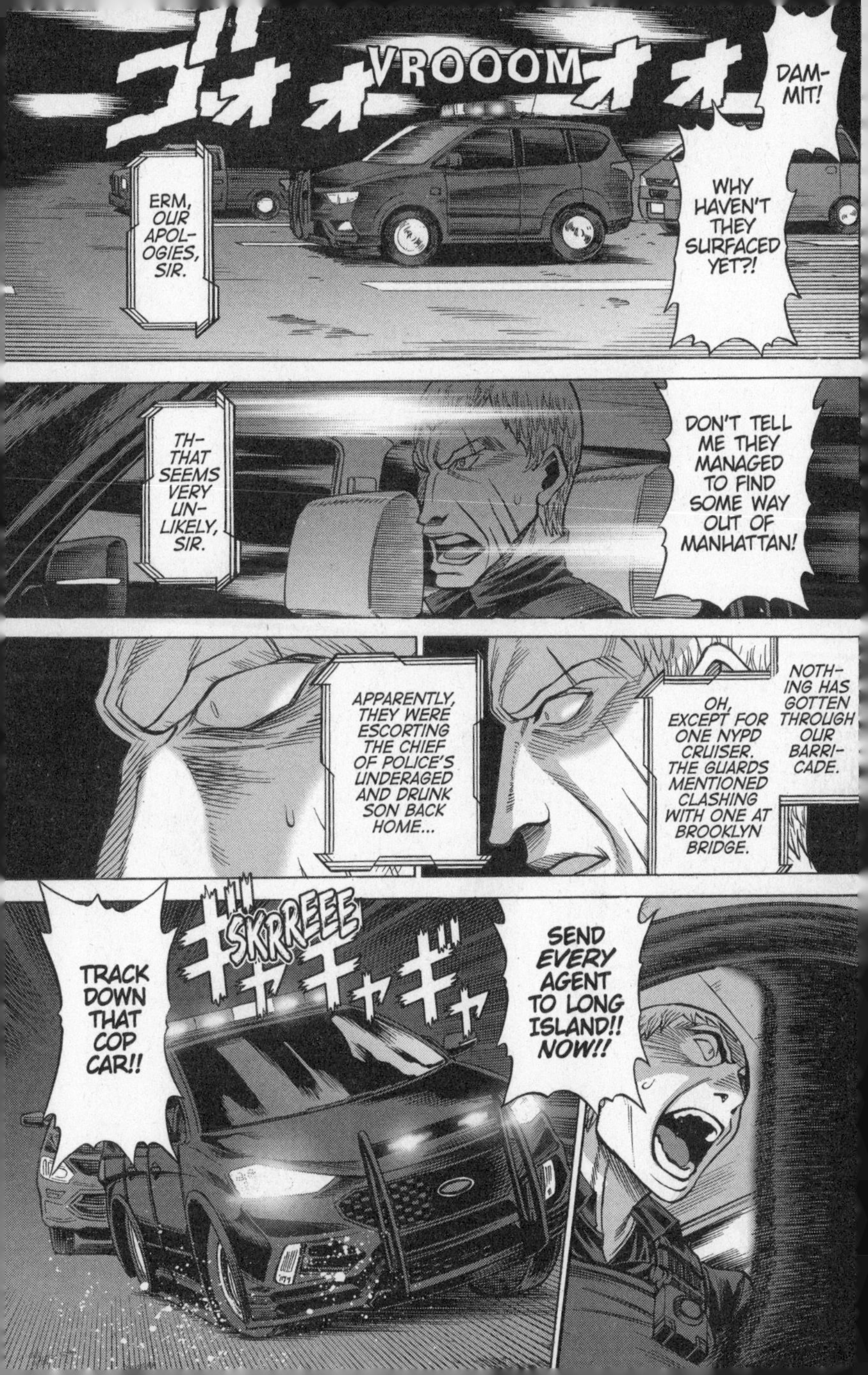
VROOOM
DAMMIT!
WHY HAVEN'T THEY SURFACED YET?!
ERM, OUR APOLOGIES, SIR.
DON'T TELL ME THEY MANAGED TO FIND SOME WAY OUT OF MANHATTAN!
TH-THAT SEEMS VERY UNLIKELY, SIR.
NOTHING HAS GOTTEN THROUGH OUR BARRICADE.
OH, EXCEPT FOR ONE NYPD CRUISER. THE GUARDS MENTIONED CLASHING WITH ONE AT BROOKLYN BRIDGE.
APPARENTLY, THEY WERE ESCORTING THE CHIEF OF POLICE'S UNDERAGED AND DRUNK SON BACK HOME...
SEND EVERY AGENT TO LONG ISLAND!! NOW!!
SKRREEE
TRACK DOWN THAT COP CAR!!

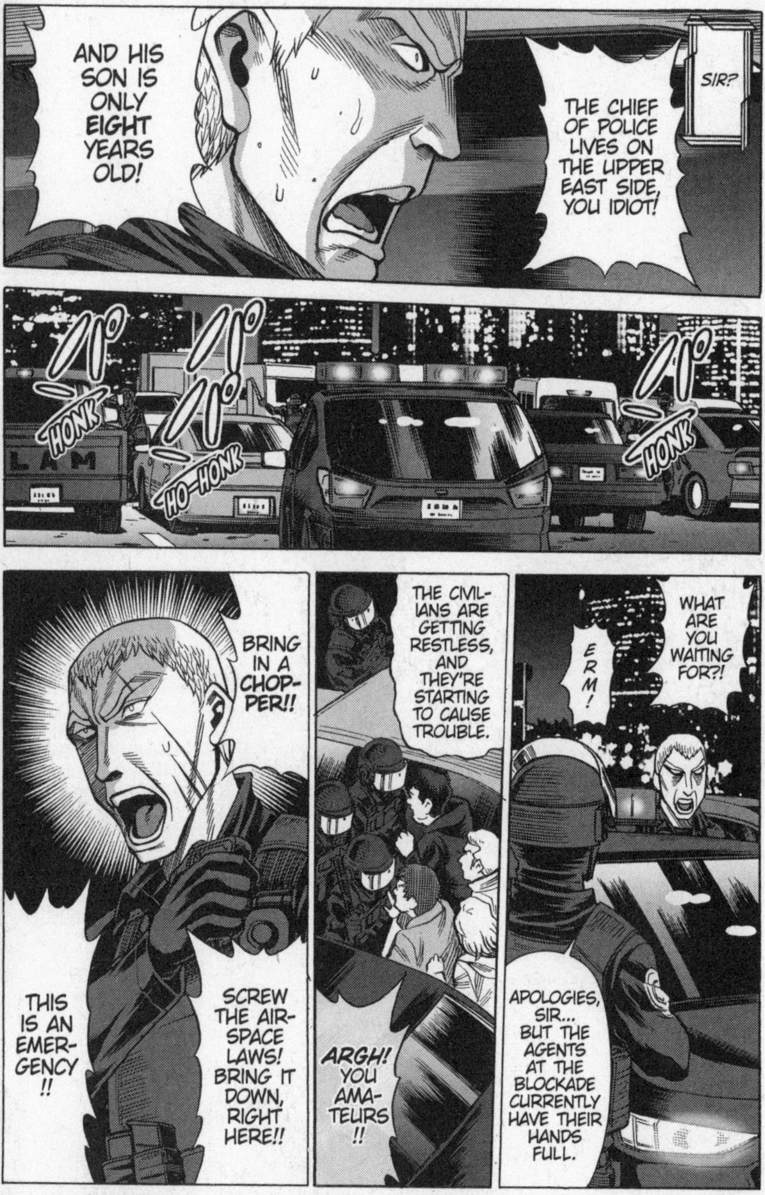
SIR?
THE CHIEF OF POLICE LIVES ON THE UPPER EAST SIDE, YOU IDIOT!
AND HIS SON IS ONLY EIGHT YEARS OLD!
HONK
HO-HONK
HONK
WHAT ARE YOU WAITING FOR?!
ERM!
APOLOGIES, SIR... BUT THE AGENTS AT THE BLOCKADE CURRENTLY HAVE THEIR HANDS FULL.
THE CIVILIANS ARE GETTING RESTLESS, AND THEY'RE STARTING TO CAUSE TROUBLE.
ARGH! YOU AMATEURS!!
BRING IN A CHOPPER!!
SCREW THE AIRSPACE LAWS! BRING IT DOWN, RIGHT HERE!!
THIS IS AN EMERGENCY!!

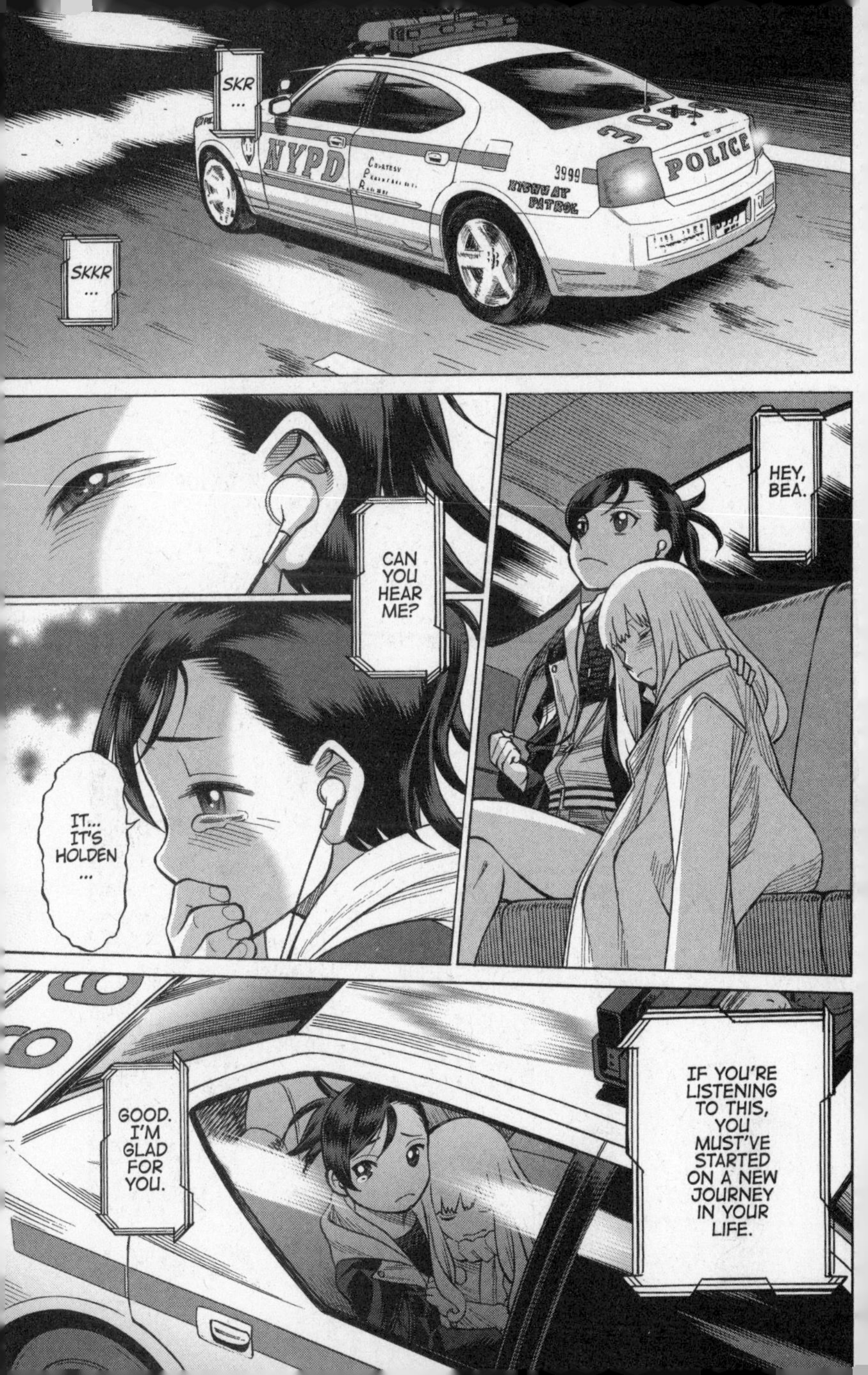
SKR ...
SKKR ...
NYPD
3999
POLICE
HEY, BEA.
CAN YOU HEAR ME?
IT... IT'S HOLDEN ...
IF YOU'RE LISTENING TO THIS, YOU MUST'VE STARTED ON A NEW JOURNEY IN YOUR LIFE.
GOOD. I'M GLAD FOR YOU.

DO YOU REMEMBER THE DAY WE FIRST MET?

YOU WERE HURT AND HUNGRY... AND SO EXHAUSTED, YOU'D COLLAPSED ON THE STREET.

IT REALLY WAS PURE WHIM THAT MADE ME DECIDE TO TAKE YOU HOME WITH ME.

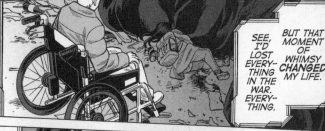

BUT THAT MOMENT OF WHIMSY **CHANGED** MY LIFE.

SEE, I'D LOST EVERYTHING IN THE WAR. EVERYTHING.

I WAS EVEN LOSING SIGHT OF A REASON TO KEEP LIVING. YOU TAUGHT ME I COULD STILL BE USEFUL TO OTHERS.

YOU ALWAYS TOLD ME THAT I'D SAVED YOU.

BUT YOU'RE WRONG, BEA,

YOU WERE THE ONE WHO SAVED **ME.**

I CAN'T IMAGINE WHERE I'LL BE OR WHAT I'LL BE DOING WHEN YOU'RE LISTENING TO THIS, BEA...

BUT THERE IS ONE THING I KNOW FOR SURE.

LIVE.

I WANT NOTHING MORE THAN FOR YOU TO BE HAPPY.

I LOVE YOU, BEA.

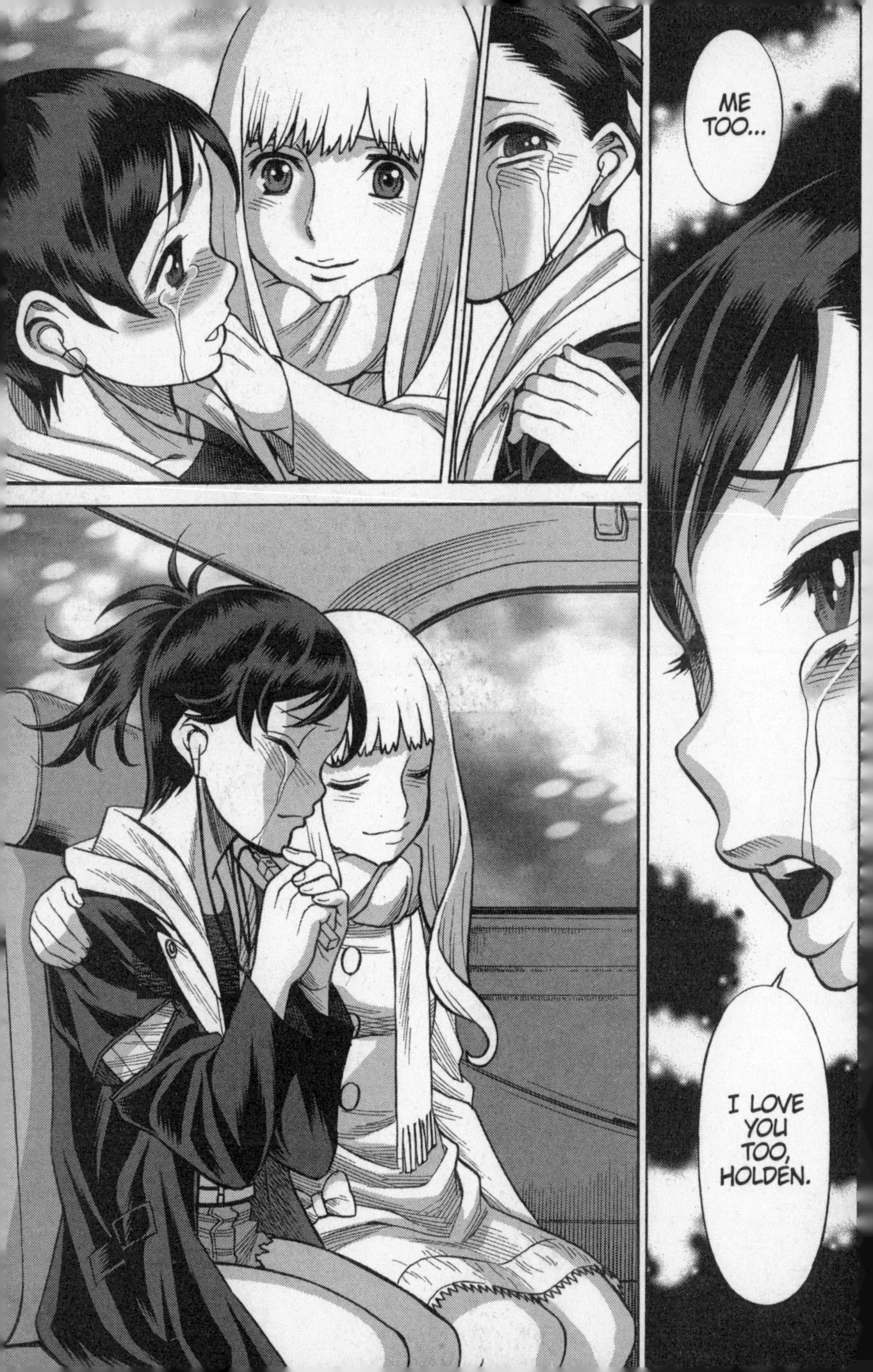
ME TOO...
I LOVE YOU TOO, HOLDEN.

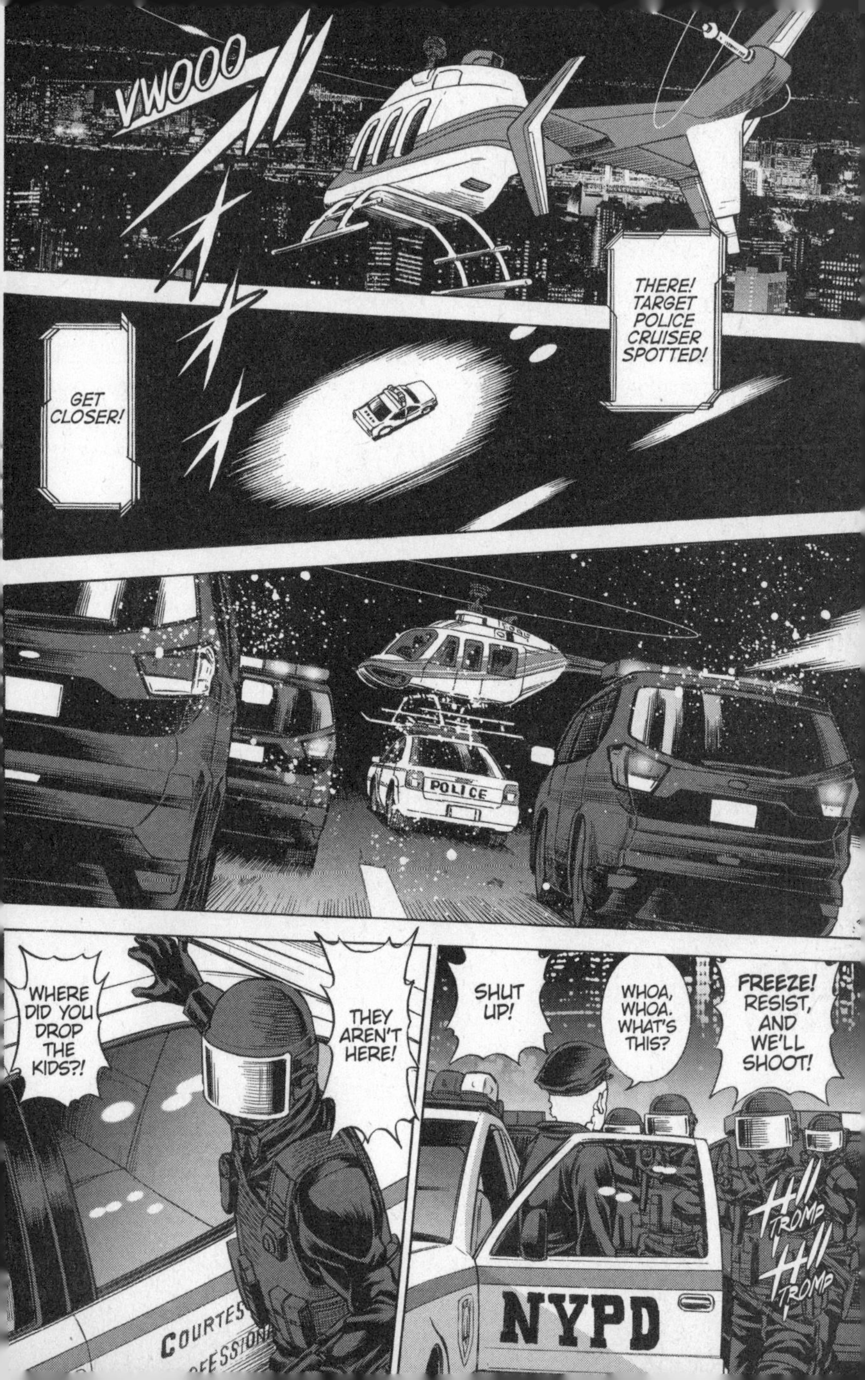
VWOOO
THERE! TARGET POLICE CRUISER SPOTTED!
GET CLOSER!
POLICE
FREEZE! RESIST, AND WE'LL SHOOT!
WHOA, WHOA. WHAT'S THIS?
SHUT UP!
TROMP
TROMP
NYPD
THEY AREN'T HERE!
WHERE DID YOU DROP THE KIDS?!

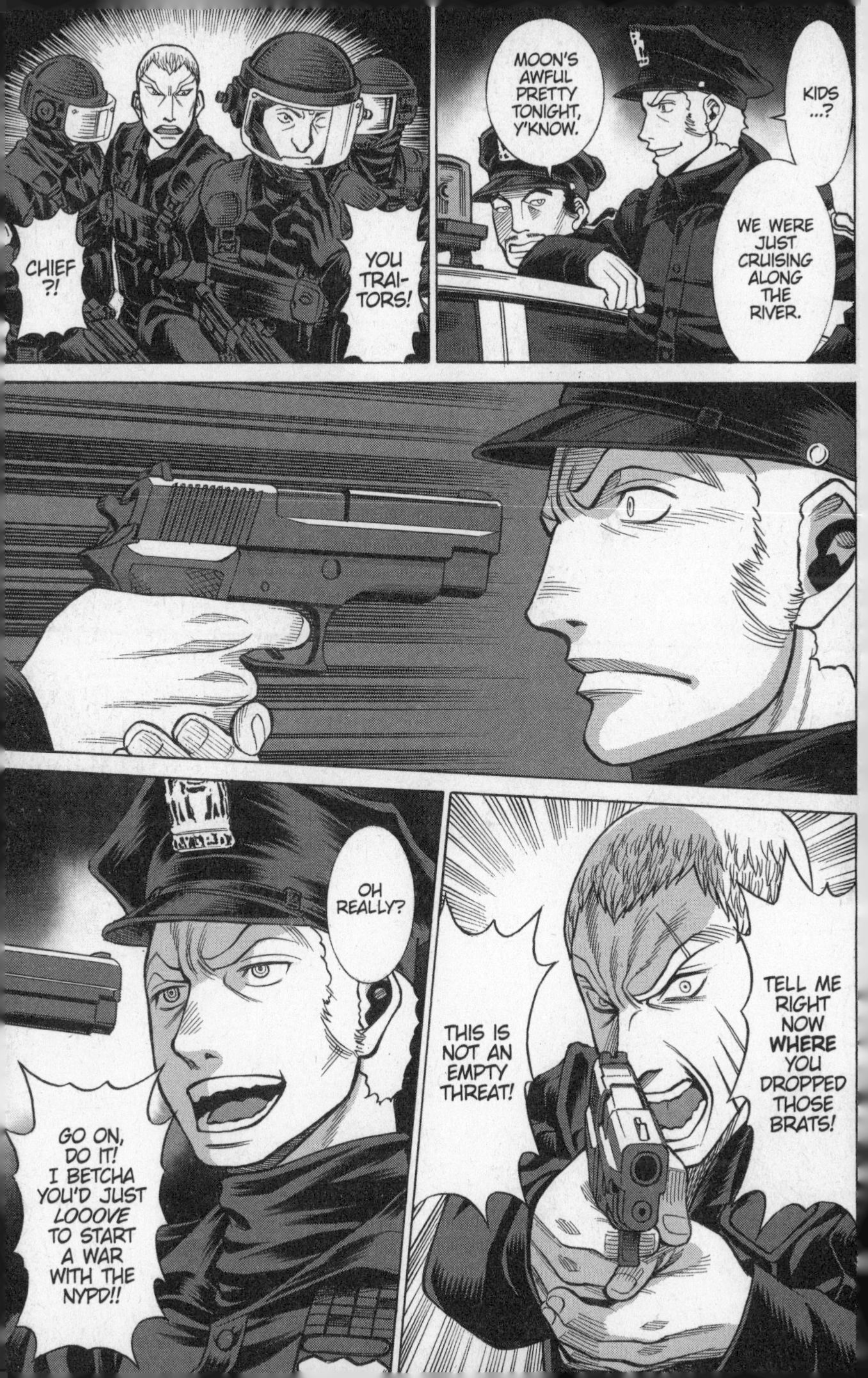
KIDS ...?
MOON'S AWFUL PRETTY TONIGHT, Y'KNOW.
WE WERE JUST CRUISING ALONG THE RIVER.
YOU TRAI-TORS!
CHIEF ?!
TELL ME RIGHT NOW WHERE YOU DROPPED THOSE BRATS!
THIS IS NOT AN EMPTY THREAT!
OH REALLY?
GO ON, DO IT! I BETCHA YOU'D JUST LOOOVE TO START A WAR WITH THE NYPD!!

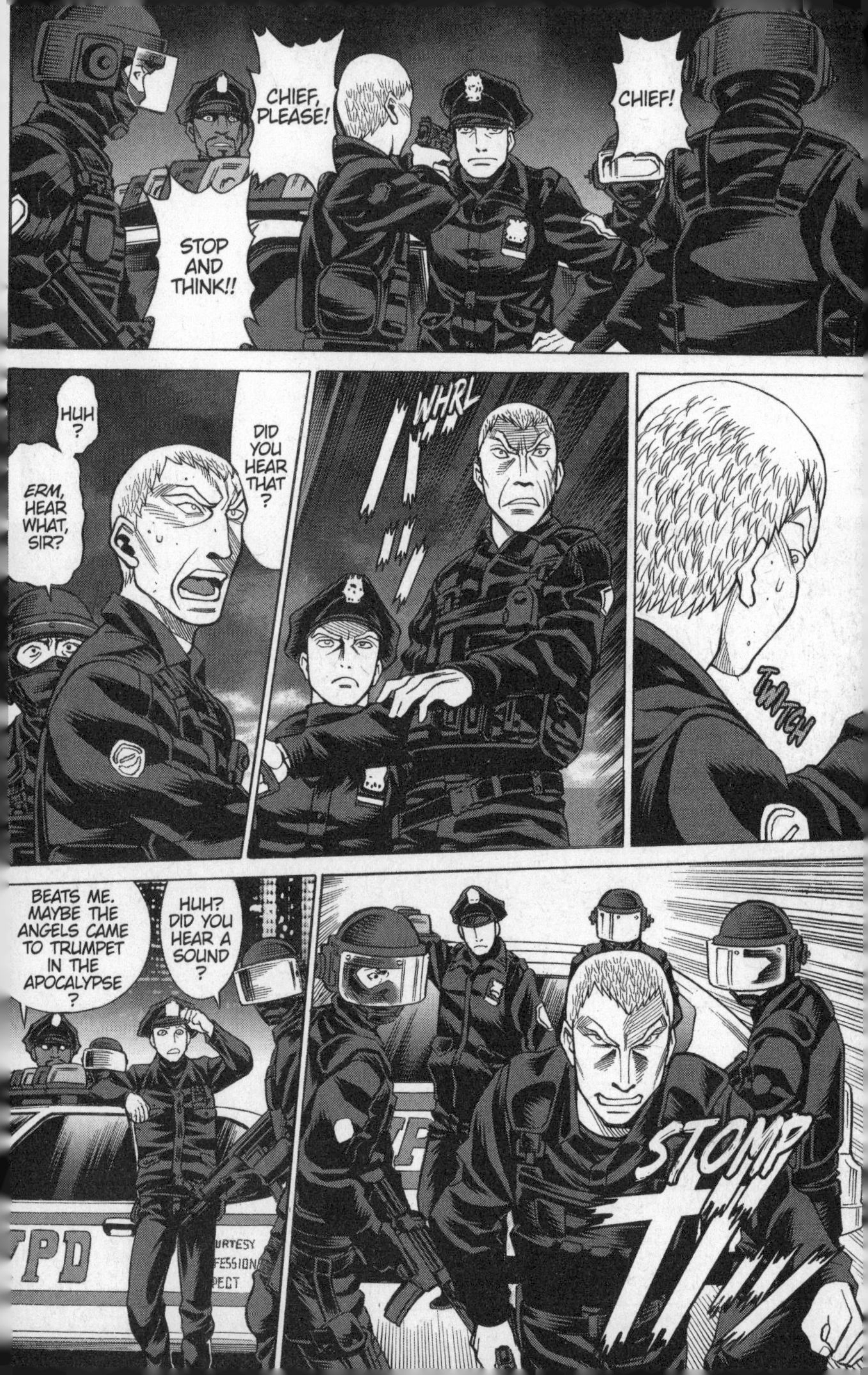
CHIEF!
CHIEF, PLEASE!
STOP AND THINK!!
TWITCH
WHRL
DID YOU HEAR THAT?
HUH?
ERM, HEAR WHAT, SIR?
STOMP
HUH? DID YOU HEAR A SOUND?
BEATS ME. MAYBE THE ANGELS CAME TO TRUMPET IN THE APOCALYPSE?

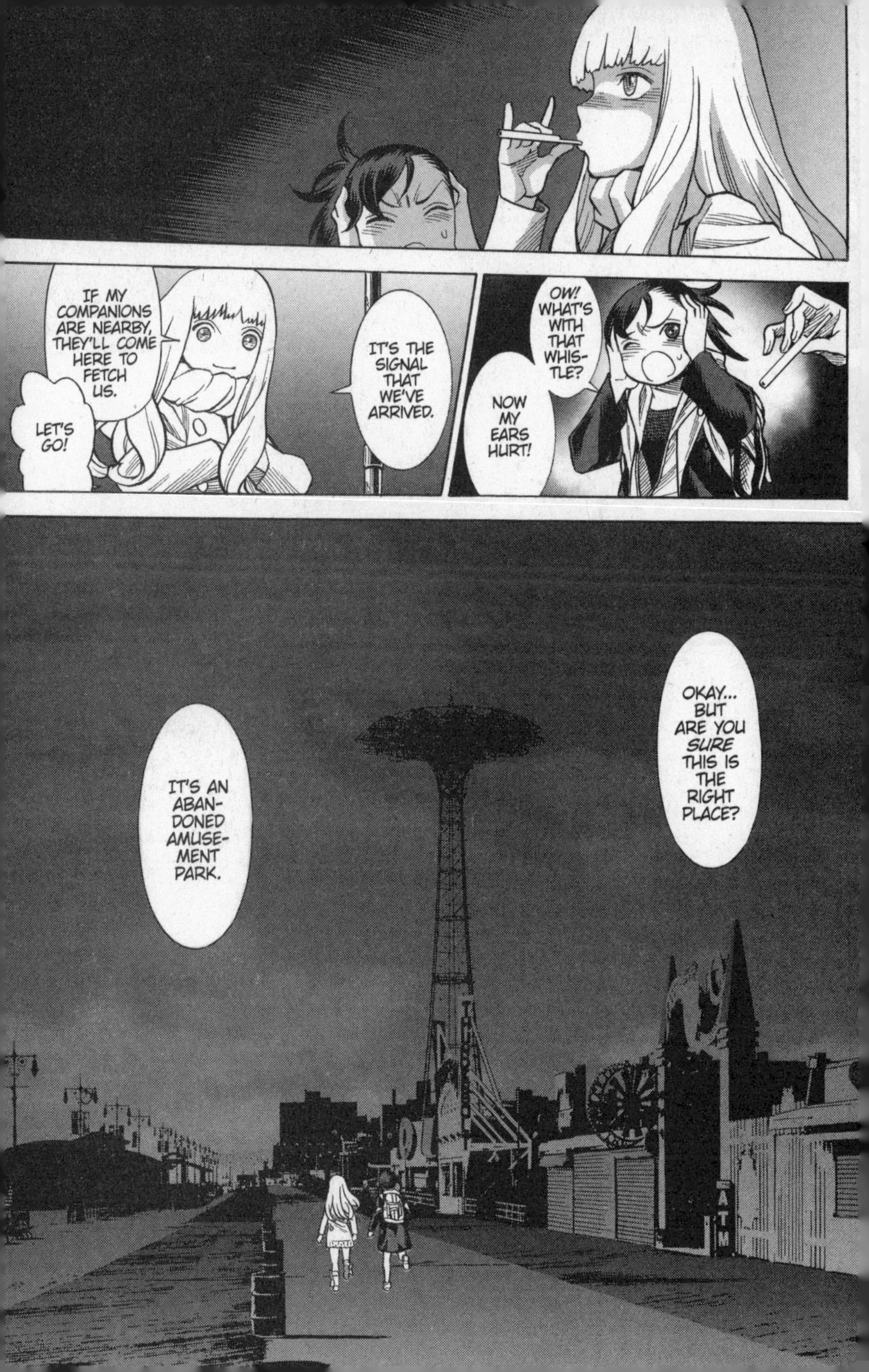
OW! WHAT'S WITH THAT WHIS-TLE?
NOW MY EARS HURT!
IT'S THE SIGNAL THAT WE'VE ARRIVED.
IF MY COMPANIONS ARE NEARBY, THEY'LL COME HERE TO FETCH US.
LET'S GO!
OKAY... BUT ARE YOU *SURE* THIS IS THE RIGHT PLACE?
IT'S AN ABAN-DONED AMUSE-MENT PARK.
ATM

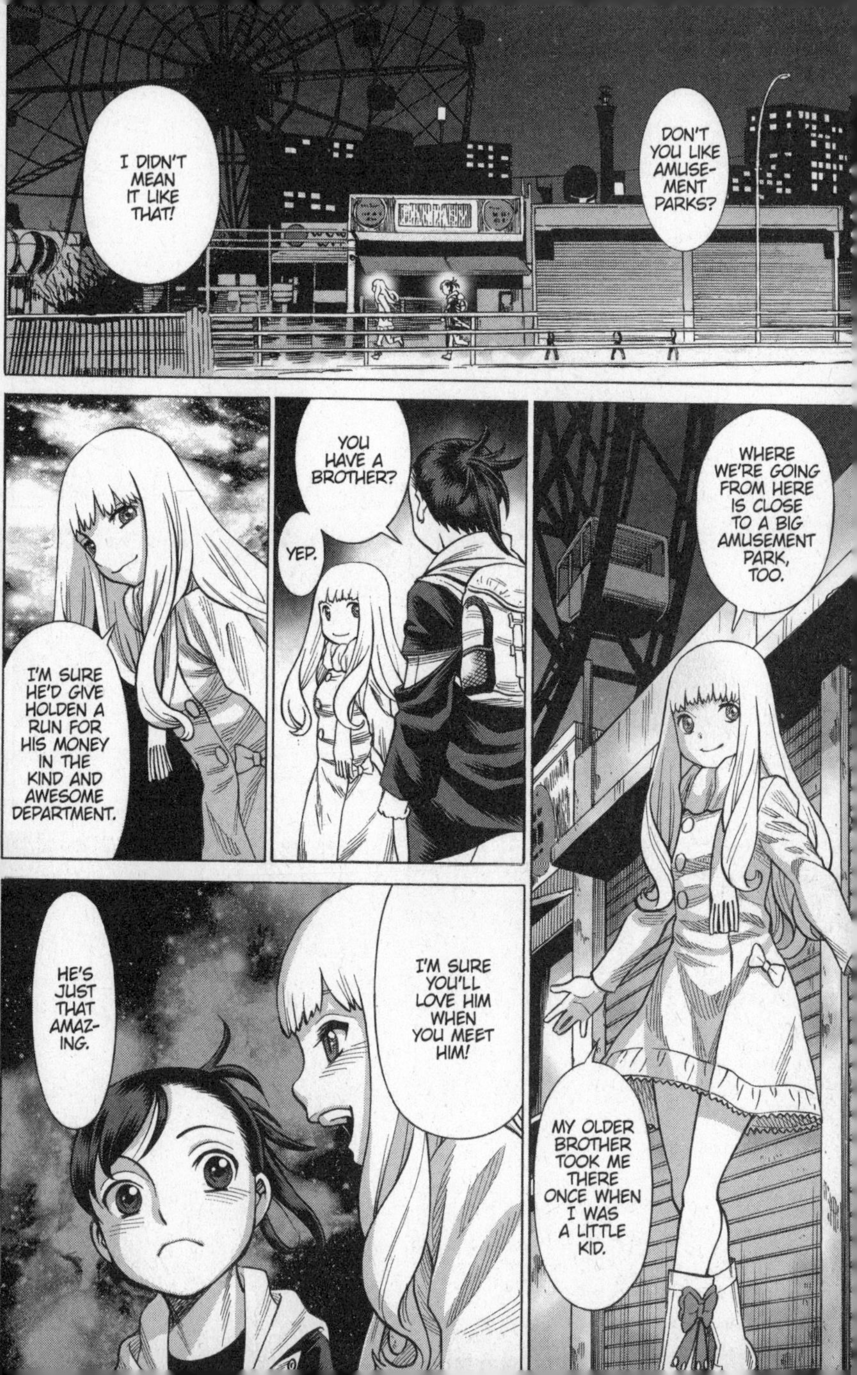
DON'T YOU LIKE AMUSEMENT PARKS?
I DIDN'T MEAN IT LIKE THAT!
WHERE WE'RE GOING FROM HERE IS CLOSE TO A BIG AMUSEMENT PARK, TOO.
MY OLDER BROTHER TOOK ME THERE ONCE WHEN I WAS A LITTLE KID.
YOU HAVE A BROTHER?
YEP.
I'M SURE HE'D GIVE HOLDEN A RUN FOR HIS MONEY IN THE KIND AND AWESOME DEPARTMENT.
I'M SURE YOU'LL LOVE HIM WHEN YOU MEET HIM!
HE'S JUST THAT AMAZ-ING.

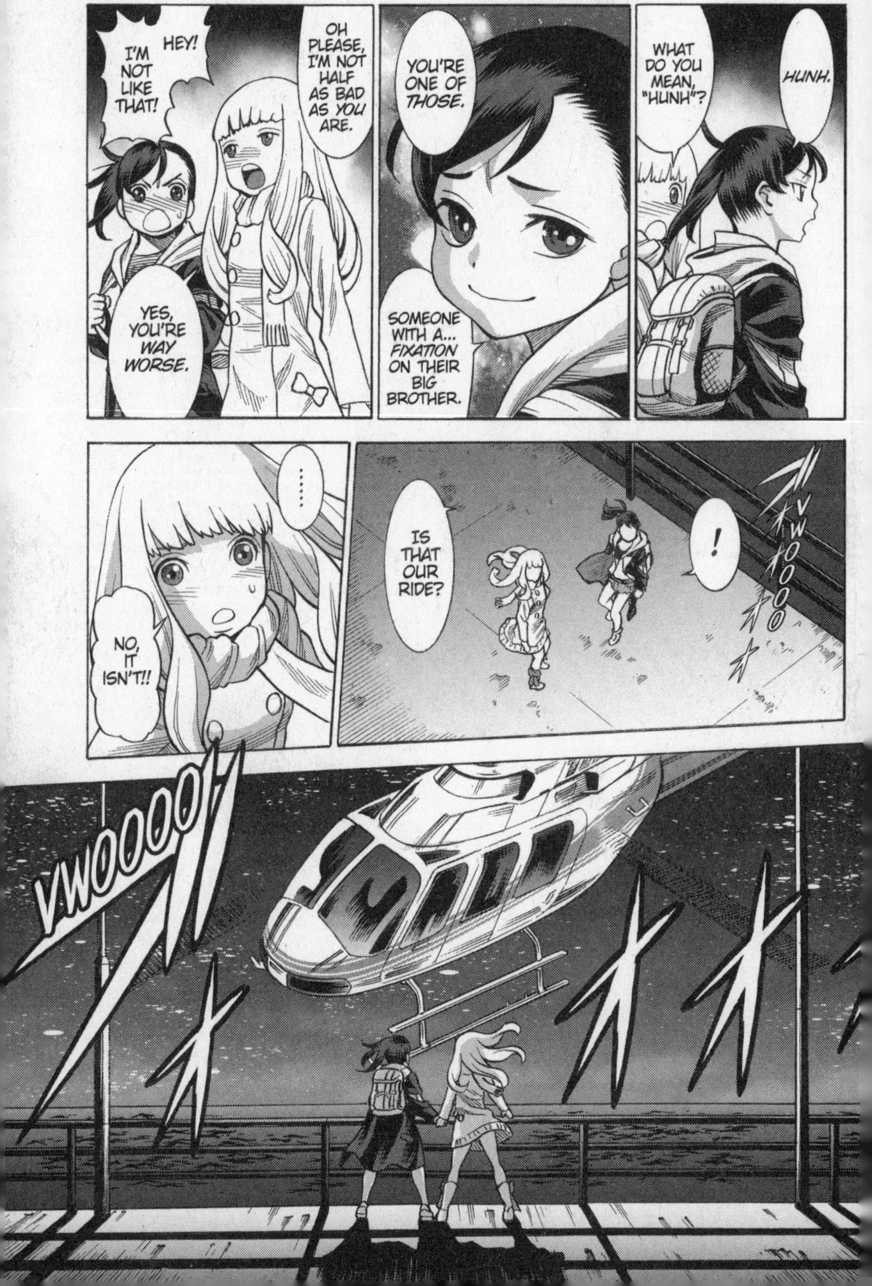
HUNH.
WHAT DO YOU MEAN, "HUNH"?
YOU'RE ONE OF *THOSE.*
SOMEONE WITH A... *FIXATION* ON THEIR BIG BROTHER.
OH PLEASE, I'M NOT HALF AS BAD AS *YOU* ARE.
HEY!
I'M NOT LIKE THAT!
YES, YOU'RE *WAY WORSE.*
VWOOOO
!
IS THAT OUR RIDE?
......
NO, IT ISN'T!!
VWOOOO

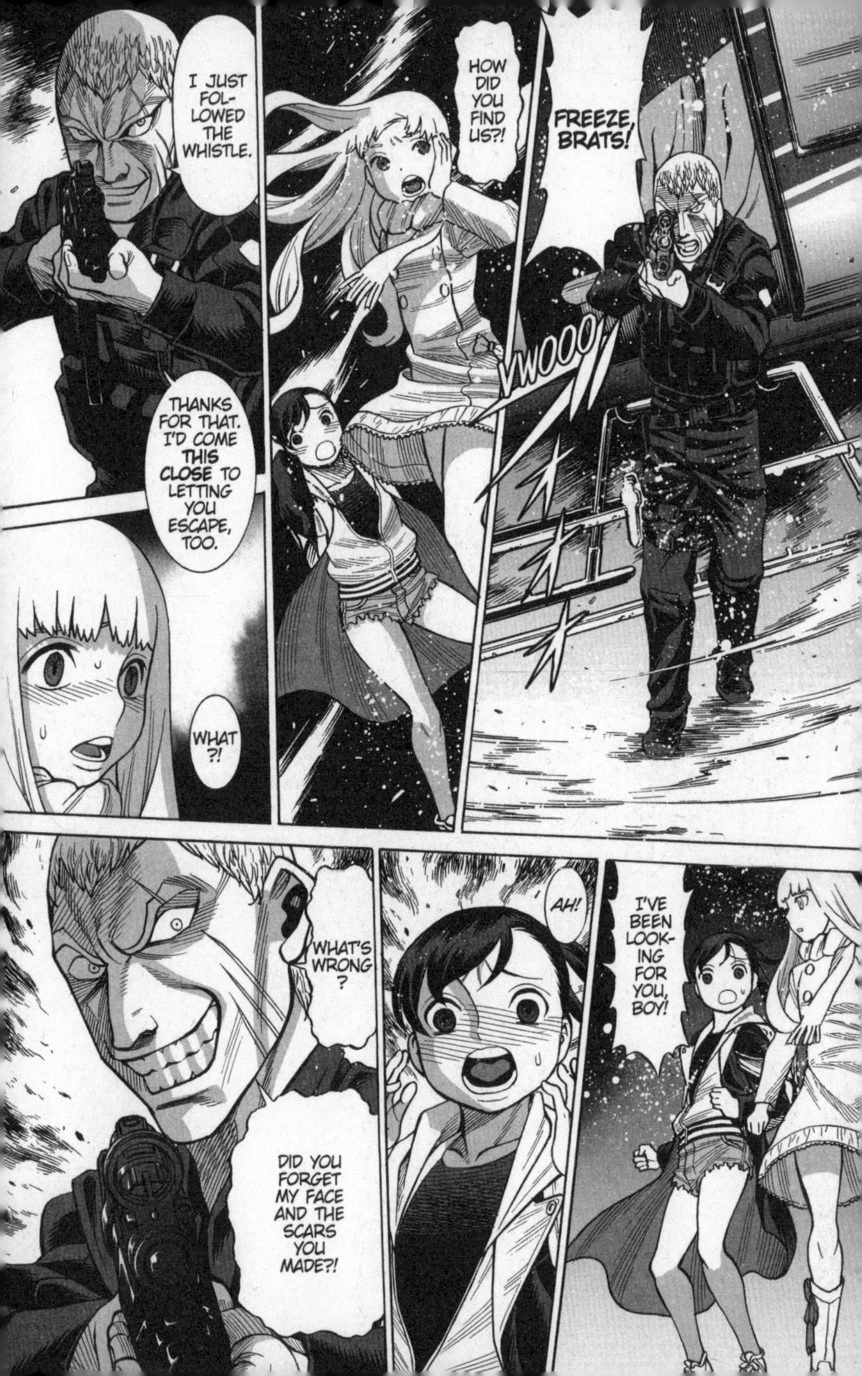
FREEZE, BRATS!
VWOOO
HOW DID YOU FIND US?!
I JUST FOL-LOWED THE WHISTLE.
THANKS FOR THAT. I'D COME **THIS CLOSE** TO LETTING YOU ESCAPE, TOO.
WHAT?!
I'VE BEEN LOOK-ING FOR YOU, BOY!
AH!
WHAT'S WRONG?
DID YOU FORGET MY FACE AND THE SCARS YOU MADE?!

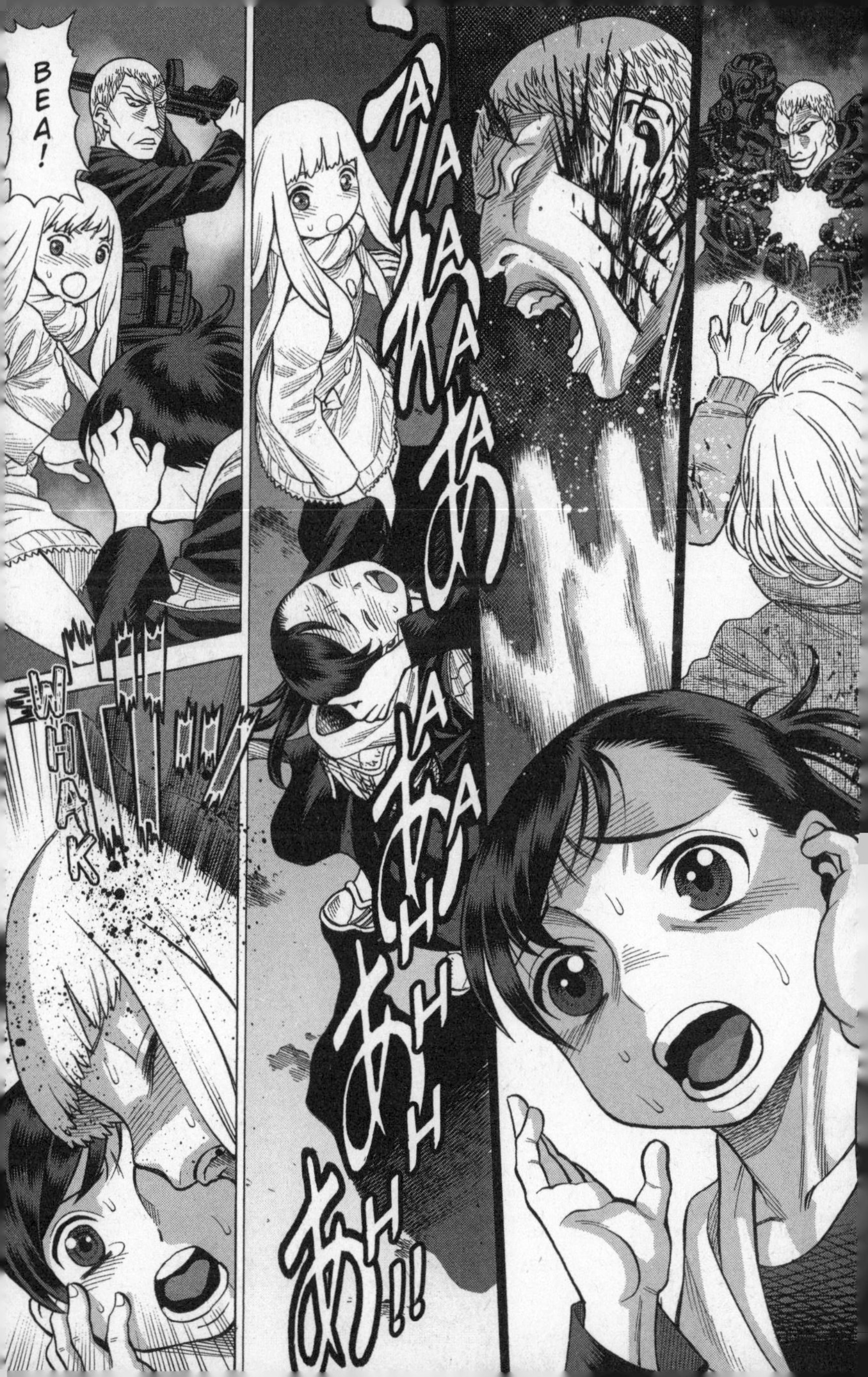
AAAAAAAAAHHHHHH!!
あああああ
BEAA!
WHAK!!

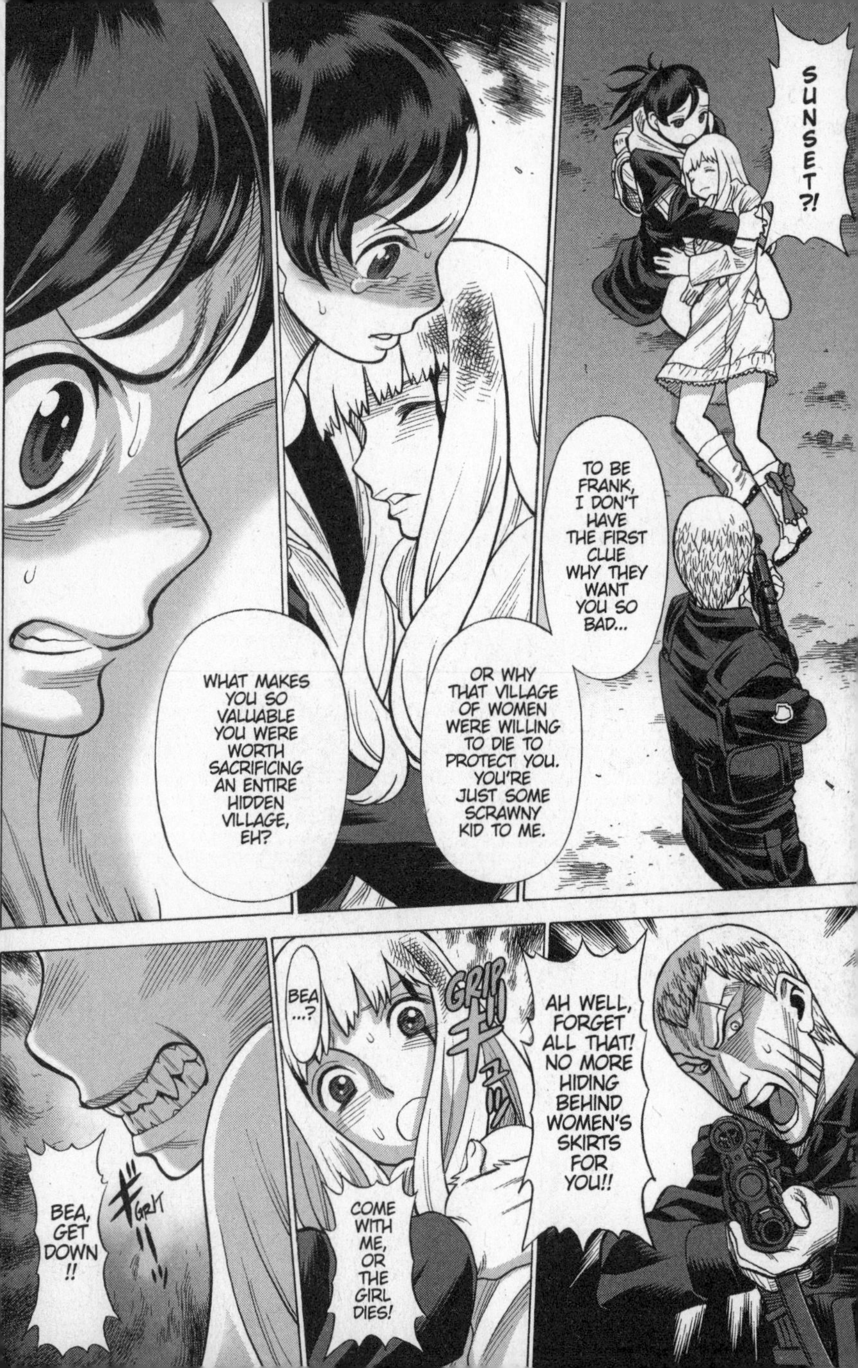
SUNSET?!
TO BE FRANK, I DON'T HAVE THE FIRST CLUE WHY THEY WANT YOU SO BAD...
OR WHY THAT VILLAGE OF WOMEN WERE WILLING TO DIE TO PROTECT YOU. YOU'RE JUST SOME SCRAWNY KID TO ME.
WHAT MAKES YOU SO VALUABLE YOU WERE WORTH SACRIFICING AN ENTIRE HIDDEN VILLAGE, EH?
AH WELL, FORGET ALL THAT! NO MORE HIDING BEHIND WOMEN'S SKIRTS FOR YOU!!
BEA ...?
GRIP
COME WITH ME, OR THE GIRL DIES!
GRIT
BEA, GET DOWN !!

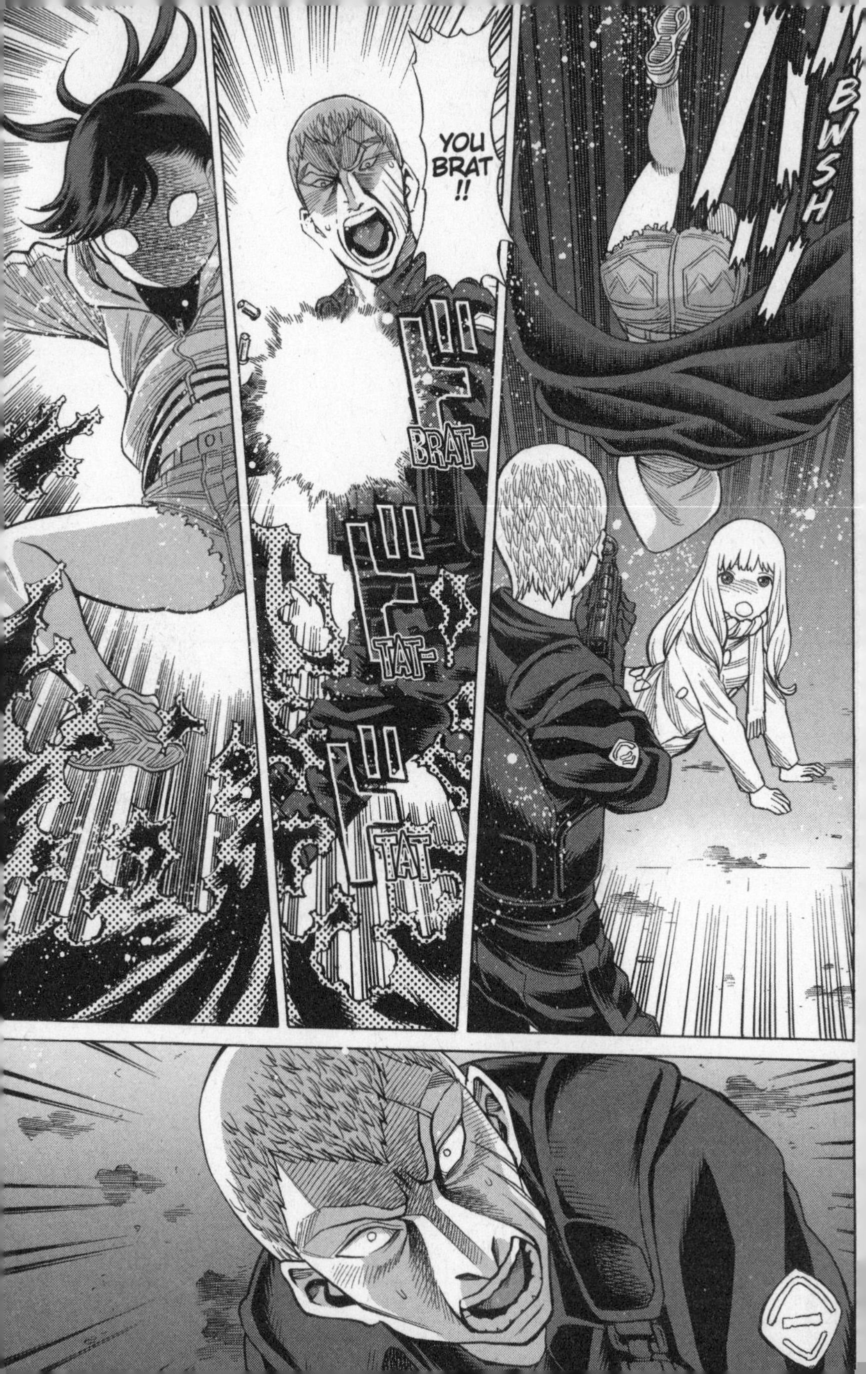
BWSH
YOU BRAT !!
BRAT-
TAT-
TAT

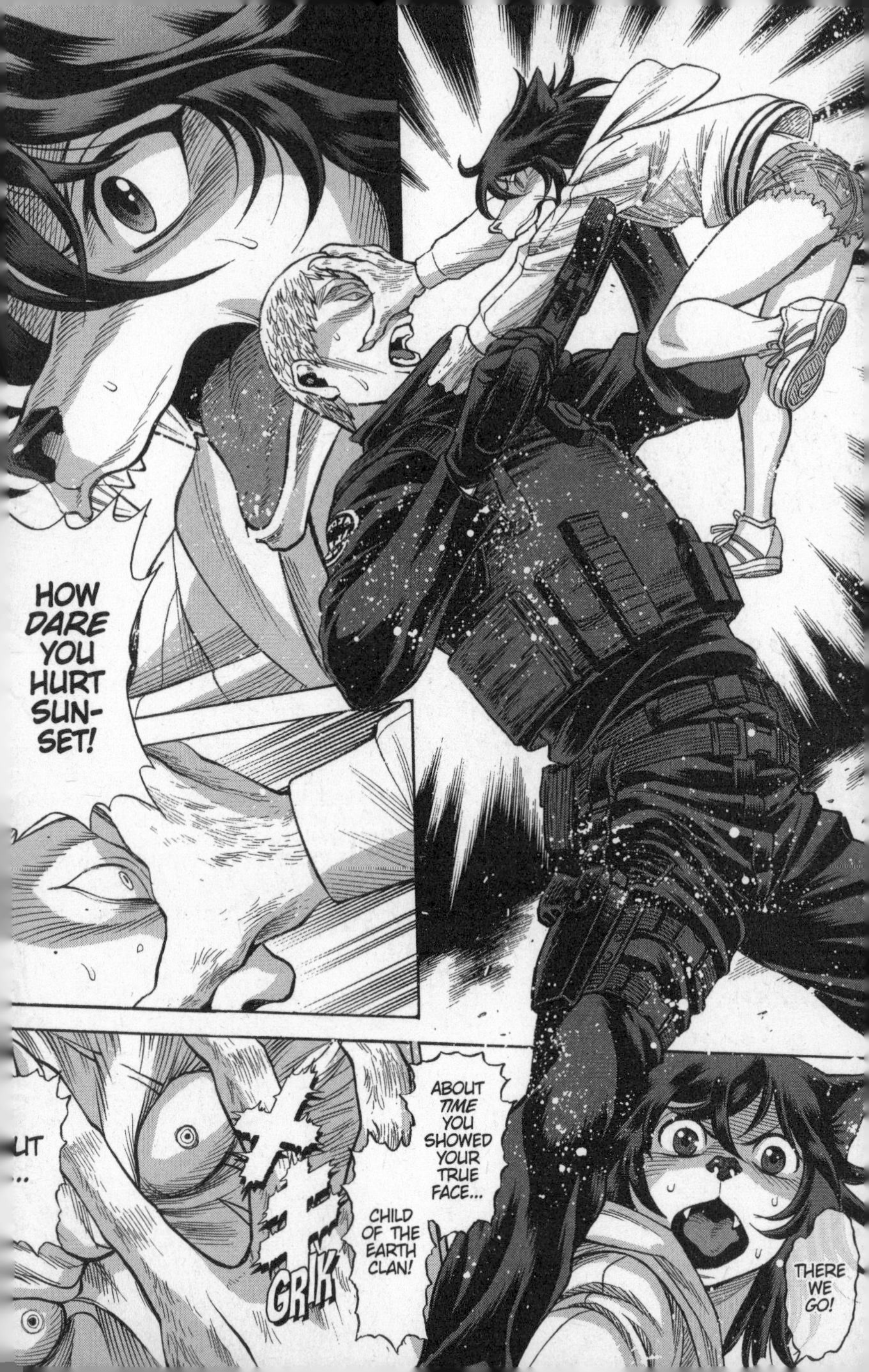
HOW DARE YOU HURT SUN-SET!
THERE WE GO!
ABOUT TIME YOU SHOWED YOUR TRUE FACE...
CHILD OF THE EARTH CLAN!
GRIK

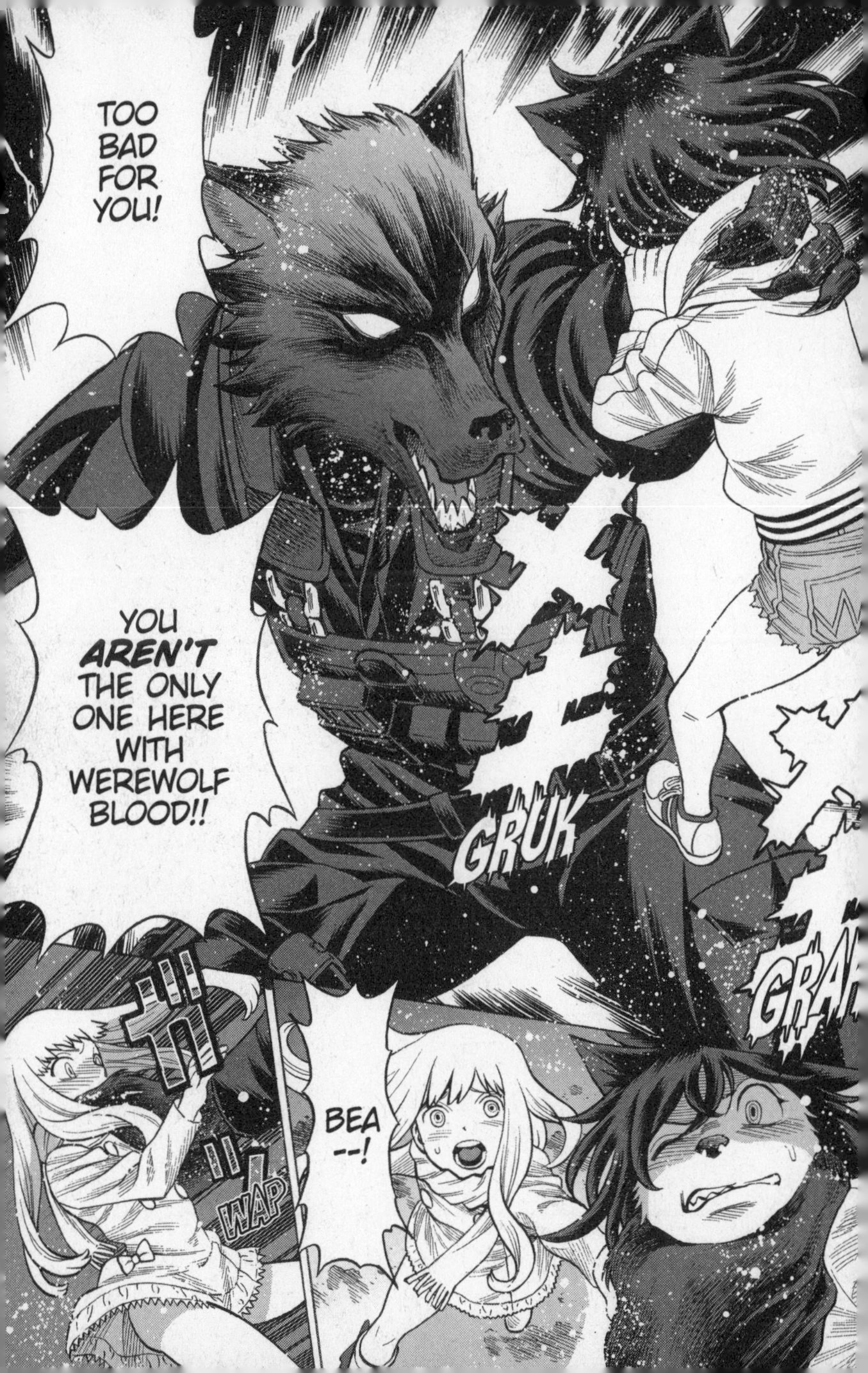
TOO BAD FOR YOU!
YOU **AREN'T** THE ONLY ONE HERE WITH WEREWOLF BLOOD!!
GRUK
GRA
BEA --!
WAP

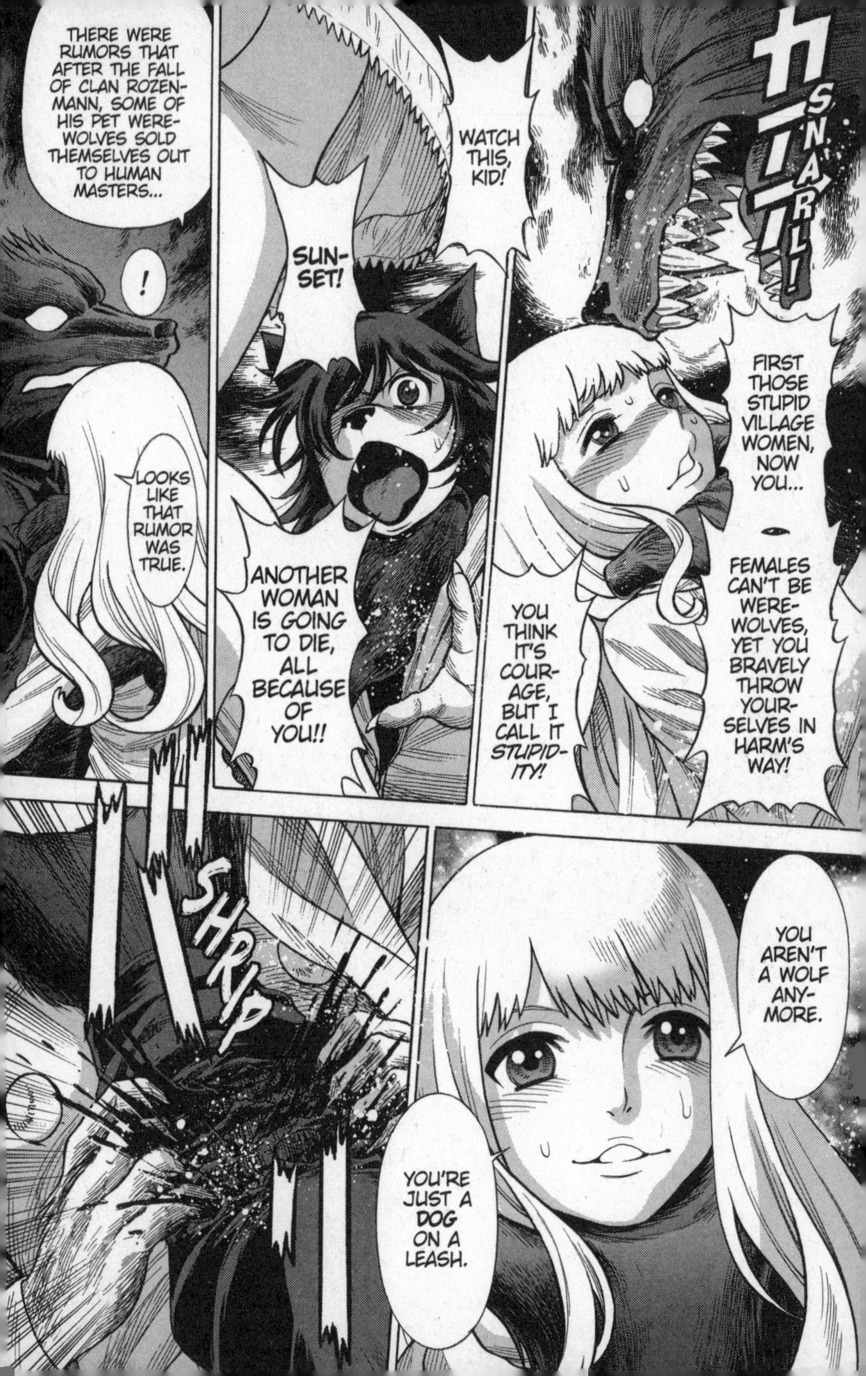
SNARL!
FIRST THOSE STUPID VILLAGE WOMEN, NOW YOU...
FEMALES CAN'T BE WERE-WOLVES, YET YOU BRAVELY THROW YOUR-SELVES IN HARM'S WAY!
YOU THINK IT'S COUR-AGE, BUT I CALL IT STUPID-ITY!
WATCH THIS, KID!
SUN-SET!
ANOTHER WOMAN IS GOING TO DIE, ALL BECAUSE OF YOU!!
THERE WERE RUMORS THAT AFTER THE FALL OF CLAN ROZEN-MANN, SOME OF HIS PET WERE-WOLVES SOLD THEMSELVES OUT TO HUMAN MASTERS...
!
LOOKS LIKE THAT RUMOR WAS TRUE.
YOU AREN'T A WOLF ANY-MORE.
YOU'RE JUST A DOG ON A LEASH.
SHRIP

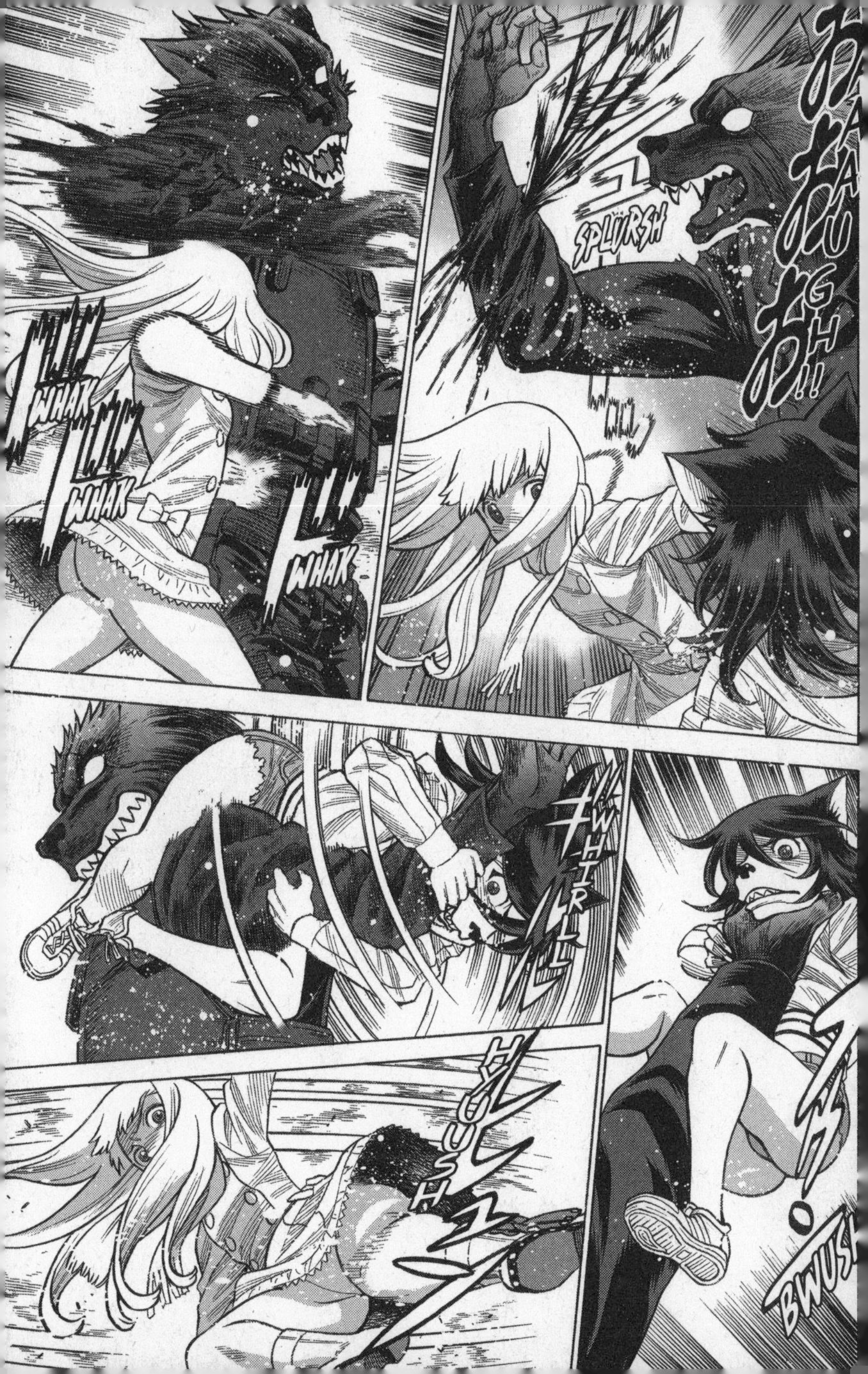
AAUUGH!!
SPLURSH
WHAK
WHAK
WHAK
WHIRLL
BWUS
HYUUSH

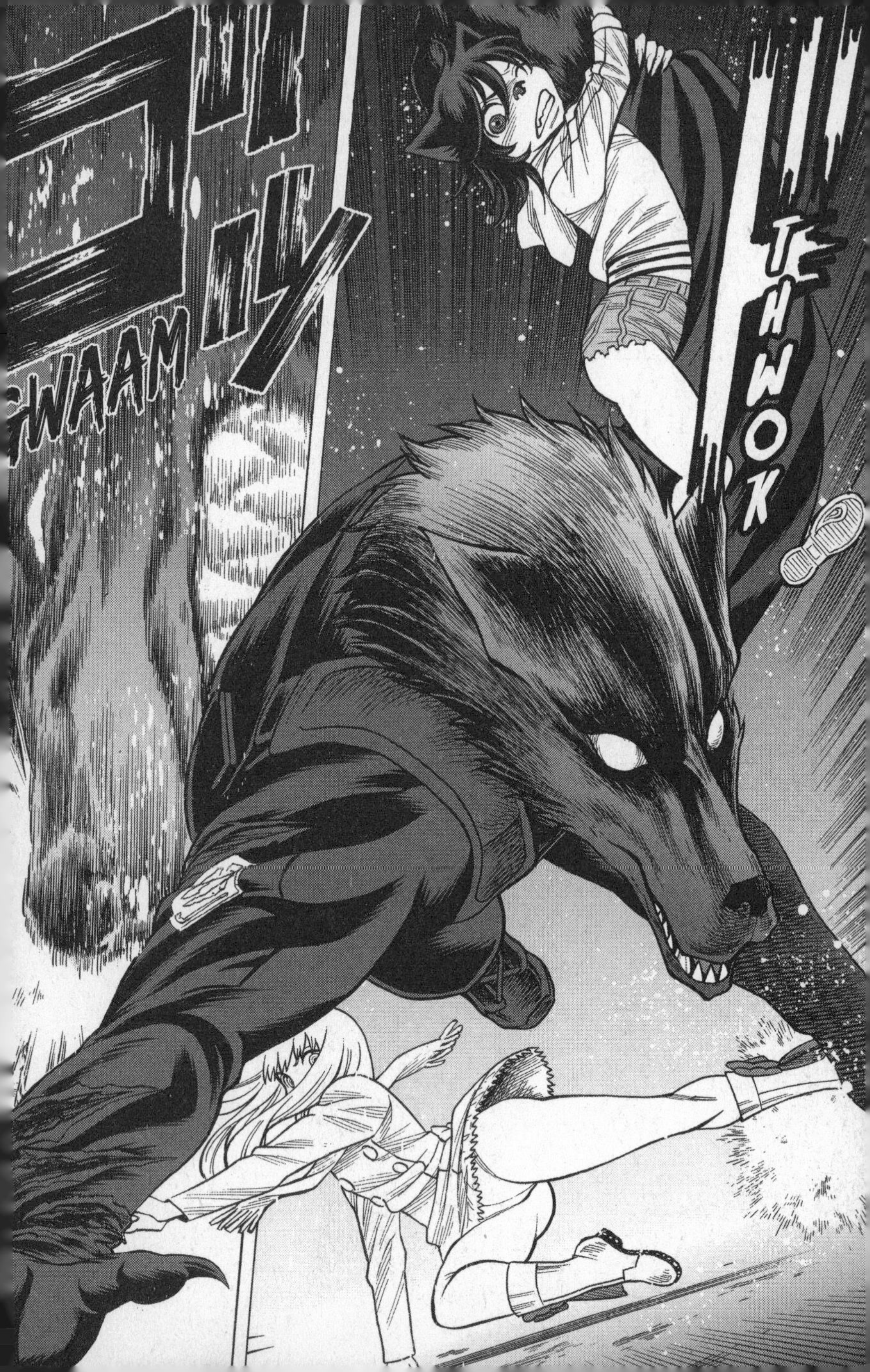
THWOK
WAAM

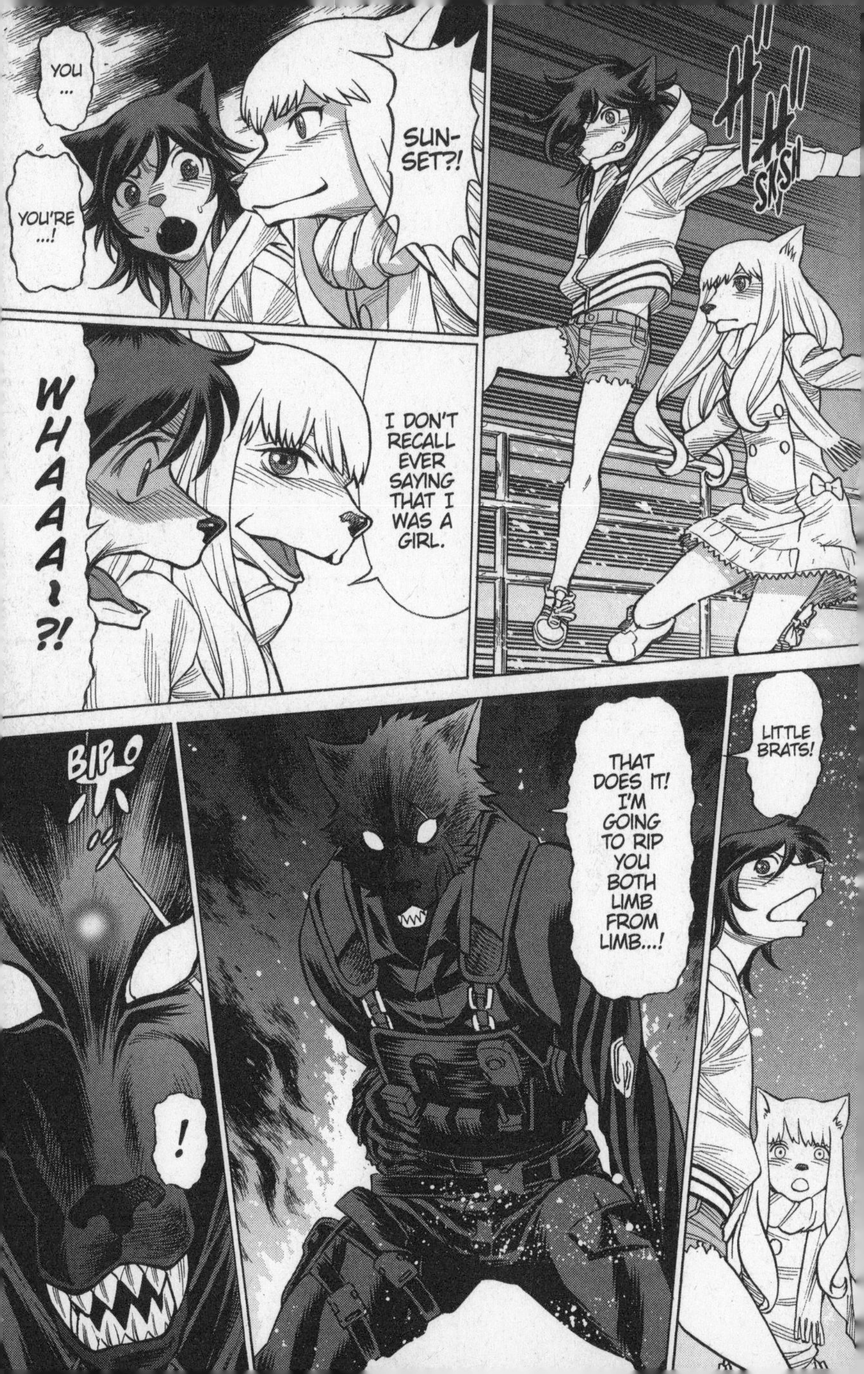
SKSH
YOU ...
YOU'RE ...!
SUN-SET?!
I DON'T RECALL EVER SAYING THAT I WAS A GIRL.
WHAAAA~?!
LITTLE BRATS!
THAT DOES IT! I'M GOING TO RIP YOU BOTH LIMB FROM LIMB...!
BIP
!

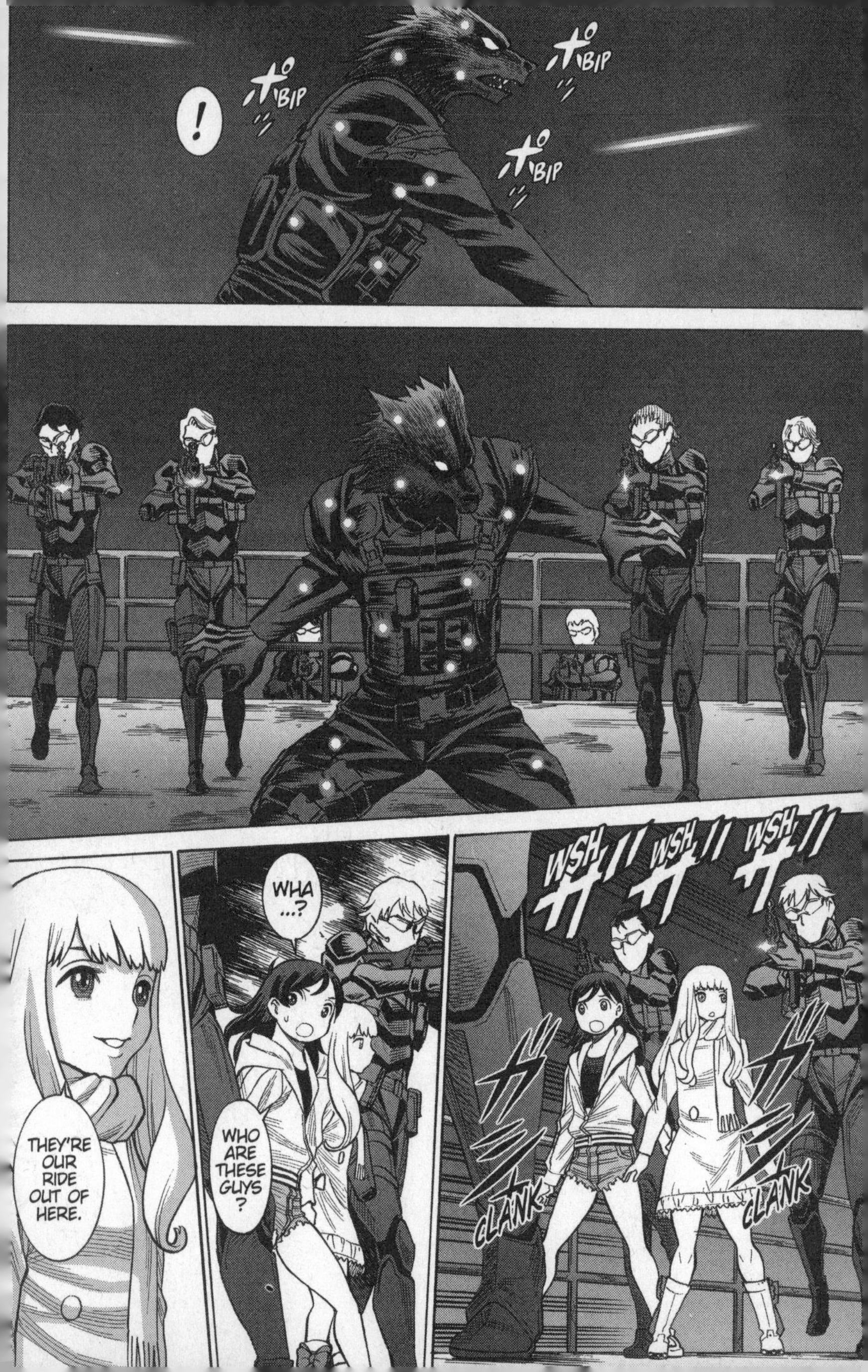

BIP
BIP
BIP
!
WSH
WSH
WSH
CLANK
CLANK
WHA ...?
WHO ARE THESE GUYS?
THEY'RE OUR RIDE OUT OF HERE.

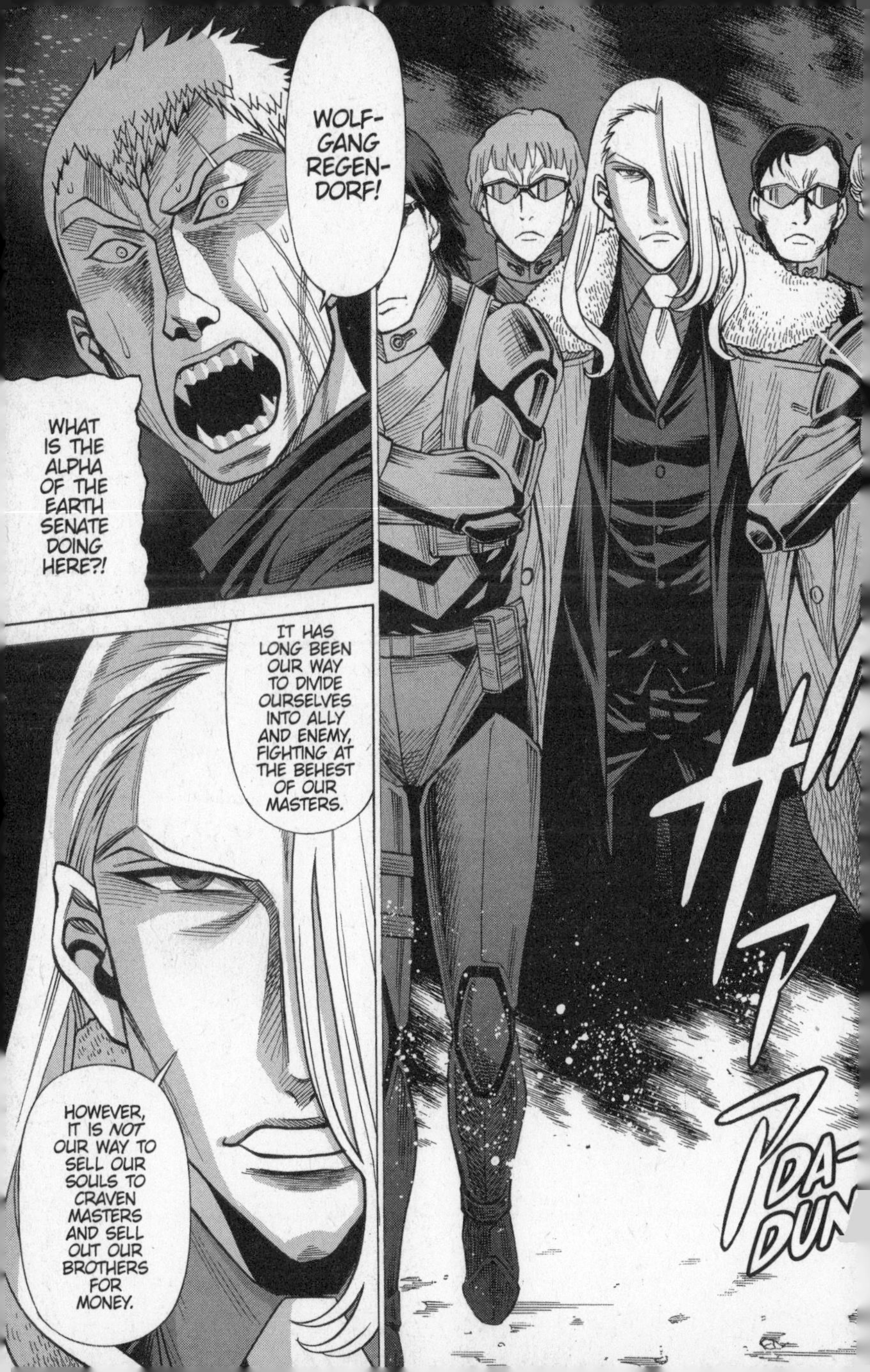
DA-DUN
WOLF-GANG REGEN-DORF!
WHAT IS THE ALPHA OF THE EARTH SENATE DOING HERE?!
IT HAS LONG BEEN OUR WAY TO DIVIDE OURSELVES INTO ALLY AND ENEMY, FIGHTING AT THE BEHEST OF OUR MASTERS.
HOWEVER, IT IS *NOT* OUR WAY TO SELL OUR SOULS TO CRAVEN MASTERS AND SELL OUT OUR BROTHERS FOR MONEY.

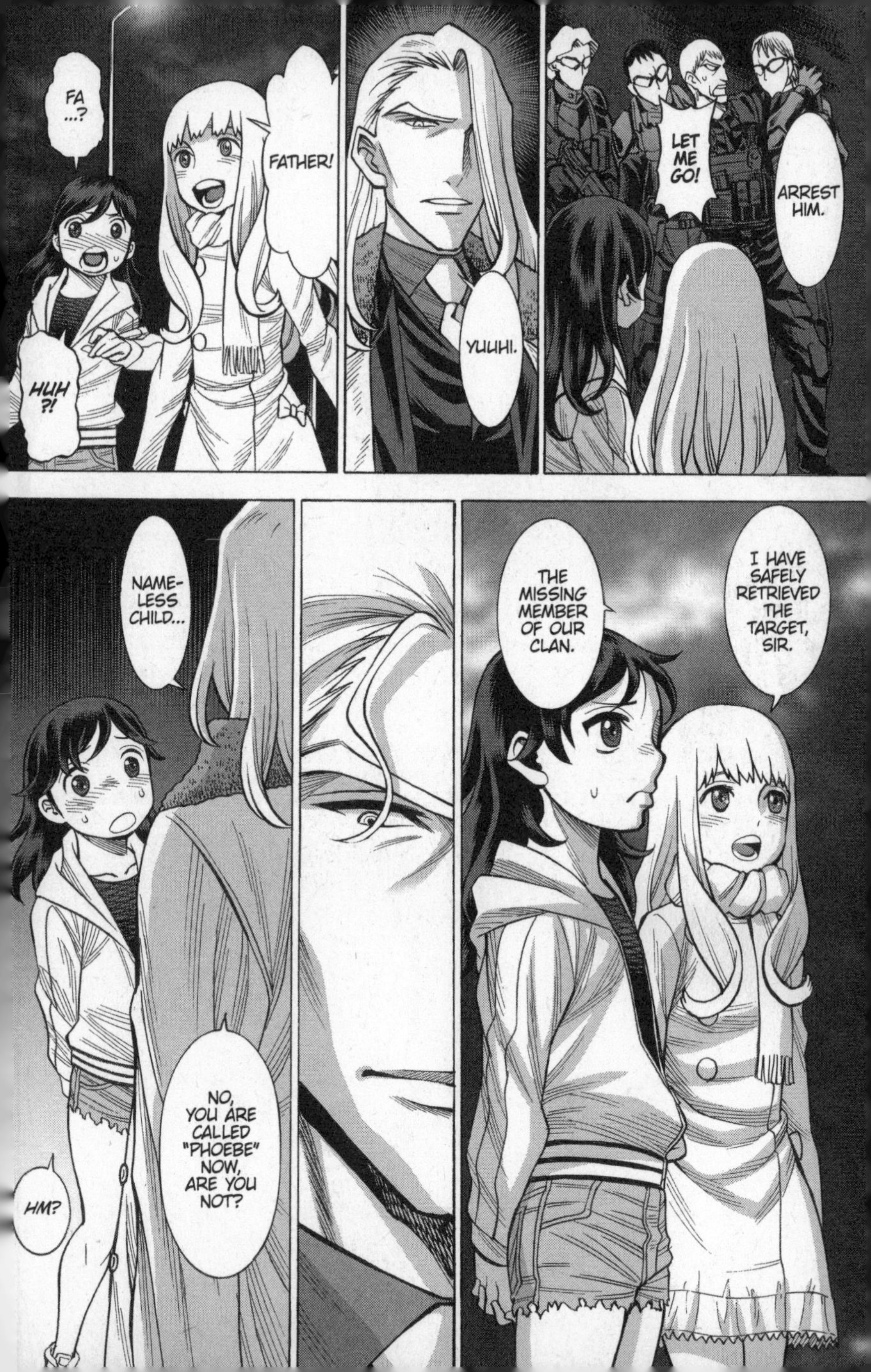
ARREST HIM.
LET ME GO!
YUUHI.
FATHER!
FA ...?
HUH ?!
I HAVE SAFELY RETRIEVED THE TARGET, SIR.
THE MISSING MEMBER OF OUR CLAN.
NAME-LESS CHILD...
NO, YOU ARE CALLED "PHOEBE" NOW, ARE YOU NOT?
HM?

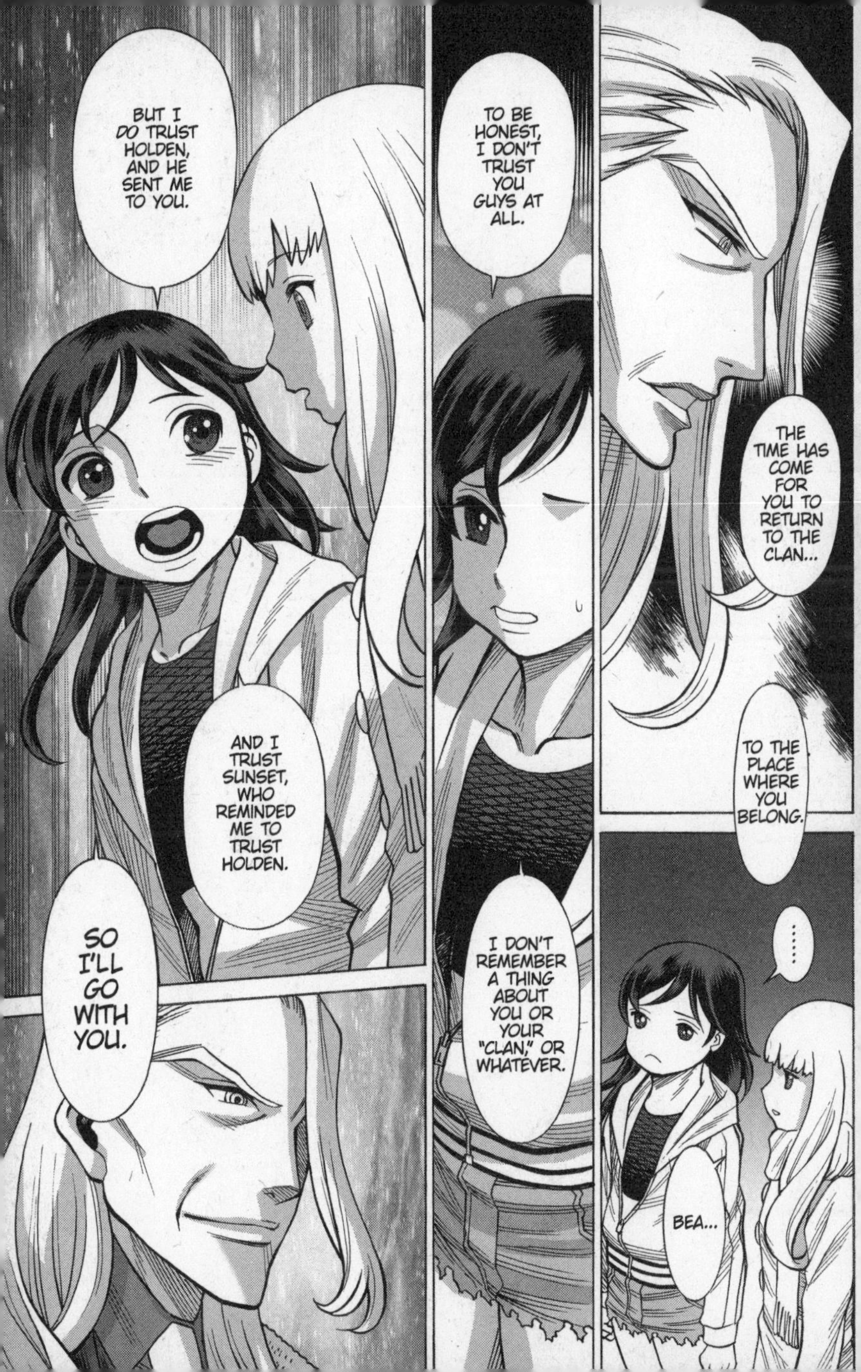
THE TIME HAS COME FOR YOU TO RETURN TO THE CLAN...
TO THE PLACE WHERE YOU BELONG.
......
BEA...
TO BE HONEST, I DON'T TRUST YOU GUYS AT ALL.
I DON'T REMEMBER A THING ABOUT YOU OR YOUR "CLAN," OR WHATEVER.
BUT I DO TRUST HOLDEN, AND HE SENT ME TO YOU.
AND I TRUST SUNSET, WHO REMINDED ME TO TRUST HOLDEN.
SO I'LL GO WITH YOU.

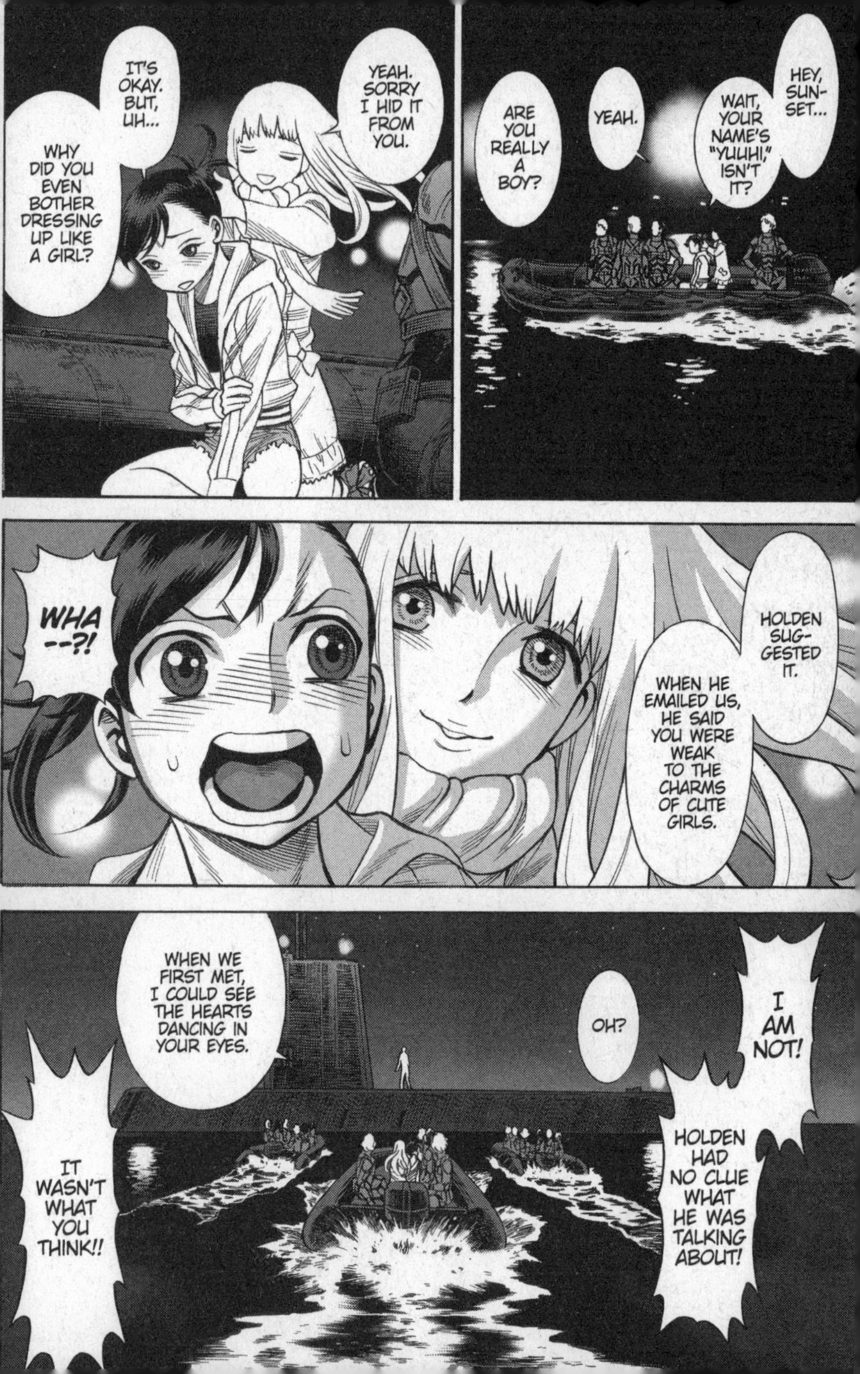
HEY, SUNSET...
WAIT, YOUR NAME'S "YUUHI," ISN'T IT?
YEAH.
ARE YOU REALLY A BOY?
YEAH. SORRY I HID IT FROM YOU.
IT'S OKAY. BUT, UH...
WHY DID YOU EVEN BOTHER DRESSING UP LIKE A GIRL?
HOLDEN SUGGESTED IT.
WHEN HE EMAILED US, HE SAID YOU WERE WEAK TO THE CHARMS OF CUTE GIRLS.
WHA--?!
I AM NOT!
OH?
WHEN WE FIRST MET, I COULD SEE THE HEARTS DANCING IN YOUR EYES.
HOLDEN HAD NO CLUE WHAT HE WAS TALKING ABOUT!
IT WASN'T WHAT YOU THINK!!

Dance in the Vampire Bund

Age of Scarlet Order

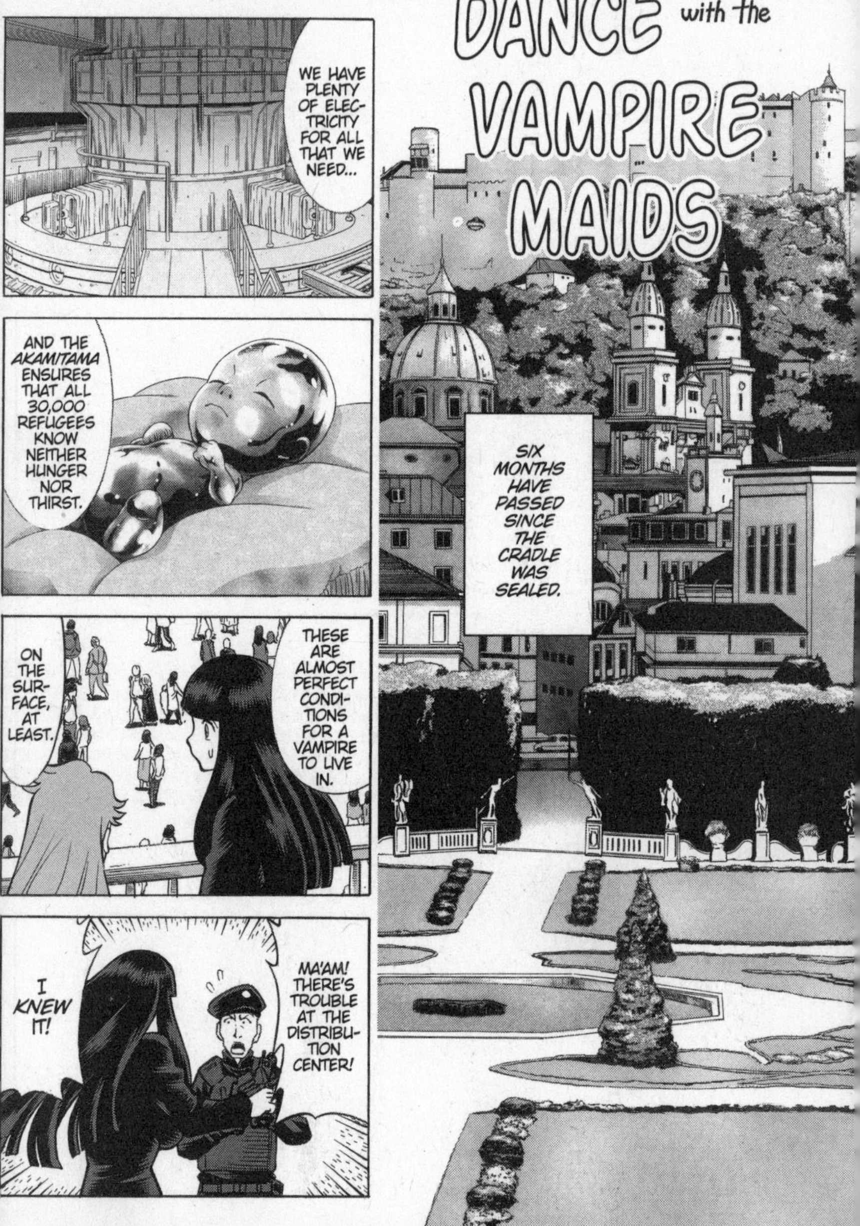
DANCE with the VAMPIRE MAIDS
SIX MONTHS HAVE PASSED SINCE THE CRADLE WAS SEALED.
WE HAVE PLENTY OF ELECTRICITY FOR ALL THAT WE NEED...
AND THE *AKAMITAMA* ENSURES THAT ALL 30,000 REFUGEES KNOW NEITHER HUNGER NOR THIRST.
THESE ARE ALMOST PERFECT CONDITIONS FOR A VAMPIRE TO LIVE IN.
ON THE SURFACE, AT LEAST.
MA'AM! THERE'S TROUBLE AT THE DISTRIBUTION CENTER!
I KNEW IT!

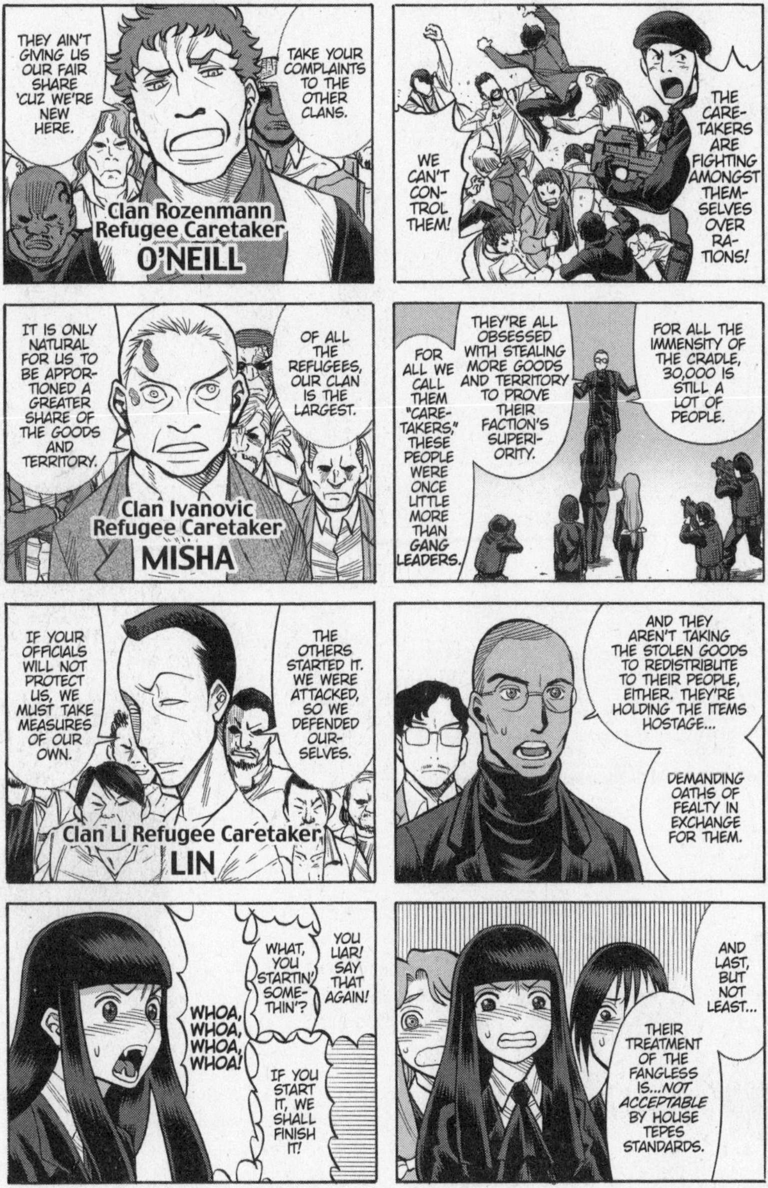
THE CARETAKERS ARE FIGHTING AMONGST THEMSELVES OVER RATIONS!
WE CAN'T CONTROL THEM!
TAKE YOUR COMPLAINTS TO THE OTHER CLANS.
THEY AIN'T GIVING US OUR FAIR SHARE 'CUZ WE'RE NEW HERE.
Clan Rozenmann Refugee Caretaker O'NEILL
FOR ALL THE IMMENSITY OF THE CRADLE, 30,000 IS STILL A LOT OF PEOPLE.
THEY'RE ALL OBSESSED WITH STEALING MORE GOODS AND TERRITORY TO PROVE THEIR FACTION'S SUPERIORITY.
FOR ALL WE CALL THEM "CARETAKERS," THESE PEOPLE WERE ONCE LITTLE MORE THAN GANG LEADERS.
OF ALL THE REFUGEES, OUR CLAN IS THE LARGEST.
IT IS ONLY NATURAL FOR US TO BE APPORTIONED A GREATER SHARE OF THE GOODS AND TERRITORY.
Clan Ivanovic Refugee Caretaker MISHA
AND THEY AREN'T TAKING THE STOLEN GOODS TO REDISTRIBUTE TO THEIR PEOPLE, EITHER. THEY'RE HOLDING THE ITEMS HOSTAGE...
DEMANDING OATHS OF FEALTY IN EXCHANGE FOR THEM.
THE OTHERS STARTED IT. WE WERE ATTACKED, SO WE DEFENDED OURSELVES.
IF YOUR OFFICIALS WILL NOT PROTECT US, WE MUST TAKE MEASURES OF OUR OWN.
Clan Li Refugee Caretaker LIN
AND LAST, BUT NOT LEAST...
THEIR TREATMENT OF THE FANGLESS IS...NOT ACCEPTABLE BY HOUSE TEPES STANDARDS.
YOU LIAR! SAY THAT AGAIN!
WHAT, YOU STARTIN' SOMETHIN'?
IF YOU START IT, WE SHALL FINISH IT!
WHOA, WHOA, WHOA, WHOA!

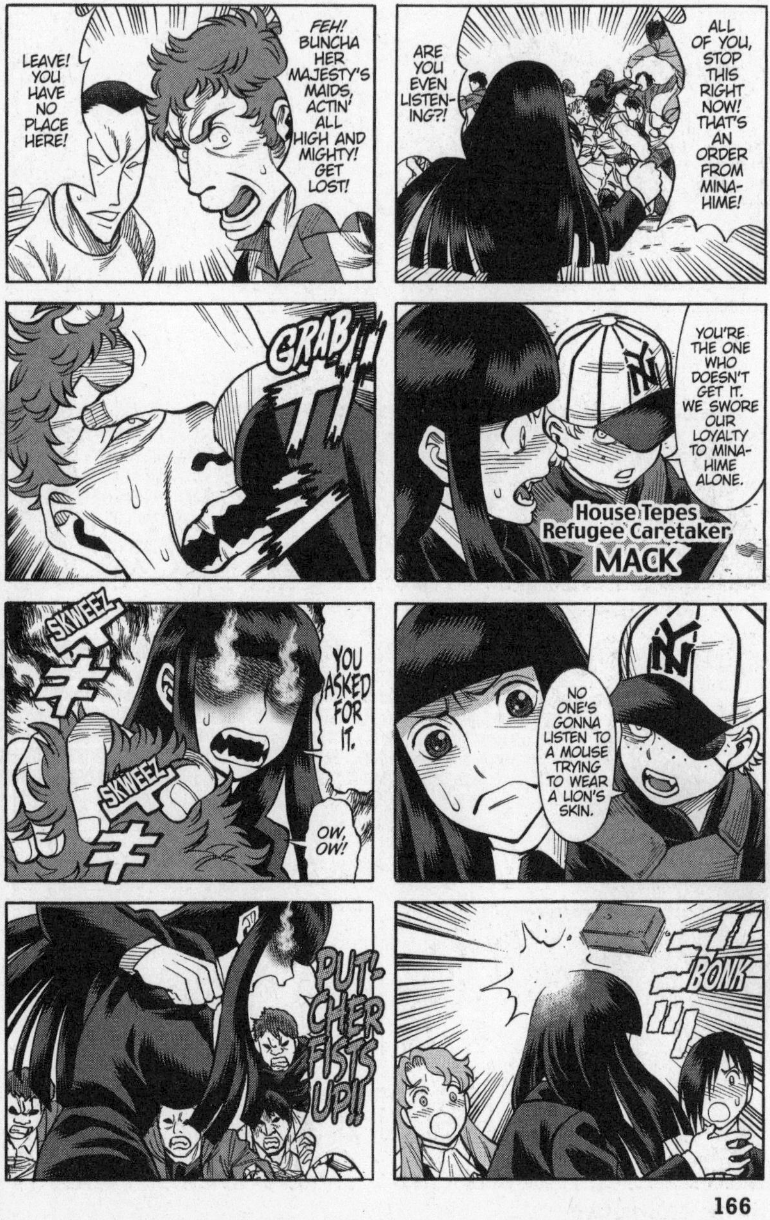
ALL OF YOU, STOP THIS RIGHT NOW! THAT'S AN ORDER FROM MINA-HIME!
ARE YOU EVEN LISTENING?!
FEH! BUNCHA HER MAJESTY'S MAIDS, ACTIN' ALL HIGH AND MIGHTY! GET LOST!
LEAVE! YOU HAVE NO PLACE HERE!
YOU'RE THE ONE WHO DOESN'T GET IT. WE SWORE OUR LOYALTY TO MINA-HIME ALONE.
House Tepes Refugee Caretaker
MACK
GRAB
NO ONE'S GONNA LISTEN TO A MOUSE TRYING TO WEAR A LION'S SKIN.
YOU ASKED FOR IT.
SKWEEZ
SKWEEZ
OW, OW!
BONK
PUT-CHER FISTS UP!!

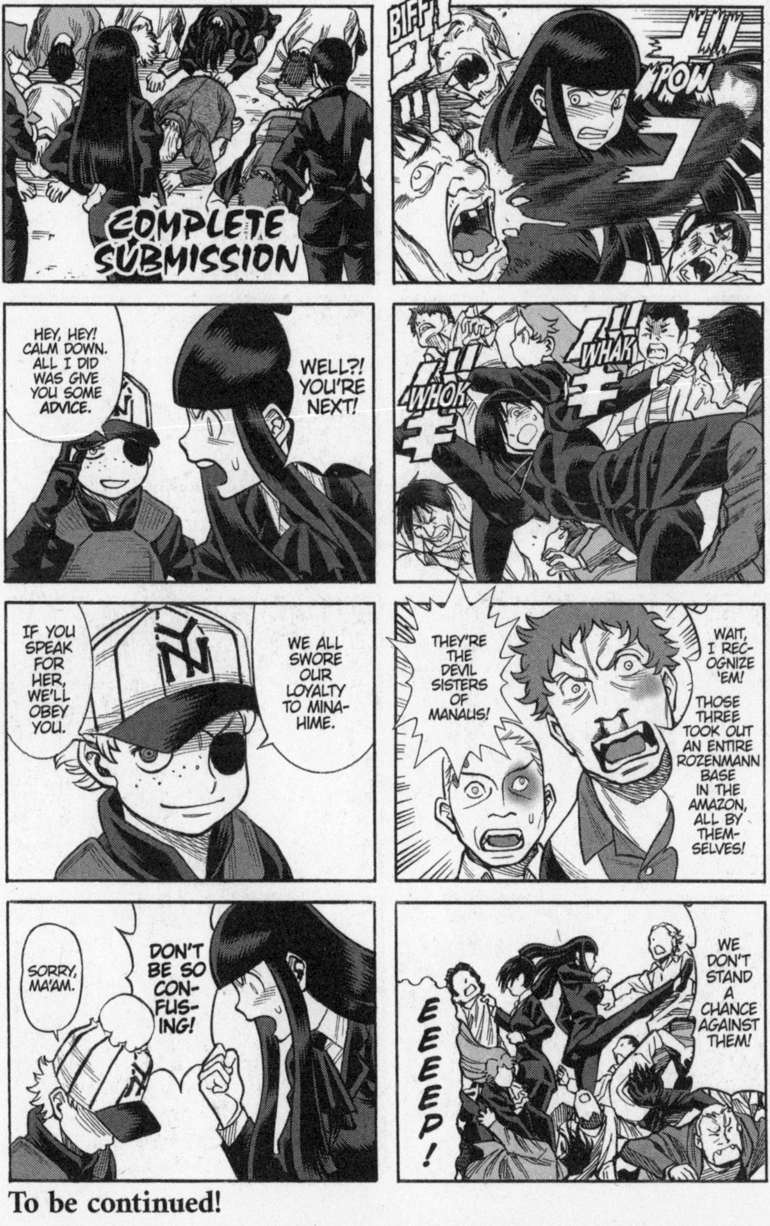
BIFF
POW
COMPLETE SUBMISSION
WHAK
WHOK
WELL?! YOU'RE NEXT!
HEY, HEY! CALM DOWN. ALL I DID WAS GIVE YOU SOME ADVICE.
WAIT, I RECOGNIZE 'EM! THOSE THREE TOOK OUT AN ENTIRE ROZENMANN BASE IN THE AMAZON, ALL BY THEMSELVES!
THEY'RE THE DEVIL SISTERS OF MANAUS!
WE ALL SWORE OUR LOYALTY TO MINA-HIME.
IF YOU SPEAK FOR HER, WE'LL OBEY YOU.
WE DON'T STAND A CHANCE AGAINST THEM!
EEEEP!
DON'T BE SO CONFUSING!
SORRY, MA'AM.

To be continued!

Dance in the Vampire Bund
Age of Scarlet Order

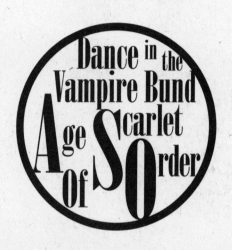

SEVEN SEAS ENTERTAINMENT PRESENTS

Dance in the Vampire Bund

story and art by NOZOMU TAMAKI

AGE OF SCARLET ORDER VOL. 2

TRANSLATION
Adrienne Beck

ADAPTATION
Janet Houck

LETTERING AND RETOUCH
Roland Amago
Bambi Eloriaga-Amago

COVER DESIGN
Nicky Lim

PROOFREADER
Danielle King

EDITOR
Alexis Roberts

PREPRESS TECHNICIAN
Rhiannon Rasmussen-Silverstein

PRODUCTION MANAGER
Lissa Pattillo

MANAGING EDITOR
Julie Davis

ASSOCIATE PUBLISHER
Adam Arnold

PUBLISHER
Jason DeAngelis

DANCE IN THE VAMPIRE BUND: AGE OF SCARLET ORDER VOL. 2

This edition originally published in Japan in 2019 by TO BOOKS., Tokyo.
English translation rights arranged with TO BOOKS., Tokyo.

Seven Seas press and purchase enquiries can be sent to Marketing Manager Lianne Sentar at press@gomanga.com. Information regarding the distribution and purchase of digital editions is available from Digital Manager CK Russell at digital@gomanga.com.

ISBN: 978-1-64505-199-2

Printed in Canada

First Printing: June 2020

10 9 8 7 6 5 4 3 2 1

FOLLOW US ONLINE: ***www.sevenseasentertainment.com***

READING DIRECTIONS

This book reads from ***right to left***, Japanese style. If this is your first time reading manga, you start reading from the top right panel on each page and take it from there. If you get lost, just follow the numbered diagram here. It may seem backwards at first, but you'll get the hang of it! Have fun!!

1
2
3
4
5
6
7
8
9

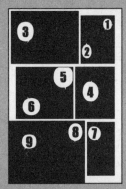